MW01710706

Qikiqtani Truth Commission

Thematic Reports and Special Studies 1950-1975

Qikiqtani Truth Commission

Thematic Reports and Special Studies 1950-1975

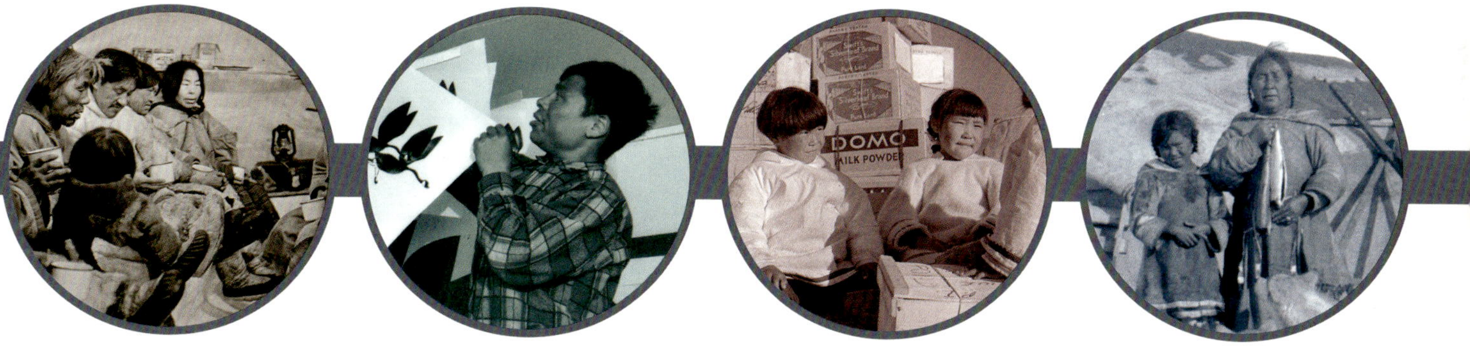

Published by Inhabit Media Inc.
www.inhabitmedia.com

Inhabit Media Inc. (Iqaluit), P.O. Box 11125, Iqaluit, Nunavut, X0A 1H0
(Toronto), 146A Orchard View Blvd., Toronto, Ontario, M4R 1C3

We acknowledge the support of the Government of Canada through the Department of Canadian Heritage Canada Book Fund program.

We acknowledge the support of the Canada Council for the Arts for our publishing program.

Printed in Canada

ISBN 978-1-927095-63-8

Qikiqtani Inuit Association

QIKIQTANI TRUTH COMMISSION

Canada

Canadian Heritage Patrimoine canadien

Contributors

The work required to plan, research, and write the studies published in this book occurred in two phases.

PHASE 1 QIKIQTANI TRUTH COMMISSION (2007 TO 2010)

The QTC phase included most of the research, producing a research database, drafting background reports, indexing of testimonies, and writing the Commissioner's report and two special studies.

Project Management

Madeleine Redfern, Executive Director, QTC, with advice and support from Commissioner James Igloliorte; Terry Audla, Executive Director, QIA; Joanasie Akumalik, QTC staff; and Paul Crowley, QTC Legal Counsel.

Historical Services

Julie Harris, Contentworks, Inc., Coordinator; Dr. Philip Goldring, Ph.D., Senior Historian; Ryan Shackleton, Historian, Contentworks, Inc.; and Joan Bard Miller, Information Manager, Contentworks, Inc.

QTC Research Strategy and Background Studies

Madeleine Redfern; Philip Goldring, Ph.D.; Julie Harris; Ryan Shackleton; Frank J. Tester, Ph.D.; and Francis Levésque, Ph.D.

Linguistic Support

Carole Cancel, Ph.D.; Jay Arnakak; and Joanasie Akumalik.

QTC Final Report: Achieving Saimaqatigiingniq

James Igloliorte, Commissioner; Madeleine Redfern, Executive Director; Brian Cameron, Editor and Writer; and Jay Arnakak, Inuit Advisor and Linguistic Support.

Analysis of the RCMP and Inuit Sled Dogs (2006) Report

Madeleine Redfern and Philip Goldring, Ph.D.

The Official Mind

Philip Goldring, Ph.D.

PHASE 2 QIKIQTANI INUIT ASSOCIATION (2011 TO 2013)

QIA managed the completion of the full set of QTC studies, as well as the preparation of materials for publication.

Project Management

Bethany Scott, QTC Project Manager, QIA; Navarana Beveridge, Executive Director, QIA; and Sandra Kownak, Director of Social Policy, QIA.

Historical Services

Julie Harris, Contentworks, Inc., General Editor and Coordinator of Research and Writing; and Philip Goldring, Ph.D., Senior Historian.

Inuktitut Translation

Jay Arnakak; Mali Curley; Julia Demcheson; Veronica Dewar; Elisapee Ikkidluak; Emily Ilinik; David Joanasie; Leonie Kappi; Pujjuut Kusugak; Nina Tootoo; and Blandina Tulugarjuk.

Authors

Julie Harris; Philip Goldring, Ph.D.; Madeleine Redfern; Natascha Morrison; Alice Glaze; Teresa Iacobelli, Ph.D.; Francis Levésque, Ph.D.; Bernadette Johnson; Joan Bard Miller; and Brian Cameron (Introduction).

Research Support

Linda Radford, Ph.D.; Pamela Gross; Anna Gilmer; Gail Cummings; Hugh Goldring; and David King.

Publishing and Art Direction

Neil Christopher, Inhabit Media; and Ellen Ziegler, Inhabit Media.

Graphic Design

Marijke Friesen.

Copy Editing

Laura Legge.

Reviewers

Mary Akavak; Olayuk Akesuk; Joanasie Akumalik; Larry Audlaluk; Stevie Aulaqiaq; John Amagoalik; Paul Amagoalik; Madeleine Cole; Yvonne Earle; Louise Flaherty; Rutie Gardner; Peter Kattuk; Sandra Kownak; Zacharias Kunuk; Mikidjuk Lyta; Annie McGowan; Rita Mike; Jerry Natanine; Yvonne Niego; Philip Paniaq; Abraham Qamaniq; Madeleine Redfern; Colin Saunders; Bethany Scott; and Craig Welsh.

Acknowledgements

There are many people who deserve thanks for their part in the work of the Qikiqtani Truth Commission and in the development of these reports.

Heartfelt gratitude to the Inuit Elders and community members whose memories and words are the foundation of this work.

Past and present Qikiqtani Inuit Association boards of directors, especially those who were members of the Dog Slaughter and Relocation Committee.

Commissioner James Igoliorte and QTC executive director Madeleine Redfern for their work in making known this part of our history and bearing witness to the stories of this region.

Julie Harris and the staff at Contentworks, Inc., especially Joan Bard Miller. Without their tremendous effort and dedication to this project, these reports would not exist.

Philip Goldring for his expertise and guidance.

Mark Poirier at SHOK Media for his work in creating the video record of the Commission.

Neil Christopher and the team at Inhabit Media for their part in the development of the QTC books.

All of the community members who provided valued and valuable feedback as the work developed.

The team of translators who put in countless hours to create the Inuktitut versions of these reports. Qujannamiimmarialuk.

Finally, thank you to the staff at QIA, each of whom supported this project in big and small ways.

Supporters

The work of the Qikiqtani Truth Commission would not have been possible without the financial support of the following organizations:

Qikiqtani Inuit Association

Nunavut Tunngavik Incorporated

Makivik Corporation

Walter & Duncan Gordon Foundation

First Air

Air Inuit

Unaalik Aviation

Kenn Borek Air Ltd.

Government of Canada, Aboriginal Affairs and Northern Development Canada

Dedication

This book is dedicated to the Inuit of the Qikiqtani region. May our history never be forgotten and our voices be forever strong.

A Note on Photographs

A PICTURE CAN BE WORTH A THOUSAND WORDS, HOWEVER . . .

Visual representation, through film and photography, is not objective. The viewer has no idea what occurred in the moments just before or just after a photo was taken, nor are they privy to what was left on the cutting-room floor. The context in which a photo was taken can affect or change what the viewer feels when they engage with the photograph. During his review of the community history of Resolute Bay, John Amagoalik, executive advisor at the Qikiqtani Inuit Association, recounted a story that drives this point home.

> The woman in this photograph is my mother. This photograph was taken when Governor General Vanier visited Resolute in the late 1950s or early 60s. A few weeks before he arrived, they came around to all of our homes and told our mothers that the children had to be clean-looking when Vanier arrived. If that meant sewing new kamiiks or parkas, so be it.
>
> The day Vanier arrived, they came into our home and ordered my mother to go out and play music for him. And they ordered us children outside to dance.

Readers are asked to be mindful of the fact that what you think you see in these historical photographs does not reveal the context in which the photograph was taken.

Also, it should be noted that most of the photographs that appear in the QTC books are from national or territorial archives. Many will seem familiar to readers. Where the information was available, names of those who appear in the photographs have been included. If you notice an error or omission, please contact QIA so that corrections can be made for future editions of these books.

Table of Contents

List of Tables

Qikiqtaaluk Communities
ELLESMERE
ISLAND
Grise Fiord
Resolute
DEVON ISLAND
Lancaster Sound
Baffin
Bay
Arctic Bay
Pond Inlet
Clyde River
BAFFIN ISLAND
Davis Strait
Qikiqtarjuaq
Igloolik
Hall Beach
Taloyoak
Gjoa Haven
Kugaarjuk
Pangnirtung
Cumberland Snd.
Foxe
Basin
Repulse Bay
Iqaluit
Cape Dorset
Frobisher Bay
Kimmirut
Baker Lake
Coral Harbour
Hudson Strait
Chesterfield Inlet
Rankin Inlet
Whale Cove
Arviat
Hudson
Bay
Sanikiluaq
Qikiqtaaluk Communities
Other Nunavut Communities
Non-Nunavut Communities
1:10,000,000
©Qikiqtani Inuit Association, 2013

Foreword

As President of the Qikiqtani Inuit Association, I am pleased to present the long-awaited set of reports of the Qikiqtani Truth Commission.

The *Qikiqtani Truth Commission: Community Histories 1950–1975* and *Qikiqtani Truth Commission: Thematic Reports and Special Studies* represent the Inuit experience during this colonial period, as told by Inuit. These reports offer a deeper understanding of the motivations driving government decisions and the effects of those decisions on the lives of Inuit—effects that are still felt today.

This period of recent history is very much alive to Qikiqtaalungmiut, and through testifying at the Commission, Inuit spoke of our experience of that time. These reports and supporting documents are for us. This work builds upon the oral history and foundation Inuit come from as told by Inuit, for Inuit, to Inuit.

On a personal level this is for the grandmother I never knew, because she died in a sanatorium in Hamilton; this is for my grandchildren, so that they can understand what our family has experienced; and it is also for the young people of Canada, so that they will also understand our story.

As it is in my family, so it is with many others in our region.

The Qikiqtani Truth Commission is a legacy project for the people of our region and QIA is proud to have been the steward of this work.

Aingai,

E7-1865
J. Okalik Eegeesiak
President
Qikiqtani Inuit Association
Iqaluit, Nunavut
2013

Preface

Many people, including Inuit and other scholars, have recognized that too much Canadian writing about the North hides social, cultural, and economic turmoil behind lovely photographs, lists of individual achievements, and nationalist narratives. In more recent years, this has been changing. Newer histories, including this QIA community-driven initiative, are putting Inuit experiences at the forefront, explaining what happened to people in a wide historical sense and in their frequent face-to-face exchanges with incomers.

From the outset, the QTC was determined to create a lasting legacy that could be used to support further research. It set out to create three parallel sets of records: a collection of historic textual materials organized in a database; digitally preserved oral testimonies with summaries; and customized histories from oral and textual sources of evidence. For this work, the QTC determined that it needed experienced professional historians who could connect stories from present-day witnesses to Inuit voices in documentary sources, and to written records produced by the government, researchers, and others. The purpose was to devise narratives linking Inuit knowledge

and experience with the kinds of evidence more generally used by the wider Canadian research community. The Qikiqtaalungmiut who commissioned, funded, and managed the work expected that it would be within the main streams of Canadian scholarship, using a wide variety of sources. They were adamant that the goal was to communicate a better understanding of the past, not to assign blame or find fault.

With only a few exceptions, as listed on the contributor's page, these histories represent the collaborative efforts of a team that was responsible for research, information management, and writing. Work for the QTC began at the end of 2007. We surveyed numerous archival collections, copying from them abundantly and scanning the results for inclusion in the QTC's database. We read deeply and widely in the literature of Inuit studies, focusing especially on individual communities. We spoke to QIA board members, attended several QTC hearings, and viewed video records, translations, transcripts, and notes from the 342 testimonies. We also interviewed academic researchers and talked continuously and repeatedly with Inuit experts. More personally, we tried to examine how our own training, motivations, and biases affected the way we read, listened to, and used the historical record. At a critical time in our work, a conference on "Sharing Authority" at Concordia University highlighted the principles and challenges of having social scientists employ evidence from community narrators—we hope that we have respected best practices.

Throughout the QTC phase of the work, from 2007 to 2010, the historical research and writing team was kept informed and challenged by the QTC's executive director, Madeleine Redfern. We also had regular communications with Commissioner James Igloliorte, QIA executive director Terry Audla, and other QIA staff, especially Joanasie Akumalik. We were also helped and queried by colleagues in numerous disciplines, such as Yvonne Boyer (Aboriginal law), Carole Cancel (linguistics), Francis Lévesque (anthropology), Marianne McLean (history), Linda Radford (education), and Frank James Tester (social work and history).

In 2012, after the Commission had issued its final report, the QIA's board of directors and President Okalik Eegeesiak chose to complete the twenty-two histories and thematic studies. During this QIA phase, we received valued guidance from QIA executive director Navarana Beveridge and QTC project manager Bethany Scott.

This project is part of the robust and intellectually stimulating tradition of studying Canadian "colonialism" in the North as something other than simple manifest destiny. Many share our view that Aboriginal rights, public memory, and government accountability have to be near the centre of studies of Canada's past. In preparing the histories, we were very aware of the important precedent set by the community approach used by the Inuit Land Use and Occupancy Project (ILOUP), a team effort led by Milton Freeman and Inuit Tapirisat of Canada (now Inuit Tapiriit Kanatami) in the 1970s. While the scope of the QTC was smaller and more condensed than the ILUOP, it also sought to underline the distinctiveness of groups in Qikiqtaaluk within a larger Inuit identity. ILUOP researchers who testified to the QTC, notably Freeman himself, Hugh Brody, and George Wenzel, had a direct impact on our work. In other ways, we also took insights from the Life Stories of Northern Leaders series and the other contemporary scholars not already mentioned above, including Nelson Graburn, Shelagh Grant, Bill Kemp, Peter Kulchyski, Louis McComber, Ann McElroy, and Peter Usher. Their publications gave us confidence and factual grounding for reporting and explaining events.

Canadians generally want truth and reconciliation to proceed together. Many people understand that bad processes and harsh consequences can occur, even where there was no desire to do harm. The QTC histories focus on Inuit experiences, but there is much more to say about the events and people who were working in the region in the service of the state, the churches, or private ventures. There are shared histories as well as separate histories that are necessary to keep dialogues going. Everyone involved in this project hopes that the QTC histories will serve as a springboard for others, especially Inuit, to return to the testimonies and the thousands of archival documents in the QTC database to carry on with the important work of incorporating Inuit knowledge and perspectives into curriculum products, scholarship, and creative works.

In 1976, the *Inuit Land Use and Occupancy Report* described its researchers' desire "to provide an explicit statement—by the Inuit—of their perception of the man–land relationship." In 2013, the QTC histories have a similar purpose concerning the relations of people with their government. It is a more fluid relationship than the one linking Inuit to their land, but it is important, and will be for years to come.

Lastly, we accept, and regret, that such histories always contain errors, omissions, and misinterpretations. We encourage readers to bring them to the attention of the QIA for future printed and online editions, and to assist anyone who wants to use the histories in their own work.

Julie Harris
Philip Goldring
Ottawa, 2013

Introduction

This work began with the breaking of a long silence. In the 1990s, Inuit made great strides in taking charge of their own affairs through the Nunavut Land Claims Agreement and the creation of Nunavut. They were then ready to examine the past, including the harm done during the period of greatest change, from 1950 to 1975. They wanted to understand more about their own lives and those lived by their parents, grandparents, and siblings in an era that was profoundly marked by game laws, residential schools, medical evacuations, substantial population movements, and broken promises about housing and jobs. One especially sensitive source of anguish and disturbing memories was the government's campaign to eliminate qimmiit (Inuit sled dogs) from the settlements. Qimmiit were often shot without warning or compensation by the RCMP and others, leaving many people without any means of winter transportation. In a culture where qimmiit were vital to hunting and travel, and valued as companions, this campaign struck very close to the well-being of every Inuit family.

For a long time, many Inuit grieved in silence. Others spoke out in anger, aware that their experiences seemed to follow a pattern that was hard to decipher, but was important for understanding the problems in communities today. These feelings led the Qikiqtani Inuit Association (QIA) to interview Elders in 2004 about various issues related to moving into settlements. In 2007, the QIA created the Qikiqtani Truth Commission (QTC), a forum where Inuit could speak openly about difficult events in the decades after the Second World War and understand more about how communities took shape and the true costs of the changes. From the outset, the QTC looked beyond discussions of qimmiit and police towards the whole spectrum of relations between Inuit and the Canadian government. More than three hundred Inuit and more than twenty Qallunaat participated in the conversation between 2007 and 2009, in addition to the interviews in 2004. Their testimonies are at the heart of this book, which brings together reports on nine topics of importance to the QIA and the Commission, as well as the QTC's Final Report, "Achieving Saimaqatigiingniq."

"Achieving Saimaqatigiingniq" summarizes what QTC Commissioner James Igloliorte and his colleagues learned from listening to Inuit testimonies as they travelled to all thirteen Qikiqtani communities in 2008 and 2009, and from the Commission's archival research. It describes the sometimes conflicting policies of the Canadian government in Qikiqtaaluk between 1950 and 1975, the lack of meaningful consultation with Inuit about the changes made to their way of life, and the lasting harm these changes caused. It also presents detailed recommendations that are intended to help heal the wounds of the past and contribute to efforts being made by Inuit to take control of their futures from now on. These recommendations were developed in close consultation with QIA executive members and staff, and were also discussed in public meetings in all the Qikiqtani communities. The QIA accepted the QTC Final Report and its recommendations in October 2010, and is currently proceeding with an implementation strategy for the recommendations.

The nine other chapters provide more detailed examinations of topics covered in "Achieving Saimaqatigiingniq."

The first of these, "Inuit Sled Dogs," examines the RCMP's 2006 report on the killings of qimmiit in communities in Nunavut and Northern Quebec between 1950 and 1970. The origins of the RCMP report date back to the late 1990s, when the deeply felt grief about the killings of qimmiit led a number of Inuit to publicly charge that the RCMP had been acting under government orders, so that they would lose their mobility and any possibility of returning to their traditional way of life. In 2005, the federal government rejected a parliamentary committee's advice to call an independent inquiry into the killings, and instead asked the RCMP to investigate itself. The resulting *RCMP Sled Dogs Report* confirmed that hundreds and perhaps thousands of qimmiit were killed by RCMP members and other authorities in the 1950s and 1960s. However, as the QTC analysis of this report points out, the RCMP took a narrow approach to their investigation. They focused on whether particular actions by RCMP members were sanctioned by legislation and concluded that the killings were legal. They also looked for but did not find patterns that might show that RCMP actions were directed towards forcing Inuit off the land and into settlements. In addition, much of its analysis was directed towards discrediting Inuit memories and interpretations of how, why, and by whom the qimmiit were killed at that time.

While the QTC also found no evidence of a conspiracy to force Inuit off the land by killing their qimmiit, it did find a series of interconnected government policies and laws put into effect and enforced by the RCMP that quickly undermined traditional Inuit ways of living. When authorities in Ottawa revised the Northwest Territory's Ordinance Respecting Dogs in 1949-50, they effectively outlawed traditional Inuit ways of handling qimmiit, wherever this seemed to conflict with the needs or practices of a growing Qallunaat population. The Ordinance was inextricably linked to other actions, laws, and policies affecting Inuit, most of whom were drawn into settlements. The standard government policy was to assume Inuit must, at their own expense, accommodate newcomers' needs and wants. The QTC's analysis concludes that the Government of Canada failed in its obligations to Inuit when it placed restrictions on their use of qimmiit without involving Inuit directly in finding ways to make restrictions less onerous or in finding mutually acceptable solutions to real or perceived threats posed by qimmiit in their new surroundings.

"The Official Mind of Canadian Colonialism" explores the beliefs of government officials who oversaw the transformation of Qikiqtaaluk. Underlying the policies they proposed and implemented in the North was a firm conviction that progress was inevitable, and that it was the government's role to ensure Inuit had access to the benefits enjoyed by all Canadian citizens. At the beginning of the period, there were two opposing views of how this should be accomplished. One was that Inuit should be encouraged to continue with their traditional way of life, while taking advantage of better health care and employment opportunities offered in the Qallunaat settlements. The second, opposing view was that Inuit were destined to leave the land and be assimilated into a new northern economy focused on military installations and mineral, oil, and gas exploitation. By 1960, the latter view had become dominant, and Inuit were increasingly encouraged to move into permanent settlements, where it was cheaper for the government to provide education, health care, and other services. The many harmful results of this transformation of Inuit life were in part due to ignorance. While officials were committed to promoting the well-being of Inuit and claimed to respect their culture, few had any experience of life in Qikiqtaaluk. Equally important, during most of this period, is that there were no serious or consistent attempts to consult with Inuit about the programs they devised.

"Schooling" describes how a centuries-old way of bringing up children was replaced by an educational system that ignored Inuit realities, culture, and expectations, and failed in its goal of preparing Inuit to find places in a wage economy. Traditional Inuit education was founded on observation and practice of the skills required for life on the land. In the first half of the twentieth century, some formal education was provided on a sporadic basis by missionaries. After the Second World War, however, the Canadian government began developing a structured, regulated system of schooling for the region, modelled on provincial education programs in southern Canada.

The construction of day schools and hostels proved to be a major catalyst for the movement of Inuit into the settlements. Initially, government officials believed that Inuit would leave their children in the hostels for the school year, and then return to their ilagiit nunagivaktangit. Parents, however, were unwilling to do this, and moved into the settlements to be near their children. The curriculum that children were taught had no relevance to life in the North, and was delivered exclusively in English. The result was a cultural and generational divide between parents and children. This divide was even sharper and more painful for families whose children were sent away to residential schools. In the words of former residential school student Paul Quassa, "We lost that knowledge that would have been transferred if we did grow up with our parents." Even on its own terms, schooling in Qikiqtaaluk was a failure in this period, because it rarely gave people the skills and knowledge they needed to fully participate in the economic changes that were planned for their communities. Men were trained for manual labour positions, and women for secretarial and institutional work, and there were never enough jobs available even at these lower levels.

For centuries, Inuit were mobile, moving seasonally in a symbiotic relationship with the land and its resources. After 1950, the nature of Inuit mobility changed dramatically. The chapter "Mobility" examines a mix of voluntary, pressured, and forced moves between 1950 and 1975, usually in response to government priorities. Many of these cases involved the coercion of families to leave ilagiit nunagivaktangit and live in settlements, or to send their children to school in settlements, often by threats of losing access to health care or family allowances. In cases of voluntary relocations, Inuit were often given assurances that they would find housing, proper schooling, income support, and health care. Some people misunderstood what they were told, but others were given empty promises. Other cases included individuals who were required to move south for extended periods for education or health care, evacuations of ilagiit nunagivaktangit to other locations in real or perceived emergencies, and the closing of communities.

Every Inuk who appeared before the QTC testified to the traumatic effects of relocations, medical evacuations, or schooling. Many expressed frustration that the government made decisions without asking Inuit and without addressing the consequences of the decisions. They felt deep cultural and personal losses resulting from severing family ties and ties to the land, and anger that a substantial amount of Inuit culture and land-based knowledge was lost in exchange for unfulfilled promises. The archival record demonstrates that Inuit were not consulted, that they did not understand the full implications of the moves they were asked or compelled to make, and that very little was done to address the negative effects of moves, especially with respect to housing.

The RCMP and Inuit have a long shared history in Qikiqtaaluk, dating back to the early 1920s when the RCMP first arrived. "Policing" documents this relationship, one that has been fraught with complications and misunderstandings. Until the 1960s, the core responsibilities of the RCMP were to visit ilagiit nunagivaktangit to report on health and economic conditions, register births and deaths, deliver family benefits, investigate complaints and game ordinance violations, and deliver the mail. The RCMP relied on Inuit appointed as special constables to guide them, feed their dogs, and interpret Inuktitut. With the growth of permanent settlements, RCMP relinquished their official social welfare duties to new administrators and focused primarily on enforcement of laws, including the Dog Ordinance, as described above. As so many testimonies to the QTC demonstrated, the killing of qimmiit proved to be one of the most damaging divides between Inuit and the RCMP. Strict enforcement of game laws, in the name of wildlife conservation, was another source of resentment and mistrust. Inuit saw RCMP officers as powerful and threatening agents in the community who could dictate to Inuit where to go, what to hunt, and how to behave. Many QTC testimonies express the sense of awe or fear (ilira) in which Inuit held

RCMP officers, which led them into doing things they did not want to do, such as move graves, tie up dogs, send children to settlement or residential schools, visit the annual medical ship, take unwanted jobs, and move from ilagiit nunagivaktangit to the settlements.

"Economic Development" examines the transformation of the region's economy from one of hunting and trapping primarily for local benefit, towards one designed by southern planners with the interests of the South in mind. Economic development was a major motive for concentrating Inuit in the thirteen Qikiqtaaluk communities. The strategy in broad terms was to build infrastructure, such as schools, housing, diesel generators, landing strips, and navigation aids; to encourage local hiring for mining and other development projects where possible; and, as in the days of the fur trade, to organize production of other exports. However, the very slow pace of development, along with the shift of people from the land to the settlements, resulted in widespread unemployment or underemployment. Exploitation of minerals, oil, and gas, in particular, did not live up to expectations in this period.

Initially, training to prepare Inuit for the new economy focused mainly on trades. However, the development of community organizations, first in Iqaluit and then in the smaller communities, helped to prepare Inuit for high-level jobs in sectors such as local retailing; trading in renewable resources; production and sale of carvings, prints, weaving, and sewing; and tourism. Co-operatives, first developed as vehicles for the sale of arts and crafts, and later expanded to market a wide range of services, proved to be successful vehicles for local economic development led by Inuit. Despite the impediments posed by settlement life, many Inuit continue to this day to value hunting as a foundation of their local economy, and where possible, combine hunting with wage employment. As expressed in a 1989 statement by the Tungavik Federation of Nunavut: "we want to design a society and economy that enables us to participate effectively in the old ways based on the land and its bounty, as well as in the new ways based on space-age technology and world-wide communication."

Government promises about the quality and cost of housing were an important factor in convincing families that it might be worthwhile to move into a settlement. One of the most consistent themes of Inuit testimony to the QTC was that these promises were not kept. The chapter, "Housing," demonstrates that successive government housing programs for most of this period failed to meet their objectives, and that Inuit were never consulted about appropriate and affordable accommodation. The Eskimo Housing Loan Program, launched in 1959, was a rent-to-own scheme that attempted to keep costs low by offering small "matchbox" houses that were unsuitable for the Inuit lifestyle and poorly constructed. These houses were unaffordable for most Inuit who subsisted on hunting and seasonal employment, and by 1965, 90% of Inuit who were contracted to buy houses had failed to make payments. This program was replaced by the Eskimo Rental Housing Program, with rentals based on income and housing type, and administered by housing councils intended to give Inuit a voice in housing options. The system was complex, and testimonies to the QTC show that many Inuit felt they had been misled by false promises of low rents that would not increase.

Government programs were never able to keep up with demand for housing in this period, and another common theme in QTC testimonies was the frequent delays finding housing once a family moved to a community. Often, Inuit spent months and even years after they moved to permanent settlements living in tents and other temporary dwellings, which were sometimes insufficiently winterized. In the 1950s, poor housing was repeatedly identified as a leading cause of high rates of illness among Inuit. Although one of the goals of government housing programs was to provide homes that would improve health outcomes, overcrowding and poor ventilation in settlement houses were major factors in high rates of TB and infant mortality.

After the Second World War, the government's recognition of Inuit as Canadians entitled to the full benefits of citizenship resulted in a new focus on Inuit health. "Health" describes the evolution and impacts of government health care programs in Qikiqtaaluk from 1950 to 1975, and the health issues Inuit faced as a result of life in the settlements. Beginning in the 1920s, the Eastern Arctic Patrol (EAP) provided limited medical services to Inuit during its annual visits to RCMP posts. With the transfer of responsibility for Inuit health to the Canadian government in 1945, the EAP and its medical facilities became crucial to carrying out the government's policy for treating an epidemic of tuberculosis (TB) among Inuit. After 1950, medical personnel on the new medical patrol ship *C.D. Howe* screened Inuit for TB and other infectious diseases or ailments, and took away those found to be infected, for treatment in southern Canada. The human cost of this policy of medical evacuation was high: Many Inuit testified to the QTC about the fear and sadness they experienced while isolated in southern hospitals, as well as the lasting pain of never seeing relatives again.

Following the creation of Indian and Northern Health Services in 1946, a chain of outport nursing stations was established in Qikiqtaaluk communities, first in Cape Dorset and Kimmirut, and later in Iqaluit (1955), Hall Beach (1957), Cambridge Bay (1958), and Kuujjuarapik (1962). In remote areas, these provided a variety of care, including some dentistry, mental health care, counselling, pre- and postnatal care, and local public health inspections, as well as public health education. In more populated communities, such as Iqaluit, nurses would screen patients and perform diagnostic tests that visiting specialists followed up on. The establishment of nursing stations, as well as a hospital in Iqaluit in 1964, reduced the need for the EAP, which came to an end in 1969. Overall, government programs in this period were relatively successful in controlling TB and improving access to regular health care for Inuit. However, the policy of centralization produced a new range of negative health effects among Inuit, including many physical ailments associated with poor nutrition and overcrowded or substandard housing, as well as high rates of suicide and substance abuse.

"Qimmiit," the final chapter, expands on the role of qimmiit in Inuit economy and culture, the management of qimmiit in the period when Inuit were moving into settlements, and the harm done to relations between Inuit and the RCMP and other government agencies by the killings of qimmiit. "Since time began, the dogs have been the most important possession of Inuit," one Inuk testified to the QTC. In winter, qimmiit pulled hunters and their equipment for long distances, helping to locate game and brought it back to ilagiit nunagivaktangit or trading posts. During storms or blizzards, qimmiit could track scents to follow paths. They were also able to recognize dangerous areas on the ice, and protected hunters against polar bear attacks.

As Inuit moved into settlements in the 1950s and 1960s, jobs, houses, and schools all worked against the keeping of qimmiit, and they began to lose their central place in Inuit life. While qimmiit were still necessary for families wanting to return to the land to hunt, the requirements of the Ordinance were difficult to comply with, and detrimental to the health of the dogs. There were no serious attempts to consult Inuit about other ways of accommodating qimmiit in settlements. Instead, qimmiit were shot when they were found loose, or when they were deemed sick. By the mid-1970s, almost every team of qimmiit in Qikiqtaaluk had been destroyed. This chapter documents the fate of qimmiit in each of the thirteen Qikiqtaaluk communities, and draws on the QTC testimonies as well as the archival record to demonstrate the anger, shame, and feelings of powerlessness caused by the killings.

In their testimonies to the QTC, many Inuit spoke of the relief they felt in unburdening themselves of the painful memories of this period. It is the QIA's hope that the chapters in this book will help Inuit and Qallunaat alike to continue the process of understanding and healing. As these studies make clear, the history of Qikiqtaaluk between 1950 and 1975 is a complex one. This book will have served its purpose if it challenges readers to further explore the significance of the personal stories and archival evidence uncovered by the QTC, and to investigate new sources that will provide insight into the period.

Brian Cameron
Philip Goldring
Julie Harris

Analysis of the *RCMP Sled Dog Report*

Editor's Note: This final report has been preserved in its entirety in order to provide the fullest possible picture of the work undertaken by the Commission. Readers may notice some repetition of material presented in other chapters. This report has not been abridged from what was presented to the QIA Board of Directors in 2010. For this reason, too, the footnotes have been preserved in the text, as they were originally presented.

Executive Summary

BACKGROUND

In March 2005, the House of Commons Standing Committee on Aboriginal Affairs and Northern Development heard witnesses describe the killing of sled dogs in Nunavik and the Baffin Region between 1950 and 1970. These incidents, which became known as the "dog slaughter," occurred during the same period as the resettlement of Inuit into a few central communities.

The Standing Committee called for a public inquiry by a superior court judge "to get to the bottom of the matter." The Government of Canada did not set up the requested inquiry. Instead, it asked the RCMP to conduct a comprehensive review of its actions regarding sled dogs in the North between 1950 and 1970. The Force presented a brief report later in 2005, followed by a 26-page final report, titled *The RCMP and the Inuit Sled Dogs (Nunavut and Northern Quebec: 1950–1970)*, to the new government in 2006. They produced a much longer compilation of evidence and commentary later the same year.

Since that time, the Qikiqtani Inuit Association (QIA) has acted on the need to understand and communicate a balanced account of what happened, which includes an Inuit perspective. The QIA established its own inquiry—the Qikiqtani Truth Commission (QTC)—independent of the government and with a broader mandate to study the whole range of government–Inuit relations during this turbulent period. The QTC completed its collection of testimonies and the majority of its research in early 2010.

During a meeting between QTC Commissioner James Igloliorte and RCMP Commissioner William J.S. Elliott held in Ottawa on 4 February 2008, Commissioner Elliott asked the QTC to review and respond to the RCMP Sled Dogs Report.

RCMP SLED DOGS REPORT (2006)

The report and compilation, referenced here as the RCMP Sled Dogs Report, exonerated RCMP members of criminal or administrative wrongdoing in the matter of killing Inuit sled dogs, by extension exonerating the federal government. The report addressed RCMP behaviour from a forensic rather than historical perspective, without examining the cultural practices and rules of Inuit society at the time. It focused on whether particular actions by RCMP members were sanctioned by legislation, and concluded that the killings were legal. They also looked for but did not find patterns that might show that actions were directed toward forcing Inuit off the land and into settlements.

QTC HISTORICAL RESEARCH (2008–10)

Although the QTC mandate addresses a smaller geographic territory (the Baffin Region) than is covered in the RCMP report, it calls for the use of a more complete methodology and inclusive social purpose that looks far beyond the issue of dog deaths to thoroughly investigate how other socio-economic trends and ill-formed government polices and practices also impacted Inuit at that time. It integrates Inuit concepts of justice (what is "right," what is "wrong," and how transgressions should be addressed) into its analysis of the responses of Inuit to dog killings and other actions of RCMP officers.

In addition to extensive archival research and listening to approximately 350 individuals (Inuit, retired RCMP, DIAND staff, scholars, and politicians), the QTC benefitted from generous access to RCMP records, including documents and administrative correspondence gathered by the RCMP for its own report.

A SHARED HISTORY: INUIT AND RCMP IN THE BAFFIN REGION

From the 1920s into the late 1950s, the RCMP was the primary face of government in the Baffin Region. Officers had four customary roles: representing Canada for sovereignty purposes; enforcing laws; exercising oversight in relations between traders and Inuit; and patrolling by boat and dog team to provide basic services, keep track of people, and report on game conditions. RCMP became knowledgeable about a region that previously only Inuit knew and controlled, thereby developing considerable understanding of Inuit culture and behaviour. They regularly visited many of the hundred or so ilagiit nunagivaktangit (camps) where Inuit lived while hunting. A large part of police work focused on making it possible for government to exercise control over the region while simultaneously encouraging Inuit to remain on the land with limited contact with traders and missionaries, and little need for government services.

Beginning in the 1950s, however, Inuit experienced tumultuous change in every aspect of their land use and annual routine. Police were also forced to adjust when new government agencies with radically new policies entered the domains of both Inuit life and police duties. At times these new civilian agencies enlisted the police to implement unpopular new measures, such as restrictions on hunting, removal of children to be educated, and rounding up of people for annual medical exams with the all-too-frequent consequence of removal to the South for treatment. These agencies competed with the police in settlements for authority and influence. By the 1970s, Inuit were living year-round in thirteen government-created settlements instead of dozens of ilagiit nunagivaktangit. The Government of the Northwest Territories delivered most social services, and RCMP members spent most of their time providing conventional southern-style policing.

One of the duties police accepted in the new state of affairs was destroying sled dogs, which had become quite numerous in the settlements. There some Inuit were less able to care for them and control them in traditional ways, because the practice of keeping dogs loose was riskier in the much larger settlements of people (and of dogs). Under pressure from non-Inuit, hundreds—perhaps thousands—of Inuit sled dogs were killed from the mid-1950s onwards, despite a confusingly contrary policy of having the police immunize dogs against disease and even import dogs to replace others lost in a canine epidemic.

With no access to decision-making or decision-makers and limited access to local officials, Inuit drew a reasonable and logical connection between the killing of their sled dogs and the detrimental effects of centralization, namely the loss of their ability to move back to the land, increasing reliance on a cash economy, and the exclusive concentration of services in settlements. By 2005, Inuit were speaking openly and forcefully about their belief that the dogs—their main means of transportation—were shot by police under federal government orders to deprive Inuit of their mobility and autonomy and to tie them to settlements.

QTC RESPONSE TO THE RCMP SLED DOGS REPORT

The RCMP Sled Dogs Report failed to fulfill the expectations of either the Standing Committee Report (March 2005) or the Minister's letter (28 April 2005). The Standing Committee, in a recommendation later endorsed by the Legislature of Nunavut, called for an inquiry to "get to the bottom of the matter." In the QTC's view, this meant more than merely confirming the killings and finding local causes and a legal excuse for them. Getting to "the bottom" would require the exploration of deeper reasons for the killings and the connections with other socio-economic trends and events, including policies, budgets, and extreme weaknesses in the cross-cultural and other job-related training given to federal agents in the North. And if hundreds of Inuit witnesses were somehow mistaken about what they saw and remembered, as RCMP analysis concluded, getting to the bottom of the matter would have to include a thoughtful examination of relations between the community and its police. It would also have required an examination of the appropriateness of the law, its interpretation and implementation, and the customary practices of Inuit with respect to dogs. This would have allowed a fuller understanding of the experience of the Elders, the discomfort of police who were expected to shoot dogs, and the consequences of the killings in the present day.

While both the RCMP and the QTC recognize that sled dogs did not pose a problem until non-Inuit began to settle in the Arctic, the RCMP report treated this Qallunaat presence and settlement living as a "given" and therefore analyzed the killings as a law enforcement issue rather than as part of a process of accelerated and disruptive social change to the Inuit way of life. Much of its analysis was directed not at understanding how Inuit and Canadian society and governance worked in this era but, rather, toward discrediting Inuit memories and interpretations of how, why, and by whom the dogs were killed at that time.

AREAS OF CONCERN

Interpreting the Killings

The RCMP Sled Dogs Report acknowledged that RCMP members and other persons in authority in the 1950s and 1960s killed hundreds and perhaps thousands of dogs, but it ignores Inuit knowledge and perspectives on these killings.

While the report carefully noted periods or episodes in which the RCMP were "dedicated to the cause of preserving the traditional Inuit semi-nomadic culture" including the use of dogs, its analysis sidestepped the impacts of the killings on Inuit at the time and since. It argued effectively that RCMP did not want to kill dogs and that the killings were never part of a "conspiracy" with the explicit motive of forcing Inuit to stop hunting and live in permanent settlements.

The QTC formed different views about the existence or absence of a "conspiracy." In place of a conspiracy, the QTC found a series of interconnected government policies and laws put into effect and enforced by the RCMP, which quickly undermined traditional Inuit ways of living. When authorities in Ottawa revised the Territory's Ordinance Respecting Dogs in 1949–50, they effectively outlawed traditional Inuit ways of handling dogs, wherever this seemed to conflict with the needs or practices of a growing Qallunaat population. The Ordinance was inextricably linked to other actions, laws, and policies affecting Inuit, most of whom were drawn into settlements. The standard government policy was to assume Inuit must, at their own expense, accommodate newcomers' needs and wants. While the Ordinance Respecting Dogs was clear to those who enforced it, hunters understood it as illogical, unnecessary, and also harmful; Inuit and dogs had existed together for uncounted generations without such restrictions being necessary.

The authors of the RCMP Sled Dogs Report, like most other writers on the subject, appeared to accept that the shooting of dogs by newcomers over more than a decade was a rational and justified activity, while the grief and resentment of the dog owners was unwarranted and worthy of criticism or at least anthropological study. In fact the considerations should not be merely cultural or emotional, but also legal, to a degree not recognized in the RCMP Sled Dogs Report. The legal implications stem from a consideration of Aboriginal and human rights. The Government of Canada failed in its obligations to Inuit when it placed restrictions on their use of dogs without involving Inuit directly in the search for ways to make restrictions less onerous, or for mutually acceptable solutions to real or perceived threats posed by dogs in their new surroundings.

RCMP Review Team and Inuit Complaints

Because the RCMP was in no position to conduct an independent inquiry, the Review Team did not receive the full trust and cooperation of most Inuit who lived through the 1950s and 1960s.

The team did receive information from a few Inuit, notably former special constables and their families. The report repeatedly deplored the fact that it received so little evidence from other Inuit. Instead of accepting the core truth in the Inuit reports of dog killings and looking for ways to understand the Inuit perspective, the RCMP Review Team set out to discredit individuals and their political organizations, although without directly accusing them of lying. Particularly negative statements were made in the RCMP Sled Dogs Report about the fact that most Inuit simply would not provide evidence to the police about the events they or their families suffered from a generation earlier. This was treated as *prima facie* evidence of political intimidation by Inuit leaders and organizations motivated by a desire for financial compensation.

Historic Inuit–RCMP Interactions

The interaction between Inuit and RCMP in the history of the Baffin Region is important to the history of both groups.

Both the RCMP Sled Dogs Report and the research and testimony gathered by the QTC provided abundant evidence of the RCMP's important role in the Inuit economy in the years before centralization. In their focus on dogs, however, the authors of the RCMP Sled Dogs Report glossed over more central aspects of the relationship between RCMP and Inuit. Inuit constituted almost the whole permanent population of the Baffin Region throughout this period and the RCMP represented government authority.

Serving the Inuit gave the RCMP a role that was essential to the Force's self-image as well as to Canada's claims to be effectively occupying the Arctic. On the long sled patrols that are part of RCMP lore, Inuit provided guiding services and hunted food for the police and their dog teams. New police recruits knew little or nothing about the North—Inuit helped them survive and learn. The police in return provided medical assistance and, albeit in paternalistic ways, delivered other social services. Less pleasant was the occasional use of police prestige and authority to direct Inuit behaviour, especially concerning the length of visits to the trading posts. Some police were known to act harshly, discriminately, and unwisely in daily interactions in communities. There were also relations between some RCMP members and Inuit women, which often resulted in offspring. The level of consent varied, depending on particular circumstances. At the end of their northern term, most officers returned South alone.

The RCMP Sled Dogs Report did not examine the way inequality of power and cultural difference affected the dynamics of RCMP–Inuit interaction in the dispersed ilagiit nunagivaktangit, on the land, sea, and ice, or around the trading establishments, either before or after centralized settlement became official policy. The statements of retired members underlined the bitterness many felt over the way other government agents took over many RCMP responsibilities after 1955. RCMP–Inuit interaction, both positive and negative, was relevant to the evolution of the settlements from Qallunaat enclaves to present-day communities.

Sled Dogs History as Collective Memory

The RCMP Sled Dogs Report reads as an exercise by the Force to sustain or create a positive collective memory of the RCMP experience in the region, with a nostalgic focus on the specific duties and circumstances of the 1950s and 1960s.

The report focused on the time, energy, and hardships required to bring the South into the North. The report ignored the more complicated story about the Force's role in Canadian appropriation of Inuit lands. Inuit, on the other hand, are still weighing—and being weighed down by—their memories of the inequalities, sacrifices, losses, shock, and bewilderment at the sudden end in a few years to a way of life that had evolved over centuries.

The problems of interpreting these overlapping histories relate not so much to law enforcement as to culture and memory, as well as to individuals' places in what continues to be a divided society. Unfortunately, the RCMP Sled Dogs Report did nothing to try to reconcile these views and experiences of Nunavut history. The report also glossed over both government records and individuals' published statements before 1975, which expressed concern over the number and manner of the dog killings. The report wrongly interpreted the lengthy public reticence of Inuit on this issue as evidence of dishonesty, when shame, grief, and other emotions connected with disempowering changes induced many Inuit to stay silent until quite recently about the loss of their dogs.

The report maintained a consistent scepticism toward the oral history of Inuit while neglecting to comment on inconsistencies and distortions within similar evidence provided by RCMP and other Qallunaat witnesses. It relied mainly on the memories of police who were not stationed at the particular places where the most systematic killings are known to have taken place. If the testimony of Inuit whose dogs were killed did not contain specific details concerning time, place, and name sufficient to support a possible criminal conviction, then the testimony was dismissed without regard for its inherent truth and value.

Public Records and Research Issues

The report fell below professional standards in its collection and identification of sources.

As an example, there are no supporting audio/visual tapes or signed statements for many interviews. Further, a more complete review of easily accessible published and public archival material would have illustrated the causes and long history of mistrust between Inuit and all government agents, mistrust in which the RCMP were inevitably embroiled even when they were not on the scene or were individually blameless in specific cases.

Prior to 1970, RCMP-generated documentation is sometimes the only written public record remaining about these communities, yet it appears that the great majority of these were destroyed along with routine paperwork. The report provided an incoherent explanation of how so much potentially relevant documentation was destroyed.

Many kinds and sources of evidence would be needed to generate a more complete and balanced understanding of the role of the RCMP and others in the disruptions Inuit society underwent between 1950 and 1975. The RCMP Sled Dogs Report shed some light and prompted the Qikiqtani Inuit Association, through the Qikiqtani Truth Commission, to add a great deal more. Nevertheless, the positive contributions of the report were undermined by a tone and spirit of scepticism and disrespect. This weakness began with the federal government's decision to encourage the Force to investigate its own role, and can be countered by increased efforts to share the task of inquiring into and explaining the Qikiqtani Region's mid-20th-century past.

Introduction

This report is the Qikiqtani Truth Commission's review of a study completed in 2006 by the RCMP titled: *The RCMP and the Inuit Sled Dogs (Nunavut and Northern Quebec: 1950–1970)*, hereafter cited as RCMP Sled Dogs Report. This review was requested by the Commissioner to help the

Qikiqtani Truth Commission (QTC) meet its mandate to seek the truth surrounding the "dog slaughter," "relocations," and other decision-making of governments up until 1980, and to document the effect of these events and decisions on Inuit culture, economy, and way of life. The review is also a response to a request made by RCMP Commissioner William J.S. Elliott during a meeting with QTC Commissioner James Igliorte on 4 February 2008 that the QTC conduct a review of the report.

The RCMP prepared its Sled Dogs Report in response to serious complaints and disclosures that were made over a number of years by Inuit whose dogs were shot during the 1950s and 1960s, a volatile period in the history of both Nunavut and Nunavik. The well-documented shooting deaths of hundreds, perhaps thousands, of sled dogs occurred at the same time Inuit were moving from the land into centres where government, religious, and commercial services were congregated. In the Baffin Region alone, more than one hundred previously autonomous groups of Inuit living on the land gathered into settlements that currently number thirteen. With no access to decision-making or to decision-makers, and limited access to local officials, Inuit drew a logical connection between the killing of dogs and the loss of their ability to move back to the land, an increasing reliance on a cash economy and the exclusive concentration of services in settlements. From the time of the shootings until the vocal complaints heard by Parliament in 2005, Inuit spoke openly and forcefully about their belief that dogs were shot by the police under federal government orders, with the intention of depriving Inuit of their mobility and tying them to the settlements.

Reading the RCMP Sled Dogs Report itself indicates that the objectives of that study were narrowly focused on refuting the assertions of illegal behaviour by the police and thereby defending the reputation of the Force and its veterans. The QTC was particularly struck by a limitation that was explained by the RCMP Sled Dogs Report's principal author to the Qikiqtani Inuit Association's executive director in February 2006:

> The RCMP is interested in obtaining only those statements that relate to possible unlawful killing of Inuit sled dogs by RCMP members. The RCMP review team has no mandate to investigate killing by non-RCMP personnel, nor is the review team interested in reviewing accounts of the killing of loose dogs that posed a potential or real public safety threat to communities and settlements, since that would have constituted destruction in accordance with the Dog Ordinance of the NWT."[1]

By accepting this limitation, or having this limitation imposed on it, the RCMP Review Team adopted what we have termed a "forensic" approach to the many historical issues that provide a context, if not justification, for the killings. It is "forensic" in the sense of limiting the inquiry to apparent offences that could form the basis of charges against individuals, instead of evaluating the many incidents as examples of failures or misapplications of federal government policies that wronged Inuit.

Despite the limitations of this forensic approach, the authors of the RCMP Sled Dogs Report did actually extend their reach to assert a general defence of the quality of services provided by RCMP in the North. Our analysis of their review examines the extent to which the evidence and process used to produce the report's conclusions achieved the desired goals stated by the authors of the report, and assesses how well the report met the goals set out by the Government of Canada. Our review also explains how alternative approaches would have been more successful, and more likely to promote reconciliation between parties who each believe they have been wronged.

---

1 Quoted in: Royal Canadian Mounted Police (RCMP), *The RCMP and the Inuit Sled Dogs (Nunavut and Northern Quebec: 1950-1970)*, 2006, pp. 148.

Background

THE DOG SLAUGHTER AND ITS INQUIRIES

The intermittent shooting of dogs began at least as early as 1957 and was never a secret in the Baffin Region. Inuit at Iqaluit spoke candidly about their losses to anthropologist Toshio Yatsushiro, who published their words in a national magazine in 1962.[2] Local politician Bryan Pearson was vocal on the issue, sharing his thoughts with the mass-circulation *Star Weekly* in 1966 and again recounting the events from his seat in the Legislative Assembly in 1973.[3] By this time there were very few dog teams left, and the killings were not prominently discussed during the years when major events such as the Nunavut Land Claim and the creation of Nunavut were consuming public attention. Yet individuals guarded their memories.[4] By the 1990s, Canadian society was more tolerant of public exposition of the past harm done by governments to individuals and groups. Accordingly, public discussion of Inuit grievances became more common. These grievances bubbled to the surface in a public meeting in Iqaluit in February 1999. The meeting had been called to build rapport between Inuit and the new RCMP "V" Division headquartered in Iqaluit, but demonstrated to the Force that the behaviour of some members in the past would undermine future relations.[5]

2 Toshio Yatsushiro, "The Changing Eskimo: A study of wage employment and its consequences among the Eskimos of Frobisher Bay, Baffin Island," *The Beaver* (Summer 1962), pp. 19–26.

3 Walter Stewart, "The shameful way we treat our Eskimos," *Star Weekly* (June 25, 1966); see also below, "Dust, Dogs and the Dump."

4 See for example, testimony of Eena Angmarlik, QTC interview QTPA03, 15 May 2008.

5 *RCMP Sled Dogs Report*, pp. 635–36, quoting an article in *Nunatsiaq News* that has not been found in the online archive; Annette Bourgeois, "Acknowledging History, the RCMP Resolves to do Better: Nunavut's Commanding Officer Chris Bothe Says the

Public discussion of the dog killings resumed. At the annual meeting of Makivik Corporation in March 1999, Nunavimmiut brought memories forward and called for an inquiry, an apology, and compensation.[6] The Qikiqtani Inuit Association (QIA), whose president had attended the Makivik meeting, quickly repeated this call. The QIA also considered bringing legal charges against the RCMP and federal government for negligence and general harm done to Inuit by killing dogs, thus limiting people's mobility. However, the Iqaluit meeting on 26 February had already stirred opinion among retired RCMP members, who vigorously denied the reports of misbehaviour in the 1950s and 1960s.

Over the next five years, the Inuit organizations in Nunavik and the Qikiqtani Region interviewed Elders, developed their policies, interpreted the evidence surrounding the "dog slaughter," and developed strategies for redress for the harm caused by the failure by government before 1970 to consult Inuit or to respect its own fiduciary obligations to Inuit in the two regions. As described by anthropologist Francis Lévesque, in 2000 the campaign became national: Organizations wrote to the relevant federal and Quebec ministers and to their local Members of Parliament. By the end of that year, leaders of Inuit organizations were convinced that the killings had been centrally organized and, Lévesque asserts, "all parties involved took their respective positions." Government admitted that some dogs had been killed, but insisted that all shootings were justified on grounds of public health and safety, while Inuit insisted that healthy dogs were killed, that government had recklessly disregarded the importance of sled dogs to Inuit culture, and that the documentary record had been tampered with to conceal government wrongdoing. The following years were spent on

---

Force is Preparing an Apology for Actions Committed by Members in the Past," *Nunatsiaq News* (February 26, 1999), pp. 1–2.

6 Francis Lévesque, "Les Inuit, Leurs Chiens et l'administration Nordique, de 1950 à 2007. Anthropologie d'une revendication inuit contemporaine" (PhD thesis, Université Laval, 2008). This paragraph draws extensively on chapter 1, pp. 68–109.

research, interviews, and quiet efforts to gather support for a public inquiry. The Inuit Circumpolar Conference supported this call in 2002, as did the *Nunatsiaq News*.[7] Research, interviews, and analysis continued in both the Qikiqtani Region and Nunavik during 2003 and 2004. Increasingly close attention was given to linkages between the dog shootings and the general government policy of moving people into centralized settlements. Lévesque identifies 2005 as the year Makivik Corporation brought the subject back into public prominence, releasing its video treatment of the period, *Echo of the Last Howl*. In short order, this caught the attention of the national press and was aired in Parliament.

In March 2005, the House of Commons Standing Committee on Aboriginal Affairs and Northern Development heard witnesses describe the killing of sled dogs in Nunavik and the Baffin Region between 1950 and 1970. These incidents, which became known as the "dog slaughter," occurred during the same period as the resettlement of Inuit into a few central communities. This led many Inuit to believe that the dogs, their main means of transportation, were killed specifically to force Inuit to abandon their life on the land.

The Standing Committee called for a public inquiry by a superior court judge "to get to the bottom of the matter."[8] The Government of Canada did not set up the requested inquiry. Instead, it asked the RCMP to conduct a comprehensive review of its actions regarding sled dogs in the North between 1950 and 1970. The Force presented a brief report later in 2005, shortly before the defeat of the Liberal government in the House of Commons and subsequently in the general election of 23 January 2006. These

7 Jim Bell, "Solid oral research needed on dog slaughter issue," *Nunatsiaq News* (August 30, 2002), accessed online 7 April 2010 at http://www.nunatsiaq.com/archives/nunavut020802/news/editorial/editorial.html#aug30.

8 Quoted in RCMP Sled Dogs Report, p. 5. Also available on the House of Commons website, http://www2.parl.gc.ca/HousePublications/Publication.aspx?DocId=1688732&Language=E&Mode=1&Parl=38&Ses=1, accessed 30 April 2010.

political events did not affect the Force's decision. It acted on its own initiative to conduct an intensive research effort that lead to a 26-page final report to the Minister in 2006, and a much longer compilation of evidence and commentary later the same year.

Scope of the RCMP Report

That compilation, which we refer to throughout this review as the RCMP Sled Dogs Report, exonerated RCMP members of criminal or administrative wrongdoing in the matter of killing dogs[9] and, by extension, it exonerated the federal government. In particular, the report addressed RCMP behaviour from a forensic rather than an historical perspective or a perspective guided by the cultural practices and rules of Inuit society at the time. The report did not explain what happened to the dogs over time or in context, but rather focused on whether particular actions by RCMP members were sanctioned by legislation. It concluded that the killings were legal. The conclusions of the RCMP Sled Dogs Report may be grouped into five main claims.[10]

---

9 This is stated in different parts of the RCMP Sled Dogs Report, beginning at page 1 in the Executive Summary: "The destruction of individual Inuit sled dogs, and other dogs, was undertaken by RCMP members for public health and safety reasons, or because of the need to contain dog disease epidemics, or at the request of the owner." A similar sentence in the conclusion to the brief final report adds the words "in accordance with the law" after the reference to safety reasons. Canada. Royal Canadian Mounted Police. *Final Report: RCMP Review of Allegations Concerning Inuit Sled Dogs*. http://www.rcmp-grc.gc.ca/pubs/ccaps-spcca/pdf/sled-traineau-dogs-chiens-final-eng.pdf, accessed 28 Dec 2009, pp. 23–24.

10 The five points outlined here were repeated a number of times throughout the lengthy report. Sample references are provided here for each: (1) RCMP Sled Dogs Report, pp. 1. (2) Ibid., pp. 2, 12, 57–63. (3) Final Report pp. 15 and Sled Dogs Report, pp.

1. That there was no "mass culling of Inuit sled dogs in Nunavik and Nunavut between 1950 and 1970, at the behest of government, with the intent to destroy Inuit culture by forcing the Inuit into settlements."

2. That numerous dogs were shot, but always for humane or public safety reasons, under the sanction of a law of general application, namely, the Ordinance Respecting Dogs.[11]

3. That RCMP members in the North used dogs themselves, vaccinated and inoculated Inuit dogs at risk of contagious diseases, and generally did much good for Inuit who wished to live on the land by continuing to hunt and trap.

4. That some of the blame falls not on the RCMP, but on the programs and policies of the federal departments responsible for northern administration, which moved hunters from the land into a handful of permanent settlements, and that the RCMP may have been mistakenly blamed for harm done by officers of that department, or by the Sureté Québec in Nunavik.

5. Finally, the RCMP Sled Dogs Report denied the truth of the current disclosures and complaints and blamed them on Inuit elected leaders, arguing that those leaders had silenced Elders and other Inuit who could have given a different version of events. The report suggested that Elders were manipulated or motivated to fabricate or exaggerate these events in order to obtain compensation.

Reaction of Inuit Organizations

The strongly negative tone of the RCMP Sled Dogs Report prompted a response from Inuit organizations, notably the Makivik Corporation and the QIA. They disagreed with the RCMP Sled Dogs Report in substance

---

274–311, *passim*, annual reports. (4) pp. 660, 663 for Northern Affairs employees, pp. 471–72. (5) p. 670.

11 A different law, a provincial Act, was in effect in Nunavik.

and tenor. They did not believe that it resolved any questions or concerns. They regretted that the police had been encouraged and permitted to investigate themselves, because this had likely influenced the way evidence was interpreted. In particular, Inuit leaders firmly rejected the notion that the dog slaughter was a fabrication designed by leaders and imposed on manipulated and muzzled Elders. It remains a fact that hundreds of Inuit who were alive in the 1950s and 1960s in these two regions have recounted experiences—first-hand or learned directly from their families—of dogs being killed, usually by RCMP members, without warning or consideration of the results.

Since 1999, media attention has helped keep both the public and the federal and Quebec governments aware that the killing of dogs in the 1950s and 1960s is an important public policy issue today. Northern media outlets have reported on the evolving claims, counterclaims, hearings, and inquiries from the outset. Major daily newspapers in southern Canada have also noted the story and, in general, have accepted that there is a case that the government has to answer. The *Nunatsiaq News* was calling for an independent inquiry as early as 30 August 2002, and on 17 June 2005 reported much of the unfavourable reaction to the internal inquiry. The RCMP Sled Dogs Report presented a selection from the twenty-six media reports and commentaries that the RCMP Review Team located up to July 2005.[12]

Scope of QTC Historical Research

The QIA has acted on the need to understand and communicate an Inuit perspective and a much broader historical context by establishing its own inquiry, independent of government and with a wide mandate to study the whole range of government–Inuit relations in this turbulent period.[13] The

---

12 *RCMP Sled Dogs Report*, pp. 113–21, 251–61.

13 The Makivik Corporation and Quebec government also appointed a retired judge to

QTC's mandate addressed a smaller geographical territory than is covered in the RCMP Sled Dogs Report, but it called for a more complete methodology. It also demanded a broad-based social purpose, far beyond the issue of dog deaths and assessing whether there were any substantiated grounds for laying criminal charges. The mandate called for a

> Truth Commission, to be known as the "Qikiqtani Truth Commission," [to] be created to conduct an inquiry to investigate facts, interview witnesses, hold public hearings, and report to the members of QIA and to the public, the truth surrounding the "Dog Slaughter," "Relocations," and other decision-making of the Government up until 1980, and its effect on Inuit culture, economy, and way of life.
>
> The Qikiqtani Truth Commission's main objective is to ensure an accurate history of the events referred to above. The truth and reconciliation process seeks to promote healing for those who suffered wrongdoings, as well as to heal relations between Inuit and the Government by providing an opportunity for uncovering all pertinent facts and allowing for acknowledgement and forgiveness. The Qikiqtani Truth Commission cannot provide compensation but will provide recommendations that will promote reconciliation.[14]

Review of the RCMP Sled Dogs Report

This review of the RCMP Sled Dogs Report is integral to the QTC's effort to understand the events that flowed from government policies in the

---

inquire and report into dog killings in Nunavik. See http://www.makivik.org/index.php/en/current/dog-slaughter, accessed online 22 Dec 2009.

14 Accessed online 3 Dec 2009 at www.qtcommission.com/actions/GetPage.php?pageId=63.

Qikiqtani Region between 1950 and 1975. There is merit to the RCMP Sled Dogs Report, but equally there are matters that the QIA and its members find troubling.[15] One persistent problem is a narrowness of purpose: the RCMP Sled Dogs Report used historical data and the historical memories of individuals in a forensic way, seeking elusive evidence of offences on which charges against individuals could be grounded. The RCMP Sled Dogs Report showed a regrettable lack of interest in understanding why individual Inuit accounts of the shooting of dogs are so numerous and geographically widespread. Its authors characterized these accounts as evidence of a deceitful and emotionally charged conspiracy instead of trying to follow the Standing Committee's desire to "get to the bottom" of Inuit reports of how their dogs—and their rights—were handled during a period of profound social and economic dislocation.

While both the RCMP Sled Dogs Report and the QTC recognized that sled dogs did not pose a problem until a Qallunaat population began to congregate at a few places in the Arctic, their two approaches are set apart by the concern of the QIA and QTC to view the dog issue as part of the social and economic currents of the times, a concern that was largely absent from the RCMP Sled Dogs Report. That report treated the Qallunaat presence as a "given" and therefore analysed the killings as a law enforcement issue, rather than as part of a process of disruptive social change.

Through a process of hearing statements from witnesses, reading published works about the period, and examining archival documents, the QTC and its research team concluded that much wrongdoing did occur, though perhaps for different reasons than many Inuit believed into the 1990s. The team also concluded that the literature on public memory and on truth and reconciliation commissions, which was disregarded by the RCMP Sled Dogs

---

15 Through the cooperation of RCMP Commissioner W. J. S. Elliott, QTC researchers reviewed the evidence gathered by the RCMP Review Team in 2005–2006. Our review provided insight into some of the internal discussions within the Force over gathering and interpreting these aspects of its history.

Report, is pertinent to this inquiry. The authors of this present review were struck by the particular relevance of what a leading Canadian theorist in the field calls "the comparative imperative." Dr. Peter Seixas of the University of British Columbia has written, "Theories of historical consciousness need to be capacious enough to account for radically different ways of understanding and using the past, from different cultures and subcultures around the world, without using a Western lens to lock them into a developmental hierarchy."[16]

Clearly, the historical perspectives of the RCMP Review Team and of the QTC would be different even if the two bodies fully agreed on the relevant historical facts. The RCMP Review Team proceeded through a formal interpretation of the actions of the Canadian authorities without applying the standards of an administrative review or considering the standard of evidence in civil cases, which is to evaluate on the balance of probabilities.[17] The details of the various amendments to the Ordinance Respecting Dogs (hereafter cited as Dog Ordinance), for example, were never explained, and neither were the inconsistencies in its application.[18] The question of

---

16 P. Seixas, "Introduction," *Theorizing Historical Consciousness* (University of Toronto Press, 2004), pp. 10.

17 By contrast, criminal convictions require proof beyond reasonable doubt.

18 See Northwest Territories, Council of the Northwest Territories, "An Ordinance Respecting Dogs," Chapter 2, 1949 (Ottawa: Edmond Cloutier, King's Printer, 1950). Among other inappropriate provisions, it was enacted that "No person shall have a dog in harness within any settlement or within one half-mile of any settlement in the Territories unless the dog has a muzzle or is under the custody and control of a person over sixteen years of age who is capable of ensuring that the dog will not harm the public or create a nuisance"—absurd restrictions for Inuit visiting trading posts. Section 9A of the revised ordinance of 30 Nov 1950, Northwest Territories, Council of the Northwest Territories, "An Ordinance to Amend an Ordinance Respecting Dogs," Chapter 18, 1950 (Ottawa: Edmond Cloutier, Queen's Printer, 1953), allowed dog officers to destroy dogs they were unable to seize, without setting a standard for determining what "unable to seize" meant.

whether the Dog Ordinance was a reasonable law under the circumstances was not explored. At multiple points in the RCMP Sled Dogs Report, contentious actions were justified by giving precedence to the urgent needs of a new transient non-Aboriginal population over established indigenous ways of life. The QTC's point of departure was the needs and practices of an Inuit society that existed in the Arctic from time immemorial, many of whose laws, beliefs, practices, and values were undermined by the behaviour and demands of newcomers. Killing dogs both with and without the sanction of the Dog Ordinance—along with the educational policy, game laws, forced relocations, painful evacuation of sick Inuit to the South, and so on—though often beneficial in a material sense, overturned a way of life with little warning and no consultation.

This transformation not only disrupted relations among individuals and within kin groups, but it also challenged the relations that already existed between Inuit and the few Qallunaat living as transients among them. On this matter, perhaps surprisingly, both Inuit testimony and the RCMP review were in agreement that the transformation had been extremely difficult and unnecessarily painful. The coming of large numbers of Qallunaat and of a wage economy in which few Inuit could take part created radical shifts in the previous relations between Inuit and the police.[19] In a very real sense, Canada's national police force and the country's northernmost permanent inhabitants have a shared history overlooked in the report. In the spirit of critical inquiry and reconciliation, the QTC has examined the RCMP Sled Dogs Report and presents this review of what that report accomplished and how it might have done better.

---

19 This is evident in much of the correspondence from retired members in *RCMP Sled Dogs Report*, pp. 514–615. See also John Matthiasson, *Living Off the Land: Change among the Inuit of Baffin Island* (Peterborough: Broadview Press, 1992), pp. 91–118.

A SHARED HISTORY: INUIT AND RCMP IN THE BAFFIN REGION

The relationship between Inuit and the RCMP grew out of the gradual encroachment of Canadian authority into what Canadians call the Eastern Arctic, early in the 20th century. For many generations, Inuit managed their own affairs, including external relations with adjoining Inuit groups and, for a few groups, with First Nations.[20] Over time, the challenge of external relations shifted to be dominated by intermittent encounters with parties of explorers, and then enlarged to include relations with, visits from, and even year-round sojourning by, British and American whalers. When whale stocks crashed around 1900, fur traders stepped in where the whalers had departed. They did not formally challenge Inuit autonomy except in matters affecting external trade, but most of these traders assumed they were working under the umbrella of British Crown sovereignty. That is because in 1577 the English explorer Martin Frobisher, and in 1818 the British naval captain John Ross, made formal acts of possession on behalf of the English and later the British Crown.[21] These acts were probably recognized only by the country that made them, but in 1880 Canada took over whatever Britain's claims amounted to and began actively to assert them through flag raising (1897), ordering regulatory and exploratory patrols by the Department of Marine and Fisheries (1903–1911), and after 1920, establishing isolated Arctic RCMP detachments.

The RCMP detachments were a formal challenge to Inuit law, custom, and practice. They were designed in part to avenge or protect Qallunaat

---

20 J. Bennett and S. Rowley, eds., *Uqalurait: An Oral History of Nunavut* (Montréal and Kingston: McGill–Queen's University Press, 2004), pp. 126–37; see additional material on relations with First Nations, pp. 137–42.

21 See W. F. King, *Title of Canada to the Islands North of the Mainland of Canada* (Ottawa: Government Printing Bureau, 1905). Along Qikiqtani shores, these acts were surprisingly rare and scattered.

who were punished by Inuit for transgressions against Inuit law. Between 1912 and 1917, the RCMP arrested and punished Inuit in the central Arctic who had put to death a pair of explorers and two missionaries who had become a danger to their hosts. When a similar clash brought about the death of a trader near Pond Inlet in 1920, the federal government established the RCMP in the Baffin Region. These detachments received supplies from the south by an annual ship, but they depended on Inuit for local travel, country food, and translation. The police in the era after 1920 had four roles, which continued until the 1960s. First, they represented Canadian authority in a formal way. Second, they checked up promptly on reported violations of the criminal code. Third, they were, with rare exceptions, stationed at the sites of existing trading posts, and were supposed to ensure that Inuit were not being exploited. Fourth, the RCMP spent a good deal of time and effort patrolling by dog team and by boat, visiting people where they lived and hunted, and checking and reporting on social, economic, and game conditions. The RCMP also provided basic medical attention to Inuit and distributed ammunition or supplies wherever these seemed to be needed. As a result, the Baffin Region ceased to be a vast tract that only Inuit knew and controlled, and became a region where the police visited many habitable areas annually. In the process, many of them developed a considerable understanding of Inuit culture and behaviour. Relative to other contact agents, the police had abundant resources and few onerous responsibilities, but they gained a great deal of prestige and authority by the services they delivered, as well as by enforcement of the criminal law, the game laws, and other regulations.[22] The RCMP would not have considered that Inuit

---

22 The Hudson's Bay Company had considerable de facto authority, especially evident in 1933–1947 when its vessels carried the government freight, and its post managers had radios, which the other agencies did not. See C.S. Mackinnon, "Canada's Eastern Arctic Patrol 1922–68," *Polar Record* 27 (161), pp. 93–101; also an unpublished paper by P. Goldring, "The Triumvirate at Pangnirtung," Canadian Historical Association Annual Meeting, 1989.

possessed a legal framework for governing themselves, but many legal anthropologists and lawyers assert otherwise.[23]

In the two decades before 1970, Inuit experienced tumultuous change in every aspect of their land use and annual routine. The police also had to adjust to change when new government agencies with radically new policies broke in on the traditional domains of both Inuit life and police duties. At times, these new civilian agencies enlisted the police to implement unpopular new measures such as restrictions on hunting, removal of children for education, forced relocations, and rounding up of people for annual medical exams with the all-too-frequent consequence of removal to the South. At other times, the new agencies competed with the police in the communities, especially after 1962 when the pressure on people to move to settlements intensified. The police initially opposed resettlement. One of the duties they accepted in the new state of affairs was the destruction of loose sled dogs, which had become quite numerous in the settlements. Here some Inuit were less able to care for and control them in traditional ways, because the practice of keeping dogs loose was riskier in the much larger settlements of people (and of dogs) that became common after 1955. Under pressure from Qallunaat, numerous sled dogs were killed from the mid-1950s onwards, despite a confusingly contrary policy of having the police immunize dogs against disease and even import dogs to replace others lost in a canine epidemic.

Inuit memories of this period tell of a serious loss and disruption of their lives. Members of the Force also tell of a change of role and direction due to their involvement in unpopular programs and competition with

---

23 See Paul Groarke, "Review: Legal Volumes from the Arctic College's Interviewing Inuit Elders Series" *Osgoode Hall Law Journal* 47:3 (2009) pp. 787–806, as well as a volume he reviewed, Mariano Aupilaarjuk *et al.*, *Perspectives on Traditional Law*, vol. 2, *Interviewing Inuit Elders*, ed. by Jarich Oosten, Frédéric Laugrand & Wim Rasing (Iqaluit: Nunavut Arctic College, 1999), also available online at http://www.nac.nu.ca/OnlineBookSite/vol2/chapters.html.

new government agents whose policies they disliked. By the 1970s, most Inuit lived year-round in thirteen towns or hamlets instead of in the former hundred or so ilagiit nunagivaktangit; snowmobiles had replaced dog teams; the Government of the Northwest Territories delivered most social services; and RCMP members spent most of their time providing conventional southern-style policing in the communities.

Although many of these developments and trends are still too controversial for this summary to be called a "consensus" history, it itemizes important, relevant historical events over seven decades in the transition from Inuit law to Canadian public law. These steps, which were very disempowering to Inuit at the time, constitute some of the background to the angry discussions that strained Inuit–RCMP relations in the decade leading up to the appointment of the QTC. A serious effort to "get to the bottom of" the dog slaughter issue must consider those tragic incidents within the context of this longer history.

WHAT THE RCMP SLED DOGS REPORT ACCOMPLISHED

The RCMP Sled Dogs Report determined that RCMP members and others did indeed kill large numbers of sled dogs in the 1950s and 1960s. It reported that these killings were not launched by a systematic policy or conspiracy and were not part of a concerted campaign to drive all Inuit into permanent settlements. Responsibility for the killings was unassigned or was assigned by implication to neglect or "passive resistance"[24] on the part of the dogs' owners.

The important accomplishment and lasting benefit of the RCMP Sled Dogs Report will likely turn out to be the gathering of new information from elderly informants and the assembly of archival information. Retired RCMP, particularly the most senior ones, provided a revealing and sometimes

24 *RCMP Sled Dogs Report*, pp. 435, 669.

critical view of their own careers among Inuit and of relations between the Force and the Canadian government, which should not surprise historians, but will help many others understand this period.[25] The RCMP Review Team's archival research, though incomplete and scarcely analysed in the RCMP Sled Dogs Report, occupied nearly one-third of the report and pointed to the rich potential of available archival records of the RCMP, the Northern Administration Branch, and other departments.[26]

To apply this approach to the dog killings, neither truth nor reconciliation can be achieved on a tight schedule. The RCMP showed clearer thinking than either the Standing Committee or the Minister when it scheduled a full year for research and analysis of historical evidence. There are different precedents and models for using historical evidence to expose maladministration and right wrongs. In the case of the dog killings, it is noteworthy that the RCMP and the Inuit have researched and told their stories separately.

Despite the report's great length, its authors failed to fulfill the expectations of either the Standing Committee Report of 10 March 2005, or the letter of 28 April 2005 from Anne McLellan, Deputy Prime Minister and Minister of Public Safety and Emergency Preparedness. The Standing Committee, in a recommendation later endorsed by the Legislature of Nunavut, called for an inquiry to "get to the bottom of the matter." In the QTC's view, this meant more than merely confirming the killings and finding local causes and a legal excuse for them. Getting to "the bottom" would require exploring deeper reasons for the killings and the connections with other socio-economic trends and public events, including policies, budgets, and extreme weaknesses in the cross-cultural and other job-related training

25 See for example, former Asst. Commissioner Robert C. Currie's condemnation of the government's "abhorrent" High Arctic relocations program, *RCMP Sled Dogs Report*, pp. 636–37 and 685–86.

26 Although much of the material is scattered and interlaced with commentary, the pages from 199–452 (32.8 percent of the total) are mainly reproduced excerpts of archival material.

given to federal agents in the North. And if hundreds of Inuit witnesses were, as RCMP analysis concluded, somehow mistaken about what they saw and remembered from the period before 1970, getting to the bottom of the matter would have to include a thoughtful examination of relations between the community and its police, in order to understand the assumptions and experience of the Elders and their consequences in the present day.

The Minister's letter to RCMP Commissioner Giuliano Zaccardelli requested "a chronology of events, a history of the issue, and an examination of all relevant RCMP records as well as current and previous RCMP reviews on this issue."[27] The RCMP Sled Dogs Report used a wide range of RCMP records, but fell short on other parts of the mandate. There was really no chronology[28] either in the short "final" report or in the full report that backed it up. Instead, analysis appeared at the beginning and the end, bracketing numerous topical sections which were then internally organized by provenance. These sections included interpretation along with evidence from documents and interviews. Three big sections that *were* organized by date—45 pages of transcripts of RCMP headquarters records, 127 pages of RCMP "G" Division records, and 45 pages of transcripts of "Indian and Northern Affairs Canada" correspondence—were so massive and so disparate in the information they contained that they did not give a clear impression of significant events in the order in which they occurred. Larger than any of these was the 147-page section of information from "Persons Contacted," sorted into eight occupational categories and arranged alphabetically, not chronologically, within those categories. The Minister had also asked for "a history of the issue," which required a broader contextual treatment of the subject matter. This was not produced or delivered.[29]

---

27 *RCMP Sled Dogs Report*, pp. 7.

28 *Oxford Canadian Dictionary* (1998:255) defines *chronology* as "**a** the arrangement of events, dates, etc. in the order of their occurrence. **b** a table or document displaying this."

29 The Minister's letter does not define "history," but it must mean something more comprehensive than the "chronology" that she also asked for. *The Oxford Canadian*

The authors of the *RCMP Sled Dogs Report* candidly admitted that in the time (one year) they were given, their relatively inexperienced team knew there "may well be limitations in this report that would not be present in an academic tome."[30] This missed the point. What is needed to advance both understanding and reconciliation is not a tome but a *treatise*, "a written work dealing formally and systematically with a subject."[31] Analysis of historical wrongs and grievances in a cross-cultural and intergenerational framework is not easily achieved.[32] The work that is still needed will deal with multiple perspectives—not only with "what happened," but with why it happened, and how to identify the long-term effects that are worthy of being understood. Five of the key historical questions are addressed in the next section of this review.[33]

Dictionary (1998), pp. 669 gives several meanings for "history" of which the relevant ones are "**2a** the study of past events, esp. human affairs. **b** the total accumulation of past events, esp. relating to human affairs or to the accumulation of developments connected with a particular nation, person, thing, etc. (*the history of Canada; the history of astronomy; has a history of illness*) [...] **4a** a systematic or critical account of or research into a past event, development, movement, etc. (*the history of broadcasting*)."

30 *RCMP Sled Dogs Report*, pp. 674.

31 *Oxford Canadian Dictionary* (1998), pp. 1546.

32 For comparison, consider the explanation by the J.W. McConnell Foundation, which funds "programs that support Canadians in building a more inclusive, sustainable and resilient society." Its projects "are often complex, collaborative efforts that involve trying out, testing and implementing new approaches," and they have "found that such innovative endeavours typically take longer to set up and operate than initially planned, and that patience and perseverance in supporting them is essential for their eventual success." www.mcconnellfoundation.ca/default.aspx?page=6&NewsId=78&lang=en-US, accessed 24 Apr. 2009.

33 In the absence of either a chronology or an analytical history of the dog killings, it is important to note that neither the Standing Committee nor the Minister called for reconciliation between Inuit and the RCMP. This silence may in effect have judged in

Areas of Concern

INTERPRETING THE KILLINGS

The RCMP View

The RCMP Sled Dogs Report acknowledged that RCMP members and other persons in authority in the 1950s and 1960s killed hundreds and perhaps thousands of dogs. It confirmed that most of these dogs were killed during the same period when Inuit were in transition from ilagiit nunagivaktangit to permanent settlements. In its executive summary, the RCMP Sled Dogs Report explained the decline:

> There was a startling drop in Inuit sled dog populations, particularly during the 1960s, but the dog population decline was the result of a number of factors, including the collapse of the fur trade, the introduction of the snowmobile, the migration of the Inuit into settlements, and their participation in the wage economy rather than living on the land. In brief, dog numbers declined because the dogs were no longer essential to the new circumstances in which the Inuit found themselves.

This analysis sidestepped the impacts of the killings on Inuit at the time and since, while noting periods or episodes in which the RCMP "were dedicated to the cause of preserving the traditional Inuit semi-nomadic culture" including the use of dogs.[34] It argued effectively that the killings were never directed by a central government plan or carried out with the explicit motive of forcing Inuit to stop hunting and live in permanent settlements.

---

advance that the RCMP would find that the dog killings were legal.

34 *RCMP Sled Dogs Report*, pp. 1–2.

The QTC View

The QTC formed different views about the absence of a "conspiracy," not all of them in full agreement with earlier RCMP or QIA positions. Granted, the killings went on far too long to be the result of a secret plan or conspiracy,[35] and they also began—in the mid-1950s at Iqaluit—several years before the federal government adopted a formal "centralizing policy" and before government was prepared to install even the rough beginnings of the housing and other infrastructure a centralized population needs. And for many individual Inuit and for all at Iqaluit whose dogs were shot in the 1950s, the mass shootings of dogs occurred long before an owner could hope to replace them with a snowmobile. While there was no secret conspiracy or policy in the 1950s of the kind that the RCMP Review Team looked for and did not find, there was a series of interconnected policies and actions, closely linked in time, by which government undermined traditional Inuit ways of living. Government resistance to traditional Inuit ways of handling dogs was one such policy and was intimately linked to other government policies.

The government and its agents presented health care and housing to Inuit in ways that exerted enormous pressure against staying on the land or returning to it. Families with school-aged children were threatened with a loss of family allowances if they did not part with their children or move into the settlements themselves. Families with Elders had to move to be near the nursing stations. Although some passages in the RCMP Sled Dogs Report appeared sensitive to the Inuit who submitted to those pressures very reluctantly, the RCMP did enforce the government's dog control policies, which were hostile to Inuit who wanted to alternate wage work in

---

35 The long duration makes redundant the RCMP Review Team's efforts to show that the RCMP in the North never had access to enough ammunition to conduct the killings in a short period. See *RCMP Sled Dogs Report*, pp. 121, 577, 665–66.

settlements with periods of hunting. As Elder Naki Ekho told anthropologist Ann McElroy in 1999: "I came here by dog team from upland with the whole family [in 1957]. . . . The reason we came here was when someone finds plentiful amounts of something, like work or food, they come to get it. They planned to stay only a year." However, police killed their dogs and they never returned to their Cumberland Sound ilagiit nunagivaktangat.[36] The new settlements were inhospitable locations for sled dogs and became places where Inuit methods of caring for dogs (and, seasonally, leaving them to care for themselves) were not accommodated by government. In the settlements, there were more people as well as more dog teams than in ilagiit nunagivaktangit. Dogs did not adapt well to being around strangers; they were more wary and potentially more dangerous. In addition, the people in settlements included Qallunaat who were either fearful or careless around sled dogs.

Under these pressures, there was no need for a conspiracy, secret or otherwise, because the authorities in Ottawa changed the law. Between 1949 and 1950, they revised the Northwest Territories' Ordinance Respecting Dogs to outlaw traditional Inuit ways of handling dogs wherever this seemed to conflict with the needs or practices of Qallunaat settlers. While the Dog Ordinance did not apply in ilagiit nunagivaktangit, in a growing list of places across the Northwest Territories (NWT) designated dog officers, including all RCMP members *ex officio*, had the discretion to destroy any dogs that they considered to be "running at large contrary to the provisions of this Ordinance."[37] When Inuit, such as Naki Ekho's husband, chose

36 Ann McElroy, *Nunavut Generations: Change and Continuity in Canadian Inuit Communities* (Long Grove Ill.: Waveland Press, 2008).

37 Library and Archives Canada, Record Group 109 (Canadian Wildlife Service), Series B.1, Volume 407, File WLU 229 Part 1, "Dogs—Generally—Rabies and Distemper", Chapters 2 and 18. Section 2(e) defined "run at large:" "means to run off the premises of the owner either when the dog is not muzzled or when the dog is not under the control

to take seasonal employment with the armed forces, they entered a world where their traditions and practices—in managing dogs as in many other matters—were in jeopardy.

Contemporary Thoughts on the Dog Slaughter

Some Inuit and RCMP understood this in the 1950s. In November 1956, the senior policeman in Iqaluit explained to his superiors in Ottawa, in this extract from a long memorandum, what he saw as the Inuit perspective:

> [4.] There are a number of dogs running loose about Frobisher Bay.... Most of these stray animals are owned by Eskimos who are employed by the United States Air Force at this point. The owners work full time and are unable to hunt seal to feed the dogs, yet they are reluctant to part with any of them. From time to time this detachment has urged them to get rid of these dogs, however, there is some deep-rooted desire to own dogs which has thus far excluded results. Probably it is prestige.[38]
>
> 5. In dealing with social problems of the Eskimo, until members of this detachment understand fully the role of custom, it's [sic] laws and varieties, they can not really effectively deal with the complicated issue which this becomes. This dog problem does indirectly affect, for instance, the economy of the Eskimo. Destruction of an Eskimo's dogs after remaining unclaimed in the pound for five days may result in him quitting his job on the air base and returning

---

of any person." "Premises" is not defined.

38 In drawing attention to prestige as a factor promoting ownership of dogs, Van Norman missed the underlying importance of sled dogs in Inuit culture; these are explored in Francis Lévesque, "Les Inuit, Leurs Chiens Et L'administration," pp. 139–75.

> to a life on the land. This would be just one of many reactions. Other Eskimos might show their dislike by offering active opposition in varied forms.
>
> 6. The Frobisher Bay Eskimos do not understand the dog problem which has developed here since the inception of the air base. Nor do they appreciate that this detachment must deal with it as outlined in the Dog Ordinance. Many of these Eskimos let their dogs run loose so they can feed in the disposal area while the owner is at work on the base. This is a perfectly reasonable explanation, and to these individuals no answer except one which will offer an alternative food supply, will have any semblance of being reasonable.[39]

The "perfectly reasonable" decision to let dogs forage was also articulated by employed Inuit to McGill University anthropologist Toshio Yatsushiro in 1959:

> Eskimos like to have dogs to use in the winter for hunting. They don't like it when the R.C.M.P. kills them. Some dogs are left untied for a week or so because they get cross when they are tied. The Eskimos understand, if they are free they will be shot, but if they are tied they cannot get food, so maybe they will die anyhow. Eskimos bring food and water to the dogs when they have it, but often they don't have it. So when the dogs go free they eat garbage—when the R.C.M.P. saw it they shot them it is not good.[40]

---

39 *RCMP Sled Dogs Report*, pp. 364.

40 Autry National Center, Institute for the Study of the American West, Braun Research Library, Collection MS 212 (Toshio Yatsushiro), Box 2, File 44, transcript of interview with Joomii, E-7-444, 26 July 1959.

Another informant asked whether "the govt. didn't want Eskimos to have dogs any more. Eskimos sometimes have dogs untied, they get hungry and run around looking for food. . . . The Eskimos can't feed them regularly because the hunting around Frobisher Bay is no longer good. Every one is working so no dog meat can be hunted for. But they need the dogs for hunting in the winter."[41]

Governance Issues

These quotations underline the fact, not sufficiently emphasized in the RCMP Sled Dogs Report, that the standard government policy was to assume Inuit must, at their own expense, accommodate newcomers' needs and wants. While the law was clear to those who enforced it, to hunters it was illogical, unnecessary, and also harmful; in addition, it was not consistently or predictably applied. Inuit and dogs had existed together for uncounted generations without such restrictions being necessary. The authors of the RCMP Sled Dogs Report, like most other writers on the subject, appeared to accept that shooting hundreds, perhaps thousands, of dogs by newcomers over more than a decade was a rational and justified activity, while the grief and resentment of the dog owners was unwarranted and worthy of criticism or at least anthropological study.[42]

In fact the considerations are not merely cultural or emotional, but also legal, to a degree not recognized in the RCMP Sled Dogs Report. The legal implications stem from a consideration of Aboriginal and human rights and the disregard of these expressed by the initiative to import Qallunaat

41 Autry National Center, Institute for the Study of the American West, Braun Research Library, Collection MS 212 (Toshio Yatsushiro), Box 2, File 44, transcript of interview with Halli, E-7-66, 29 Aug 1959.

42 The RCMP Sled Dogs Report, at pp. 35–39, discusses the Inuit sled dog in Inuit culture. The complex and ambivalent role of dogs in Qallunaat cultures is left unexplored.

transient workers and military men and officials. The Dog Ordinance was designed primarily to protect Qallunaat from Inuit dogs. (Later a need was shown to protect Inuit children as well.) The Government of Canada failed in its obligations to Inuit when it placed restrictions on their use of dogs without providing the means to make those restrictions less onerous, or involving Inuit directly in finding solutions. There was also a practical element: tying, chaining, or confining them in pounds was not good for the dogs themselves. Chained dogs could not exercise, socialize, or forage, and employed Inuit could not hunt for them. The burden of complying with the Dog Ordinance was placed on Inuit. Exceptional officers, such as Cpl. Van Norman, understood that family economies would be severely disrupted unless the government provided a means for feeding dogs, while their movement was restricted and their owners were occupied on what was, in most cases, government business. While some of Yatsushiro's informants sounded laconic and fatalistic in their comments about the loss of their dogs, others were not. One admitted, "First I thought of killing the policemen. But I don't mind now. Maybe afterwards there won't be so many dogs, since the police are shooting them. In five years there may be none at all. Maybe the police will kill Eskimos then, just like the dogs."[43]

In the RCMP Sled Dogs Report, a great deal of attention was also paid to public health motives for killing dogs that were known to be ill or at risk of transmitting contagious diseases to other animals. This became almost a routine practice for the police and other dog officers, and was frequently carried out without ensuring that the dogs' owners understood and agreed to the destruction, and in disregard of the Inuit practice of giving sick dogs

43 Quoted in Toshio Yatsushiro, "The Changing Eskimo: A study of wage employment and its consequences among the Eskimos of Frobisher Bay, Baffin Island," *The Beaver* (Summer 1962), pp. 20–21. Yatsushiro's own gloss on the policy was that "the RC.M. Police detachment stationed in Frobisher Bay has been exterminating unleashed dogs owned by Eskimos, on the ground that such animals constitute a menace to the community, especially the white residents."

time to recover. The question of faulty translations is dealt with at a number of points in the RCMP Sled Dogs Report and contributes to the report's message that the police always acted within the law, but may have been misunderstood by Inuit who were harmed by their actions.[44]

Gaps in the Analysis

QTC researchers found a number of problems in the way information about dog maulings and dog slaughter were reported and explained in the RCMP Sled Dogs Report. There was a lack of clarity about why dogs were suddenly viewed as an uncontrolled danger in regions of Nunavut where this had not previously been a problem. Certain anecdotes were repeated twice or more, including at least half a dozen references to a single fatal mauling, that of Maggie Clay in 1924.[45] Toshio Yatsushiro commented that dogs were chiefly a danger to Qallunaat, not to Inuit, but the RCMP Sled Dogs Report—which listed Yatsushiro's work in the bibliography, but did not quote it—ignored this rather obvious line of inquiry.

It might be expected that the migration of non-Inuit women and children into the Arctic would raise consciousness of the potential dangers from dogs, especially if these incomers were unprepared, but there was no attempt at gender analysis. Even employees received little or no orientation to Inuit culture or Arctic living conditions. The RCMP Sled Dogs

44 RCMP Sled Dogs Report, pp. 686, 46: "Many former members reported instances where they gave a lengthy explanation to the Inuit for a decision being made, only to witness the interpreter reduce it to several sentences. The assumption by the members was that the interpreter conveyed only the decision, not the explanation."

45 This is dealt with in detail below. The RCMP Sled Dogs Report did not discuss how real risks are misrepresented and misunderstood by using unrepresentative examples. For a non-expert review of scientific literature on this subject, see Dan Gardner, *Risk: the Science of Politics and Fear* (Toronto: McClelland and Stewart, 2008), pp. 62–76.

Report documented examples of Qallunaat families trying to make pets of sled dogs. One of these cases almost ended fatally when a small boy had to be medivaced from Arviat to Churchill in 1960. He was sleeping outdoors in a playpen while his mother, a missionary's wife, was socializing with a policeman's wife indoors. The missionary's own pet husky broke loose and inflicted life-threatening injuries on his child. Although this reflected a high level of maladaptation to actual conditions in the region, and no Inuit or Inuit-owned sled dogs were involved, the Superintendent commanding "G" Division advised all detachments to be extra vigilant and "where husky dogs are loose . . . take action at once." He added a warning against making pets of these animals.[46]

A more serious gap was the lack of chronological treatment of extended episodes of dog killings. The provisions of the Dog Ordinance were extended to DEW Line sites and to all settlements in August 1955,[47] and shortly afterwards efforts were made to crack down on loose dogs around Iqaluit. The killings there were numerous and quite widely commented on. A decade later in Pangnirtung, according to an RCMP source, that region experienced comparable killings. Smaller instances of shooting dogs were recorded in Igloolik around 1960, when a Northern Service Officer took action in the absence of a police detachment. How these episodes fit into the long-term trend of reducing teams almost to zero might affect how specific incidents are interpreted.

While the Dog Ordinance made it unnecessary for government to hatch a conspiracy, and many or most of the killings can be explained due to that law being enacted by an external, unelected legislature, the social context of the killings and the resulting damage to the prestige of the RCMP in the North were not thoroughly examined in the RCMP Sled Dogs Report. Its authors seemed to take it for granted that every bulge in the statistics of dog killings was carried out in accordance with the law and was therefore,

---

46 *RCMP Sled Dogs Report*, pp. 327–28.

47 *RCMP Sled Dogs Report*, pp. 58–59.

apparently, not worthy of detailed investigation or contextual analysis by the Force's researchers. As a result, the reader—and the Inuit whose dogs were killed—received little explanation of local and particular circumstances, either of the necessity of the killing or the communication, if any, with the dog's owners.[48] Also unexamined is the possibility that there were distinct patterns of dog killings across time: for example, in Iqaluit in the 1950s it was primarily employed Inuit whose dogs were killed, but elsewhere in the late 1960s, some of the victims were people who had just relocated to settlements without jobs.

THE RCMP REVIEW TEAM AND INUIT COMPLAINTS

Because it was in no position to conduct an independent inquiry, the RCMP Review Team did not receive the full trust and cooperation of most Inuit who lived through the 1950s and 1960s. The RCMP Review Team did solicit information from Inuit, notably former special constables and their families. The report repeatedly deplored the fact that it received so little evidence from other Inuit. This kind of evidence existed in the testimony that Inuit would have been prepared to give to a judicial inquiry or had already given in confidential statements to Inuit beneficiary organizations.[49] A certain amount was already on the public record,[50] yet this was dismissed

48 See especially RCMP Sled Dogs Report, pp. 226–27 where the Administrator of the Arctic discussed the RCMP's apparent reluctance to administer the Dog Ordinance; "My own feeling is that if the R.C.M. Police are asked to enforce the Ordinance, and agree to act, *they are likely to shoot stray dogs but would make little effort to round up and impound strays*. I would like to see a very serious effort made to have stray dogs impounded, and have the owners charged for their release." [Emphasis added.]

49 RCMP Sled Dogs Report, pp. 148–49.

50 The RCMP Sled Dogs Report provides summaries of statements from newspapers

by the RCMP Review Team because of minor inconsistencies or because information lacked particulars about names and dates at a level of detail that would warrant laying charges against individual perpetrators. The report also pointed out that Inuit could not have known the detailed inner workings of government and therefore did not have first-hand evidence to link the policy of centralization with the policy of dog control.

Instead of accepting the core truth in the Inuit reports of dog killings, and looking for ways to understand the Inuit perspective and its related cultural and situational differences, the RCMP Review Team set out to discredit the witnesses and their political organizations, although without directly accusing them of exaggerating or lying. A tense situation developed that Inuit had anticipated when asking for an independent inquiry—the statements of witnesses who came forward were attacked. Particularly negative statements were made in the RCMP Sled Dogs Report about the fact that most Inuit simply would not provide evidence to the police about the events they or their families suffered from a generation earlier. In its "Review Findings," the report treated this as *prima facie* evidence of intimidation, motivated by desire for financial compensation, as the RCMP Review Team asserted:

> The QIA had instructed Inuit not to cooperate with the RCMP review of the allegations; refer to page 145. This placed the review team in a difficult situation. Inuit could be presumed to be reluctant to contradict the allegations being made by their leaders and be equally reluctant to disregard the direction of non-collaboration.
>
> The review team had to be cognizant that, in the small Arctic communities, it could be anticipated that there could be serious repercussions for any Inuk who spoke out and in any way under-

and witnesses before Parliament; see especially pp. 113–21 and 123–45.

> mined the allegations that had been made. The RCMP therefore refrained from aggressively soliciting the direct collaboration of Inuit, preferring to respect the position in which they found themselves; refer to page 492.[51]

That passage exhibited a serious misunderstanding of Inuit cultural relations by failing to examine patterns of Inuit deference to Qallunaat authority. Instead of examining the serious issues around an inquiry conducted by the RCMP into its own members' behaviour, the RCMP Sled Dogs Report alleged that the real rift was between Inuit and their elected leaders.

> At this juncture, it is essential to make a distinction between "the Inuit" as a people, and "Inuit leaders/organizations." There are only a few Inuit making these allegations. Those most vocal are the Inuit leadership and two of the four Inuit organizations; the Nunavut Tunngavik Inc. and the Inuit Tapiriit Kanatami have not been vocal on this issue in the public forum. It may be that significant numbers of Inuit do not believe the allegations are true, but are unwilling to contradict their leadership or fellow Inuit.[52]

Not only were these comments disrespectful toward the possible reasons for the reticence of Elders and other witnesses, but they were also uninformed by any consideration of how groups that are affected differently by events will view the causes and character of those events differently. While the RCMP Sled Dogs Report successfully demonstrated that there was no central conspiracy to kill dogs to force people into settlements, it overlooked the very high probability that the control of loose and sick dogs was done in a way that was unintelligible to Inuit, was hostile to their customs and

51 RCMP Sled Dogs Report, pp. 660.

52 RCMP Sled Dogs Report, pp. 663.

beliefs, and was carried out without their consent. The way different parties remember these events is significant.[53]

HISTORIC INUIT–RCMP INTERACTIONS

Sled Dogs and the Reputation of the Force

The RCMP Sled Dogs Report was primarily about dogs, but also exhibited an underlying preoccupation with the RCMP's reputation in the communities where they still serve. In particular, the RCMP Review Team adopted from RCMP veterans a strong desire for respect and acknowledgement of their service and sacrifice in the North during the transitions of 1950–1970. While accusations about the dog slaughter in 1999 were felt to be particularly hurtful, memories of bureaucratic defeats and a change of role in the 1960s also emerged in the editorial content and supporting documentation of the RCMP Sled Dogs Report. Those feelings of resentment against both the federal government in the 1960s and the Inuit in the 1990s were defining characteristics in pages 514 to 615, where the memories of more than 130 veterans were asserted against those of protesting Inuit.[54] The RCMP Sled Dogs Report also devoted a remarkable amount of space to proving that senior officers *did not* apologize to Inuit in 1999, despite two separate oral statements that seemed to suggest that the Force regretted its roles in the hardships Inuit endured. Although the evidence of repeated non-apologizing is fairly convincing, the whole issue seemed important to the

53 As noted above, the limited scope of this inquiry prevented discussion of how Inuit were involved in decisions affecting the treatment of their dogs. See RCMP Sled Dogs Report, pp. 148.

54 See RCMP Sled Dogs Report, pp. 516, "Members were so incensed by these allegations, reported in the media, that they came forward in significant numbers, simplifying the process of locating them."

RCMP Review Team for three reasons:

- It provoked a storm of protest from retired RCMP members, which infuses the RCMP Sled Dogs Report.
- It brought into the open the fact that many Inuit, most of whom lived through the events complained of, believed the RCMP to be capable of extremely prejudicial acts.
- It shaped the RCMP reaction to the fact that Inuit, by and large, would not tell their side of the story to a self-investigating body that they believed to be biased.

A trigger for many of the indignant outbursts from retired members was the report in the *Nunatsiaq News* of a meeting where Commissioner Philip Murray tried to get off on the right foot during the creation of Nunavut. The *Nunatsiaq News* reported:

> These words confirm what the head of Canada's police force already knows—that RCMP [sic] have a sordid past with the Inuit of Nunavut and that past is still a vivid memory for some. "I think it's very important from our point of view, as the new territory is created, that we have a very real sense of the history of the relationship between the RCMP and the community," Murray said.[55]

The QTC research team was also influenced by recognition that the RCMP and Inuit have lived together in the North for many decades and that a good relationship between a police force and the communities it serves is very important. This was recognized in the Force's official report to Parliament on the sled dogs, although difficulties were glossed over.

> It is important to note that the relationship between Inuit people and the RCMP in "V" Division today is positive and cordial. However, there would be great value to Canada and the RCMP

---

55 Quoted in RCMP Sled Dogs Report, pp. 635.

> to explore the possibility of some form of dialogue with the Inuit community aimed at reconciling any differences the alleged sled dog issue[56] may have highlighted and strengthening the relationship with a community whom the RCMP is proud to serve.[57]

Enforcing the Dog Ordinance: Iqaluit 1956–1959

The Northwest Territories Dog Ordinance developed in the 1920s to deal with conditions in the Mackenzie Valley, where there were both dog teams and privately owned pets. As late as 1954 this ordinance was not applied to the Baffin Region, except around the United States Air Force base at Iqaluit and at a weather station in Kimmirut.[58] On 19 August 1955, it was applied to all places within one-quarter mile from any "building" of a DEW Line station or within the same distance of "any dwelling in any settlement in the Keewatin and Franklin Districts." This included the whole Baffin Region. With inadequate consultation with Inuit and some misgivings from officials on the spot, the police and administration were drawn into a rigorous enforcement of the Dog Ordinance in Iqaluit. This now included a 1950

56 Two comments are needed here: It would be more accurate to say that positive and cordial relations are highly desirable but that relations remain ambivalent, and the word "alleged" is at odds with the good intentions shown in the rest of the statement.

57 Canada. Royal Canadian Mounted Police. *Final Report: RCMP Review of Allegations Concerning Inuit Sled Dogs*. http://www.rcmp-grc.gc.ca/pubs/ccaps-spcca/pdf/sled-traineau-dogs-chiens-final-eng.pdf, accessed 28 Dec 2009, pp. 23–24.

58 Library and Archives Canada, Record Group 109 (Canadian Wildlife Service), Series B.1, Volume 407, File WLU 229, Part 1, "Dogs—Generally—Rabies and Distemper," Chapter 18, An Ordinance to Amend an Ordinance Respecting Dogs, 30 Nov 1950; see the "SCHEDULE Description of Areas" naming Lake Harbour and Frobisher Bay and any place within one quarter mile of any "dwelling" in the settlement.

amendment that allowed, "Where an officer is unable to seize a dog that is running at large contrary to the provisions of this Ordinance" he could "destroy" that dog and the owner would be entitled to no compensation.

Official anxiety over loose dogs in the Eastern Arctic surfaced as early as 1954 at Coral Harbour, where a new Welfare Teacher asked for authority under the Dog Ordinance to seize or destroy dogs that the Inuit did not keep chained. The Chief of the Arctic Division in Ottawa ordered the teacher to get the consent of Inuit before Ottawa would change the law. "It is almost axiomatic that laws that do not have general public support are difficult to administer" and made it clear he did not expect Inuit to agree.

> I have mentioned that the views of the Eskimos should be obtained but I fully realize that this is not a simple matter to carry out. It has been noted by people who have studied primitive cultures and the impact of civilization that when one thread in the fabric of the culture is disturbed the whole weave is affected. This is true whether the thread in question is an economic matter or whether it concerns clothing, marriage, handicraft, health or religious aspects. We cannot lightly issue orders in such a matter as the restraining of dogs. We must remember that these animals are important to the Eskimo in many ways, that they have always run at large and that keeping them tied up will bring up several new considerations. One interesting and possibly significant point of view that has been put forward on occasion by people experienced in the north is that chaining dogs makes them much more dangerous.[59]

---

59 Library and Archives Canada, Record Group 85 (Northern Affairs Program), Volume 1321, File 530-25, Part 5, "Dog Ordinance, NWT," letter from F. J. G. Cunningham, Director, to James R. Whitford, Welfare Teacher, 24 Dec. 1954. This letter is quoted at length because it is not in the RCMP Sled Dogs Report where logically it should appear with related correspondence at pp. 206–07, and because the issues of Inuit consent and

Coral Harbour (where there was no RCMP detachment) remained a flashpoint. Late in 1956, when a new teacher ordered ammunition to shoot loose dogs, he was sternly warned not to act without specific permission from Ottawa. But he also received permission to shoot any dog actually attacking a person, and to requisition five boxes of .22 long ammunition. A surprising marginal note reveals that the letter had been "Read to and approved by" four of the most senior officials in the Northern Administration and Lands Branch—an indication of how seriously the matter was being taken.[60]

The situation in Iqaluit came to a head after senior officials visited the town in autumn 1956, and the medical staff of the DEW Line project office complained about treating bites inflicted by "ownerless strays"[61]—although these were, in fact, dogs belonging to Inuit employees of the military. The Chief of the Arctic Division advised his director:

> Mr. Nicol recommends that our Northern Service Officers be given authority to dispose of dogs. We prefer that such enforcement jobs be done by police. Our officers cannot be successful in their efforts at community organization if they have to act as policemen. If we want to instruct the police at Frobisher in this matter we must do it through "G" Division, and that puts fat into several fires. We would much prefer to adjust the matter locally. . . .[62]

Inuit culture raised in December 1954 were only weakly raised and then overturned in discussions about Iqaluit two years later. Cunningham's letter was drafted by his immediate subordinate, Chief of the Arctic Division Bent Sivertz, but the contents suggest input from Alex Stevenson or James Cantley.

60 "Read to and approved by Adams, Jacobson, Brown & Stevenson. F. J. G. C."

61 NWT Archives, Series G-79-003 Box 163, File 3, former Northern Administration Branch file 530-25-1, letter from H. Graham Ross, M. D. to B. G. Sivertz, 13 Nov 1956.

62 NWT Archives, Series G-79-003, Box 163, File 3, former Northern Administration Branch file 530-25-2, B.G. Sivertz to Director [F. Cunningham], 9 Oct 1956.

Whatever the qualms about bringing "G" Division in Ottawa into the discussion, NSO Archie Flucke and Cst. R. Van Norman quickly put together a plan, which they shared with their superiors in Ottawa. It included an information poster in Inuktitut on the law requiring dogs to be tied up, a public meeting on 24 November at which all adult Inuit would be lectured on dog control, and the purchase by Flucke of materials for a dog pound to hold and feed up to twelve dogs at a time. Enforcement proceeded through the next two months and was duly reported to Ottawa as a success: twenty dogs were impounded, two men were fined for letting their dogs run loose, and "three or four dogs" were shot after five days. Inuit were critical of the chains, which were too short. Flucke believed that feeding the dogs was "an acute problem" because commercial dog feed lacked essential nutrients, especially fat. Inuit who were chaining their dogs were losing them to cold and malnutrition while other dogs, which ran free, grew fat on waste food from the Air Force dump. Flucke concluded that the only solution to the problem would be a costly one—two large compounds near the air base, where dogs could be easily fed and watered.[63] Just a month later, the detachment reported that impoundments and prosecutions were continuing and loose dogs were no longer a problem in Iqaluit.[64]

This was a temporary solution, backed by the threat of force. The director of the Northern Administration and Lands Branch confided to Superintendent Henry Larsen his determination to introduce "a new regimen with respect to these large and dangerous dogs." This was qualified by an admission that "Eskimos have a long history of association with dogs, and they have strong feelings on the subject of shooting dogs without cause that is sufficient in their view." The director's concluding emphasis on the "importance of carrying the Eskimos with us in these new ways" was an un-

63 NWT Archives, Series G-1979-003, Box 163, File 3, Memorandum from A.F. Flucke, Northern Service Officer to Chief, Arctic Division, 5 Feb 1957.

64 NWT Archives, Series G-1979-003, Box 163, File 3, RCMP Report forwarded by W.J. Fitzsimmons, Inspector, G Division, 4 March 1957.

mistakeable warning that Inuit preferences had less weight than southern precautions.[65]

It is not clear what happened in 1958 because files are incomplete, but a policeman told a visitor in May 1959 that 286 dogs were shot the preceding year.[66] Certainly in 1959 the arrangements carefully worked out by Flucke and Van Norman were no longer effective. Inuit were letting their dogs roam free and forage for food in the traditional way, even though dogs were being shot in large numbers. In September, Archie Flucke's successor wrote from Iqaluit that there was no need to appoint a new dog officer because "the Eskimos [were by then] quite familiar with the rough outlines of the Dog Ordinance, if not the details. Most of them conscientiously keep their dogs tied, and [were] unhappily resigned to the fact that loose dogs [would] be destroyed. Approximately two hundred dogs or more [had] been destroyed in [a] year and those that [were] left [were] valued by the owners."[67] Two hundred dogs represents between fourteen and twenty-five teams, or the destruction of essential tools needed by hunters to support between seventy and one hundred people. With the 286 reported shot the previous year, those numbers approach forty teams and two hundred people. Inuit found it impractical to chain their dogs. Many ignored a law that was in conflict with their own laws and practices, which developed not only for their own welfare but also for that of their dogs. In the face of this re-

65 NWT Archives, Series G-1979-003, Box 163, File 3, Letter from F.J.G. Cunningham, Director, to H.A. Larsen, Superintendent, Officer Commanding G Division, RCMP, 26 Nov. 1956; drafted by Sivertz, copies were sent to Flucke in Iqaluit and to medical officers of the DEW Line and the Indian and Northern Health Service.

66 Library and Archives Canada, Record Group 85 (Northern Affairs Program), Volume 1473, File 201-1-8, Part 6, "Reports re: Arctic Inspections," P. Godt, Acting Chief, Co-operative Development, Report, 21 May 1959, "Trip to Cape Dorset."

67 Library and Archives Canada, Record Group 85 (Northern Affairs Program), Series D-1-a, Volume 1220, File 530-25-2, Part 1, "Dog Officer—NWT (Appointments)," Memorandum from J.F. Delaute, A/Regional Administrator of the Arctic, 21 Sept 1959.

sistance, the authorities overcame their reluctance to engage in large-scale shooting. Arctic veterans such as A. J. "Moose" Kerr might argue the case for respecting Aboriginal customs, but in a losing cause.

> The Eskimos or Indians, even if agreeable to having their dogs in an enclosure, would expect the White residents to feed them. From experience in the North I personally do not think that "Wandering" dogs create any greater hazard than does the normal automobile traffic of southern Canada. In the south we warn our children of the necessary safe-guards and there is no reason why we can't do the same in the North. It is also my experience that a tied up dog, if approached by children, is more dangerous than a "Wandering" one. However, the law, poorly worded as it is in the case of the Quebec Dog Ordinance, and ignoring the Eskimos [sic] and Indians [sic] right to an accepted (By them) [sic] traditional custom in their own land, should be enforced on the grounds that it is the law.[68]

Although the argument concerning traffic accidents had some supporters, fatalities such as the mauling of an Inuit translator's son at Apex in 1960 ensured that the advocates of shooting loose dogs would keep the upper hand.[69]

---

68 RCMP Sled Dogs Report, pp. 225.

69 NWT Archives, Series G-1979-003, Box 183, File 4, Memorandum from C. M. Bolger, Administrator of the Arctic, to Deputy Commissioner of the NWT, with attachment, 8 Nov. 1960.

Gaps and Omissions in Describing the Relationship, 1950–1975

Both the RCMP Sled Dogs Report and the research and testimony gathered by the QTC provided abundant evidence of how valuable the RCMP was to the Inuit economy in the years before centralization. Authors of the RCMP Sled Dogs Report especially emphasized the programs of vaccination and inoculation of Inuit sled dogs, evidence in their view that the police were not part of a conspiracy against the survival of the breed and that they made considerable individual efforts, in settlements and in ilagiit nunagivaktangit, to keep teams healthy.[70] This focus on dogs arguably led the RCMP Review Team at times to gloss over more central aspects of the relationship.

Other aspects were, admittedly, scattered through the report. The following is a candid, if extremely one-sided, acknowledgement of this.

> It is also essential to remember that particularly in the 1950s and earlier, the RCMP officer was often the only Qallunaat [sic] in a settlement employed by the federal government and, as such, had the full authority of the government to manage the delivery of all government services, a situation far different from the reality today. Therefore, the Inuit in the settlement were, in fact, the member's responsibility: They were "his Eskimos" to look after.

---

70 The RCMP Sled Dogs Report, pp. 14, notes that the RCMP Review Team believed it was overreaching its mandate by going into these matters. "The review team became aware of the magnitude of the work done by RCMP members in the north, including their key role in the Inuit sled dog vaccination program, much of which was virtually unknown to history. It was considered to be essential that the work done by the members to promote and preserve the Inuit culture be told, and accordingly, the scope of this report was expanded to this limited degree." The RCMP Review Team's narrow interpretation of its mandate has been commented on above.

> The Inuit themselves, without modern media access and being otherwise exposed to Qallunaat culture, relied on the RCMP officer to look after their needs. There were elements of authority, respect, fear, and dependence in the relationship.[71]

Inuit constituted almost the whole permanent population of the Baffin Region throughout this period and the RCMP represented government authority. Serving the Inuit gave the RCMP a role that was essential to the Force's self-image as well as to Canada's claims to be effectively occupying the Arctic. On the long sled patrols, which are part of RCMP lore, Inuit provided guiding services and hunted food for the police dog teams. Many new recruits had received equestrian training at Regina, but knew little or nothing about the North—Inuit regarded them at first as similar to children and performed an essential service to Canada by helping them learn the ways of the North. The police in return provided medical assistance and, albeit in paternalistic ways, delivered other social services.

Less pleasant was the occasional use of police prestige and authority to direct Inuit behaviour, especially concerning the length of visits to the trading posts. Perhaps it is significant that the Review Team chose to omit from its selection of annual reports the following statement concerning families considered by the constable in charge to be "bums and scroungers." "They were informed during their visit to the settlement that unless they moved from this location they would receive no further Family Allowance, they were further advised that relief and assistance to all members of that camp had been discontinued. All the natives of this camp agreeed [sic] to move." [72]Also missing from the RCMP Sled Dogs Report, although very familiar

71 RCMP Sled Dogs Report, pp. 633.

72 Library and Archives Canada, Record Group 18 (RCMP), Series 1985-86/048, Volume 55, File TA 500-8-1-11, Conditions Among Eskimos—Pangnirtung, Memo to Officer Commanding from H.A. Johnson, 1955. The annual RCMP reports on "Conditions Amongst the Eskimos" were required to report, for each detachment area, whether

to northerners (including witnesses who spoke to the QTC), were the daily interactions in communities, including relations between individual police and Inuit women.

The RCMP Sled Dogs Report did not examine the way inequality of power and cultural difference affected the dynamics of RCMP–Inuit interaction in the dispersed ilagiit nunagivaktangit, on the trail, or around the trading establishments, either before or after centralized settlement became official policy. It also left it mainly to the statements of retired members to underline the bitterness many felt over the way other government agents, especially Northern Service officers, took over many of the RCMP's responsibilities after 1955. This loss was also explored in a slim book by an anthropologist who went North specifically to study the role of policing in the Baffin Region.[73] This interaction, whether positive or negative, was relevant to the evolution of the settlements from Qallunaat enclaves to present-day communities. The report also did not explain how the RCMP used its increased funding to benefit Inuit. The RCMP budget north of 60° grew from $881,000 in 1953–1954 to $2,291,721 in 1968–1969.[74] No doubt much of the increase was spent outside the Baffin Region and some on services that chiefly benefited Qallunaat. Additional funds were certainly required for conventional law enforcement as crime increased in the settlements. Unfortunately, the report missed this opportunity to explore the way the Force took on new roles and deployed new resources in Inuit communities.

The QTC research team deals with some of these issues in more detail in

---

members felt that "loitering" was a problem. Loitering meant remaining at a trading post after completing the commercial purpose of the visit, and deserves its own study in the history of intercultural relations. See Adamee Veevee. Testimony before the QTC, Pangnirtung [QIPA13].

73 John Matthiasson, *Living on the Land*, especially pp. 91–129, "The coming of the Bureaucrats" and "A Changing Political Paradigm, and the Impact of New Statuses."

74 Figures derived from appendices in the annual report by the Advisory Committee on Northern Development on *Government Activities in the North.*

a background paper on intercultural communications. They make it clear in ways that should have been important to the RCMP Sled Dogs Report that relations were not just marked by "authority, respect, fear, and dependence" as that report acknowledged, but were tainted by systematically maintained colonial inequality whose intimidating impact is often summed up in the Inuit language as illira[75]—a word that does not appear in the RCMP Sled Dogs Report. (Pond Inlet Elder Anaviapik explained to Hugh Brody that illira is the characteristic of "people or things that have power over you and can be neither controlled nor predicted. People or things that make you feel vulnerable, and to which you *are* vulnerable.") This extreme diffidence, and the impairment of ordinary human interactions that flowed from it, are essential to explaining a number of factors the RCMP Sled Dogs Report dealt with, including the reluctance of Inuit to resist the killing of their dogs in the first place and their reticence in avoiding the self-investigation launched by the Force in 2005.

SLED DOGS HISTORY AS COLLECTIVE MEMORY

Promoting RCMP History

The RCMP Sled Dogs Report was more than a report on investigating possible wrongdoing. It was an exercise by the police to sustain or create a positive collective memory of the RCMP experience in Nunavut, with a nostalgic focus on the specific duties and circumstances of the 1950s and 1960s. The RCMP Sled Dogs Report used documentary sources and personal reminiscences to elaborate a view of the RCMP's services to Inuit around the middle of the last century as a kind of golden age.

---

75 H. Brody, *The Other Side of Eden* (Vancouver and Toronto: Douglas and MacIntyre, 2000), pp. 43.

> The review team became aware of the magnitude of the work done by RCMP members in the north, including their key role in the Inuit sled dog vaccination program, much of which was virtually unknown to history. It was considered to be essential that the work done by the members to promote and preserve Inuit culture be told, and accordingly, the scope of this report was expanded to this limited degree.[76]

This version of a collective memory for Northern Canada emphasized the RCMP as benefactors who made great sacrifices to protect Inuit against both the harsh environment and unwise government policies.[77] While the collective memory is consistent on important points, it is not monolithic: the rifts mostly concern relocation and centralization. In particular, retired Assistant Commissioner Robert Currie's repeated denunciation of the "abhorrent policy" of High Arctic relocation stands out as an example of divergent opinion without, however, challenging the emphasis on the RCMP's benevolence.

Unfortunately, the RCMP Sled Dogs Report did nothing to try to reconcile this view of Nunavut history with one commonly understood by Inuit—a history in which the existence of inequality was taken for granted, and

76 RCMP Sled Dogs Report, pp. 14. The assertions in this paragraph were amply supported in the report by e-mails and interviews involving retired RCMP members who served in the North.

77 Getting this recognized is not a new problem. See the *Ottawa Journal* review of the Glassco Report in 1962: "It is disappointing, too, to see the Report show so little awareness of the role of the Royal Canadian Mounted Police in the North. Such reference as is made is lacking [sic, i.e. *not* lacking] in accuracy, but there is no proper recognition of the RCMP's great work up there. The Mounties are more than mere police in the North and a tribute to them was in order." Undated clipping on file, circa mid-Nov 1962, in Library and Archives Canada, Record Group 85 (Northern Affairs Program), Volume 1654, File NR1/1-12, Part 1.

benevolence was sometimes negated by unexplained behaviour that might have caused distress or hardship.

Understanding Inuit History

What is missing from this exercise was the needed appreciation of Inuit as actors in their own history. They appeared intermittently as special constables or as more or less passive—and by implication now ungrateful—recipients of the RCMP's skill and compassion. The RCMP Sled Dogs Report valued the contributions of only one group of participants in a complex social and cultural exchange. This treatment raises serious questions about whether, as a matter of either historical understanding or of public policy, there is merit in fostering a collective memory that elevates retired policemen as a group by marginalizing the memories of a much larger number of Inuit.

Past patterns of inequality, as well as present ones, encourage development of different group identities and rival forms of historical consciousness. It would be tempting for the QTC to delineate a rival Inuit collective memory in opposition to that of the RCMP Review Team. However, the QTC's mandate requires it look for both truth *and* reconciliation and therefore to look for elements of a common history that do not exclusively emphasize division and disagreement. Because the RCMP did, as the RCMP Sled Dogs Report argued, provide services to Inuit as individuals and as groups, some grounds do exist for writing a shared history.

A major flaw in the RCMP Sled Dogs Report was its lack of curiosity or respect toward very complex and sensitive issues surrounding historical memory. The RCMP Review Team, on finding no evidence of an illegal conspiracy, seemed to jump immediately to the conclusion that Inuit were lying about the dog slaughter. Alternative explanations were left virtually unexplored.[78] The discussion in this section of our review accepts that the RCMP had a legal rationale for killing most of the dogs its members disposed of from 1950 to 1970, and it accepts that the police doubted the wisdom of the government's centralization policy. However, our analysis also asserts that hundreds of Inuit suffered severe losses at the hands of government agents, including the police, because administrative policies were carried out in ways that were sometimes cruel and generally insensitive. Some cases probably constituted wrongdoing, such as the actions of a settlement manager in Igloolik who without warning killed the dogs of a man who had just arrived to trade. The killings were so extensive in Pangnirtung in 1966 that RCMP headquarters authorities themselves cautioned the constable against a repetition.[79] (In addition, the likelihood that some or all of the dog slaughter constituted a breach of the government's fiduciary obligations towards Inuit[80] is examined by the QTC in another paper.) In other words, while technically the police generally acted within the law, Inuit do have legitimate grounds to claim that there was wrongdoing, possibly including illegal acts by individuals.[81]

The two parties in this debate were so obviously focused on different aspects of their shared past that there is no need to assume that either side is lying. The RCMP look at their investment of time and energy and the hard-

---

78 One passage suggests that interpreters, usually special constables, passed along instructions, but not explanations or choices. See RCMP Sled Dogs Report, pp. 46, 685.

79 For the Igloolik incident around 1959, see evidence of Maurice Arnatsiaq; for Pangnirtung, see the section below, "Cst. Jack Grabowski and the dogs of Pangnirtung, 1966."

80 Mr. Justice J-J Croteau has concluded that there were breaches of the fiduciary responsibility in Nunavik.

81 The question of whether there is "wrongdoing" without a breach of statutes or ordinances is one on which the QTC research team and the RCMP Review Team would probably not agree. The position adopted here is that when people in authority perform lawful acts in an arbitrary or disrespectful manner or without regard for harm done to individuals, a wrong has occurred, even if no specific law has been broken.

ships they endured to bring the South into the North—to be the vanguard of official Canadian appropriation of Inuit lands while delivering services to Inuit, including those who were not ready to follow the modernist program. Indeed, until about the mid-1960s, many RCMP had a particular soft spot for Inuit who were not ready to join the "modern world." Inuit, on the other hand, are still weighing—and being weighed down by—their memories of the sacrifices, losses, shock, and bewilderment at the sudden end in a few years to a way of life that evolved over centuries. The problems of interpreting these overlapping histories relate not so much to law enforcement as to culture and memory, as well as to individuals' places in what continues to be a divided society.

In a section of the RCMP Sled Dogs Report dealing with the reliability of witnesses, the RCMP Review Team's attacks on the Royal Commission on Aboriginal Peoples, the Inuit who testified before it, and the commissioners, went well beyond the boundaries of respectful disagreement. The implication of that passage[82] was that Inuit witnesses were clever enough to deceive a retired Chief Justice of Canada, but not clever enough to fool the RCMP Review Team. At no point did the RCMP Review Team deal with the fact that since 1997 the oral history of Aboriginal peoples has a privileged place in Canadian jurisprudence where it can be admitted as proof whether or not it is corroborated by written records.[83]

In a brief and puzzling digression,[84] the RCMP Sled Dogs Report dealt with the difficulty of using eyewitness evidence, citing only a very brief

82 RCMP Sled Dogs Report, pp. 454–67.

83 The landmark Supreme Court of Canada ruling on this principle is Delgamukw vs Regina, 11 Dec 1997. It has generated an enormous literature, including the very accessible book by Dara Culhane, *The Pleasure of the Crown: Anthropology, Law and First Nations* (Burnaby: Talon, 1998). The QTC is preparing a background paper on the fiduciary obligations of the federal government, which will contain further analysis of Delgamukw.

84 RCMP Sled Dogs Report, pp. 197–98.

article in an RCMP house organ, the *Gazette*. "The article was intended to caution police officers to exercise considerable care in accepting eye-witness testimony, even in relation to recent events." This two-page article summarized the expertise of two American psychologists and denounced "instituting legal [i.e. criminal] proceedings solely on the basis of eyewitness testimony."

Although the RCMP Sled Dogs Report said little in an organized way about the strengths or even the weaknesses of individual and collective memories of historical events, it did include and base its conclusions on written and oral interviews with retired RCMP and other non-Inuit northerners. Some of this material showed evidence of distortion, suppression, and exaggeration. Later in this section, three examples will illustrate this point.

Collective Memory and Public Policy

Collective memory is one of the terms social scientists use to describe and analyse how the past is understood and explained by groups of people, either through their formal state institutions or as families, religious communities, local and regional units, and social and political movements. (Public memory, historical consciousness, and memory studies are related phrases.) In the case of the sled dogs, two affected communities—a) the RCMP and its veterans, and b) Inuit whose dogs were shot and the children and advocates of those Inuit—are using forms of collective memory to explain the past and solidify support in the present. In doing so, their historical statements and inquiries have defined separate and rather hostile ways of dealing with rival histories of the same events. The QTC's mandate, which involves reconciliation as well as truth, encourages a different perspective, one that may allow all parties to see the complexity of the mid-century centralization of people into the present thirteen settlements.

Studies of collective memory draw on history, psychology, and other academic disciplines, but they are largely concerned not with what academic researchers do, but with "the beliefs of everyone else."[85] Not only do different communities have their own ways of understanding the past, but also those understandings can change, especially if they were based on inadequate or misleading information. As new evidence emerges or new developments take place, people come to believe that they must change their former views of trends, causes, and effects. Memory studies may also deal with aspects of "forgetting" or delayed disclosure.[86] For example, shame, grief, and other emotions connected with the disempowering changes in their way of life induced many Inuit to stay silent about the loss of their dogs until quite recently. Although memory studies originate in post-1918 reflections on the Great War, and much of the theoretical groundwork was laid by research on the Shoah, studies of collective memory have taken root in Canada in recent decades and have begun to be used to analyse many dimensions of how Canadians use their pasts. As Roger Simon of Toronto pointed out in a volume of essays edited by Peter Seixas:

> Aboriginal communities across North America have been producing written and oral testimony as part of an attempt to contribute to a historical awareness and understanding of the history of Aboriginal-settler relations and the its [sic] impact on the lives lived in its wake. A central aspect of this history has been government-initiated removal of native peoples from lands they had been living on for centuries.[87]

---

85 Peter Seixas, "Introduction," in *Theorizing Historical Consciousness* (University of Toronto Press, 2004), pp. 5.

86 Michael G. Kenny, "A Place for Memory: the Interface between Individual and Collective History," *Comparative Studies in Society and History* 41:3 (July 1999), pp. 420–37, esp. 423–26 concerning "cultural amnesia."

87 Roger Simon, "The Pedagogical Insistence of Public Memory," in Seixas, ed.,

Another contributor to the Seixas volume proposed a hierarchy of four types of historical consciousness, "each representing a different stance towards the past as a means of moral orientation in the present." Seixas summarized these:[88]

- The "traditional" type: supports the continuity of fixed and unchanging moral obligations, without acknowledging any significant change over time.
- The "exemplary" type: draws on particular events and people from the past as a source of cultural universals, which apply across temporal change, as in the celebratory history of heroes to inspire strong character in the present.
- The "critical" type: turns towards the past in order to break from it, as in women's history that helps to undo the past's oppressive gender relations.
- The "genetic" type: acknowledges the ongoing legacy of the past, at the same time comprehending radically changed present circumstances and mores.

The RCMP Sled Dogs Report was mainly concerned with the "traditional" type of history, while the complaints of Inuit Elders represented a step towards "critical" history. The QTC's mandate favours a "genetic" approach. This generally conforms to the encouragement Peter Seixas gave to people to make a commitment to certain values, including openness to change and acceptance of others, when using history, as they should in other public behaviour:

Theorizing Historical Consciousness, pp. 191.

88 Peter Seixas, "Historiographies and Historical Consciousness," in Seixas, ed., *Theorizing Historical Consciousness*, pp. 22–23.

> These requirements are particularly difficult to reconcile with practices of collective memory that seek to draw immutable boundaries round groups by establishing fixed identities based on biological differences or on moral codes rooted in the revelations of canonical texts. Some forms of historical consciousness that may have been acceptable for relatively homogenous cultures pose obstacles to the negotiation of inter-group relations and adaptation to rapid change that characterize postmodern global culture.[89]

This does not imply that Canadians should be served an inoffensive, blurred consensus history. It is foreseeable that two different narratives of northern Canadian history will endure, one which remains optimistic about the future while still fully conscious of loss and injustice, the other preferring to praise past governments for whatever benefits they conferred. Yet Roger Simon has warned that study of difficult questions should reopen the way individuals and groups acknowledge the past. When people in the majority culture hear traumatic narratives, they need to "incorporate them into an intelligible past, while recognizing that there is an insistence in their stories that calls for reopening the present to reconsideration."[90] This may call for "a change in the way non-Aboriginals view their shared history with native peoples. For this change to happen, we will have to learn to listen differently, take the measure of our ignorance, and reassess the terms on which we are prepared to hear stories that might trouble the social arrangements on which we presume a collective future."[91] This kind of approach by all concerned, rather than a hardening of lines around legalistic interpretations of past behaviour, offers a better future for Nunavut.

---

89 Seixas, "Introduction," pp. 15.

90 Simon, "Pedagogical Insistence of Public Memory," pp. 195.

91 Simon, "Pedagogical Insistence of Public Memory," pp. 197. Conversely, Inuit understanding of the past may need to change to take into account further insights into Qallunaat culture.

Cst. Jack Grabowski and the Dogs of Pangnirtung, 1966

Memories of dog slaughter are strong in Pangnirtung. Many people from this district travelled to nearby Frobisher Bay to work in the 1950s and some of their dogs were shot during their stay. Later, a cyclical episode of canine distemper in 1961–1962 south of Pangnirtung evoked a much stronger reaction from the authorities than the same disease had done in Kimmirut a few years earlier. Many Inuit believed that some dogs had a good chance of surviving the distemper, but that police shot them unnecessarily while trying to stop the spread of the disease. Later, a well-documented culling of sled dogs in the settlement occurred in 1966. Reporting to "G" Division headquarters, Cst. Jack Grabowski stated, as quoted in the RCMP Sled Dogs Report and the RCMP Report to Parliament in 2005, that:

> The dog population decreased rapidly over the past year. Some Eskimos disposed of their own dogs when they were able to purchase ski-doos, while a good number were destroyed in contravention to the Dog Ordinance. Referring to the latter, numerous requests were made by myself and members of this Detachment to the Eskimos to keep their dogs adequately tied, or penned. When these requests went unheeded I gave instructions that all dogs at large were to be shot, and in the period of slightly over one year, I would estimate that some 250 dogs have been shot. This too, does not seem to have the desired effect, as almost daily, dogs are still seen at large. A new approach to the apparent passive resistance of the Eskimo has been taken, whereby the owner will be sought out, and he will be prosecuted.[92]

92 *RCMP Sled Dogs Report*, pp. 435–36. His superiors in "G" Division headquarters believed he had over-reacted and after a short review he was informally disciplined for this. The RCMP Review Team used this incident in the final report to Parliament as

Grabowski had a keen interest in problem dogs. Jim Cumming, the Hudson's Bay Company (HBC) manager at the time, shared this observation with the RCMP Review Team in July 2005: "Cpl. Jack Grabowski on a Sunday shot probably five dogs. He stated that Cpl. Grabowski couldn't get out of his house at one point because of the dogs." But a woman who cooked for two decades at Pangnirtung's St. Luke's Hospital told the RCMP Review Team by telephone on 25 October 2005 that she "[did] not recall any RCMP members shooting dogs or even hearing that they shot dogs in the settlement."[93]

In these three first-hand accounts, a coherent view of a campaign to control loose dogs by shooting emerges only in the one contemporary document, which was written by the man responsible for it. By contrast, Mr. Cummings did not mention the campaign and gave a severely limited account of Cst. Grabowski's personal involvement in the actual shooting. He suggested that nothing out of the ordinary happened. The cook's statement may be technically true—she might have been oblivious to many things that happened in the settlement—but the three statements taken together suggest that memories, perhaps unintentionally, were adjusted after the fact to align the witnesses' statements with others who shared their place in society, and to avoid acknowledging the occurrence of things that were hurtful to Inuit.

Dust, Dogs, and the Dump

One vocal participant who smoothed nothing over, but told his community's story from different points of view over time, was long-time Iqaluit resident and former mayor Bryan Pearson. In 1966 Mr. Pearson voiced his concern over the way dogs were being controlled to a reporter from the *Star Weekly*

---

evidence that the RCMP did not condone indiscriminate or systematic slaughter of dogs.

93 RCMP Sled Dogs Report, pp. 631.

and in the legislature in 1973 he recalled his time on the community council as a time when, as he expressed it later, elected local authority dealt mainly with the three Ds: dust, dogs, and the dump.[94]

Now, in just going over the history, when I first came North which was not very long ago, 1956, in a community like Frobisher a conflict had started, the conflict of the dogs, and Frobisher like many other communities was just one seething mass of dogs. They were everywhere, and of course shortly round about 1958 or 1959 regulations that existed were then enforced, and that was that nobody may leave his dog loose otherwise it would be shot. In 1959 I recall vividly seeing squads of cars going out on Sunday afternoon in particular with shotguns shooting dogs and in October of 1959 the RCMP in that month alone shot 280 dogs.

These are facts, okay. And then this conflict went on for many, many years, because the hunters who were then the Eskimo people were coming into the community and bringing their families in from the camps. They were coming in with their dogs and dog teams and these regulations were being enforced in all of these communities. Regulations said, "tie up your dogs or we will shoot them," to which they would reply, "well, we cannot tie them up, they have nothing to eat, they have got to scavenge around to get food." That is where one of the greatest conflicts that ever happened in the North began when the Eskimo people, I do not know if the same applies here, but the Eskimo people in the Eastern Arctic then began to wonder about the wonderful white man and his wonderful system. And gradually we eliminated the dogs, eliminated them completely. There are no dog teams in any community on Baffin Island, the nearest dog team that I know of is at Igloolik.

In his communications with the RCMP Review Team in 2005, Mr. Pearson was critical of Inuit complaints against the dog slaughter and sceptical of individual complaints. His communications were especially critical of the interpretation that dogs were slaughtered to force people into settlements.

---

94 RCMP Sled Dogs Report pp. 502.

He does not seem to have repeated his comments about "one of the greatest conflicts that ever happened in the North" or his earlier indication that the way the authorities handled dogs discredited white people in the view of Inuit. The different views, expressed three or four decades apart, underline how in speaking of past events, a person may choose different facts and present a different point of view, in response to a changed context.

While the later statements do not directly contradict the earlier, they have a very different tone. Closer to the events, Mr. Pearson spoke of the dog killings as bungled and likely to discredit the Qallunaat in the eyes of Inuit generally. More recently, he has emphasized the dangerous nature of sled dogs and has singled out individual complaints as being unjustified. While his statement to the RCMP Review Team did not repudiate any of the facts in his earlier discourse on the dog issue, the tone of these recent statements is very different.

The Most Famous White Woman in Eastern Arctic History

Pond Inlet resident Rosie Katsak told the QTC of an experience her father Ishmael related to her. Before his recent death, he explained to his daughter how his dog team was destroyed by a mounted policeman when Ishmael moved his family into the settlement, probably in the late 1960s.

> [A]ll of his dogs were killed by RCMP. He told me that one of the RCMP's wife was attacked by a dog team and then that the police was shocked, so he asked the police to shoot all the dog teams—that is what he told me.
>
> All of his dogs were killed by police. Somewhere in Nunavut police's wife was killed by the dog team....
>
> I think it was when they starting [sic] to move people to a larger community when that lady was killed.[95]

95 Rosie Katsak. Testimony before the QTC (19 Dec 2008) Pond Inlet [QTPI20].

The policeman's wife did not die in the 1960s. In fact, Maggie Agnes Clay[96] died of her wounds more than thirty years before and more than 1200 kilometres away from where Ishmael's dog team was sacrificed in her memory. But Ishmael was not the only person to learn a version of her story. It spread across the Arctic, a vital part of both the oral and written culture of the Qallunaat in the North. The incident appeared repeatedly in the RCMP Sled Dogs Report, almost always recounted by Qallunaat and always employed as sensationalist evidence that sled dogs can be lethal. Maggie Clay was possibly the only adult killed in Nunavut by sled dogs in the past century, but her story lives on. She is the most famous white woman in the history of the Eastern Arctic, where she lived for less than a month.

The story is brief, and tragic. During her first month in the Arctic, while her husband was away on a long patrol by boat, Maggie Clay walked out to feed or play with the dogs on the beach near the detachment house. For unknown reasons, the dogs knocked her down and stripped the flesh from one leg before people intervened. With no medical personnel within a thousand miles, two of the half-dozen white people on hand amputated the victim's leg with her consent, but she died shortly afterwards. After the mauling, as the report to RCMP headquarters stated, "of course all dogs connected in the matter were at once shot."[97]

The RCMP Review Team used the story of Maggie Clay's demise as a basis for one of their many criticisms of Inuit oral tradition.[98] The RCMP

---

96 The name is taken from her grave marker at Chesterfield Inlet. Officially she was, of course, "Mrs. S. G. Clay" and some sources call her "Marie Agnes Clay."

97 Library and Archives Canada, Record Group 18 (RCMP), Volume 3301, File HQ-660-G-1, Petty to O/C "F" Division, Prince Albert, 30 Sept 1924.

98 Two official files on this tragedy are held by Library and Archives Canada, Record Group 18 (RCMP), Volume 3301, File HQ-660-G-1, Mrs. Marie Agnes Clay wife of S/Sgt. S.G. Clay—Chesterfield, Northwest Territories—Death of from wounds received when attacked by sled dogs; also Record Group 85 (Northern Affairs Program), Volume 612, File 2816, Parts 1, Mrs. S.G. Clay—Killed by dogs—Appt. of Staff Sgt. Clay as J.P. and

Sled Dogs Report commented that one Inuk living as far away as Gjoa Haven, Cst. Mark Toiak, had heard the story in outline. In October 2005, Cst. Toiak told the RCMP Review Team that:

> His father, a local Shaman, always advised his son to tie up his dogs in settlements where the white men lived or they would shoot his dogs if they were loose. His father also told him that many years ago loose dogs attacked and killed the wife of a Mountie in Chesterfield Inlet and that the RCMP then shot all dogs in the settlement.... He does not know the year, or in fact if this actually happened.

Based on a seven-page internal report on Arctic history in 2005, the RCMP Review Team concluded that not all the dogs in the settlement had been killed, but only a few teams that were on the beach at the time of the attack. The review continued:

> This confirms that oral history is not immutable. In fact, on the following page, the facts [sic] of the killing of the sled dogs involved in the mauling of the wife of S/Sgt. Clay in Chesterfield Inlet in 1924 are presented. Compare that with the oral history account given by a former Inuit RCMP member, which he heard from his father, a shaman, that all of the dogs in Chesterfield Inlet were killed as a result of this attack.

The disparagement of oral history continued in a footnote: "According to the internal report, only the 19 dogs on the beach were destroyed, and

---

Coroner Outside Dates: 1922–1936. For a recent tribute, see http://www.rcmpgraves.com/vetcorner/vetmonth-feb.html, accessed online 25 June 2009. By far the best account of the incident is from the private papers of Cst. Stallworthy by William Barr. See his *Red Serge and Polar Bear Pants: The Biography of Harry Stallworthy, RCMP* (Edmonton: University of Alberta Press, 2004), pp. 60–71.

they were owned by the RCMP, the HBC, and the Special Constables. The story could have become embellished over time, becoming a well-recited and universally accepted 'tundra tale.'"

The RCMP Review Team's concern with "facts" did not extend to consulting all the available documentation. It would have raised concerns about how few dogs there were in the Chesterfield Inlet "settlement" in late September 1924, as well as other doubts about the superiority of written reports to "tundra tales."[99]

Undoubtedly sled dogs can be dangerous to humans, especially to vulnerable people such as small children, but the official RCMP report on the death of Maggie Clay contained this significant phrase: "A catastrophe of this nature was anticipated by no one, as there is no record of a grown person ever being attacked before in this District."[100] Nor was the incident repeated: In 1961 a senior officer wrote that there had been no subsequent attack on a member's wife or child in the North.[101] It is therefore important to understand how this horrific but isolated incident became a landmark of collective memory for eighty years.

First, it is not surprising how quickly the story spread. It received newspaper coverage as soon as news reached Prince Albert and Ottawa, the headquarters going so far as to issue a press release. Maggie Clay was soon memorialized by a stone cross at Chesterfield Inlet and by a plaque in the chapel at the RCMP Depot in Regina. A prolific American writer of non-fiction gained access to the official file to include the story of her death in a book called *The Silent Force*, published in 1927.[102] In 1930, the woman

99 The RCMP Sled Dogs Report deals with Mark Toiak's account and Mrs. Clay's death at pp. 290–91, 607 and 684 note 81.

100 Library and Archives Canada, Record Group 18 (RCMP), Volume 3301, File HQ-660-G-1, Petty to O/C "F" Division, Prince Albert, 30 Sept 1924.

101 Library and Archives Canada, RG 18 (RCMP), Volume 3301, File HQ-660-G-1, Insp. J.T. Parsons to Commissioner, 29 Dec 1961.

102 T.M. Longstreth, *The Silent Force* (New York: The Century Company, 1927).

who preceded Maggie in the married quarters at Chesterfield Inlet retold the story in a published memoir. There must have been many unofficial channels of communication as well. A 1936 article in the *Canadian Medical Association Journal* stated, somewhat inaccurately, that "a woman [...] in 1924, was eaten alive at Chesterfield when she fell and hurt herself."[103] A senior departmental official assured a salivating journalist that this was indeed "based on actual facts."[104] The story continued to be told and retold over the years. It was cited repeatedly in the RCMP Sled Dogs Report, rarely with much detail and seldom with any indication by the report's authors that only a single incident was being referred to, over and over again.[105]

It is instructive to identify questions that are generally not asked, either in the literature or elsewhere. First of all, unlike the official report and the Inuit memory, very few press or book accounts referred to what happened to the dogs—authors were quite rightly preoccupied with the human victim. Second, from the very beginning, there was a common aversion to assigning blame to anyone, including the dog owners and the victim herself. The official report carefully made it clear that, apart from the fact that sled dogs were not known to attack adults, these dogs were very well fed and in excellent condition. In other words, the detachment had not abused or neglected its animals, which perhaps could have explained aggressive behaviour. The unwanted inference might be that Maggie Clay somehow brought the accident about by her own carelessness, but this is only very slyly suggested in the memoir by Luta Munday, the previous RCMP wife at Chesterfield. She mentioned her brief meeting with Maggie Clay in a chapter entitled

---

103 I. Rabinowitch, "Clinical and Other Observations on Canadian Eskimos in the Eastern Arctic," *Canadian Medical Association Journal* 34:5 (May 1936), pp. 497.

104 Library and Archives Canada, Record Group 85, Volume 612, File 2816, McKeand to Morrison, 4 June 1936.

105 The RCMP Sled Dogs Report reported aspects of the Clay tragedy at eight separate points, including a detailed discussion in one of the endnotes. See pp. 60, 119, 191–92, 273, 568, 607, 616 and 684.

"The Dogs: My Greatest Friends." The implication was that Mrs. Munday got along very well with these sled dogs, as most sensible people would.[106]

Intriguingly, it was not until 2004 that information was published hinting that the absent S/Sgt. Clay might have inadvertently contributed to his wife's tragedy.[107] A biography of one of the men on the spot, Corporal Stallworthy, reported the victim's account of her encounter with the dogs. "She hadn't been in the least afraid of them as they ran and jumped playfully around her. But it was the black dog Clay had brought from Labrador that had snatched at her coat, then took a nip at her leg. Then she knew she was in trouble." And she insisted that the dogs involved in the attack be shot. Stallworthy and Petty did this and Norman Snow, the HBC manager who helped the missionary perform the amputation, shot a number of his dogs too. The detachment and the HBC suffered from a severe lack of transport until a dozen more dogs could be brought in from Labrador the following spring.

It is quite possible that not all the dogs were shot. The RCMP Sled Dogs Report speculated that dogs belonging to Inuit were shot and compensation was not paid, but this is unconfirmed. First-hand accounts suggest few or no Inuit were on site at the time and according to Luta Munday, there was only one privately owned dog. It is not clear whether the Mission, the only other likely sled dog owner at Chesterfield Inlet, actually possessed any and if so whether they were shot. The purpose of this lengthy digression on the tragedy of Maggie Clay is to underline the unfairness of the RCMP Sled Dogs Report in taking Mark Toiak's oral evidence to task even though his father's memory preserved the rarely acknowledged fact that the dogs

---

106 Luta Munday, *A Mounty's Wife: being the life story of one attached to the Force but not of it* (London: The Sheldon Press, 1930), pp. 192–96, 210–11. Munday's account is the only one reviewed to date that states that Maggie Clay disliked Chesterfield Inlet and was afraid of the country and the Inuit. All others make her out to be positive and cheerful, even when facing death.

107 William Barr, ed., *Red Serge and Polar Bear Pants*, pp. 62–71.

were destroyed and, bare of details though it was, lacked the inconsistencies and distortions that mar a number of Qallunaat publications on the subject before 2004.[108]

Summary of Public Memory Issues in the Case of the Sled Dogs

The RCMP Review Team gave only the most superficial treatment to problems of witness reliability. It paid even less attention to the issues of why communities remember the historical facts that they do and retell them (or suppress the retelling of them) in ways that are particular to culture and local circumstances. The RCMP Review Team exhibited several different approaches to the use of evidence. The testimony of Inuit whose dogs were killed was generally undervalued because they were not specific enough to warrant laying charges with a high probability of obtaining a conviction, as if reticence or inability to remember precise details of time, place, and names deprived the memory of all truth and value. The report maintained a consistent scepticism towards the oral history of Inuit while neglecting to comment on inconsistencies within the similar evidence provided by non-Inuit. The *RCMP Sled Dogs Report* seemed to assume that because an ordinance existed authorizing police to kill dogs in certain circumstances, all killings that occurred met those circumstances and were therefore justified and, by implication, the fault of the dogs' owners.

---

108 See also the comments attributed to Iqaluit businessman and historian Kenn Harper in 2006, RCMP Sled Dogs Report, pp. 616: "He thought that some dogs may have been shot by authorities when they shouldn't have been. There was no doubt, in his view, that there may have been over-conscientious police or others in authority that remembered the "Mrs. Clay" incident, the wife of an RCMP officer who was mauled to death by sled dogs, or other deaths and/or serious injuries inflicted by loose sled dogs that caused these authorities to be overly aggressive in destroying loose dogs."

The underlying weakness in the use of evidence, however, is the odd mixture of a law enforcement approach to Inuit accusations of wrongdoing and a "collective memory" approach to RCMP image and memory. The RCMP Sled Dogs Report showed more interest in glorifying the RCMP's service in the Arctic than in trying to understand the harshness with which change was imposed when the government's policy swung from dispersing Inuit in the 1950s to concentrating them in settlements in the 1960s. Both versions of the history of this period contain substantial elements of truth. These divergent histories do not exist in isolation from the societies that nourish them. They reinforce the group identities of different elements in the population, chiefly those for whom Nunavut is a frontier to be colonized and others for whom it is already a homeland.

It is obvious that these two groups experienced change differently in the past and will remember it differently in the future. Canadians as a whole would not be well served by a history that lets one of these versions drown out the other. They will be better served by an approach that acknowledges the ongoing legacy of the past, and at the same time chooses carefully from differing memories to meet the needs of both groups to deal with present circumstances in a shared future.

PUBLIC RECORDS AND RESEARCH ISSUES

Loss of Unique Historical Community Records

The RCMP Sled Dogs Report missed an opportunity to broaden and deepen Canadians' understanding of the part their national police force played in administering the Arctic around the middle of the 20th century. In addition, the RCMP Sled Dogs Report provided an incoherent explanation of how so much potentially relevant documentation came to be destroyed.

For several generations, RCMP detachments created what were almost the only public records of the local, regional, and national affairs of communities in the Baffin Region. Because there were no separate municipal or territorial public bodies in that region, the whole of public life—to the extent that there was any—passed through the office of the RCMP. This gives the detachment records a historical importance much greater than police records anywhere south of 60°. Yet it appears that the great majority of these records are gone, destroyed along with other paperwork considered to be of transitory value, which no government office can or should keep for long. Although documenting the killing of sled dogs is important to many today, it may have been regarded as "routine or not of historical value, either at the RCMP or by Archives Staff" two or more decades ago.[109]

According to a small inventory in the Library and Archives of Canada (LAC), each detachment must have created considerable documentation every year. This judgement is based not only on the survival of RCMP material in other fonds (notably patrol reports and correspondence in LAC's RG85, Northern Administration Branch), but also on inventories of a very small selection of "G" Division records, which were transferred in the 1990s to the National Archives (now the Library and Archives Canada). "These records include operational records, letterbooks, daily journals, daily diaries. Some of the records in this series are from such Northern Detachments as Lake Harbour, Chesterfield Inlet, Bache Peninsula and Fort Resolution."[110] The Lake Harbour [Kimmirut] records include daily diaries from the years 1935–1960, which apparently were created in Kimmirut, but were collected by "G" Division in Ottawa. The same inventory refers to "The monthly, weekly and patrol reports of the divisions concerning their day to day activities

109 This view was expressed to the QTC research team by Glenn Wright, former Archivist (LAC) and Staff Historian (RCMP) in a memorandum datred 23 June 2010.

110 LAC website, online description of MIKAN No. 158663. Accession: ROYAL CANADIAN MOUNTED POLICE / GENDARMERIE ROYALE DU CANADA (123-000691-5), accessed 22 June 2009 at http://collectionscanada.gc.ca/.

[which] are located in the Official correspondence sub-series, part of the Commissioner's office series, (RG18-B-1)." Such material is extremely sparse in the LAC's inventories of RCMP Arctic records. The inference is that these few volumes were kept simply as a sample of what was once typical, but is now lost.

Useful information survived in hands other than those of the RCMP. Government departments received information from each other and the chance of a particular document surviving, somewhere, is better than if only one copy had existed. So while researchers might never find the local RCMP records that document that the RCMP destroyed 286 dogs in Iqaluit in 1958, the tally itself has survived in the records of a sister department.[111] In addition, the RCMP Review Team sought additional records—and created valuable new ones through interviews—to fill some of the gaps. Nevertheless, QTC researchers believe there would have been public benefit for Nunavut, for the Force, and for Canadians generally, if more effort had been made to inventory records that are still in detachment offices and in private hands. It would not be possible to release all records immediately to the public, but a more visible commitment to curating the public record would be a benefit. In this vein, it is unfortunate that the RCMP Sled Dogs Report gave such cloudy explanations of the destruction of records.

Disposition of Records under the National Archives Act

The RCMP Sled Dogs Report approached the apparent destruction of important public records defensively, strongly asserting that no records were destroyed to cover up wrongdoing, and that numerous detachment records, and perhaps some headquarters records, were destroyed to comply with a

111 Library and Archives Canada, Record Group 85 (Northern Affairs Program), Series D-1-a, Volume 1473, File 201-1-8, Part 6, Reports re: Arctic Inspections; this document is not included in the RCMP Sled Dogs Report.

federal law. In this section, the QTC research team has kept an open mind concerning the RCMP Sled Dogs Report's assertion that no incriminating records were destroyed. Once a document is destroyed, its importance can only be assessed through discovery of copies or references to its contents in some other reliable source. QTC researchers cannot prove that there was incriminating material in the wide range of documents that are thought to have been destroyed.[112]

The RCMP Review Team also asserted that a large number of records were destroyed because this was required under federal legislation, namely the National Archives Act of 1987 and the relevant federal acts and policies that preceded it. In this version of events, the RCMP was merely performing a duty imposed on it by legislation. The QTC research team found different explanations of the working of that act that indicate the destruction of Nunavut community public records took place under the authority of the RCMP itself, though generally with advice from the National Archives.

Destruction of public records is one of the most necessary and least understood aspects of public administration. The benefits of retaining certain records are obvious not only to historians, but to anyone needing to ascertain a chain of operational decisions affecting public or private interests. This should be especially evident when the records relate to Aboriginal people, towards whom the government has a fiduciary duty. But the cost of retaining records is also high, both with regard to physical control (including storage and a tracking system that allows retrieval of a specific box in a reasonable time) and intellectual control (knowing what is in each box and why it is being kept). In 1980, passage of the Access to Information Act and the Privacy Act greatly increased the cost of intellectual control because it

112 Wrongdoing does not necessarily leave a paper trail. Only if record creation and retention rules were strictly followed can the integrity of the whole record be guaranteed. The official record would be unreliable if decisions were made in person or on the telephone, if correspondence was treated as personal, failed to be placed on any official file, or was subsequently removed by any person.

exposed departments to the obligation to search their holdings for a variety of new and often sensitive reasons. In recent years, more than 95 percent of government paperwork is routinely destroyed when it is thought to have neither operational use nor historical value. With such a large proportion destroyed, sceptical citizens may easily believe that the destruction served a corrupt purpose. The QTC research team has no evidence of inappropriate motives for destroying RCMP records, but deplores the loss of so much historical material.

The RCMP's description of its records disposal processes is not consistent with an explanation of that policy given by the National Archivist, Ian Wilson, in 2000.[113] The records in question, created between 1950 and 1975, had to be managed under the authority of a series of federal policies and laws.[114] According to general principles explained by Wilson, records that were under RCMP control in 1950, and all records created by the Force after that date, have been subject to administrative controls called "scheduling," which means "taking official inventories in order to manage the life cycle of records." Only since 1987 has the National Archives possessed authority to forbid the destruction of records it deemed historical, or to take possession of them.

Otherwise, departments and agencies of the federal government have always had ultimate responsibility for deciding what to retain and what to

---

113 Ian Wilson, "The Fine Art of Destruction Revisited," *Archivaria* 49 (Spring 2000), pp. 124–39. At the time Wilson wrote, the authority he exercised was in the National Archives of Canada Act, as amended in 1988. At present, similar authorities exist under the Library and Archives of Canada Act of 2004; for a description of the disposition process, see http://www.collectionscanada.gc.ca/government/disposition/index-e.html, accessed 23 June 2009.

114 Until 1966, departments could consult a Public Records Committee, which oversaw the destruction or preservation of records referred to it. From 1966 to 1987, a Treasury Board directive, the Public Records Order, required departments to consult the Dominion Archivist before destroying their own records.

destroy. It is apparent that some local RCMP records were either shipped elsewhere or destroyed locally, possibly after quite a short time.[115] If the National Archives did not consider a record to be of national significance, the creating department still had to evaluate whether it was important to keep for its own business processes, including accountability. Dr. Wilson explained, "when I authorize government institutions to carry out their records disposal plans [. . .] I am not ordering the destruction of the remaining records."[116] When the RCMP Sled Dogs Report described destruction of operational records, it described something that was probably permitted by law, but even this cannot be convincingly shown from the selection of evidence in the RCMP Sled Dogs Report.

Dr. Wilson's explanation published in 2000 gives readers a somewhat different view of departments' responsibility for destroying records than the one offered in the RCMP Sled Dogs Report.[117] That report asserted that "the review team found absolutely no evidence of records being improperly destroyed." But because of the nature of cooperation between archivists and departments through the scheduling process, it would be hard to define what was "improper." The RCMP Sled Dogs Report alluded to the existence of schedules, but the Review Team did not provide any information concerning their contents, so it remains unclear whether they included a full range of detachment records surviving at that time and, if so, whether items deemed not historic or archival by the National Archives were in fact destroyed.

Regrettably, it was possible in that period to destroy information that was historically important or of continuing business value because, as Dr. Wilson acknowledged, archival staff were not always adequately prepared:

---

115 See RCMP Archives Management Section, file TP-400-18, Mills to CO G Division, 22 Nov 1965, concerning the lack of written records to document recent attacks by dogs on humans.

116 Wilson, "Fine Art of Destruction Revisited," pp. 133.

117 RCMP Sled Dogs Report, pp. 64–66.

"Notably over the last twenty years or so, we have been either avoiding or ignoring the tough decisions involved in the undertaking of records destruction. . . . by records managers often without appropriate support."[118] In addition, decisions about historical value were made far from the sites where the documents were created. Because the RCMP Sled Dogs Report gave no information about the contents of the RCMP records schedules, readers also lack information on what documentation originally existed, or what disposition was made of it. This comment says nothing about motives. As the RCMP Sled Dogs Report asserted, the destruction may well have been motivated by the high cost of management and not by worries about what the records might reveal.[119]

The RCMP Sled Dogs Report also cited an unrelated passage in the National Archives Act to suggest erroneously that the destruction of records under departmental control was somehow under the authority of the national archivist. In fact the subsection quoted (4 [3]) relates to records already under National Archives control and thus has no relevance to the detachment records under discussion. The RCMP Sled Dogs Report also alleged that records relating to destruction of dogs in Pangnirtung in 1955 "would have been destroyed in 1957, in accordance with the policies established between the National Archivist and the RCMP." But the RCMP in 1957 could not act in accordance with legislation passed thirty years later. And it is equally misleading for the RCMP Sled Dogs Report to continue, "The destruction of certain RCMP records was done in accordance with its statutory obligations, pursuant to the National Archives of Canada Act."[120]

For the sake of better historical understanding, it would have been desirable for the RCMP Review Team to research and describe the records schedules that were created over the years, along with lists of which records were, in fact, destroyed. The QTC's researchers believe that these record

---

118 Wilson, "Fine Art of Destruction Revisited," pp. 136.

119 RCMP Sled Dogs Report, pp. 65.

120 RCMP Sled Dogs Report, pp. 66.

schedules do exist and that disclosure of all relevant decisions could help to clear the air. The RCMP had a statutory right to destroy records, but it was not obliged to do so. The destruction that is thought to have taken place was unfortunate. In addition, if any records have survived in detachment files, in private hands, or in hitherto-unsearched places in the National Capital Region, knowledge of their existence and a plan for their management would be welcome. They would not only help Canadians understand the hardships Inuit experienced, they would also enrich our understanding of the contributions of Canada's national police force to sovereignty and effective occupation on the frontiers of Canadian expansion in the mid-20th century.

What Was Missed?

The RCMP Review Team reported having read an estimated 42,000 pages of files, publications, and similar information sources. Though substantial, this needs to be put into perspective. It is equivalent to 140 books or, more relevant here, perhaps as few as 20 archival boxes.[121] For many historical studies—academic or governmental accountability research—20 boxes would be little more than a good start. The sources cited, for example, did not include departmental correspondence concerning the Eastern Arctic Patrol. This series contains first-hand comments by a variety of observers, among which we located a document from 1959 that was extremely critical of the RCMP's conduct in dog control. The volume also documents apparent cruelty and misdeeds from which the RCMP evidently did not protect Inuit, including this statement from the DEW Line site at Qikiqtarjuaq:

121 A standard 12-inch archival box could hold anything between 1,000 and 3,000 pages, generally single-sided, often with multiple copies of the same document, and some of it blank or of little interest.

> Broughton Island: The Station Chief, Mr. Al. Watson said that there was a dog problem in the area because the dogs were breaking into the food supplies. He had warned the Eskimos to tie up their dogs or else he would have to shoot them. He had already shot several and received no complaints from the Eskimos.[122]

Mr. Watson had reasons for acting as he did, but he was probably not a dog officer under the Ordinance and his actions, taking place 200 kilometres from the nearest police detachment, seem irregular. This case from Qikiqtarjuaq, like other evidence in these and related files, helps illustrate the causes of mistrust between Inuit and all government agents, mistrust in which the RCMP were inevitably embroiled even when they were not on the scene or were individually blameless in specific cases.

The review of secondary literature could also have been differently handled. In particular, the review of anthropological writing is wrong to say, "The silence of academia on the subject of systematic dog slaughters by the RCMP is a strong indicator that these allegations cannot be substantiated."[123] This is not necessarily true. Anthropologists, like other social scientists, pursue a particular research agenda and do not necessarily digress, especially on subjects that are apt to offend one party or another in a dispute. (It is also possible that dog officers, including police, were careful not to shoot dogs when visiting scholars were around.) Furthermore, Toshio Yatsushiro of McGill University, whose work appeared in the bibliography of the RCMP Sled Dogs Report, wrote in some detail and with sympathy for the Inuit point of view on the Iqaluit dog killings of the 1950s.[124] John

122 Library and Archives Canada, Record Group 85, Volume 1473, File: 201-1-8, Part: 6 "Reports re: Arctic Inspections," A. Stevenson for RAJ Phillips, Ottawa, Memorandum for Mr. Brown, "Eastern Arctic Patrol Report Pangnirtung District, 2 Dec 1958."

123 RCMP Sled Dogs Report, pp. 162.

124 In addition to an official government report and an article in *The Beaver*, QTC researchers located a file of government correspondence with Yatsushiro, and his inter-

and Irma Honigmann noted that in 1963 the Iqaluit radio station broadcast warnings against letting dogs run at large, but did so almost exclusively in English. Also relevant to the RCMP Sled Dog Report's concern with the reputation of the Force is John Matthiasson's *Living on the Land*, which addresses Inuit–RCMP relations, and which the RCMP Sled Dogs Report did not mention.[125]

Future users of the RCMP Sled Dogs Report will be hindered by the RCMP Review Team's practice of reproducing documents without indicating their provenance. The bulk of the quoted material from official records is not linked to any archival references—an elementary failure in a research project of this kind. While QTC researchers do not challenge the careful transcription of these documents, neither historical scholarship nor Canadian courts accept such casual presentation of evidence. To have evidentiary value, a document must be clearly attributed, on its face or on its back, to a specific archival fonds, box, and file. Scholars would also find fault with the practice of transcribing a document without the handwritten marginal comments that indicate its file location, cross-filing, initialling by those who have read it, and detailed minutes by the recipient and other officials with expertise or authority on the subject. For example, Paul Godt's indignant account of the dog slaughter by police at Apex in 1959 is annotated by numerous colleagues in Ottawa, all of whom blamed Inuit for the difficulties there. At a minimum, researchers have a right to an accurate, detailed reference to each transcribed or quoted document so that they may locate it, verify the transcription, check the marginalia, and examine other documents in the same file in their own pursuit of additional information.

A more comprehensive review of the existing literature and a full citation of manuscript sources would not have required the RCMP Review Team to change any conclusions, but should have suggested a change of

---

view transcripts, in a library in California.

125 John Matthiasson, *Living Off the Land*, pp. 91–118. A nn McElroy's interview with Naki Ekho, discussed above, was published after 2006.

approach. Profound questions remain to be answered about the conflict between Inuit traditional practices and Canadian law, and the inability of the federal government and its police force before 1975 to resolve these conflicts in a less confrontational and ultimately harmful fashion. The complexity of these issues is apparent in much of the RCMP Sled Dogs Report's resource material, but the discussion stopped well short of explaining the history of the period.

Summary of Issues Related to Documentation

The QTC research team developed considerable respect for the effort and accomplishment of the RCMP Review Team in locating and arranging documents that may contribute to a more careful examination and a more subtle understanding of past relations between the RCMP and Inuit in the Baffin Region. However, QTC researchers could not help but notice how much of this information, if differently analysed, could contribute to at least tentative explanations of the profound differences in outlook between Inuit and police and other government agents in their approach to the enforcement of the Dog Ordinance.

Conclusion

The 2006 RCMP Sled Dogs Report was not a conventional work of history. It sacrificed broad analysis to its pursuit of limited interpretations of complex events and their consequences. It closely focused on reports of a widespread slaughter of sled dogs in the 1950s and 1960s. Much of the analysis was directed not at understanding how Inuit and Canadian society and governance worked in this era, but towards discrediting Inuit memories and interpretations of how and why dogs were killed by the authorities, chiefly the RCMP, at the time.

The report has methodological and interpretive flaws in areas including the explanation of record retention practices of the RCMP, and in its failure to document the cases, probably very numerous, when police or other dog officers may have killed dogs without complying with the letter of the Dog Ordinance, especially regarding warnings, seizure, and impoundment. It was also cursory and dismissive towards the strengths and limitations of written and oral evidence after the lapse of forty or more years, denying the validity of most Inuit oral evidence yet presenting the views of non-Inuit with little negative comment. The RCMP Sled Dogs Report neglected, throughout its considerable length, to look for deeper meanings or nuances in the way events were recorded as they occurred, written about afterwards, or recalled by participants after the passage of decades.

For these and other reasons, the 2006 RCMP Sled Dogs Report significantly delayed the process of seeking a balanced history of how different state and private actors took part in the great transformation of Inuit life in the Baffin Region between 1950 and 1970. The effort invested in the RCMP Sled Dogs Report therefore delayed the use of elements of that shared history in the cause of reconciliation.

The Official Mind of Canadian Colonialism

Editor's Note: This final report has been preserved in its entirety in order to provide the fullest possible picture of the work undertaken by the Commission. Readers may notice some repetition of material presented in other chapters. This report has not been abridged from what was presented to the QIA Board of Directors in 2010. For this reason, too, the footnotes have been preserved in the text, as they were originally presented.

Executive Summary

From 1950 to 1975, Canadian officials saw the Qikiqtani Region (formerly the Baffin Region) as an isolated, underdeveloped, and problematic area that they wanted to incorporate economically, socially, and politically into the rest of Canada. Until about 1969, Ottawa was delivering federal, territorial, and municipal services to a small, dispersed population. In this period, the problems of the North were usually defined by people with little or no personal experience of the Arctic. These same people developed solutions without asking advice from Inuit. A greater understanding of Ottawa's motivations and ideas will help explain how events unfolded in the Baffin Region and explain which results were intended and which were not.

Canadian officials were part of a generation that believed the future would be better than the past, that Canada was a decent and progressive country, that education and training were keys to a better life, and that any remnants of cultural traditions among Canada's Aboriginal groups were likely to end due to forces beyond the control of governments. The archival record and Qikiqtani Truth Commission (QTC) testimonies also show that officials with first-hand knowledge of the North were less certain about applying southern solutions and expectations to northern conditions, but that they were usually overruled by those with less understanding but more power.

Two issues were high on the federal agenda for the North in the 1950s, 1960s, and 1970s. The first was planning for economic development—especially exploitation of minerals, oil, and gas. Before 1950, to support future development, the federal government performed extensive aerial mapping and mineral resource surveys that covered most of the Arctic. Early in the period under discussion, it promoted defence projects that developed the Frobisher Bay townsite in Iqaluit, as well as runways and weather stations at selected Arctic locations. These investments were expected to provide new jobs to replace the traditional land-based economy for a portion of the Inuit population, to reduce social assistance costs and to generate wealth for the whole country. Officials admitted, however, that there was no certainty that the effort would lead to a sustained increase in wage employment for Inuit.

The welfare of the people—the "human problems"—provided the second area of major concern. Three central worries concerned officials: health, possible scarcity of game animals, and a belief that Inuit needed intensive retraining for the industrial economy. Almost none of the decision-makers had any experience of living among Inuit, and consultation with Inuit above the most local levels ranged from non-existent in 1950 to hesitant and imperfect in 1975, the end of the period under review. As a result, stereotypes and externally generated priorities set the agenda for the North. Ottawa promoted change by increasing its own involvement in almost all aspects of Inuit life, from areas of expected government interest, such as education, healthcare, and employment, to more personal concerns, such as child-rearing strategies and housekeeping.

The cheapest way to expose Inuit to modernizing trends and to provide critical government services was to require them to congregate in a few places chosen for southern convenience. In particular, an epidemic of tuberculosis was addressed by sending patients to the South. As well, a southern approach to schooling was introduced, which required the dismantling of a whole way of living and bringing up children. These planned changes required Inuit, who wanted and needed access to services, to settle in permanent communities, mostly around the sites of existing trading posts in places chosen by government agents.

Throughout this period, remote officials claimed to respect Inuit culture. By the 1960s, they were no longer speaking about civilizing "primitive" people; they were describing their intentions to promote community development by delivering universal social programs, new technologies, and investments that would benefit both Inuit and southern Canadians. However, most of their investments did not yield an immediate financial return. Furthermore, this desire to benefit Inuit was imposed by outsiders in the name of Canada and its cultural norms. It largely denied Inuit opportunities to define the main problems as they saw them or to apply traditional environmental knowledge or Inuit Qaujimajatuqangit to the search for solutions.

Introduction

In the 1950s, it became fashionable to say that Canada's destiny would be shaped in the North. Canadians generally looked south to the United States and east to Europe for cultural and economic stimuli, and yet the North, ever since the Klondike Gold Rush, also offered them a bundle of images affirming the country's separate existence, mainly as a storehouse of resources waiting to make us prosperous. It seemed, quite wrongly, that latitude was destiny or at least that climate shaped national character.[1] What, then, did Canadians think about Inuit, the living bearers of cultures that had survived for millennia in the Arctic?

Canadians learned, from time to time, about the peoples whose homeland was in the North. Inuit sometimes appeared in the inside pages of the *Globe and Mail* or the *Toronto Star*, but they were generally dismissed as a special responsibility of the missionaries or of the Hudson's Bay Company. Impressions were generally favourable but simplistic—southerners recognized Inuit as resilient and cheerful people who were capable of surviving in a land of extreme hardship. Other stereotypes were not so positive. Inuit were imagined to be incapable of long-term planning or of recognizing or adjusting to important changes in their environments, such as trends in game shortages. Southerners recognized that Inuit were fascinated by the intrusions of capital and technology, but did not interpret this as a willingness among Inuit to engage with modernization on their own terms. Instead the non-Inuit, mostly white population—Qallunaat to the Inuit—feared that Inuit were balanced on a precipice, facing either starvation or dependency. After 1950, the interests of those people—the "peculiar and

1 Northern scholars have begun to distance themselves from earlier insistence on Canadian nordicity. See especially K. Coates, W. Lackenbauer, W. Morrison and Greg Poelzer, *Arctic Front: Defending Canada in the Far North* (Toronto: Thomas Allen, 2008).

difficult human problems that arise in the North"[2]—began to compete more successfully for public, parliamentary and official attention as part of the hunt for ways to make the North profitable to southern Canadians. In this spirit, Prime Minister St. Laurent in 1953 rose in Parliament to announce a new Department of Northern Affairs and National Resources, with civil administration as part of its mandate.[3]

In doing this, St. Laurent commented somewhat misleadingly that Canada had never established a department specifically for this purpose: "It has been said that Great Britain acquired her empire in a state of absence of mind. Apparently we have administered these vast territories of the north in an almost continuing state of absence of mind."[4] It is fascinating that St. Laurent (or his speechwriter) borrowed this expression of mock innocence from an era when Great Britain was dominating South Asia and had just seized control of Egypt. St. Laurent's new Northern Affairs department expressed no loud imperial ambitions, because it already assumed that northern lands belonged to Canada, but it raised the profile of the northern territories to the point where an official later noted that the 1953 debates

---

2 Canada. Department of Northern Affairs and National Resources. "Human Problems in the Canadian North" in *Annual Report Fiscal Year 1954–1955*, p. 9.

3 An important product of this work is Moira Dunbar and Keith Greenaway, *Arctic Canada from the Air* (Ottawa: Defence Research Board, 1956). See also "Mineral Resources and Mining Activity in the Canadian Eastern Arctic," *Canadian Geographical Journal* 29:2 (Aug. 1944), pp. 55–75; Y. O. Fortier, "Activities of the Geological Survey of Canada in the Arctic Islands, 1947–1953," *The Arctic Circular* 8:3 (March 1954), pp. 25–33.

4 Canada. House of Commons Debates, Session 1953: vol. 1, p. 698. British historian Sir John Seeley actually said, "We seem, as it were, to have conquered and peopled half the world in a fit of absence of mind." In Margery Sabin, *Dissenters and Mavericks: Writings About India in English 1765–2000* (Oxford University Press, 2002), p. 90, Sabin calls this the "best-known reference point for the false innocence of British imperialism [...] the notorious sentence frequently extracted from [...] [Seeley's] 1883 book *The Expansion of England*."

"gave northern development a new respectability like other national institutions beyond the range of attack by prudent men."[5] It was an accurate way to describe a mentality that did not embrace many of the challenges of northern development and administration, but allowed concerned public servants a new freedom of action.

The Official Mind: What Does It Mean?

"Official mind" is a shorthand expression used by some historians to describe a set of beliefs, values, goals, knowledge and fears that are widely shared by the small number of people who make and carry out public policy. The concept of an "official mind" emerged in the 1960s to help describe how Great Britain expanded overseas to control territories that did not seem strategically important or profitable.[6] An official mind is not always unanimous on methods or details, but it filters information and interprets events in fairly consistent ways, then has the power to translate this outlook into government action—or inaction. Although this interpretive tool is mainly used by British historians, it offers insights for explaining Canada's 20th-century efforts in the North.

Canada's possessions in the Arctic are often rightly described as colonies.[7] Colonialism can be defined as "the exploitation or subjugation of a

---

5 R. A. J. Phillips, *Canada's North* (Toronto: MacMillan and Co., 1967), p. 162.

6 See especially Ronald Robinson and John Gallagher with Alice Denny, *Africa and the Victorians: The Official Mind of Imperialism* (London: MacMillan, 1961), p. 25.

7 The practice may have entered the mainstream with Kenneth Coates, *Canada's Colonies: A History of the Yukon and Northwest Territories* (Toronto: Lorimer, 1985).

people by a larger or wealthier power."[8] In a colony, an external authority dominates much of the economic, social and political life of the inhabitants, who are generally (as in the case of Nunavut) culturally distinct from the colonizing nation, and lack strong representation in national political institutions. Colonizing countries and individuals have many different motives for wishing to control the territory of others. These motives usually include national pride, denying opportunities to rival countries, the possibility of future profit for business, revenue for government, or employment for citizens. It is also quite common for the external power to believe it has a mission to provide a more secure present and future for the indigenous people of less developed or "backward" regions.[9] Colonialism does not necessarily require a large settler population, military force, or even formal political control, if the colonizing power can meet its objectives more cheaply or with less effort. In the case of Canada's North, the Qallunaat population remained small and the military presence was largely supplied by another country; only political control was persistently applied by Canada from 1950 to 1975.

Because Canada's colonized northern regions, including Nunavut, are internationally recognized as part of Canada's sovereign territory, they are "internal colonies."[10] Officially, Canada has always avoided calling its remote

---

8 *Oxford Canadian Dictionary* (Toronto: Oxford University Press, 1998), p. 280.

9 See also the observation by political scientist Mark Dickerson in *Whose North?* (University of British Columbia Press, 1992), pp. 61–63. "If, by colonialism, one means state control through a bureaucratic apparatus on the ground, the 1950s represent the period when it started."

10 For a discussion of internal colonies, see Jack Hicks, "On the Application of Theories of 'Internal Colonialism' to Inuit Societies." Presentation for the Annual Conference of the Canadian Political Science Association, June 5, 2004, accessed online at http://www.cpsa-acsp.ca/papers-2004/Hicks.pdf; for a later version with an extensive bibliography, see "On the Application of the 'Internal Colonial' Metaphor to Inuit Societies," accessed 19 Jan. 2010 at http://www.jackhicks.com/e107_files/downloads/Hicks%20J%20WRSA%202006.pdf.

regions "colonies." From the 1950s to 1970s, officials, even when writing confidentially, took it for granted that Canada had sovereign rights over Arctic lands and peoples, and intended to treat them as fairly as they treated any other citizens. Yet because of the real inequality of power and the absence of concern for Aboriginal rights during most of the period studied here, this report uses the word "colonialism" with the meaning outlined in these paragraphs.

Today, a study of the official mind might seem outdated: colonial and postcolonial histories are preoccupied not so much with the way outside forces planned and directed change and control as with actual cross-cultural relations inside a "contact zone," a social space where "disparate cultures meet, clash, and grapple with each other, often in highly asymmetrical relations of domination and subordination."[11] The Qikiqtani Truth Commission (QTC) has been inspired in part by a need to get away from a history that is written from the outside. In Canada, some studies of what happened inside the contact zone have been produced by anthropologists,[12] many of whom excel at explaining the results of colonialism, but do not necessarily explain how colonialism in a particular place took the form that it did. For that, a study of the tone and spirit of the collective mind of politicians and officials remains an essential tool for understanding the flows of capital, legislation,

---

11 This definition of the contact zone is offered by Mary Louise Pratt in *Imperial Eyes: Travel Writing and Transculturation* (London and New York: Routledge, 2nd ed. 2008), p. 7. See also Ania Loomba, *Colonialism/Postcolonialism* (London and New York: Routledge, 1998).

12 Significant works on Inuit Nunangat include Hugh Brody's *The Peoples' Land: Whites and the Eastern Arctic* (Harmondsworth: Penguin, 1975). A quarter century later, he revisited this analysis in *The Other Side of Eden: Hunters, Farmers and the Shaping of the World* (Vancouver: Douglas and McIntyre, 2000). See also works written or edited by Robert Paine, including *The White Arctic: Anthropological Essays on Tutelage and Ethnicity* (St. John's: Memorial University of Newfoundland, Social and Economic Papers No. 7, 1977).

and contact agents onto the frontier, where they might begin to carry out the changes desired by the decision-makers at the centre of the colonizing venture.

Therefore, this report explores the beliefs of high-ranking officials, elected politicians, and chosen intellectuals who set the framework for Canadian expansion on the Arctic frontier. To do this, an effort has to be made to set clear boundaries in space, time, and hierarchy.

- Chronologically, this survey covers the period 1950–1975, which is based on the QTC's mandate. This bridges the transfer of administration from Ottawa to Yellowknife after 1967.
- Geographically, the focus is the Baffin Region (now the Qikiqtani Region). The Mackenzie Valley has a very different and better-known recent history. Much of what is written elsewhere treats the Eastern Arctic as an afterthought. This report tries to avoid that bias.
- Hierarchically, evidence of the official mind is looked for in writings by civil servants, politicians, and selected intellectuals. This includes their official publications, confidential official correspondence, and post-retirement writings.

These viewpoints are worth examining in their southern isolation, because they had a profound impact on the way the colonial encounter unfolded away from the centre, inside the contact zone. This separate study is worthwhile because:

- the centre mobilizes support for ventures, and obtains and distributes funds and personnel;
- the centre tries to coordinate policy nationally despite differences that exist in the field;
- the centre selects, trains, and gives direction to the contact agents who engage in—or avoid—face-to-face relations inside the contact zone; and
- the centre is responsible to other citizens, and to posterity, for what happens.

This does not suggest that the official mind was unanimous or always successful in the goals it pursued. In fact, much of the period was marked by competition between different points of view. Jim Lotz pointed out that during a career in northern programs lasting a decade, he "never saw any evidence of a deliberate plan to destroy the North or its people." Indeed, he continued:

> I never came across a deliberate plan to do anything in the North. I saw instead the continuous reaction to a series of crises, a simple equation of development with resource exploitation, a lot of ego-tripping as individuals pushed their ideas and their programs as the final solution to the problems of the North, and much bureaucratic in-fighting in government agencies charged with northern development. . . . I saw a lot of selfish opportunists make money out of the miseries of the North. I also saw a lot of dedicated, selfless people give a great deal of themselves to help to create, in the North, a saner, more humane society than the one in the South. Whether the exploiters or the idealists did the more harm in the North needs to be determined in the perspective of history.[13]

Before surrendering to the pessimism of Lotz, however, readers can review a more tactful explanation from Peter Jull, another participant in the events of those years:

> In terms of material commitment, Canada's investment in improvements for people in the NWT can hardly be faulted. Many painful, even tragic mistakes have been made, but the aims and the persistence of government have been clear and well-intended. Nevertheless, in the vital matter of enabling men and women to take charge of their lives—a prerequisite for mental and social

13 J Lotz, "Northern Alternatives," in *Arctic* 28:1 (March 1975), pp. 4–5.

> well-being—delay has been recognized as the most effective form of denial.[14]

Many now challenge the view that "Canada's investment [...] can hardly be faulted" because budgets were often inadequate even for the flawed programs that developed in the South to address problems in the North. This was probably in large part because nobody in the South foresaw an immediate financial return on investments, particularly in the Eastern Arctic. While Inuit have always been subject to taxation on what they earn or the costly imported goods they consume, the cost of delivering services in such an isolated area generally outweighed public revenues from mining licenses or permits to explore for oil and gas.

The diversity, sometimes bordering on incoherence, of official views on key subjects, has already been mentioned. The most widely recognized example of this is the conflict in opinions, policies, and programs concerning whether Inuit should remain dispersed on the land in one hundred or more little settlements as self-sufficient primary producers, or be concentrated in a few settlements as a reserve labour force for administration and projects to exploit non-renewable resources. The policy of dispersal, still influential in 1950, was battered by the massive influx of Qallunaat who built and then maintained the DEW Line. Within a decade, the Inuit, who did not even have a federal or municipal vote at this point, received the full impact of policy, programs, and infrastructure investments that still underpin the current thirteen communities. In outline, this can be seen not as policy incoherence, but as a rapid and decisive evolution. One thread of incompatible views running through this period was the issue of how to involve Inuit in public policy debates on changes that so profoundly altered their lives. Throughout the period a handful of departmental officials who had lived in the North and spoke Inuktitut insisted that even where change might

14 Peter Jull, "Inuit Politics and the Arctic Seas," in Franklin Griffiths, ed., *Politics of the Northwest Passage* (Montreal: McGill-Queen's University Press, 1987), p. 53.

be necessary, it would be ineffective and unjust if Inuit were not involved. While such men as Graham Rowley, Alex Stevenson, and Keith Crowe could add knowledge and wisdom to the government's decision-making, at the highest levels there was less tolerance and more impatience. As an example of continuing divisions within the federal establishment, Inuit from across the Arctic gathered at Coppermine (Kugluktuk) in mid-July 1970 "to discuss their mutual concerns." The meeting, organized by a Toronto-based NGO, was opposed by the Department of Indian Affairs and Northern Development, but received an indispensable $15,000 travel grant from the citizenship branch of the Department of the Secretary of State. The NGO reported that "several matters discussed at the conference clearly indicated the incompetence and indifference of the Department [...] in administering the affairs of the North."[15] Government "ambivalence" towards consultation and Inuit rights would continue, along with the pressure for development.[16] The Baffin Region's institutions of governance in place in 1975 were still largely designed and implemented from outside the region, although by then, some institutions of the Territorial government had begun to empower Inuit at the local level in ways that the federal government had resisted. By this time, economic policy had been firmly reoriented in favour of development, without much progress towards the kinds of cultural retention and community development that had once found favour with participants in official decision-making.

---

15 P. Cumming, "Arctic Power!" *Indian-Eskimo Association of Canada Bulletin* 11:4 (Oct. 1970), p. 1.

16 Another report for the QTC will look in more detail at the background to a vague but important document published two years later: Canada. Department of Indian Affairs and Northern Development, *Canada's North 1970–1980* (Ottawa: DIAND, 1972).

Some Continuities

The history of the Canadian North is often written as a story of opposing paired concepts. The Arctic is either an icebox or a treasure chest, a homeland or a frontier. The official mind also saw a choice of futures that tended to be binary—a population policy that would encourage either dispersal or centralization and, therefore, would favour either a "traditional" economy based on hunting or a "modern" one based on wage employment. At times these seemed to be stark alternatives, while at other times it seemed that individuals would be allowed to make their own choices from a range of possibilities. A certain number of concepts were commonly held throughout the period, and may help explain the approach in this report.

One disturbing feature of the whole period of Canadian expansion into the North was the widespread use of the word "settlement" to describe tiny enclaves of transient people and their buildings, while much more populous places where Inuit lived were termed "camps." This language was so common that most readers quickly adopt it, despite its racialized, hierarchical overtones. It conveys a feeling, sometimes entirely intentional, that clusters of permanent buildings occupied by Qallunaat deserved recognition in ways that the seasonal habitations of Inuit did not.[17] Today, "hamlet," "settlement,"

---

17 Not all social scientists adopted this vocabulary. One who did was the government-employed geographer J.L. Robinson, in "Eskimo Population in the Canadian Arctic," *Canadian Geographical Journal* 9:3 (Sept. 1944), pp. 128–42. Jacob Fried was more analytical in "Settlement Types and Community Organization in Northern Canada," *Arctic* 16:2 (June 1963), pp. 93–100. He describes many of today's hamlets as "spottily and partly planned administrative outpost settlements where Eskimo communities are being formed" (pp. 93–94) and said that "all settlements dealt with in this paper have come into being to satisfy some special need or purpose of southern Canadian civilization." He notes the transient nature of the Qallunaat population (p. 95). Recent work by Mathhiasson and by McElroy employs the word "outpost" to describe the Qallunaat centres in

or "community" are all used to describe these places, now permanent, where most Inuit live.[18] Even the Nunavut Land Claim Agreement defines residential places away from settlements as "outpost camps." How outposts staffed by transients[19] came to be called "settlements" while multi-family, multi-year settlements came to be called "outposts" deserves to be discussed elsewhere. This report, somewhat reluctantly, accepts the prevailing usage and for the historical period uses "settlements" and "camps" with their usual if somewhat illogical meanings, while also using an Inuktitut term, ilagiit nunagivaktangat, in some references to camps.

Another of the strongest forces unifying Qallunaat thought, including the official mind, was a preoccupation with dependency. Modernists and anti-modernists alike generally assumed that Inuit would quickly surrender their attachment to traditional ways of life when they gained access to the convenience of imported material culture, an abundance of processed food, and the other attractions that came from interacting with a wealthy Qallunaat population. This fear was part of a general belief in the superiority of Qallunaat cultural norms, but there was a contrary fear among non-Inuit that these benefits could be withdrawn at any time, leaving some Inuit unable or unwilling to return to hunting and, therefore, dependent

---

the 1960s. See John Matthiasson, *Living Off the Land: Change among the Inuit of Baffin Island* (Peterborough, Ont.: Broadview Press, 1992), p. 91; and Ann McElroy, *Nunavut Generations: Change and Continuity in Canadian Inuit Communities* (Long Grove Ill.: Waveland Press, 2008), p. 12.

18 The major exception is Iqaluit, a "city." George Wenzel explored some implications of using "settlement" and "community" to describe Inuit residential places in "Clyde Inuit Settlement and Community: From Before Boas to Centralization," *Arctic Anthropology* 45:1 (2008), pp. 1–21.

19 For transiency see Fried, "Settlement Types and Community Organization," p. 97, and P. Goldring, "The Triumvirate at Pangnirtung: Career Paths and Cross-Cultural Relations, 1921–1945," unpublished paper delivered to the Canadian Historical Association annual meeting, June 1989, pp. 27–29.

on social assistance. In the 1940s, this feeling among Qallunaat revealed itself in strange debates over topics such as whether to allow Inuit to live in wooden houses. By the 1950s, it evolved into a profound critique of the effect of the DEW Line and the hazards of involving Inuit in short-term employment without providing long-term opportunities. A prevailing fear was that the new economy was even less sustainable than the mode of production that preceded it, but that Inuit were on the point of willingly and totally abandoning the hardship of life on the land and collectively losing all knowledge or skill of how to recover that life. This fear was shared by both anti-modernists who thought Inuit should be banned from living closer than 20 miles from Qallunaat establishments and by advocates of community development who acknowledged how hard it would be to develop the North economically at a pace that would absorb the people who were being encouraged to leave the land.

It is customary to say that Qallunaat had a great faith in the superiority of their own culture, or what is often called western civilization. Although this attitude permeates much of the official and unofficial writing of the time, it is worth emphasizing the evidence that by 1960 this feeling fought with a fear that Inuit would not benefit from their exposure to modern, southern culture. At best, by 1960 the superiority was thought of as technological rather than moral. In Inuit Nunangat (the land, water, and ice inhabited by Inuit),[20] missionaries had always singled out the white man as a source of sin and exploitation, while traders and administrators were less dogmatic. After 1945, what gripped the Qallunaat both inside and outside the contact zone was a sense that change was inevitable and would not be reversible. Speaking pessimistically in a conference session on the North in 1961, anthropologist Henry Hawthorne apologized for making a statement that he thought might be misunderstood as "an attack on the Eskimo

---

20 The term and definition have recently been adopted by Inuit Tapiriit Kanatami; see http://www.itk.ca/publications/maps-inuit-nunangat-inuit-regions-canada, accessed 10 May 2010.

language and sense of identity. The impersonal events of history have themselves constituted such an attack."[21]

Moreover, it seemed to many that those seemingly "impersonal events" caught southerners in their unpredictable rush as much as they did Aboriginal northerners. A senior official mused after a conference in 1960:

> It would, of course, be very helpful if one could peer into the future of the industrial community of the North American continent and know just where the organizational man will have led us all, say three or four generations hence, in response to the inexorable and extremely rapid processes of scientific, industrial and social development. I get the distinct impression that some of our colleagues at the Conference became so deeply immersed in the study of allegedly immutable characteristics of ethnic personality they were failing to comprehend the fact that the whole nation, together with all its aboriginal and other racial groups, is being subjected to change at a rate never before even approached. Many of us may recognize this great speed, but I am not sure we are used to thinking of it in comprehensive terms. . . .[22]

If officials were aware of the challenges of rapid modernization, they did not accept that it was out of all control, or that Qallunaat should concede much autonomy to the different wisdom of the Inuit. Official writings and speeches showed infrequent awareness of the interdependence of Inuit and Qallunaat in either the short- or the long-term. The decision-makers did not seriously consider Inuit to be immediately useful or competent as

---

21 Comments as a discussant in a workshop on "The significance of communities and social capital in resource development in frontier regions," *Proceedings of the Resources for Tomorrow Conference* held in Montreal, October 23–28, 1961, vol. 3, p. 372.

22 LAC: RG85, vol. 1661, file NR 4/3-14, Indian-Eskimo Association of Canada—V. F. Valentine—Personal files, Bent Sivertz to R. H. Dunning, 22 June 1960.

partners, let alone leaders, in planning the response to change. In fundamental ways, most officials do not seem to have really believed in the potential of either the North or its people, yet they felt responsible for rescuing those people from a multitude of social and economic ills, and shouldering the burden of telling Inuit how to prepare for the future.

Reading the Official Mind

The published history of northern Canada already says a great deal about government activities in the North between 1950 and 1975. Without debating the work of earlier writers, this report is organized around a few key themes that are particularly relevant to the QTC's work. Specific government programs are described in other QTC background studies.

During the 1940s, strategic concerns about the North ensured that the Qikiqtani Region would always receive a certain amount of attention at even the highest levels of government—the Cabinet, central agencies, and deputy ministers. The puzzle for officials after 1950 was not what to possess, but how to administer the territories Canada already claimed to own. Historian Shelagh Grant explained the development of a generation of "northern nationalists," senior officials, and intellectuals who, in the 1940s, asserted a need to maintain and exercise Canada's Northern sovereignty, and in the early 1950s designed the administrative machinery to achieve this.[23] To their credit, their hopes, plans, and fears for the Arctic included concern about the problems that development would create for Aboriginal inhabitants north of 60°, including the stepped-up pace of American military activity. Although the politicians and officials were determined to appropriate the peoples' land and were not at all sure whether or why to appropriate

23 Shelagh Grant, *Sovereignty or Security: Government Policy in the Canadian North 1936–1950* (Vancouver: University of British Columbia Press, 1988).

their labour, the impetus to control and exploit the land inevitably brought responsibilities towards its people. And as more journalists found their way into the North, these government responsibilities would be enforced in the court of public opinion if the government fell back into the habits of neglect shown in the interwar years.

As the 1950s wore on, there was considerable growth in the Arctic responsibilities of lower echelons of public life as well. Patrick Nixon's incisive analysis of federal administration in the North from 1954–1965 observed that the administration in the early 1950s was extremely small, largely idealistic, and generally unhampered by interference from politicians. But their success was their downfall. They appear to have oversold their "northern vision" to the Diefenbaker Conservatives, and in the process attracted the public scrutiny and bureaucratization that come with large budgets.[24] In the process, the small group of expert policy-makers expanded in ways that empowered a much wider circle of stakeholders within the government. This emphasized the division of authority that remained after creating the Department of Northern Affairs and National Resources, and aggravated existing divisions within Ottawa. This incoherence, in Nixon's view, continued and grew through the 1960s. It fuelled a campaign to separate the Mackenzie Valley from the less developed Eastern Arctic. This movement failed, but spurred the devolution of programs to the territorial government in Yellowknife, where a new and slightly different "official mind" began to develop.

24 Nixon interviewed central figures in the Northern Administration, including former deputy minister Gordon Robertson. His findings have not been published in a monograph, but are accessible in a short doctoral thesis, "Eskimo Housing Programmes, 1954–65: A case study of representative bureaucracy," [microform] (Ottawa: National Library of Canada, Canadian Theses on Microfiche Service, 1984), especially chapter 3, "The Context of Eskimo Housing Policy," pp. 44–73; also P. G. Nixon, "Bureaucracy and Innovation," *Canadian Public Administration* 30:2 (Summer 1987), pp. 280–298; also "The Politics of Government Research," in K. Coates and R. Morrison, eds., *For Purposes of Dominion: Essays in Honour of Morris Zaslow* (Toronto: Captus Press, 1989), pp. 5.

From the discussion above, it is apparent where evidence of an official mind will not be found. The mass media, which in the 1950s still largely meant newspapers, was not a dependable reporter, commentator, or stimulator of broad public interest in the North, let alone a strong influence on policy choices. While *Maclean's* Magazine, under its editor Ralph Allen, seemed like a positive influence to officials,[25] and the *Globe and Mail* could pull its readers' heartstrings with articles such as "Stone Age Just North of Moosonee" about a 1956 epidemic in the Belcher Islands,[26] news of the Inuit was erratically received. The Canadian Broadcasting Corporation (CBC) was not regularly broadcasting into the Eastern Arctic, let alone out of it, until the 1970s.[27] Without strong media interest, the relatively small community of investors with assets or markets in the North were also not a major influence on policy, although exploitative ambitions were voiced—often in Parliament—and standardization of products such as housing and shipping favoured regular suppliers over the less structured efforts of earlier times.[28]

It is important to acknowledge that the perceptions of the "men on the spot" receive little emphasis in this report. These individuals were chosen, recruited, assigned job titles and duties, and generally empowered to carry out federal policies on the "frontier." They could report back with information to help refine the government's strategies, but their powers were limited. Those actors are highly worthy of the study they receive in other QTC reports.

This survey of the official mind focusses on the federal department responsible for northern administration: the Department of Resources and

---

25 Donald Snowden, interview with P.G. Nixon quoted in Nixon, "Eskimo Housing Programmes," p. 80.

26 *Globe and Mail* (16 Aug 1956), p. 25.

27 The progressive extension of broadcast services into the Arctic was reported on annually in *Government Activities in the North*, the regular roll-up of all departmental activities published by the Advisory Committee on Northern Development.

28 P.G. Nixon, "Eskimo Housing Programmes," pp. 86–88.

Development (1950–1953), Department of Northern Affairs and National Resources (1953–1966), and the Department of Indian Affairs and Northern Development (1966–present). Because the department was the hinge between southern aspirations and northern conditions, and it had to obtain financial and other resources for the North and oversee their expenditure, a considerable amount of this report is based on publications of the Department and the quiet machinations of its senior officials. Public statements had to be vetted at a senior level. The director for much of this period, Bent Sivertz, took an interest in scholarly as well as administrative debates; as a result, he is often quoted directly in this report. More colourful and original characters in the department, such as R. A. J. Phillips or Vic Valentine, appear less frequently, although they may also have helped write the pronouncements of more senior figures.

Contemporary commentary by non-officials, like later scholarship, is not evidence of the official mind, but it does sometimes offer information or helpful insights. Reports of the Royal Commission on Aboriginal Peoples are helpful, as are the numerous short writings of political scientist Patrick Nixon, who interviewed officials to help him explain the opportunities and limitations facing the Department in the 1950s and 1960s.[29] Two important books by Frank Tester and Peter Kulchyski explore some failures of northern policy-making, especially in the 1950s,[30] and a recent work by anthropologist David Damas documented the major policy shift in the 1960s, from a "policy of dispersal" in which Inuit were encouraged to remain "on

29 Nixon's studies bypass some of the principal facets of government-driven change in the Eastern Arctic, including health care and schooling, but his thoughts on housing and income security are presented as evidence that senior departmental officials established a framework for government policy and at least initially set some of their own goals.

30 Frank Tester and Peter Kulchyski, *Tammarniit (Mistakes): Inuit Relocation in the Eastern Arctic 1939–63* (Vancouver: University of British Columbia Press, 1994); also, *Kiumajut (Talking Back) Game Management and Inuit Rights 1900–70* (Vancouver: University of British Columbia Press, 2007).

the land," to a "welfare state" policy that saw Inuit concentrated into a much smaller number of year-round settlements where schooling and social services were concentrated.[31]

Most of the historical scholarship deployed on this period to date, as well as anthropological writing in a historical vein, follows this development only to the achievement of centralization, which was almost complete throughout the region by 1970. Only a few writers attempt to bridge the period from the 1960s to 1970s because of the interpretive and documentary challenges posed by that period. These challenges were the change of personnel and focus when responsibility moved from Ottawa to Yellowknife, and the change of life and culture in Nunavut as one hundred small communities merged into thirteen larger settlements. The rapid change in governmental structures since 1970, culminating in the creation of Nunavut, means that broad historical overviews will be scarce and harder to conceptualize. Today's challenges for public government remain the same as those of the 1950s—to protect Inuit culture, autonomy, and rights, while carving out a place in an increasingly complex international economy.

Ottawa's Northern Bureaucracy: Membership and Viewpoints

Prime Minister St. Laurent's desire for a single coordinating department for the North was not translated into action. Uncertainty continued as different departments designed, adopted, and implemented government programs

31 David Damas, *Arctic Migrants, Arctic Villagers: The Transformation of Inuit Settlement in the Central Arctic* (Montréal: McGill-Queens University Press, 2002). Damas's belief in a major policy shift concerning where Inuit would live is now widely shared among scholars, though the incoherence of that policy is also accepted.

for the North. Some departments, notably National Defence, were largely independent, but others had to struggle if they wanted to coordinate their work at the levels of policy and logistics. The key questions concerned the pace of cultural change and the development of centralized settlements, a policy that some departments adopted sooner than others. In addition, the old Arctic powers—the Hudson's Bay Company and rival missionaries from the Anglican and Catholic churches—were never chased from the field, and they continued to have influence over the policy-makers and administrators.

THE NORTHERN ADMINISTRATION BRANCH

Through several name changes, a single federal administrative unit oversaw northern affairs from 1921 until the late 1960s. This unit was mainly concerned with land and resources, but because it combined federal-, provincial-, and municipal-type responsibilities in its mandate, and because Inuit were not consistently regarded as wards of the Crown, it was unavoidably accountable for a wide range of programs and regulations affecting Inuit. In the Qikiqtani Region before 1950, the department made an annual patrol by ship, sent out the occasional field scientist for a year or more, paid the doctor in Pangnirtung, and delivered other services through the Royal Canadian Mounted Police (RCMP) or, where there were no police, through the Hudson's Bay Company. From 1947 there was steady growth in field staff, starting in the Western Arctic with "welfare teachers" and spreading to include Northern Service officers, later called Area Administrators. These officials on the ground oversaw the growth of the thirteen present-day Qikiqtani Region communities.

In Ottawa from 1921 to 1936, the director of the branch responsible for northern administration reported straight to the Deputy Minister of the Interior. After 1936, Northwest Territories (NWT) and Yukon affairs were pushed at least one additional layer farther down in the hierarchy, while

Arctic affairs, when they eventually had their own unit, were buried even deeper. This status meant that personnel overseeing northern policy or operations were generally not distracted by too many additional responsibilities. An important change occurred after 1970 when the devolution of "people" programs to Yellowknife left Ottawa with little except a strong focus on economic development.

Throughout this period, senior personnel were often involved in developing programs and overseeing their implications, briefing their deputy minister or minister, dealing with the press, and generally setting the tone for Canada's handling of social and economic programs in the territorial North. Many departmental publications, including some signed by ministers, were written by these thoughtful and diligent officials. P.G. Nixon has described them as well-trained and strongly influenced by a British tradition of service to the public. He describes the emergence of a "representative bureaucracy," that is, one that took on the task of speaking for clients who lacked direct or effective representation at the centre.[32] Because few Northern Affairs officials spoke Inuktitut, and Inuit rarely paid more than brief visits to Ottawa, administration of the Baffin Region offered a natural opening for a "representative bureaucracy" to take shape.

The northern administration staff based in Ottawa grew from three or four in the 1920s to over three hundred in the 1960s. They helped develop and implement the visions that imagined Inuit, initially, as a primitive people whose way of life should be disturbed as little as possible, but later as vulnerable people who needed to be integrated quickly to avoid being crushed by economic development. Canada never put Inuit under the Indian Act, which would have acknowledged them as wards of the Crown, while forbidding them to control land or other property. Instead, most administrators and parliamentarians saw Inuit as British subjects and Canadian citizens, but also felt they needed special protection. To make matters more awkward, the Supreme Court in 1939 ruled that Inuit were "Indians" under

32 P.G. Nixon, "Eskimo Housing Programmes," introductory chapter.

the British North America Act. This confirmed the obvious fact that Inuit are an indigenous people, while also stating an untruth. The decision had little real effect outside of Quebec, where it excused the provincial government from paying for social programs for Inuit.

In fact, until after 1970, Ottawa made up its own rules about how to manage its responsibilities towards Inuit. As an RCMP officer remarked complacently in 1952, "I think the view generally held now is that Eskimos are not wards of the Government but have complete citizenship rights. There was a Supreme Court decision holding that Eskimos and Indians were in the same category but I do not think that is the opinion held by Northern Administration officials."[33] Strange but true—senior officials and their ministers, whether confused, negligent, or simply repelled by the risks of subjecting Inuit to the Indian Act, disregarded much of the Supreme Court decision and swayed between nominal egalitarianism and excessive paternalism. Retired officials who have spoken to the QTC emphasize that most senior officials lacked faith in Inuit and desired to keep paternalistic structures in place almost indefinitely.[34] Because Inuit lacked either economic or political power, Northern Affairs exercised as complete an authority over them as Indian Affairs did over First Nations peoples.

One effect of this ambivalent policy was that Canada never had a clearly named "Eskimo Affairs" bureau, like the one that managed Indian

---

33 LAC: RCMP, Accession 85-86/048 Box 42, file D-1512-2-4-027 (1952), Memorandum to The Commissioner, RCMP from Asst. DCI J.A. Peacock, 27 Sept. 1952; QTC Document A05116.

34 In particular, Walter Rudnicki, who was first head of the Northern Affairs Welfare Division, and Gene Rheaume, who worked for Rudnicki and was later the NWT Member of Parliament, described to the QTC their encounters with a paternalistic attitude that was different from the cautious optimism about long-term change that official departmental statements exhibit. Rheaume once told Gordon Robertson that Inuit might not be ready for the franchise, but they would be ready the day after they were given it.

Affairs.[35] Instead, the organizational structure carried names such as Arctic Division that suggested all citizens had the same rights and were subject to the same laws and regulations. The Eskimo Affairs Committee (1952–1962) was tightly managed by the department, and was purely advisory. One peculiarity was that until 1966 the federal Northern Administration branch managed local affairs in the Inuit regions of Quebec. Although specific programs such as the Eskimo Loan Fund (1953) and the Eskimo Housing Program (1965) targeted the specific needs of Inuit, the tendency was to conceal federal and territorial programs for Inuit, along with those used mainly by Qallunaat, under racially neutral terms.

In the Territories, the federal government assumed all municipal- and provincial-type responsibilities, and therefore the official mind found it hard to perceive that underlying Aboriginal rights were at stake. In an era of developing social programs, Inuit were regarded not primarily as wards, but as an ethnically homogenous rural and isolated population whose needs might be met—or ignored—as they were by lower levels of government in the South. In Parliament, poorly briefed leaders debated Inuit status between 1924 and 1951 in a confused and confusing manner: ministers made illogical and contradictory statements. In fact, parliamentarians barely exhibited any concept of Aboriginal rights anywhere, as Members of Parliament tried to apply various historical, logical, or Canadian legal tests to explain why Inuit should not submit to the restrictions of "Indian" status. For many members an economic factor—that Canada was unlikely to appropriate Arctic land—seemed to justify a different status for Inuit.[36] The

---

35 Around 1950, a few members of the Northern Administration and Lands branch were briefly identified as an "Eskimo Research Unit."

36 See Diamond Jenness, *Eskimo Administration: II. Canada* (Montreal: Arctic Institute of North America Technical Paper No. 14, May 1964), especially pp. 40–48; see also occasional debates in Parliament on the status of Inuit in Canada. *House of Commons Debates*. 1924, pp. 440–911, 3823–27; 1930 pp. 1091–99; 1950, pp. 3810–16. See also Peter A. Cumming and Neil H. Mickenberg, eds., *Native Rights in Canada; second*

fact that Canada already had appropriated Inuit land did not seem to occur to anyone.

ROYAL CANADIAN MOUNTED POLICE

The RCMP served as markers of Canadian sovereignty. They also served as monitors of economic conditions and of relations between Inuit and the traders who carried on year-round business among them. No other southern agency in the North had such slender duties or such abundant resources for carrying them out.[37] While the list of official duties is impressive, most were nominal except when an annual ship arrived. Their major duties were to keep official records of the Inuit population, to visit and report on conditions in each ilagiit nunagivaktangat at least once a year, to provide and if necessary deliver relief supplies to people in distress or long-term poverty, and to assist other public servants with logistics and advice. The RCMP placed stress on the self-reliance, hunting ability, and survival skills of Inuit. They believed that too much contact with traders (and later, with rivals such as Northern Service officers) would demoralize the entire population. At the same time, their positional authority endowed them with an overwhelming prestige and ability to secure agreement without true consent. Over time, the RCMP lost many of their paternalistic roles and their focus changed from protecting the hunting economy to imposing social control and enforcing the criminal law within the large and unstable settlements, which grew up around schools and nursing stations.

---

edition (Toronto: The Indian-Eskimo Association of Canada, 1972), pp. 132–69.

37 R. A. J. Phillips wrote of the typical Mountie that "his objective at first was simply to exist," *Canada's North*, p. 126.

People were still trying to dodge the *C.D. Howe* as late as 1965.[42] By that time, however, the worst ravages of TB had been broken. If communities had nursing stations, their staffs provided essential care while also eroding the independence of Elders by forbidding them to leave the settlements and return to their ilagiit nunagivaktangat, and in later years by pressuring pregnant women to deliver their babies in southern hospitals. Mortality declined, but the mentality of medical staff did not permit them to relieve many of the psychological pressures this disempowerment and style of treatment placed on Inuit families and culture.[43] The federal government withdrew from medical care in stages, beginning in the early 1970s and completing devolution to the NWT in 1988.[44] Throughout, medical policies offered the same outlook as many other social services, treating the Inuit, but blocking their ability to live anything like a traditional life on the land.

ELECTED POLITICIANS

The elected arm of the national government did not usually focus closely or for long on northern issues. For historians, the risks of relying on politicians' unscripted words are evident in a parliamentary statement by Resources and Development Minister Robert Winters in 1950, comparing Inuit to First Nations people:

---

42 Milton Freeman, interview with P. Goldring for QTC, 4 June 2009.

43 See J.D. O'Neill, "The Politics of Health in the Fourth World: A Northern Canadian Example," in K.S. Coates and W.R. Morrison, eds., *Interpreting Canada's North* (Toronto: Copp-Clark, 1989), pp. 279–98; also Betty-Anne Daviss-Putt, "Rights of Passage in the North: From Evacuation to the Birth of a Culture," in Mary Crnkovitch, ed., *Gossip; A Spoken History of Women in the North* (Ottawa: Canadian Arctic Resources Committee, 1990), pp. 91–114.

44 This paragraph includes material prepared by Dr. Frank Tester for the QTC in April 2008.

> They live under conditions different from the Indians, and a great attempt has been made to assimilate them into modern ways of life and so on. They are not the same type of wards [of the federal government] as Indians are, and the over-all conditions are sufficiently different that it would appear to be the proper thing to do. . . . to have them included in the northern administration of this department."[45]

Winters understood the general thrust and direction of recent policy initiatives, but he was not reliable on details. Politicians, however, occasionally seized an opportunity for headlines, especially when the Conservative government under John Diefenbaker made northern development a campaign theme in 1958,[46] or when the entire House of Commons Standing Committee on Indian Affairs and Northern Development flew to Resolute in 1969 to rendezvous with the American experimental oil tanker, *SS Manhattan*.[47] Especially as time went on, parliamentary debates could expose some southern Canadians to the injustice and inefficiency of contemporary Arctic governance. This is especially evident in the 1960s, when more politicians became knowledgeable and the federal riding in the Northwest Territories elected an articulate and anti-bureaucratic Métis veteran of the Northern Administration, Gene Rheaume, who knew the shortcomings of the Administration first-hand.[48] Rheaume's intervention earned enough

45 Canada. House of Commons Debates, 1 June 1950, p. 3104.

46 Although Diefenbaker's "Northern Vision" became a campaign slogan and is remembered as part of his effort to distinguish himself from his Liberal predecessors, an authoritative survey of Canadian general elections did not mention it among the defining issues. J.M. Beck, *Pendulum of Power: Canada's Federal Elections* (Toronto: Prentice-Hall, 1968), pp. 291–328.

47 William D. Smith, *Northwest Passage* (New York: *New York Times*, 1970), pp. 99–101.

48 See for example, Canada. House of Commons Debates. 7 July 1964 for Rheaume excoriating the exclusion of northerners from their own governance; also 24 July 1964,

support to block dividing the NWT, a bipartisan initiative that he believes was designed to prolong indefinitely the colonial restrictions on the Eastern Arctic, which Ottawa was gradually loosening in the more developed Mackenzie District.[49]

Politicians became more prominent when elected members were added to the Council of the Northwest Territories. As a result, that subordinate legislature gave increasing scope for action by members who lived in the North and whose whole public life focused on the North. This tendency became stronger when the seat of government moved to Yellowknife in 1967 and, over time, a wide range of social and economic programs were delegated to the territorial government.

COMMISSIONER AND COUNCIL OF THE NORTHWEST TERRITORIES

The NWT, including present-day Nunavut, was governed throughout the period under study under a constitution enacted by Parliament, initially with a Deputy Minister as "Commissioner" of the NWT. The territories and their governments had no independent or entrenched constitution. Local laws were passed by a council, which was, for the most part, made up of senior federal officials or their appointees. Their laws were not acts but "ordinances." The seat of government until 1967 was in Ottawa, and was accountable only to federal authorities. While the Council could act as a sounding board, its actions were dominated by the concerns of the growing non-Aboriginal settlements in the Mackenzie Valley. In every other respect, it was simply one of the tools the department could use to administer Canada's northern dependencies.[50]

---

pp. 5965–71, QTC Document A07358.

49 E. Rheaume, telephone interview with QTC researchers and staff, 8 March 2010.

50 Inuit regions first elected members in 1966. In 1951, the Mackenzie Valley was al-

The nominal head of this unrepresentative external legislature was the Commissioner, a figure whose office changed partway through the period under review. Between 1921 and 1963, the Commissioner was always the deputy minister of the department responsible for northern affairs. Thus he was a very senior official with time-consuming responsibilities beyond his role in the North. At times administrators found it expedient or necessary to manage an issue through the Council and its commissioner, but, except for the passage of ordinances concerning local government services, there were generally better ways to get things done. In 1965, the post of commissioner was downgraded to a full-time position held by a lower-level official. This commissioner, Bent Sivertz, focused more on the North, but was a less powerful figure in Ottawa.[51]

Gradually, Council members came to represent geographical districts, and some members were elected in districts that had large educated populations. As the elected membership grew, members who were independent of the federal government became more active, and the published debates reflect a better sense of some northerners' concerns and diversity. In 1965–1966, the Pearson government appointed the Advisory Commission on the Development of Government in the Northwest Territories. Its report was only a speed bump on the long road to Nunavut, but by delaying division of the NWT, it offered Inuit the mixed blessings of being administered from Yellowknife instead of from Ottawa. At the time Carruthers offered the cautious

---

lowed to elect three of approximately eight members. The role of the Council is usually either ignored or misrepresented in memoirs and histories of this period. For a good summary, especially with regards to the mining districts of the western Arctic, see K. Rae, *The Political Economy of the Canadian* North (Toronto: University of Toronto Press, 1967), pp. 34–40. Gordon Robertson described his duties as Commissioner in *Memoirs of a Very Civil Servant* (Toronto: University of Toronto Press, 2000), pp. 146–64.

51 R.A.J. Phillips *Canada's North,* p. 246; see also the autobiography of Bent Sivertz, *The Life of Bent Gestur Sivertz, A Seaman, a Teacher and a Worker in the Canadian Arctic* (Victoria: Trafford Publishing, 2000), pp. 127–43.

men in Ottawa a short-term vision of how to prepare the NWT "not [for] provincehood but [for] the means of growth to provincehood," with decentralization as an achievable goal and division as merely a distant possibility.[52] The importance of this to the evolution of the official mind is that the Carruthers Commission recommended removing the legislature and some of the administrative machinery from Ottawa. It proposed the Council be renamed the Legislative Assembly (though some members would remain unelected). It redesigned the office of Commissioner to combine many of the functions that in a province are exercised by a lieutenant governor, speaker of the Assembly, and premier. This was adopted, and only since 1980 has the Commissioner, in Yellowknife and later in Iqaluit, withdrawn to a ceremonial role very like that of a lieutenant governor. The shifting power and prestige of the office, with its confusing sequence of real powers and ceremonial duties, illustrate the constitutional evolution of legislative authority as planned from Ottawa.

OTHER FEDERAL DEPARTMENTS

Numerous federal departments sent officials to the Arctic, conducted surveys and studies there, funded researchers heading North, or provided central agency support and direction. One of the main departments was the Department of Transport, which oversaw aids to navigation, ran the icebreaker service and chartered the great fleets of sea-lift vessels whose appearance offshore at permanent establishments became an annual routine each summer. The independence and high-handedness of this department were especially noticeable in its management of the supply vessel and hospital ship, the *C. D. Howe*.

The Department of National Defence, with its American allies and their numerous "contractors" in the Arctic, had a policy of "non-fraternization,"

52 Canada. Advisory Commission on the Development of Government in the Northwest Territories, *Summary of the Report* (Ottawa: 1966) pp. 5–6.

but still employed a large number of Inuit and had a wider impact through infrastructure development. The departments of External Affairs, Fisheries, and Justice had small roles in Qikiqtani Region affairs and had variable impacts on events inside the contact zone. The departments responsible for mining did their best to stimulate economic development, while the national museums conducted fieldwork including, in the 1960s, an "urgent ethnology" program based on the premise that traditional cultures in Canada would soon die out. In the 1970s the CBC emerged as part of the government's agenda to modernize the region and make it more attractive to southern workers, but it gradually developed as a platform for the empowerment of Inuit as well. All these activities were faithfully reported in the annual reports of the Advisory Committee on Northern Development (ACND), a good source of official information on mandates and budgets from 1953 to 1978.

ESKIMO AFFAIRS COMMITTEE

The Eskimo Affairs Committee, 1952–1962, was an advisory group created by the department to forestall the creation of representative institutions for Inuit. The Committee, which first heard from Inuit in person in 1959, enlisted veterans of northern fieldwork to advise it on administrative and program ideas. Because the RCMP, Hudson's Bay Company, and churches were all represented on this committee, the administration could float schemes in front of agencies that had the power to obstruct Arctic initiatives that threatened their own operations. These schemes included secular schools, the appointment of field officers, and the chartering of cooperatives. Eventually the Northern Administration prevailed and with its own new policy capacity in Ottawa, Northern Service officers in the field, and greater backing from the political level, the Administration disbanded this public–private advisory body. In Peter Clancy's view, by empowering the traditional non-Inuit contact agents at "a time when formal channels between Ottawa and indigenous arctic interests were virtually non-existent, the committee ... is an apt reflection of the administrative colonialism then prevalent in the North."[53]

INDIAN AFFAIRS BRANCH, INUIT STATUS AND THE INDIAN ACT

Significantly missing from this list is the federal Department of Indian Affairs. The officials who managed northern affairs lived in a legal fog where Inuit were sometimes treated as a special responsibility of the Crown in the same manner as First Nations peoples were, and at other times were said to have the same rights and responsibilities as any other citizens. At Confederation there were no Inuit in the three British colonies that combined to form Canada, but thousands were added in 1870 with the annexation of Rupert's Land and the North Western Territory. For most of the next century, official rhetoric suggested that Inuit in the NWT were not wards of the Crown, and had the same rights as any other Canadians, but sometimes needed additional management because of their poverty and the fragility of their resources. This was the strongly held view of the northern administration in the 1920s.[54] The legal situation was further clouded by a 1939 Supreme Court decision that said Inuit in Quebec were "Indians" and, therefore, under federal protection and jurisdiction; and yet a 1951 amendment to the Indian Act specifically exempted Inuit from that law. Parliamentarians grappled with this inconsistency in 1950 when giving Inuit the right to vote in federal elections, while refusing it to people living on First Nations reserves:

---

53 Peter Clancy, "The Making of Eskimo Policy in Canada, 1952–62: The Life and Times of the Eskimo Affairs Committee," *Arctic* 40:3 (Sept. 1987), p. 192.

54 D. Jenness, *Eskimo Administration. II Canada*. Finnie is quoted regularly on Inuit status, pp. 32–37.

> Mr. Carroll: Are the Eskimo and the Indian in the same category as far as being a ward of the government is concerned?
>
> Mr. Gibson: They are accepted as wards of the government in the estimates of the health and welfare department where they are handled jointly. I am sure the minister who looks after that matter will confirm what I say.
>
> Mr. Carroll: The Indians are wards of the government and are supported by the government, and I should like to know whether the Eskimos are in that same category.
>
> Mr. Gibson: They are definitely wards of the government and have been accepted as such.
>
> Mr. Ward [sic]: I think the hon. Member is wrong, the Eskimo is not a ward of the government.
>
> Mr. Gibson: Maybe we should have a ministerial statement on this.[55]

The confusion in this long-running debate came from an almost total lack of any sense of Aboriginal rights. Members imagined that the rights of status Indians came from the Crown and Parliament, partly through treaties and partly through legislation. A major obstacle to understanding that Inuit had Aboriginal rights was that they had not signed treaties surrendering any of those rights. Thus, before about 1960, the discussion did not focus on what afterwards came to be termed "Eskimo birthright." It muddled around with questions about treaties, reserves, voting rights, taxation, and relief (social assistance).

55 Canada. House of Commons Debates, Session 1950, vol. 4, 19 June 1950, pp. 3811–12.

Few members wanted Inuit to sign treaties or be assigned reserves. This attitude arose partly from a sense that the existing administration of Indian affairs was inefficient as well as unjust, and partly because, as opposition leader George Drew stated in 1950, there was no economic need for Canada to have treaties with Inuit. "It is difficult to imagine that the areas occupied by the Eskimos had a substantial land value. Conceivably, at some future time minerals may be discovered in some of the Eskimo areas, although this has not yet happened so far as I know."[56] The official stance remained that Inuit were ordinary citizens, although over time they became subject to closer and closer paternalistic supervision.[57]

Debate had not moved much further fifteen years later, when the NWT Council discussed whether "Eskimo birthright" (Aboriginal rights) existed, and how it could be dealt with in the NWT. The member for the Mackenzie Delta, Mr. Trimble, kicked this off by observing, "I feel myself that the Eskimo people have the same birthrights as the Indian people, although there were no treaties made with the Eskimos. I am interested to know who is considered to be an Eskimo and what privileges and birthrights they do have." The commissioner, Bent Sivertz, took this opening to denounce recognition of Aboriginal rights. If rights were recognized, government might have to control the exercise of those rights through an Eskimo Act along the same lines as the Indian Act. He opposed this because "categorization of people intended to confer some special privilege or benefit upon them very often acts in the reverse way." Besides, education and employment opportunities were developing so fast that special status "might well overtake any kind of provisions that are intended to

---

56 Ibid., p. 3816. Five months earlier, Gibson himself was Minister of the responsible department.

57 A prominent example of this is the "non-fraternization" clauses in the governance of major defence projects, notably article 13, "Matters Affecting Canadian Eskimos" in the Canada–USA "Statement Of Conditions To Govern The Establishment Of A Distant Early Warning System In Canadian Territory."

be benefits to Eskimos, but might actually result in their disadvantage."[58]

By raising the threats of an Eskimo Act or a reserve system, Sivertz fell into line with a growing preference for addressing inequalities in society through education and economic development without addressing questions of rights. (This was at the core of the 1969 White Paper on Indian policy.) This discourse became obsolete with the broader acceptance of Aboriginal rights in the 1970s, which made official confusion about Inuit status somewhat irrelevant. However, it was largely irrelevant already because the federal government enjoyed provincial- and municipal-type powers throughout the NWT.[59] It could, therefore, intervene directly in people's lives in multiple ways, regardless of whatever "birthright" might exist. In this sense, the confusion over whether Inuit were "Indians" or ordinary citizens was irrelevant. One enduring benefit of the confusion is that Inuit were kept separate from the tradition-bound and overtly racist Indian Affairs bureaucracy, leaving the Northern Administration staff to devise measures without regard to the very different traditions prevailing in the sister department.

INTELLECTUALS

Academics had few formal roles in making and carrying out government policy in the Arctic, but most officials were not anti-intellectual. The secretary of the ACND was university-educated, was well-grounded in anthropology, and had lived with Inuit for several years. There was a long tradition of information exchange between officialdom and the professional staffs of the Geological Survey, the National Museum, and similar bodies.

58 Council of the Northwest Territories. Twenty-ninth Session. *Debates*. 8–17 February 1965. vol. 1, pp. 90–91.

59 This was the only realm in which the federal government exercised such responsibilities for a large civilian population except, significantly, for the constitutional responsibility for Indians and lands reserved for Indians.

Sivertz had a reading knowledge of Margaret Mead's work on Samoa and used it to generalize about cultures closer to home. In the 1950s, relatively few consultants were used to inform social policy. Some participants felt that the Department's scientists were underused in the policy sphere.[60] This separation of research from action gradually changed, and in 1961 the important *Resources for Tomorrow* conference was addressed by, among others, anthropologist Henry Hawthorne from the University of British Columbia, and McGill University geographer and Arctic expert Trevor Lloyd.

Government-supported research in the Arctic was reported on annually by the ACND. Leadership in research clearly rested with the Defence Research Board and the Department of Mines and Technical Surveys, including the Polar Continental Shelf Project. Each year the National Research Council had up to five projects in applied science, while Northern Affairs and National Resources (NANR) itself sponsored or conducted research through the Wildlife Service and the archaeology or ethnology programs of the National Museum of Canada. It is important to note that National Health and Welfare sponsored only one research project in this era, and the RCMP none. This suggests that aside from NANR, bodies with an operational presence in the North relied on their in-house expertise to understand conditions and make plans.[61]

NANR in these years created a Northern Social Research Group (NSRG), which by 1973 filled huge gaps in Canadians' previous knowledge of the North. The group's "mandate was to encourage, fund, and engage in social science research on the traditional and contemporary economy and cultures of Canada's north. The intent was to form a base of research from which an orderly social, political, and economic modernizing of the

---

60 LAC: RG85, vol. 1654, file NR 1/1-13, part 1, "Glassco Commission—Royal Commission on Government Organization," G. W. R. to Deputy Minister (Graham Rowley to Gordon Robertson), 15 Nov 1962.

61 J. R. Lotz, *Government Research and Surveys in the Canadian North 1956–61* (Ottawa: Northern Coordination and Research Centre, 1961).

north could be drawn."[62] The NSRG "gained an international reputation as a source of generally top-quality social science work." At times their published work became a critical audit of the Department itself.[63] Unfortunately, with the devolution of many programs to Yellowknife, the NSRG suffered organizational changes in 1968 that were, as Graham Rowley told Nixon, "meant to be dysfunctional."

Economy and Culture: Twin Dilemmas in Planning for the North

The whirlwind that overtook the Qikiqtani Region in the 1950s was not unique to that place or time. Recently, Canadian historian Anthony J. Hall has written:

> Two immense, opposing forces [which] are pulling at humanity as we move beyond the millenarian fever during this time of great transformations. One historical impetus is tugging down old linguistic, cultural, national, economic and political boundaries. The other pressure is seen in the struggle by many of the world's peoples against assimilation and in support of those values, insti-

62 P.G. Nixon, "The Politics of Government Research," pp. 37–46.

63 See for example, D.K. Thomas and C.T. Thompson, *Eskimo Housing as Planned Social Change* (Ottawa: 1972); and David Omar Born, *Eskimo Education and the Trauma of Social Change* (Ottawa: 1970); and, especially, Peter J. Usher's demolition of government credibility in the Western Arctic, in *The Banks Islanders: Economy and Ecology of a Frontier Trapping Community*. 3 vols. (Ottawa: 1971).

> tutions, and political rights they believe are essential to retain or secure a distinct place on this planet.[64]

To the official mind of Canadian colonialism fifty years ago, it was not supposed to be this conflicted. The orthodoxy of the time said that economic development could be given by the developed to their dependencies, would be welcomed as the subordinated peoples embraced economic opportunities, and could be achieved simply by letting obsolete cultural norms and identities wither. While this now seems as problematic as other 20th-century slogans such as "the war to end war" or "the end of history," many expressions of optimism and good intentions were wrapped around the steady encroachment of southern government and economy on Inuit society.

One characteristic of official interest in the Qikiqtani Region from 1950 to at least 1970 was how forward-looking much of it was. Coupled with a sense of urgency over medical and other challenges was an understanding that northern societies could not absorb, and southern taxpayers would not support, the kind of sudden change that had swept through Yukon during the Gold Rush of 1896–1898 and again during the military emergencies of 1941–1945. In Qikiqtani Region in 1950, officials were pressed between two views of the future.

The first was that Inuit should continue to live a "traditional life," as some imagined they still did, while making some necessary adjustments to the perceived shortage of game animals, adopting new standards in public and personal health, and reaching out to grasp the increasingly complex opportunities and demands posed by the swelling migrant population in the North. These fears and preferences were common among missionaries and the RCMP.

An opposing view was also common: Inuit seemed destined to abandon the land and embrace wage labour in a modern, industrializing North

64 Anthony J. Hall, *The American Empire and the Fourth World* (Montreal: McGill-Queen's University Press, 2003), p. 59.

marked by rapid investment in military installations and exploitation of minerals, oil, and gas. For a variety of reasons, and despite the shortage of clear indications of probable success, the second view—the view based on assimilation and economic development—grew increasingly strong as government invested in schools, housing, military infrastructure, and other efforts to bring the southern way of life into the North. New infrastructure, particularly schools, clinics, and housing, was meant to compensate Inuit for leaving the land. The federal authorities saw formal schooling and technical training as the essential hinge between economic development and the future social well-being of Inuit. Development was seen as absolutely inevitable, in which case the stark choice for Inuit was between schooling and segregation.[65] "Education is the greatest barrier which the Eskimos and Indians have to overcome," a departmental pamphlet on *Peoples of the Northwest Territories* intoned in 1957. It also warned that isolating Inuit from "the new settlers with their unsettling ways" was segregation. "This has been the solution in other countries, but it will not be the Canadian solution. Segregation has not found favour in Canada."[66] With great regularity, departmental publications and official pronouncements made education the great hope for the future. By setting up segregation as the alternative to profound cultural change, official pronouncements grasped a major North American public issue and put Canada's northern administrators firmly on the side of virtue.

From then on, elementary schooling for children and technical training for adults were top objectives in the official statements published for

---

65 It is interesting that segregation, not oppression or exploitation, was portrayed as the ultimate evil to be avoided. See Canada. Department of Northern Affairs and National Resources, *Annual Report Fiscal Year 1954–1955*, "Human Problems in the Canadian North," p. 12; also Canada. Department of Indian Affairs and Northern Development, *Canada's North 1970–1980* (Ottawa: 1972), p. 34. "The need to rid northern communities of all forms of segregation is axiomatic."

66 Canada. Dept. of Northern Affairs and National Resources. *Peoples of the Northwest Territories* (Ottawa: 1957), p. 36.

the Canadian public. Because teachers were appointed for the permanent settlements, not the ilagiit nunagivaktangat, whole families moved into settlements to avoid being split up, a relocation that officials did not seem to foresee. Officials sometimes admitted that rapid change was disruptive to established social relations, and would deprive many Inuit of the meaningful roles they held in society, especially Elders and hunters. Many of the current imbalances in Qikiqtani Region communities can be traced to government attitudes and actions from the 1950s to 1970s, which failed either to protect the hunting life or replace it with enough meaningful jobs.

All these trends weakened the "traditional life" that so many Qallunaat in the 1950s said they respected and wanted to save. That "traditional life" was partly a southern invention, because for a long time Inuit had been adopting or developing new practices, which they hoped would not overwhelm valued cultural traditions. (A major recent adaptation was the fur-trapping economy: the fox and the imported goods it bought had never been staples of pre-contact existence.) In addition to this misunderstanding, Qallunaat admiration for traditional ways contained a hefty dose of anti-modernism. They viewed Inuit as the ultimate frontiersmen, and admired their balanced obligations within networks of kin and community, which were said to resemble Christianity. The anti-modernists, however, predicted that Inuit culture would be destroyed by contact with the harmful side of Qallunaat society, negative forces such as venereal disease and dependence on social welfare. The anti-modernists, especially common among the RCMP and the churches, possessed little sense of Inuit as competent economic actors on a wider stage.

Government was so dependent on the Hudson's Bay Company that a serious critique of the commercial system was slower to develop after the Second World War than it had been after the First World War. In 1924, a government official told the *Toronto Star*:

> While they have been in touch with civilization for 100 years... and while they are capable and keen to learn, the Eskimos, beyond

> learning from the missionaries to read and write their own language, are poor linguists. They don't as a rule speak English, and few English people speak Eskimo. The interchange of ideas is therefore very slow. The net result is that while they have taken hold of a great many of the man's ideas, they have got nowhere commercially. It is a fair statement that there is not one Eskimo in Baffin Land who has any idea of the real value of his own products. Their position now is that they are in the best possible frame of mind to learn, and anxious to do so.[67]

By 1950, such critiques of the Hudson's Bay Company were rarely uttered aloud. The Company had become profitably entangled in the government's own service delivery, transporting the Eastern Arctic Patrol from 1932 to 1947, owning almost all the two-way radios at establishments, providing "relief"—food or ammunition—to Inuit in need and, after 1945, distributing the supplies Inuit families received under the Family Allowance program, a universal social program that provided a high proportion of the nominal money income of every Qikiqtani Region community.

Fuzzy thinking about family allowance should not be underestimated as a facet of the official mind. In 1950, social transfers made up over 40 percent of Inuit income at eight trading posts visited by the Eastern Arctic Patrol, with family allowance alone accounting for over 45 percent at three Baffin Island locations.[68] By comparison, furs made up another 29 percent of reported income. Although the value of country food was not counted in this survey, it is nonetheless apparent that the Inuit economy was to a significant degree integrated with the wider national economy. It was also sometimes noted that the major commodities produced by Inuit, such as

67 The interview, printed 3 Dec. 1924, was vetted and approved by the Deputy Minister. See LAC: RG85, vol. 755, file 4687, "L.T. Burwash—Report as Exploratory Engineer."

68 LAC: RG85, vol. 1207, file 201-1-8, part 3, attachment to J. Cantley to A/Chief, 19 Nov. 1952.

fine furs and later art works, were luxury items for which both supply and demand were unreliable. These awkward realities were seldom dealt with in any nuanced way in official publications at the time. Instead, these publications wrote off the present as if it were more or less unsustainable and then offered a choice of futures designed for Inuit rather than with them.

The official sense of anxious responsibility was clearly expressed in a number of places during the 1950s. In an article meant for a wide public audience, RCMP Commissioner L. H. Nicholson bluntly asserted the need for government intervention, not in the trading economy but in the social lives of people:

> We cannot today accept the harshness of nature's laws. Thirty years ago the death of a few Eskimos by starvation would have attracted no attention, or at most would have been a matter of interest only. Such deaths were looked upon by Eskimos themselves as inevitable and the population was in this hard way held to what the country could maintain. The Eskimos may still accept this rule—we cannot.[69]

Earlier, a speech prepared for Bent Sivertz described the traditional life as part of the "balance of nature" and mused about the government's interference in previous cycles of prosperity and famine.[70] Sivertz found it "incompatible with the responsibility of the modern state" to allow its citizens to feel "expendable" by exposure to the dangers of the traditional life. As a result, in Sivertz's view, the help that government directed to those in danger interfered with the balance of nature and thus allowed the

---

69 L. H. Nicholson, "The Problem of the People," *The Beaver* (Spring 1959), pp. 20–21. Of 11 articles in this number of *The Beaver*, this is the only one written by a public servant.

70 NWT Archives. Alexander Stevenson fonds, Accession N-1992-023, box 23 file 7. "Development of the North—Sociological Developments (speech by Mr. B. G. Sivertz)", 25 Oct. 1954.; QTC Document A00024.

population to grow rapidly, with the unintended result that existing game supplies dwindled alarmingly.[71]

Sivertz continued, "Bringing education to Eskimos is a formidable task." While southerners usually think of schools in settlements, "if the Eskimos are brought together in settlements they will starve unless the government provides food, clothing, and shelter—and extreme paternalism of this kind would destroy the people." This prophetic speech was critical of proposals to encourage all Inuit to move South, and offered assimilation and employment for those who wanted it along with increased support and appropriate levels of intervention for those who wanted to "continue the primitive life in regions where game is plentiful." What he apparently failed to foresee was how difficult it would be to design and finance programs that would respond to individual desires and local challenges, to train or recruit people with the flexibility to deliver those programs, and to resist the tendency to bring the people to health care and educational institutions rather than the other way around.

One reason for this disappointing result was that economic development was the top priority when plans for the future were implemented. This should not be portrayed as a particularly reactionary approach or a uniquely Canadian one. The seeds of this kind of thinking were present in a range of international policy-making after the Second World War and were expressed in Article 73, the part of the United Nations (UN) Charter devoted to colonial administration. Article 73 somewhat euphemistically referred to colonizing powers as "Members of the United Nations which have or assume responsibilities for the administration of territories whose peoples have not yet attained a full measure of self-government." It stated that "the interests of the inhabitants of these territories are paramount."[72]

---

71 These speaking notes show no awareness that population figures were possibly much higher before virgin soil epidemics harrowed the populations at first contact, starting around 1840.

72 Article 73 is part of Chapter 11, the "Declaration Regarding Non-Self-Governing

However, Article 73 is silent on "internal colonies" of larger powers or what came to be called the peoples of the "fourth world," but the spirit of promoting peace through economic development and self-government permeated the document. It might almost have provided the foundational text for the speech by Sivertz quoted above.

The document, however, linked development and culture in a way that clearly made the retention of culture subordinate to the economy. UN members pledged:

> a. to ensure, with due respect for the culture of the peoples concerned, their political, economic, social, and educational advancement, their just treatment, and their protection against abuses;
>
> b. to develop self-government, to take due account of the political aspirations of the peoples, and to assist them in the progressive development of their free political institutions, according to the particular circumstances of each territory and its peoples and their varying stages of advancement.[73]

For a population such as Inuit whose livelihood was organized around harvesting wild animals across large tracts of territory, subordinating culture to development exposed that culture to tremendous pressures by cutting people off from the scenes of their most prized activities and the sites where they educated their children in the values and practices of their Elders.

In general, the course of development policy was uneven, especially in the Kivalliq Region, which was noted for its mineral potential, but also for alleged game shortages, and in the Qikiqtani Region, which had relatively abundant game, but almost no economic minerals. In the Qikiqtani Region,

---

Territories." Accessed online at http://www.un.org/en/documents/charter/chapter11.shtml, 17 May 2010.

73 Ibid.

therefore, the main hopes for economic stability or development lay in the direction of artistic production and handicrafts, developed first at Cape Dorset about 1950; construction for defence projects and administrative services, focused on Iqaluit from the mid-1950s onwards; and tourism, particularly catering to hunters and fishermen. By the end of the 1960s, there were commercial char fishing camps on the beautifully scenic Cumberland Sound (where a national park was to be established in 1972) in line with a forecast by Sivertz in 1961, that changes in the game laws

> would permit the hunting of walrus and other sea mammals in the wide list of attractions that will bring tourists and their money into the many depressed areas in the Eastern Arctic. In this way the recreational use of the wildlife of the North can bring much greater economic benefit to residents than is now derived from domestic or subsistence use. This revised system of utilizing wildlife can be an effective conservation technique.[74]

Only later would wilderness adventure and hunting be joined by the community-based tourism initiatives that became a cornerstone of NWT government policy after 1984.[75]

The lack of adequate consideration of the renewable resource economy is one of the missed opportunities of the development plans of the 1950s and 1960s, especially when weighed against Article 73's endorsement of "due respect for the culture of the peoples concerned." It was never going to be easy to centralize services and hence people, and at the same time preserve a way of life that required a high degree both of dispersal and of

---

74 B.G. Sivertz, "The North as a Region," in *Resources for Tomorrow: A Series of Background Papers for Discussion at the Resources for Tomorrow Conference* (Montreal: October 1961), p. 572.

75 Gillian Corless, "Community Based Tourism Planning And Policy: The Case Of The Baffin Region, Nunavut." PhD Thesis. (Montreal: McGill University, 1999).

continuous use of land to harvest game and instruct youth. The federal government conducted a series of Area Economic Studies in the mid-1960s, which inventoried the concentrations of game animals and which, not surprisingly, were largely carried out by talking to Inuit. However, government support for hunting was largely passive, which George Wenzel has suggested may have been due to the fact that a number of communities already earned income from the skins of ringed seals. This was an animal (unlike the Arctic fox) whose products could be both eaten and traded. Therefore hunter-support programs were not in place when international pressures killed the sealskin trade in the early 1980s. David Natcher argues, "Despite the predictions of their eventual demise, subsistence economies continue to demonstrate considerable resilience and remain integral to the health and well-being of northern Aboriginal communities." The survival of the sector depends largely on the efforts of Inuit themselves, which are paradoxically facilitated by the failure of any other large-scale enterprise, except government itself, to take root across the region.[76]

Cultural Change and Continuity

This report has already quoted, with some bewilderment, Minister Robert Winters's statement in 1950 that "a great attempt has been made to assimilate [the Inuit] into modern ways of life." In fact, at the official level before that year, only feeble and equivocal efforts had been made to assimilate Inuit. In keeping with the anti-modern attitudes of many contact agents, the HBC's need for hardworking trappers, and the spirit of the UN's timid steps towards decolonization, Canadian officials in the 1950s seldom spoke

---

76 See David C. Natcher, *The Social Economy of Canada's Aboriginal North*, accessed 19 Jan 2010, at http://www.nrf.is/Open%20Meetings/Anchorage/Position%20Papers/Natcher%20NRF%20Submission.pdf.

directly about assimilating Inuit to southern cultural standards. Instead they welcomed every evidence of Inuit showing an interest in wage labour. While government steadily undermined the material bases of previous socio-economic structures, they never clearly articulated a view they probably held, that not much of the Inuit's land- and kin-based social, economic, and spiritual systems were of value to the Qikiqtani Region of the future. In outline, it appears that officials did not know what to expect from the future in the 1950s, then became resigned after 1960 to the notion that development must prevail against older Inuit practices.

By the mid-1960s, this cultural pessimism blossomed into a kind of civic optimism. Inuit would be encouraged, through cooperatives and local councils, to have more influence over their own local affairs. Missionaries, traders, health workers, and other officials all wanted to consign to history's dustbin the majority of practices and beliefs that set Inuit apart from their new neighbours. Officials, therefore, found it convenient to believe that Inuit would make the same choices, and their distinctiveness would be blurred in a common citizenship with other Canadians. In a speech devoted mainly to exploitation of natural resources, Minister Arthur Laing in 1965 shared his faith that the "special problems" of Inuit would cease to trouble Canada before long, as they abandoned their "precarious" economy based on trapping, to acquire mechanical and technical training and business skills. Then "the very real benefits to them in their social, political and economic development are of even greater value in coming to grips with their problems of transition." Without generally using the word "assimilation" or worrying overtly at what would happen to those who preferred a more traditional path, Laing declaimed that "the job of developing Canada must always go on, but the day that the Eskimos can develop in the same framework as the people in the provinces is fast approaching." This was all to be achieved by merging the Inuit in a common citizenship with other Canadians. "The development of the Eskimos in the Arctic will continue until they themselves achieve the rights and responsibilities which they seek and deserve—the heritage of Canadian citizenship."[77] Readers may recognize a foreshadowing of a more famous document issued four years later, generally known as the White Paper on Indian Policy, which invited First Nations peoples to exchange their rights for a vague promise of equality of economic opportunity:

> The policy promises all Indian people a new opportunity to expand and develop their identity within the framework of a Canadian society which offers them the rewards and responsibilities of participation, the benefits of involvement and the pride of belonging.[78]

In a similar fashion, official statements about Inuit shied away from outright denunciation of core elements of the culture and instead deflected attention toward opportunities for Inuit to acquire new skills and to commodify parts of the existing culture through tourism and artistic production. Official statements generally avoided talking about the fate of Inuit beliefs, lifeways, and social structures that were not attuned to the modern world, but the subject was important to academic and museum anthropologists, and some of their debates spilled into the official sphere.

In one corner of the discussion were a number of older anthropologists who took an essentialist view of Inuit culture and deplored its loss. In 1959, E. S. Carpenter of the University of Toronto publicly denounced the "tragedy

---

77 Canada. Dept. of Northern Affairs and National Resources, "The Potential of the North," An Address by the Honourable Arthur Laing, March 18, 1965, pp. 12–14. Mimeograph in Library and Archives Canada, Amicus No. 9098272.

78 Canada. Dept. of Indian Affairs and Northern Development, *Statement of the Government of Canada on Indian Policy 1969* (Ottawa: 1969), p. 7. The same document dismissed comprehensive claims as "so general and undefined that it is not realistic to think of them as specific claims capable of remedy except through a policy and program that will end injustice to Indians as members of the Canadian community," p. 11.

of misunderstanding and ignorance" whereby romantics and bureaucrats were preventing any movement to "assist [Inuit] in their adjustment to modern life and, at the same time, to preserve their ancient culture in book and film."[79] He denounced the "little old ladies" who he ridiculed as "defenders of the igloo" for wanting to "insist that the Eskimo regain" the precarious life of other times. Carpenter praised recent government initiatives to treat Inuit as human beings and he mocked the view that they were being "destroyed." But he denounced the Northern Administration for failing to support academic fieldwork, failing to "put on record the meaning of life to these arctic peoples." He went on:

> Now that Eskimo culture has fallen before our needs and power, and the Eskimo themselves are abandoning their ancient traditions, these are offered to us, briefly, at this moment. If we seize this opportunity and preserve these traditions in book and film, we enrich our own lives and, perhaps not incidentally, reaffirm that minorities, if not in flesh, at least in tradition, can survive in a modern democracy.

Inuit dignity and the enriching of the dominant society both seemed to Carpenter to require the program, which came to be known (and tolerably well-funded) as the "urgent ethnology" program of the National Museum of Canada. But in general he stood on the same ground as Canada's pre-eminent student of the Inuit, Diamond Jenness. Nearly eighty years old and retired from government service since 1948, Jenness in 1966 published a stinging indictment of administrators who had made Inuit "the pawns of history" and—in his biased view—extinguished them as a separate race or culture. His essay in R. St. J. Macdonald's collection, *The Arctic Frontier*, is simultaneously defeatist, anti-modern, and assimilationist. Canada, he

---

79 E.S. Carpenter, "Eskimo Culture: A tragedy of misunderstanding and ignorance," *Canadian Commentator*, 3:4 (Apr. 1959). QTC Document A00717.

said, had allowed Inuit to corrode in idleness because she could not make up her mind what to do with them:[80]

> The true Indians, the true Eskimos, have passed into history, to join the Romans of Italy . . . and the Normans who conquered and settled in England. . . . Are we not duping ourselves, then, when we persistently talk about, and even legislate for, "Canadian Eskimos."[81]

Bitterness and pessimism might fund a film series or collect traditional legends, but it did not add up to giving direction to public policy. The official mind was not closed to the contributions of anthropology. Sivertz in 1959 wrote a circular memo to his staff praising the insights of American anthropologist Margaret Mead, whose views provided a good fit with some of the assumptions of high modernism. Sivertz alerted his staff to an ongoing struggle between his Branch and the RCMP to design the pace and direction of social change in the Arctic, and strongly asserted their Department's belief in rapid change. (Commissioner Nicholson had proposed a buffer zone forcing Inuit to live more than 20 miles from any settlement.)

> One point at which our philosophy diverges from that of Commissioner Nicholson is in respect of the speed at which it is possible for cultural adaptation to take place without destroying the integrity of the group or the individual. We believe, and have ample evidence for it, that people from practically a stone age culture can enter a very different way of life such as that common in Canada, generally in the space of one generation. This in fact is the basic

80 D. Jenness, "The Administration of Northern Peoples: America's Eskimos—Pawns of History," in R. St. J. Macdonald, *The Arctic Frontier* (Toronto: University of Toronto Press, 1966), p. 126.

81 Ibid., p. 128.

> premise of the ferment in the minds of aboriginal people all over the world who have been living in something less than the status of full citizenship in their own countries. Their demands at this moment are very insistent and may be briefly summarized as a desire for the maximum advantages human knowledge and the most developed institutions of civilization can bring. The legitimacy of these demands is being widely recognized and we have felt that it would be incompatible for Canada to use one point of view with respect to under-developed peoples in other lands and a different one in respect of similar problems within her own borders.[82]

The appeal to the authority of Mead followed:

> Incidentally, social anthropologists have traditionally advocated a policy of gradualness in cultural change, but many leaders in this field such as Dr. Margaret Mead now favour an accelerated programme of change, provided only that the individuals and groups in question have a place in the new culture that is secure and satisfactory to them economically, vocationally and socially. In this view, the people must have economic opportunity and social acceptance,—they must have a real place in the new society,—it is fatal for them to spend time in an in-between void.[83]

This preoccupation of the official mind with theoretical aspects of assimilation was expressed again in the important Resources for Tomorrow conference in 1961. Northern development was a major theme, with Sivertz himself a key speaker and British Columbia anthropologist Henry Hawthorne

---

82 NWT Archives, Alexander Stevenson fonds, Accession N-1992-023, box 17 file 7, "Memo to Field Staff for Information, re: Eskimo Affairs", B.G. Sivertz, Director, 11 March 1959. QTC Document A00003.

83 Ibid.

disseminating Mead's views in a careful presentation on "Problems of Cultural Adjustment."[84] Also citing Mead, Hawthorne set out a program for the responsible imposition of rapid culture change. He foresaw a North whose population would be disproportionately young and town-based, where the existing educational system might be flawed in ways not yet understood, but where "the new centres may become centres of unusual intellectual, scientific and artistic growth."

Hawthorne offered six goals for moving a person from "a tribal outlook to one which fits the contemporary world," which can be summarized—not quoted—here:

1. ability to speak, read, and write some "world language," that is, a language that will make participation in international conferences and free movement about the world possible;

2. a grasp of the framework of Western economy, use of money and credit, and a recognition of the implications of living in a contract rather than a status society;

3. a modicum of cross-cultural sophistication that will enable the individual concerned to work among people with different codes and standards without taking offence or becoming disoriented;

4. a working acceptance of the state of mind roughly summarized in such phrases as "the scientific attitude," and an ability to show this attitude in public interpersonal contexts, whether political, economic, or technological;

5. some conceptualized view of history that makes it possible to deal with the time perspectives (towards the past and the future) of the great civilizations; and

6. a sufficient independence of the living mesh of their own culture to be able to exist outside it without crippling nostalgia.[85]

---

84 H. B. Hawthorne, "Problems of Cultural Adjustment in Relation to Northern Resources Development," in *Resources for Tomorrow: A Series of Background Papers for Discussion at the Resources for Tomorrow Conference* (Montreal: October 1961), pp. 597–606.

85 H. B. Hawthorne, "Problems of Cultural Adjustment," pp. 601–02.

Taken all together, Hawthorne's talk sent messages of optimism rather than the usual prevailing anxiety, but offered this at a high cost to hunter-gatherer cultures. However, he accurately foresaw that change would move people off the land and into "centres [. . .] more highly urbanized than the rest of Canada." He argued that this would require rapid and consensual change if Canada were to avoid "the hapless growth of ethnic slums and the sort of human relations they imply [which] would be indefensible." Some other salient features of the presentation were:

- Hawthorne noted the importance of adult education in this process. "[U]nless the goals of education are accepted as distant ones several generations away, there must be inducements and opportunities to learn for the parent generation also."
- He did not seem to foresee much intercultural growth for the non-Inuit contact agents.

Given the primacy Canada assigned to economic development over cultural retention, and the proposed penetration of non-Inuit culture into almost every individual, familial, and communal aspect of Inuit life, it is not clear what part of traditional Inuit culture was predicted to survive, with or without "crippling nostalgia." Perhaps this contradiction is what soon propelled Hawthorne into a new concern for "the survival of small societies." One of the things foreshadowed by his 1961 presentation was a growing awareness that effective social change would have to be guided by Inuit preference and participation. Officials sensitive to this fact, notably Graham Rowley,[86] were more successful in getting senior officials at least to pay lip service to this principle, though in fact it had begun to emerge as early as 1959 when two Inuit—both government employees—attended the

---

86 NWT Archives. Alexander Stevenson fonds, Accession N-1992-023, box 17 file 8, Memo, J. B. Bergevin, ADM Indian and Eskimo Affairs to "Mr. MACDONALD" [perhaps Deputy Minister John A. MacDonald], 22 Oct. 1969, summarizing and praising G. W. Rowley's paper on policy requirements for a sound Inuit policy. QTC Document A01859.

meeting of an interdepartmental Eskimo Affairs Committee.[87] The government, rather like the whalers a century before, began to identify Inuit who could act as cultural intermediaries and perhaps even as role models in accommodating a new economy.

The role of anthropologists in influencing official policy, and of Inuit in shaping the agenda, took a new and perhaps unexpected turn in 1973–1975 when the Department of Indian Affairs and Northern Development funded the Inuit Tapirisat of Canada to conduct a land use and occupancy project. This supported Inuit identification of rights to lands and resources they had actually used within their traditional territories. The fieldwork was entrusted to teams of younger anthropologists whose interests included hunting, and who took it for granted that, despite problems of underdevelopment and pressures on traditional practices and beliefs, the communities of the Qikiqtani Region were still inhabited by Inuit and not by some deracinated underclass of former Eskimos. This ecological approach provided both government and Inuit with a clear picture of the full geographical extent of historic and recent land use, and created an expanded scientific documentation for debating the future of resource management in what has since become Nunavut.[88]

---

87 Richard Diubaldo, *The Government of Canada and the Inuit, 1900-1967* (Ottawa: Indian and Northern Affairs Canada, 1985) pp. 1-7, 155; P. Clancy, "The Making of Eskimo Policy in Canada, 1952–62: The Life and Times of the Eskimo Affairs Committee," *Arctic* 40:3 (Sept. 1987), pp. 191–97.

88 This exercise accomplished for the Eastern Arctic something similar to what Berger's *Northern Frontier, Northern Homeland* did for the west. See Milton Freeman Research Limited, *Inuit Land Use and Occupancy Project*. 3 vols. (Ottawa: 1976); Milton Freeman, interview with P. Goldring for QTC, 4 June 2009. This research led at least indirectly to federal acceptance of Nunavut as a separate government and territory, and its revelations continue to inspire discussion in literature on the unique institutions and future of Nunavut.

Summing up: The Trajectory of the Official Mind, 1950–1975

The official mind of Canadian colonialism in the North showed some of the characteristics of post-1945 decolonization movements, but also a relentless desire to control the land and its people in the interests of the larger Canadian state. This survey has emphasized fear and mistrust because departmental officials were by no means naive in certain important matters. They grasped the complexity of the changes they were trying to control, and also understood that they were, themselves, being driven forward by international modernizing forces they did not control. The urge to prevent harm to Inuit—the impulse to rescue—was the single most universal feeling shared by anti-modernists and modernizers alike. Their preoccupation with their own responsibility to offer Inuit physical safety dampened any interest in taking minor financial or policy risks to protect or promote the survival of Inuit ways of life.

Although certain official desires prevailed through the entire period, there were distinct chronological stages. Until the late 1950s, there was much fear in official circles that the 20th-century economy of the Qikiqtani Region was doomed by overhunting of game resources, epidemic TB, and slumping fur markets. The federal government had no thought of completely abandoning the people to market forces, which were failing them already and failing to prepare them for change. In a revealing statement by a senior official, a serious criticism of the Inuit way of dwelling in the Arctic was that it "requires the full time of the entire family."[89] Viewed in this light, the traditional life, characterized by highly mobile multigenerational family life, was inconsistent with compulsory schooling, specialized skills training, and various forms of migrant labour.

---

89 B. G. Sivertz, "The North as a Region," p. 561.

In 1959, having persuaded the Diefenbaker government to make the North a high priority, the Northern Administration accepted highly convenient theories offered by some recent anthropology about embracing rapid social change as both necessary and wise. They tended to ignore the caveats—especially the budgetary implications—that came with those theories. However, budgets became large enough to empower southern engineers and other advocates of modernization, and to demand change at a speed that precluded involvement of Inuit in key decisions. The emphasis on schooling for children and training for adults developed without actual employment opportunities in the cash economy.

Though funding levels rose, they were never adequate for the resulting experiment in social engineering. One consequence of inadequate budgets was that by 1961 the Northern Administration was publicly distancing itself from the idea of delivering social services to Inuit in ilagiit nunagivaktangat. People were to live in settlements, and oil and minerals were to provide the "principal economic base for a northern population."[90] By the mid-1960s, the accelerated pace of change and the constitutional discussions in the Western Arctic began the shift of responsibility for social policy from Ottawa to Yellowknife. The result, which eventually favoured Inuit empowerment in the medium term, was that Ottawa's attention increasingly focused on non-renewable resources while it was left to the Yellowknife government, though not an Aboriginal government, to begin to temper the promotion of development with a renewed interest in actual conditions in communities and on the land. The federal role remained strong, both in providing program funding to the Government of the Northwest Territories and in targeting specific programs such as national parks and the CBC.

Throughout this period, economic development was a strong preoccupation of officials, and "the human problem" came to function as both an obstacle and a rationale for accelerated development. In a remarkably short time, officials shifted from regarding hunting as the basis of survival

---

90 B. G. Sivertz, "The North as a Region," p. 567.

to seeing it as at best a specialized occupation for a minority. The Resources for Tomorrow Conference underlined the growing but untested expectation that northern development, especially oil, would pay its own costs and also solve the human problem.

The prevailing pessimism about traditional Inuit culture and economy was offset to a certain degree by official interest in community development, including market-oriented instruments such as co-operatives. The official mind had a strongly international cast. Internationally, it was the decolonization of the Third World (if not of the Fourth) that sensitized governments to the material needs of Inuit. It was left to Inuit themselves, and to a small corps of advocates in the South, notably anthropologists, to make the case for a more humane and rights-based approach to foster the survival of elements of traditional culture into an uncertain future. It was another kind of external event—the Supreme Court's recognition of Aboriginal rights as the basis for legitimate claims—that began the subsequent chapter in the rivalry between Ottawa and the Inuit for the dominant say in how the future of the region and its people would unfold.

Illinniarniq

Schooling in Qikiqtaaluk

This report focuses on the implementation of a formal schooling system by the Government of Canada (and later the Government of the Northwest Territories) in Qikiqtaaluk from 1950 to 1975. This period's constant changes in formal schooling generally took the direction of having more children in school, without—at least until after 1975—important and needed advances in policy, curriculum, and teacher training.

Rapid changes in this period had far-reaching effects on Inuit life. The catalyst was, more often than not, the provision of a school and a school hostel. The facilities were installed in settlements with the expressed purpose of taking responsibility for the teaching of children away from parents and Elders in ilagiit nunagivaktangit to the teachers employed by the government. The government saw schools as one rung on the ladder towards acculturation. In a typical example of internal colonial thought, a former Northern Services Officer wrote in a government publication in 1963 that "the stiff requirements of job-holding in competitive Canadian enterprises" would require Inuit to have:

> a great deal more than simply knowing sixth or even eighth grade arithmetic, or of having acquired the ability to read a few school books. It will depend much more on the degree of acculturation he has reached; on the extent to which he has become aware of the qualities expected in a worker by Canadian employers; on his recognition of the attitudes and values he must acquire if he is to become a respected and welcome member of Canada's labour force.

Until the 1950s, education by Qallunaat in Qikiqtaaluk had been scattered and inconsistent. Many people used the knowledge attained from missionaries visiting their ilagiit nunagivaktangit or during seasonal visits to missions to learn and teach others how to read and write Inuktitut in syllabics (an Inuktitut writing system developed by missionaries stationed in the Arctic). By 1945, the federal government had begun planning for a structured, regulated system of schooling for the region, modelled on provincial education programs in southern Canada. It experimented with schooling delivered by travelling teachers, but the decision to focus instruction in fixed classrooms in settlements was fully in place by the early 1950s.

The period studied here has to be understood as one of continuous change for individuals and institutions. Many communities had never seen a teacher before the 1950s; in others, instruction was given only from time to time, depending on the talents and energy of the clergy or their wives. Throughout the 1950s, formal schooling was scarcely available except to the daughters and sons of a handful of Inuit who worked full-time in the settlements. According to figures assembled by Diamond Jenness about 1961, 727 pupils were enrolled in schools in the "Arctic District" that year, but 677 of these, or 93%, were in Grades 1 to 3. Only two were above Grade 5, and none above Grade 7. Typically, boys started school around age nine and dropped out at twelve, when old enough to make a serious contribution to hunting for the family. Progress was uneven [See Table 1]. By 1970, every school offered at least Grade 6, and four offered Grade 8 or above.

At the same time, schools were driving community development. An ambitious program designed in Ottawa in 1965 to build or enlarge schools included a budget for teachers' houses, small hostels, electric generators, and many more infrastructure improvements for communities. Equally, the omission of Paallavvik from that plan gave early warning of the complete withdrawal of government services from that community, which occurred in 1968.

All these plans for northern education lacked the essential ingredients of its southern counterparts: a reliable local funding base, equal opportunity for all students to attend schools, adequately prepared teachers, and elected school boards made up of local residents who could speak to the unique needs of their communities. As a result, Inuit were expected to make do with inexperienced teachers, books and subjects of no relevance to their lives, shoddy school buildings, and lack of opportunities to make changes to programs.

The key factors in ensuring that schools supported acculturation objectives were the teaching of English; the schools' role in enticing families to live in settlements; and the content of curricula that ignored Inuit realities, culture, and expectations. A lasting legacy of this system, over three or four generations, has been the distancing of Inuit children from their culture, language, and land, and the removal of children from family settings at critical moments in their development. Schooling rarely gave people the skills and knowledge they needed to fully participate in the economic changes that were planned for their communities, while simultaneously negating their Inuit identities and damaging their sense of self-worth. For some people, learning to read and write English and to "think like white men" gave them skills and knowledge to gain positions with the federal or territorial governments or in the private sector.

This chapter examines the history and impact of schooling from the perspectives of Inuit students and parents, as well as Qallunaat administrators. The evidence comes from archival records, from oral histories and memoirs given by parents, teachers, and former students, and from books and articles. Former students and parents testified directly to the Qikiqtani Truth Commission (QTC) and the Qikiqtani Inuit Association (QIA) on the impacts of the government's education programs on their lives, and on their children and parents' lives. Their words are quoted often in this chapter.

The following list of terms helps clarify the types of programs that are discussed in this chapter.

Education refers to the act of acquiring knowledge, by either formal or informal means; this knowledge can be imparted by family, through practical experience, or within a formal classroom.

Schooling refers exclusively to the education received in an institutional setting using a common curriculum.

Federal day schools are publicly funded schools established in settlements by the federal government, and before 1960 were attended primarily by children of the few families who lived year-round in those settlements.

Residential schools in Qikiqtaaluk were of two kinds: small hostels designed to accommodate about one dozen pupils in the settlements nearest to where their families lived and hunted, and large hostels made to accommodate eighty or more students from a much wider territory. There was no large hostel in Qikiqtaaluk until 1971. Before then some pupils were sent to Chesterfield Inlet and (after 1964) to the Churchill Vocational Centre.

Southern schooling experiences refer to programs that sent Inuit children south for schooling, usually as boarders in Qallunaat homes. One was the Experimental Eskimo Education Program, a federal program that operated briefly in the early 1960s to train selected Inuit children to become leaders.

Welfare teachers are federal employees who were responsible in the early 1950s for a variety of government programs within settlements. The term "teacher" is used generally before 1958 although not all had formal teaching qualifications.

Education in the North: A Timeline

TRADITIONAL INUIT LEARNING

Prior to the era when Inuit attended government schools, children learned skills through observation, practice, and everyday experiences integrated into daily life. They also moved very quickly from childhood to adulthood. For a young man, an ability to hunt successfully signalled his readiness to become a husband because he could now support and feed his own family. For a young woman, knowledge of traditional skills, such as sewing tents and clothing and caring for children, made her more desirable as a wife. Young couples usually lived with one set of parents for several years until they were self-sufficient. As July Papatsie, an Inuit artist, recalled during his QTC interview in 2008, "We are very good with our hands because we had to be. That's why a man who did not know how to make an iglu could not marry a wife and a woman who could not sew could not marry a man."

The process of learning in Inuit families is fully and eloquently described in Heather McGregor's book, *Inuit Education and Schools in the Eastern Arctic*. Learning by observation, practice, and "being" gave Inuit knowledge about their environment, personal responsibilities, and beliefs that persisted across generations. It also placed Elders in a position of authority. Asked at the QTC hearings how he learned to hunt, Qimmiataq Nungusuituk described going on hunting trips with his father and stated that, "We didn't like asking too many questions so we had to learn how by seeing what they do." Girls worked side by side with their mothers and grandmothers. Nangaq Idlout of Resolute described her experience of learning to sew at the age of nine, stating, "Because our parents were perfectionists when we were growing up, we had to do everything properly.

We had to imitate them, to get it done the way they do, because you have to stretch the pelts properly in order to fit them as clothes, and those are the things we start learning."

MISSIONARY SCHOOLING

As soon as Anglican and Roman Catholic missionaries arrived in Qikiqtaaluk in the early twentieth century, usually in concert with traders, they began to teach Inuit how to read and write in Inuktitut using syllabics and, less often, in English or French using Roman orthography. With very small grants from the government and more extensive support from English and Canadian donors, missionaries generally visited Inuit families living in ilagiit nunagivaktangit. They also saw them whenever they would come to trading posts during religious holidays such as Christmas and Easter to attend services and join in communal celebrations and games. While the missionaries influenced ideas about marriage, shamanism, and parenting in particular, Inuit continued to speak Inuktitut, live on the land, and follow most Inuit practices while simultaneously absorbing many Christian ideas.

Missionaries were not trained educators—they focused more on religious ideas than on math, science, and social studies. They taught basic syllabic literacy to give converts the skills needed to read and assimilate religious teachings from the Bible and Western moral codes embedded in storybooks. Inuit recount that missionary teaching allowed them to enjoy high rates of Inuktitut literacy, with most people being able to read and write syllabics. Beyond basic literacy, however, the missionaries could offer very little because they lacked the means to provide a curriculum-based schooling system that was reliable and staffed with trained teachers. In one of many pieces of correspondence with government officials about the pitiable state of schooling in the Arctic, Dr. A. L. Fleming, Anglican Bishop of the Arctic, described government grants for education as "hopelessly inadequate."

The timing of the letter—1946—coincided with the beginning of the period when the government was turning its attention both to its responsibilities for the well-being of Inuit and to its interest in the economic development of the North.

LEGAL CONTEXT FOR GOVERNMENT INVOLVEMENT IN INUIT EDUCATION

The federal government's decision to direct schooling in Qikiqtaaluk was not the result of a simple evolution of thinking on the part of bureaucrats. It flowed from the Supreme Court of Canada's ruling in 1939 (in a decision commonly referenced as "Re: Eskimos") that Inuit were to be treated as "Indians" under the Indian Act. Prior to this decision, the federal government took advantage of the confusion about its responsibilities for Inuit. Since the 1880s, the government had provided services for "destitute" Inuit in parts of the Arctic through mission schools and medical attention. With an obvious need to deal with infectious diseases in the Arctic, especially tuberculosis, the government amended the Indian Act in 1924 to give the Indian Department responsibility for "Eskimo Affairs." The meaning of the term "Eskimo Affairs" remained undefined, and the government continued to back away from any interpretation that meant that it was responsible for the people themselves. Even after the government transferred responsibility for Inuit affairs to the Northwest Territories Council, the Indian Act made no reference to Inuit.

Into the early 1930s, Inuit across the Arctic were provided with relief from time to time by the Department of the Interior. A dispute between the governments of Canada and Quebec (which was the only province with an Inuit population) about who should be responsible for the costs of assisting destitute Inuit finally reached the Supreme Court of Canada, and led to the 1939 ruling. The federal government immediately appealed to the

Privy Council in London, but the start of the Second World War delayed the case. While the 1939 ruling effectively became law, the federal government carried on delivering a minimal level of services (specifically health, education, and welfare) to Inuit through various agencies without the benefit of a policy or legislative framework specific to Inuit.

During the 1940s, the Second World War focused the government's attention on sovereignty issues, rather than social ones, and the "Re: Eskimo" decision had little effect on the delivery of government services or programs for Inuit. In 1945, however, the responsibility for the health of First Nations and Inuit was transferred to the Department of National Health and Welfare and "'officialdom for the first time publicly recognized the Eskimos as citizens of the Dominion by distributing among them family allowances to which a bill enacted a few months before had entitled all Canadian citizens.'" Such family allowances became representative of the government's national social welfare programs, like health care, which were being developed during the postwar years in lieu of funding charities established by religious organizations.

FEDERAL SCHOOLING

In March 1947, the new deputy minister at the Department of Mines and Resources established a permanent program designed to build community day schools and remove Church influence from schooling across the Arctic. Progress towards both objectives was slow, although by 1950, eight new schools for Inuit were opened in the Northwest Territories and Northern Quebec. As one example, the school at Cape Dorset—the first in Qikiqtaaluk—experienced its share of challenges. Attendance in the school's first two years can be best described as sporadic. Many children in the settlement or surrounding area of Cape Dorset simply did not attend, and a measles outbreak closed the school in early April 1952. Later that year, J.H. Houston conducted a "tent school" near the community, but even this effort only lasted a short time.

As part of the program, the federal government did not just build schools—it ran them. While some church personnel continued to teach at federally funded schools, federally appointed teachers, initially known as welfare teachers, soon outnumbered them. Welfare teachers had responsibilities far beyond their classrooms as they also took over other aspects of the government's relations with individual Inuit, including administration of relief. These multiple roles often took time away from the actual job of teaching. As A. F. Applewhite, the first welfare teacher at Cape Dorset, pointed out to his superiors in 1951, he could not find the time to commit to intensive teaching while the community was also dependent on him to hand out family allowances, repair machinery, and solve other problems as they arose.

At times, the teachers in these early schools were allowed to experiment. Not all stayed in the settlements; some travelled to the ilagiit nunagivaktangit as well. When Margery Hinds arrived in Cape Dorset, she decided to forego the existing schoolhouse in favour of visiting children in their ilagiit nunagivaktangit or waiting for them to arrive at the trading post. She travelled with her own supplies and set up her school in a tent. When she returned to the settlement, she welcomed eager students who came with their parents to have work corrected and new assignments sent out. This type of teaching became known as the Cape Dorset Experiment. Hinds personally opposed hostels or residential schools that required the children to leave their families during their formative years and to miss out on Inuit skills and knowledge that were so important to survival and cultural fulfillment.

In 1952, the Department of Northern Affairs established the Subcommittee on Eskimo Education. The Subcommittee was comprised of government officials and professional educators, as well as senior churchmen who had a strong stake in the old ways of providing northern education. By the mid-1950s, the government began to design services that could only be delivered in a handful of centralized places. Advocates of centralization argued that costly modern health care, communications, transportation, social benefits, economic development, and schooling could only be delivered in a few places—the settlements where staff and facilities would be made available. The northern officials were rightly suspicious of the model provided by Canada's Indian Residential Schools system, and put most of their initial effort into expanding day-school programs for the handful of Inuit already living year-round in settlements and for the larger numbers expected to join them there.

At a 1954 meeting, the Subcommittee on Eskimo Education considered a number of recommendations presented by E. N. Grantham, an inspector and education officer. Following an inspection of school facilities in the Eastern Arctic in the summer of 1954, Grantham made several interesting suggestions, including the creation of a settlement council to deal specifically with issues of education. He proposed that the council be composed of selected Inuit operating under the guidance of Qallunaat leadership. In promotion of this idea, he wrote that, "It may be found in time that Eskimo people themselves have some worthwhile ideas to contribute." It is important to note that this proposal fell far short of an elected school board, and nevertheless, went unrealized. Like Hinds, Grantham believed that education should be adapted to community-specific needs.

Throughout the 1950s, the foremost questions of schooling in the North continued to center on the very real problems of vast distances between settlements, Inuit patterns of seasonal moves, a lack of appropriate knowledgeable and motivated teacher recruits, and the roles of English and Inuktitut languages. Government administrators supported the creation of hostels and a limited number of residential schools. A 1954 report by the Subcommittee referenced the "nomadic character" of Inuit and stated: "The residential school is perhaps the most effective way of giving children from primitive environments experience in education along the lines of civilization leading to vocational training to fit them for occupations in the white man's economy."

The idea of building small or "family-type" hostels was suggested in the Mackenzie District in 1957. There was some early hope these hostels might be community-run, perhaps encouraged in Qikiqtaaluk by the Eskimo Loan Fund, but government ownership became the rule. The benefits of small hostels versus large residential institutions were debated into the early 1960s. Some argued that larger residential schools could perhaps lead to more rapid assimilation. Others noted that small hostels offered the benefits of flexible, community-specific teaching and continued links to family and home life. In the end, the government opted for small hostels for primary students, and planned to move them to larger residential institutions as the first wave of students moved up through the grades.

It was felt that hostels could help boost attendance at day schools by accommodating children whose parents continued to live and hunt on the land. They were also intended to provide a more humane option for younger children than the residential schools forced upon First Nations children in the south. The hostels were staffed by Inuit to emulate a home environment. Mosesee Qappik and his wife testified at the Commission hearings that they supervised children at a hostel in Pangnirtung for three years, beginning in 1964. Mosesee said that, along with his wife, he was responsible for eight children each year and loved them as if they were his own children.

From 1960 to 1964, a rapid construction campaign of both day schools and hostels showed the government's continued uncertainty about how education plans fit with the future of the traditional Inuit economy. Day schools were designed to bring conventional schooling to as many young Inuit as possible, but the hostels were built to allow the older generations, and particularly the parents of pupils in school, to remain on the land. By 1963, there were small hostels serving day schools at Igloolik (twenty-four beds), Cape Dorset (twenty-four beds), Pangnirtung (twenty-four beds), Qikiqtarjuaq (twenty-four beds), Sanikiluaq (twelve beds), and Grise Fiord. Despite the government's intentions, there were early warnings from the communities that the hostels could disrupt the traditional economy. A 1961 RCMP report from Clyde River forecast such trouble:

> [If] the camp Eskimo children started to attend school regularly there could be some trouble with loitering. The main reason for the loitering would be parents being reluctant to leave their children in school, as this would tend to "break up" the family, as the Eskimos refer to the situation. It is felt that most of the trouble would come from the Eskimo mother.

Despite these concerns, a major new school and hostel building program was designed in 1965, and included plans for additional small hostels at Kimmirut (twelve beds), Arctic Bay (twelve beds), Clyde River (twenty-four beds), and Pond Inlet (thirty-six beds), along with a pair of hundred-bed hostels at Pangnirtung and Igloolik. The government completely miscalculated the impact its program would have on Inuit families and mobility patterns. An RCMP officer at Pond Inlet warned that same year that:

> The only foreseen problem in the immediate future . . . will be the mass migration from the camps to the settlements. This has been quite noticeable this year in Pond Inlet . . . This is brought about mainly by the parents wishing to be close to their children, when they leave the camps to attend school in the settlement. Because of the close-knit Eskimo family, this will continue to be a problem, and in the future, I would imagine a very great one. This past year a whole camp moved into the settlement, the only reason given, to be close to their children attending school.

The opening of hostels and day schools sped up the growth of settlements as Inuit parents relocated whole families, and at times, entire ilagiit nunagivaktangit, to be closer to their children attending school. The tight-knit kinship bonds so prevalent in Inuit society simply would not withstand government-imposed separation between parents, children, siblings, grandparents, and extended family members.

Numerous witnesses told the QTC that their decision to relocate to a settlement was driven by separation from school-age children. Within a few years, officials were admitting that the existing hostels were mostly being used for other purposes. Out of thirty-two small hostels in the Arctic District, only twelve were actually in use as pupil residences, the cause being the "very rapid urbanization in the Arctic District settlements." Speaking of his own decision to move from his ilagiit nunagivaktangat to the Pond Inlet community in 1967, Gamailie Kilukishak stated that he decided to move because his eldest child was expected to attend school. Unless the family moved, his son would be living in a hostel. Gamailie explained to the QIA interviewer Davidee Qamaniq, "No one told me [to move], I don't remember being told but because I wanted to follow for the love towards my child and I didn't want to be separated, I voluntarily moved here."

Large hostels were very different from small ones as they typically served large day schools that drew their pupils from many parts of the Northwest Territories. There were no large hostels in Qikiqtaaluk until 1971, when a high school, the Gordon Robertson Educational Centre (GREC), opened in Iqaluit and an old air force barracks became the Ukkivik Residence. This was not the only experience Qikiqtaaluk Inuit had with the larger residential schools, though: previously, some students from Qikiqtaaluk had attended the Joseph Bernier Day School and lived at Turquetil Hall in Chesterfield Inlet. Later, the Churchill Vocational School (CVC) in northern Manitoba offered occupational training for older students from the Eastern Arctic and Nunavik. The opening of Ukkivik and GREC made the closure of CVC possible.

Agents of the federal government, priests, RCMP, or day school teachers generally selected students for residential schools. The anxieties of parents were heightened by the fact that in most cases there was no real consent given to have their children taken to residential schools. Students' feelings of isolation were often magnified by the vast physical distances between themselves and their parents, as well as by the profound social and cultural dislocation that came from being in a foreign location. Ooloosie Kopalie of Qikiqtarjuaq was one of many students from Qikiqtaaluk who was sent to CVC for further academic and vocational training. In a 2005 QIA interview, Kopalie spoke of missing her home during her years at residential school, stating that, "I used to be so homesick because I didn't know the environment, so I used to yearn to return to Paallavvik [the settlement that was her original home]!" The population of Paallavvik, about forty in a typical year, was much smaller than the number of teenagers at CVC.

Other students had more positive experiences, especially at Churchill. This institution brought Inuit students from many communities together where they were directly exposed to emerging ideas about civil rights and anti-colonial movements. The educational and social opportunities at CVC allowed many students to become aware of their political rights, and to receive the education needed to take positions in the territorial government and campaign for land claims. As John Amagoalik of Resolute Bay described:

> The attitude was different, and we had excellent teachers. To this day, we still talk about them … They treated us as ordinary people. We had never experienced this sort of attitude before and it was, in a way, liberating to be with new teachers that treated you as their equal.

GREC, the first secondary school in the Qikiqtaaluk, opened its doors in 1971. While still separating children from families from outside Iqaluit, GREC and its companion hostel, Ukkivik, did offer the advantage of permitting students to remain in the region. For the Government of Canada, GREC provided both a cheaper and administratively easier option, especially when it came to transferring students to and from their home communities. GREC was a junior and senior high school, as well as a vocational school.

GREC earned some respect from Inuit because it was established in an era when courses in traditional Inuit skills and the Inuktitut language began to be offered. However, the high school disappointed and frustrated many Nunavummiut in other respects. GREC was located in Iqaluit, the largest community in the Eastern Arctic, with the highest Inuit and Qallunaat population. Iqaluit had a poor reputation among Inuit as a disorderly community, with problems with violence, drugs, alcohol, and other abuses. Without consultation and without true consent, parents were expected to send their children to reside in this community, and risk exposing them to vices for long periods of time. RCMP authorities also recognized the problems associated with GREC. In a 1973 Inspection Report, A. M. Cart, then Chief Superintendent of G Division, noted that:

> The older Eskimos are experiencing and suffering some disillusionment with what is defined as progress . . . The problem arises when the children are sent to [Iqaluit] to continue in the higher grades. There, they are subjected to outside interests and influences not compatible with their home environment and way of life. When and if they return, many of the older students are changed and create problems because of new attitudes and in some cases due to the inordinate use of alcohol and drugs.

Students from GREC returned to their home communities with tales of violence and disorder, and as a result, dropout rates at the school were high.

It is worth noting the profound cultural differences that were experienced by a small group of students who were involved in the Experimental Eskimo Education Program. As part of this government initiative, a small number of Inuit students considered to be academically gifted were taken out of their communities in the early 1960s and sent to southern Canada. The purpose was both to further their education and to test their ability to compete academically among their southern Canadian counterparts. Some of these students thrived both socially and academically, and acknowledge the positive benefits that resulted from their participation in the program. This included a competitive education that allowed them to eventually return north and take on important leadership roles. Because of their immersion in southern Canadian society, often when these students returned home they proved to be indispensable in helping to bridge the gap between the people of their home communities and government authorities. Many of these students also went on to be trailblazers in fighting for Inuit rights and recognition. For example, Peter Ittinuar, who attended high school in Ottawa for two years, became the first Inuk Member of Parliament in the Canadian House of Commons. Despite his success, Ittinuar also admits that for many the program had mixed results. In his autobiography, he writes that fellow student Zebedee Nungak always said that "he has never regretted the experience, but he has also never recovered from it." The QTC heard from other former students of the Program who spoke of a profound sense of cultural dislocation. Loseeosee Aipellee was made to attend high school in Ottawa from 1963 to 1965, and he described his experience as "traumatizing."

The Commission also heard the story of Jeannie Mike, who was only seven years old when she was sent to school in a small Nova Scotia village, along with two other girls. Mike has little information on her southern school experience. When asked why she was sent away, she responded, "My dad said he was told that we were to go to school, but I don't know the whys and hows and for what purpose." Mike testified that it was only in 2006 that she even discovered that the decision to send her to Nova Scotia was a federal one, and not one made by her parents. In her hearing testimony, she went on to describe her pain:

> Finding out that it was the federal government who had sent us there made me very angry…The hardest part of it was re-integrating back into Inuit society … I came back thinking more like a Qallunaat than an Inuk and people noticed that. I remember being in my

> teens and feeling very isolated because . . . I didn't feel Inuk among the Inuit, and because I looked [Inuk] so I was not accepted by the Qallunaat . . . It was always like trying to walk a fine line between both worlds . . . They might as well have sent me to the moon, because the environment, the culture was so different . . . Sometimes I really wish, I dream of the day that I can sit across from some policymaker within the Government of Canada and say "Here, this is what your policy, and your decision has done to my life."

One of the lasting consequences of her experience was an inability to leave her community again for post-secondary school. Her academic aptitude led her to be taken out of the community, but the trauma she suffered stopped her from ever taking advantage of her schooling or intellectual abilities.

POST-1970: TERRITORIAL TAKEOVER OF EDUCATION

In April 1970, the federal authorities in Ottawa transferred authority for the administration of education in the territories, including Qikiqtaaluk, to the territorial government in Yellowknife. The transfer was part of a general delegation of powers over social programs from the federal to the territorial government. One result of the change was an increased interest in providing Aboriginal "cultural content" in courses in community schools and more proposals to involve parents in choices about education. As McGregor has cautioned, however, these trends did not defeat the administration's respect for traditional southern curricula. In addition, the idea of multiculturalism that was used to justify some experimentation in classrooms was highly inappropriate in parts of the Arctic where the "minority" that was being accommodated was not a minority at all but made up over 90% of the population.

As shown by McGregor, the resulting curriculum incorporated some aspects of Inuit language and culture, while also formally stating that the continuation of traditional Inuit practices should be accommodated through the education system. The accommodation was difficult to achieve, however, because decision-making power about education was still largely in the hands of Qallunaat authorities. A 1974 article by Desmond Sparham, a former settlement manager at Cape Dorset, records signs of change in that particular community by making reference to a "steering committee" of five local Inuit who acted as an advisory board on matters of education. As Sparham went on to acknowledge, much more effort was needed to make education relevant to the entire community. It was only in 1982, with the creation of regional boards of education with greater Inuit representation, that Inuit were finally allowed a more significant role in the decision-making process for education. Even with this change, broader educational policies were still set in Yellowknife, with little community input. To this day, local access to decision-making power remains a challenge of northern education.

The government effort to educate every child in the North, from teachers to classroom methods to curriculums, had profound consequences for Inuit children, families, communities, and culture. Some of these consequences were intentional, and some were not.

Cumulative Impact of Education

The primary goal of government-sponsored education in Qikiqtaaluk was to create good Canadian "citizens." In practice, this meant creating individuals who could adapt and contribute positively to the changing northern environment, in part by learning English, and by becoming employable in the new northern economic ventures. In sum, it required Inuit to assimilate and "catch up" with the practices of the rest of Canadian society. As a government official noted in an internal statement in 1949:

> In this task of interpreting the Canadian way of life, education is certainly the key point. In order that the Eskimo may accomplish the adjustment to civilization successfully, the education set-up must afford understanding of, and practice in, Canadian and democratic ways of living. Development towards citizenship should be the chief criterion in judging the success of our educational program, and other factors such as the development of specific skills or techniques, while important, should be subordinated to this end.

The Department of Northern Affairs attempted to reconcile a standard southern-style curriculum with the protection of Inuit culture, which appears to have meant the capacity to live and work in the North, sustained by some language, folklore, and craft skills. The same 1949 memorandum commented:

> The Northwest Territories Administration has the opportunity to bring these people into civilization without the maladjustment and loss of independence and initiative which have resulted in many parts of the world when a similar task was attempted amongst other primitive races.

However, in spite of the rhetoric and the promise not to divorce Inuit children from their culture, the policy of assimilation seems to have prevailed once the children began schooling.

The first serious debates about curriculum took place in the mid-1950s in connection with the Alberta curriculum used in the Mackenzie District of the Northwest Territories. Further east, teachers were allowed to adapt other provincial curricula. This practice cost the Department nothing, and familiar curriculum smoothed the way to recruiting teachers from the south to work in a challenging natural and social environment. It was also argued that a recognized provincial curriculum would allow Inuit students to pursue further education in the southern provinces. In fact, however, most Inuit students would never study in southern Canada, and if they tried, would find their way blocked because standards were lower in the Arctic than the equivalent grades in the south. Despite these considerations, the curriculum they were being taught had little actual relevance to their lives in the North. This proved especially true in Qikiqtaaluk, where Inuit were even less exposed to southern life and values than their Aboriginal and Inuit counterparts elsewhere in the Northwest Territories.

As early as 1955, there was a recognized need for a northern curriculum that referenced the values and traditions of the North; the problem was that the stated goals of the new curriculum often seemed confusing and even contradictory. In 1955, the contradictions were laid bare in a memorandum from J.V. Jacobson, Superintendent of Education. He described the two main purposes of revisions to the curriculum: "to prepare the pupil to return to his own native way of life" and "to prepare a student for occupations in the white man's economy." To this end, classes in game and conservation were proposed, as well as courses in marksmanship and trapping. These courses were almost never delivered since teachers did not have the skills needed to teach them. In addition to an academic curriculum, vocational training after Grade 7 was offered for those students with less academic interests or abilities. While the motives behind vocational training might have been to give students the skills required to thrive in the evolving north and oncoming wage economy, in some respects vocational training also limited the opportunities available to Inuit youth. By preparing students to enter into the "white man's economy," the government was typically offering students opportunities for manual work, often directed towards the growth of oil exploration or other construction activity. Inuit students were typically trained to be machine operators rather than professionals, managers, business owners, policy analysts, or decision-makers. Vocational training limited the types of opportunities for Inuit as they grew older, especially if manual labour became too difficult. In effect, they were set up to be servants, assistants, or dependents on their own land. It amounted to systemic discrimination.

The Eastern Arctic District curriculum was given even less attention than its counterpart in the Mackenzie District, where there were a greater number of Qallunaat children. Teachers relied on a mixed curriculum from Alberta, Manitoba, Quebec, Ontario, and Newfoundland. Bland materials such as the "Dick and Jane" series of readers repeatedly referenced people and situations that had no relevance to Inuit experiences. In addition to learning to read English, children were expected to learn entirely new concepts and a new worldview. Many who went through the educational system remembered being made to forget their Inuit roots. Speaking to the QIA in Pond Inlet, Kaujak Kanajuk said that he was encouraged to forget his prior life experience. "We weren't allowed to draw dogs or tell stories about them, anything that had something to do with being Inuk, about iglus or anything, as soon as we came [to Pond Inlet]."

The lives of Inuit students and the experiences of those depicted in schoolbooks (as well as the life experiences of the teachers) were worlds apart. Inuit students knew little about farm animals, trains, cities, and wartime. Teachers had no direct experience with Inuit environments or beliefs. In southern Canada, teachers typically shared similar cultural values, language, customs, and connections to location as their students. This was simply not the case in Qikiqtaaluk schools and it did have consequences.

To help bridge the gap between curriculum content and student experience, educational theorists called on teachers to incorporate examples of northern culture in their everyday lesson plans. In a 1961 article entitled, "The Opening Door," R. A. J. Phillips, Chief of the Arctic Division in Ottawa, suggested teaching arithmetic by counting walruses rather than cows, a suggestion that was probably not needed by any competent teacher. Phillips explained that these types of cultural references would reinforce the value of schooling to students. However, he also recognized that northern teachers were expected to teach pride in a culture which they themselves knew very little about. As one former teacher noted, "A lot of teachers tried to incorporate these things [aspects of Inuit life] in the curriculum to the extent that they understood it themselves, which, in most cases, wasn't very much."

Most teachers arrived in the North with a southern education and preconceived ideas about Inuit and what should be taught to them. Experience and orientation, which ranged from one day to two weeks, failed to prepare them for the cultural and language barriers that they encountered and could not overcome. Motives for enlisting were mixed, but experiences were similar. In the early 1960s, Diamond Jenness found that the 30% annual turnover clearly showed the results of hiring people who "seem incapable of enduring the hardships and deprivations of a northern life." He speculated about the roots of the failure:

> [I]ts cause lies deeply rooted in our New World civilization, which demands an educational system that will train our children to earn their livelihood and perhaps enrich their pockets, but does not require that it should simultaneously enrich their minds and their lives . . . A government can easily select well-trained teachers by studying the papers they submit in support of their applications. But how is it to determine whether they possess also the temperaments to rise above the difficulties of an arctic life, and the problems of teaching children who, however lovable, still speak and think in a different tongue?

With teachers staying for only one or two years, students experienced frustration with inconsistent teaching quality, lesson plans that were repeated year after year, and gaps in the curriculum.

One of the solutions that had been proposed since the 1940s to reduce teacher turnover was the training of Inuit as teachers. As one southern Canadian teacher who went north in 1966 reflected, "I think perhaps a lot more value would result in terms of cultural inclusion from having more and more Native people entering the teaching profession, not so much as classroom assistants, but as regular teachers." The vision of indigenous teachers working in the classroom would not be realized until years later. The Northwest Territories Teacher Education Program was established in 1968 with the goal of increasing First Nations and Inuit staff in schools. This program was supposed to improve communication between teachers and students, increase Aboriginal employment, and improve teacher retention and continuity in the schools. The program received substantial investments throughout the 1970s, but only succeeded in training Inuit as teachers' assistants, not as teachers. In addition, differences in objectives and issues over curriculum between the various parts of the Territory plagued the program, resulting in the creation of a separate Eastern Teacher Education Program in Iqaluit in 1979.

It is important to note, however, that Inuit teachers were intended to solve staffing problems, not to provide Inuktitut instruction. Few, if any, teachers could have taught Inuit children in their own language. Unlike the missionary teachers before them who needed to speak Inuktitut to proselytize, government teachers conducted their work in English. Typically, they lived separate from the Inuit community and socialized with other Qallunaat—nurses, government administrators, and RCMP officers.

For both practical and ideological reasons, English-language instruction was the foundation of the curriculum. For the most part, Inuit were very eager to have their children learn English and looked forward to the benefits of these programs as they were promised by government administrators. As remembered by one Inuk parent, Taqtu:

> Later on the children had to go to school, which was all right too—they had to learn if they were not going to be staying out in camp. They had to take jobs, which was also all right. There was really no choice, and I accepted it gladly because our children had to learn.

> I wanted them to learn English so that they can have good jobs when they [grew up].

The practical obstacles to bringing Inuktitut into classrooms were addressed in 1964 by the Director of the Northern Administration Branch:

> [W]e simply are not equipped to have Eskimo language teaching in the schools. We have far too few teachers with a command of the Eskimo language to make it possible for them to teach the language, and we still must wait several years before there is a body of Eskimos who have had time for sufficient education to pursue teaching careers.

While the lack of Inuit language delivery was recognized as a major factor inhibiting the success of Inuit students, no language-training programs, even at a basic level, existed for teachers (then and in 2013). In fact, the Department openly discouraged the use of Inuktitut in the classroom. As one former teacher recalled that at his orientation for northern teaching he was advised not to learn Inuktitut by Gordon Devitt, the District Superintendent of Schools. The former teacher stated that Devitt cautioned:

> 'Don't you dare learn Eskimo—that would be the worst thing you could possibly do.' The children would have no incentive to learn English because they would know that even though you weren't going to speak to them in the classroom in Eskimo, you could understand them anyway and have that crutch, so there would be no real impetus for them to learn English.

Another teacher who had taught in Kimmirut confirmed this statement:

> It was [the] policy of the department at that time that there was to be no native language used—you had to use English as much as possible—and to drive to get the English language skills there. And I'll admit it on tape that we didn't follow the policy if we thought it was to the benefit of the kid if we used his language. We used interpreters if we had to and the older kids helped.

Many teachers accepted the departmental preference and forbade the use of Inuktitut both in and out of the classroom. For some, it was a way to "civilize" the child. A number of former students testified to the QTC about physical and mental abuse when they were unable to learn English quickly enough, or when they used Inuktitut among their own peers. Cape Dorset resident Quppirualuk Padluq remembered: "It was very scary to speak in Inuktitut because we were punished if we spoke in Inuktitut unexpectedly. Our teacher always told us not to speak any Inuktitut whatsoever in class." Geela Akulukjak of Pangnirtung wept as she related the story of her abuse:

> I was told to go to school here and tried my best to go to school. Ever since then I was scared of Qallunaat because a teacher I had would slap me, would slap the children who could not speak English, with a ruler stick, with a yardstick; she was a woman. That always hurts me, because I couldn't speak English, she forced us to be able to speak English.

July Papatsie also testified about similar abuse she experienced in the same school:

> Children who spoke Inuktitut were punished. I remember their first punishment: they had to put their hands on the desk and got twenty slaps on the back of their hand. The second time they got thirty slaps on their bare bum in front of all the class. They were

> forced to eat a bar of soap. They would throw up for two to three days. They were told that it was because they spoke an evil language.

The frequency of corporal punishment was especially traumatic, since spanking was rarely used in Inuit culture and young children were typically treated gently and showered with affection.

The extent to which Inuktitut was deliberately suppressed as a means of acculturation is difficult to establish with certainty. In 1967, for the *Edmonton Journal*, Robert Williamson, an elected representative to the Council of the Northwest Territories and a former federal bureaucrat, described the federal government's previous position that Inuktitut "should be allowed to die" as both "prevalent" and "abhorrent." The author of the article also stated that, "One of the most serious charges filed against the federal government's territories education system is its refusal to recognize [Inuktitut] as a language in school."

Even if the intentions were not clearly stated, it was predictable that children were more likely to lose proficiency if they did not use a language at an early age. The impact of the loss of Inuktitut through continuous exposure to English was intensified by changes in what children ate or how they dressed when they attended school. This was particularly true for children in large hostels.

Students at residential schools were steered away from eating country food, such as raw meats that were a staple of the Inuit diet. The government often stated that it wanted to eliminate the risk of trichinosis, but it continued to provide all types of meats common to Qallunaat diets, such as pork, that needed to be cooked.

Staff at the large hostels also threw away the children's traditional clothing when providing them with school uniforms. Similar pressures existed at the day schools in Qikiqtaaluk. As Elizabeth Kyak of Pond Inlet testified to the QTC in 2008, "When we were going to school, if there was a blizzard in winter and we go to school with wind pants on, we were slapped and sent to go home and go put on a skirt, in a blizzard we would go home, change to a skirt." Elizabeth went on to recall how members of her community attempted to maintain some of their traditional ways of life, even when discouraged from doing so. Speaking specifically to the issue of food, Elizabeth testified:

> The Inuit were encouraged not to eat traditional foods back then . . . They used to hide if they were eating quaq, [or other] traditional food . . . If they heard somebody coming in, they would hide it right away because they were encouraged not to eat traditional foods. If a white man was coming in, they'd sneak around, they would pretend they were not eating.

Despite some of the children's best efforts to hold onto their culture, what often resulted was a deep cultural and generational divide between students away at school and their parents, as well as further diminishment of the value of Inuit knowledge. Children who had lost the ability to speak in Inuktitut could no longer communicate with parents, grandparents, or other adults who knew little to no English. Children who were raised in schools with southern foods and values went home and questioned, challenged, criticized, or denigrated their parents' customs and values. Furthermore, the knowledge of Elders was perceived as outdated, unnecessary, or uncivilized. This new cultural divide often proved hard to repair. In the words of former residential school student Paul Quassa, "We lost that knowledge that would have been transferred if we did grow up with our parents." All formal schooling, especially residential schooling, disrupted traditional family life. These changes had a profound impact and contributed to a sense of confusion regarding traditional gender roles and identity within Inuit culture.

In the 1970s, as Inuit gained representation in the territorial legislative council in Yellowknife and the Council took charge of educational policy, community leaders in the Eastern Arctic became articulate critics of the school system, demanding local control. Sympathetic Qallunaat shared these ideas and offered an even more fundamental denunciation. Language teacher Mick Mallon wrote in 1977:

> Our school system is alien not only because it has been developed and is being run by non-Inuit: it is alien because it is a system. There were no places in traditional Inuit culture where children were herded together for a set number of hours a day to learn how to become functioning adults; there was no sub-set of adults who devoted their lives to instruction ... To put it as extremely as possible: the mere building of a school could be said to be an alien act of cultural aggression.

As Mallon implied, Inuit parents had very little opportunity to provide input into questions of curriculum, language, teaching methodology, teachers, or the location of their children's education. Nonetheless, they were often very receptive to change. Inuit parents were optimistic that the promises about the quality and value of Canadian education as explained by government officials would come true. They knew by observation and their own experience that inability to speak English was a drawback economically. The receptiveness of Inuit to change, and their ability to adapt to changing circumstances, emerged clearly in research at Iqaluit sponsored by the Department in 1963. John J. and Irma Honigmann published *Eskimo Townsmen* after six months of intensive observation, and noted that in almost every area of life, Inuit "have successfully, often easily, learned much new behaviour, many tastes, and increasing responsibilities." The Honigmanns went on to attribute their millennia of survival in the Arctic to this ability to adapt and learn. They also noted that some of the children with the best school attendance records came from the most traditional families.

However, even parents who let their children be educated by the government did not understand the full extent of cultural loss that would result. Many parents believed that knowledge and culture could be sustained in spite of formal schooling. The demands of classrooms and hostels challenged all assumptions. In the end, Inuit parents were denied the fundamental right to have their children educated in accordance with some of their own cultural beliefs and values. For some parents, the guilt over sending their children away for education remains to this day. Speaking to the QTC in 2008, Louis Uttak of Igloolik described his deep regret:

> I hate myself for agreeing to send my children out to Chesterfield Inlet. I am sorry I was not smart at that time, smart enough to know what I had to do. It was good for a while; our children started learning another culture. We tried to be parents to them, but they were growing up so they changed too. The parenting part then was broken and we didn't know how to fix it. But the two cultures, the Qallunaat and the Inuit culture, are so different from each other, so they were using this culture and we couldn't quite be in contact with them anymore.

In some cases, Inuit children returned home and asked their parents how they could have agreed to send them away from their families and allow them to have been abused. Years after dealing with the trauma of being sent away for school at age seven, Jeannie Mike recalled for the QTC a confrontation with her mother. Looking at her own children at seven years old, Jeannie stated she felt compelled to ask her mother, "How could you let me go?" In response her mother replied, "when Qallunaat asked for something there [was] no choice of refusal."

These mothers were not alone in offering little or no resistance when government authorities ordered them to send their children away to school. There are reasons to explain this appearance of submitting to authority. The first reason is a concept named by Inuit as "ilira." Ilira can be described as "a great fear or awe," and Inuit use it to describe the feelings that they once held towards Qallunaat. This sense of fear or awe made even the notion of questioning the authority of RCMP officers or government administrators unthinkable to Inuit, especially during the period in question. Furthermore, Qallunaat, for the most part, projected an air of absolute authority, and most Inuit did not have a sufficient understanding of southern Canadian society or their own rights to challenge them. In describing her experience with the RCMP, Mary Battye of Pangnirtung stated, "The Qallunaat would go to the camps. We were scared even though they didn't do anything wrong . . . We went out of our way to do our best because we were so scared of the RCMP." When Elisapee Ootoova was a young child, she felt these same anxieties around Qallunaat. Ootoova recalls seeing RCMP officers, Hudson's Bay Company (HBC) staff, and Anglican and Catholic priests while in Pond Inlet. She remembers, "It seems they were really scary, and they were so clean, they smelled so clean, and very tidy. We used to sit very still when we were visiting." She also went on to describe Qallunaat in the Grise Fiord area as being very "bossy" and "controlling." Based on these past experiences, Ootoova says that she completely "caved in" when it came time to send her own children to Churchill for an education.

Parents also told the QTC and QIA that they were threatened with the loss of Family Allowance payments if they refused to send their children to school or move into settlements. Family Allowance payments began across Canada in 1945. Payments generally ranged between $5.00 and $8.00 per month, depending on the age and number of children per family. In the North, as in the South, family allowance was intended to promote the nourishment and general well-being of children. However, in the North, paternalism was also ingrained into this program. Payments were used to force parents to send their children away to be educated or to force entire families to permanently move into settlements. By 1950, many Inuit families relied heavily upon these payments, especially when hunting or trapping was poor. The threat of having payments cut off was taken very seriously. As Peterosie Qarpik stated at the QIA hearings in 2005, his own move to Pangnirtung was motivated by a government agent:

> We started to be told that our children needed an education and they said that if we did not agree, they would stop paying us the child tax and we felt we had no choice but to move here to Pangnirtung. We felt we had no choice as we had some children and that was our only income. It was like they were trying to scare us using the money that we received.

Likewise, Annie Paingut Peterloosie moved her family to Arctic Bay for related reasons:

> We moved because the children had to go to school, we were told that if we didn't move we would not be receiving any child tax benefits, that time we were receiving children benefits when we were still in the camp, and we moved so that we would not lose the money we were getting.

Similarly, many families were also offered housing, either free or at a fixed low rate, as an added inducement to moving to settlements and putting their children in day schools. Many people also testified that housing promises went unfulfilled, as the QTC report *Igluliriniq: Housing in Qikiqtaaluk, 1950–1975* explains in more detail.

For their part, local administrators in the North and RCMP officers saw the threat of suspended Family Allowances as one of their only effective tools for getting parents to send their children to school. While the Family Allowance Act did require that children be in school in order to receive payment, there was never an official policy sanctioning its suspension in isolated settlements. Nevertheless, the government was aware that this practice was used by local officials as an "economic hammer," as Milton Freeman described in his QTC testimony.

In the 1950 to 1975 period, public schools in Qikiqtaaluk gave the luckiest students, including many Inuit leaders, access to new knowledge and skills, while also retaining Inuktitut language skills and remaining fully in touch with Inuit knowledge and practices. When this happened, however, the school system played no part—it was due to the efforts of Elders, parents, and individual teachers, or to exceptional personal strengths. The overwhelming result of the government education programs and policies was failure in terms of the number of children who enjoyed school, maintained a sense of community and family, and found ways to apply the knowledge learned to daily life and material well-being.

Many parents in Qikiqtaaluk were convinced by government administrators to give up their children for schooling with the promise that the end result would be both a good education and a chance to participate fully in future opportunities in the North. In the early 1950s and 1960s, parents were optimistic that government-provided education would resolve some of the challenges of living in settlements, even though they were always reluctant to leave children in small hostels or allow them to be sent to residential schools.

Evidence of Inuit resistance to formal schooling and its impact on Inuit language and culture is present over and over again in archival records and in the testimonies to the QTC. The top-down method of managing schools and setting policies, however, meant that parents had little or no influence on the way children were taught or how formal education was integrated with Inuit culture and language. The testimonies of Inuit at the QIA and QTC hearings showed how damaging and long-lasting the effects of these practices have been. Through tears, former students spoke of cultural dislocation and confusion, of abuse, and of missing their homes. Parents spoke of the horrors of watching their own children be taken away, of feeling forced to choose between a livelihood on the land, or a move to the settlement if only to be near their children. Together, they spoke of losing their traditions and practices, maintained so strongly in generations before.

Inuit community leaders and political leaders in the 1970s were very vocal about the problems with the education system (controlled by then in Yellowknife) and its assimilation objectives. They sought to secure a role

for Elders in the classroom, and asked that more grades be offered in communities so only older students would need to go to Iqaluit. Even with these changes, however, the underlying school curriculum and administration was based on English-language instruction and a standardization of approaches across the Territory.

Reasons for the poor results of government schooling efforts and the suffering they caused among several generations in Qikiqtaaluk include inadequate funding, a lack of serious commitment towards curriculum development, no strategy for training Inuit teachers, and hostility towards the use of Inuktitut and Inuit culture. The government aimed to change Inuit through formal education for a wage economy, so that, in the eyes of the government, Inuit would be like other Canadian citizens. At best, the government failed to provide an appropriate standard of education to achieve this goal. However, more devastatingly, the government imposed unquestioned Eurocentric values and, in the process, marginalized Inuit. Changes in education were brought too quickly and too forcefully. Attempts to consult Inuit about how they would like their values represented within their own education system came too late and were imperfect.

SCHOOLS IN QIKIQTAALUK
1962, 1970, 1979

Place	**1962**			**1970**		
	Teachers	**Students**	**Grades**	**Teachers**	**Students**	**Grades**
Arctic Bay	1	13	1 to 4	3	66	1 to 6
Cape Dorset	3	76	1 to 6	9	163	1 to 8
Clyde River	1	37	1 to 5	3	79	1 to 6
Grise Fiord	1	20	1	2	31	1 to 6
Hall Beach	No school			3	57	1 to 6
Igloolik	3	50	1 to 5	8	187	1 to 6
Iqaluit	16	237	1 to 10	35	572	1 to 10
Iqaluit – GREC						
Iqaluit – Nakasuk						
Iqaluit – Nanook						
Kimmirut	No school			2	61	1 to 6
Nanisivik	-	-	-	-	-	-
Paallavvik	1	15	1	School closed 1968		
Pangnirtung	2	59	1 to 6	10	198	1 to 6
Pond Inlet	1	34	1 to 6	6	117	K to 8
Port Burwell	Not reported			2	36	K to 6
Qikiqtarjuaq	2	34	1 to 3	5	97	1 to 8
Resolute Bay	1	26	1 to 6	3	51	1 to 7
Sanikiluaq (Belcher Islands)	1	18	1 to 5	No Report; not in Baffin Region in 1970		

SCHOOLS IN QIKIQTAALUK
1962, 1970, 1979

Place	1979			
	Teachers	Students	Grades	Hostel
Arctic Bay	6	114	K to 8	-
Cape Dorset	11	220	K to 9	-
Clyde River	6	123	K to 8	-
Grise Fiord	1	26	K to 8	-
Hall Beach	5	121	K to 8	-
Igloolik	13	290	K to 9	-
Iqaluit	See below – separate schools			92
Iqaluit – GREC	22	312	7 to 12	-
Iqaluit – Nakasuk	23	379	K to 6	-
Iqaluit – Nanook	4	66	K to 6	-
Kimmirut	4	76	K to 8	-
Nanisivik	3	70	K to 8	-
Paallavvik	School closed 1968			
Pangnirtung	16	322	K to 10	-
Pond Inlet	9	204	K to 9	-
Port Burwell	Not reported			
Qikiqtarjuaq	6	130	K to 8	-
Resolute Bay	3	59	K to 8	-
Sanikiluaq (Belcher Islands)	6	115	K-8	-

Nuutauniq

Moves in Inuit Life

Mobility has always been part of Inuit culture. Anthropologist Hugh Brody explains that "hunting families travel familiar routes and reoccupy sites that have been important to their people for generations. The seasonal rounds occupy grooves of cultural history, and draw upon archives of experience and knowledge." For the Qikiqtaalungmiut, the seasonal cycle of harvesting that naturally took advantage of weather conditions, animal migrations and cultural linkages continued into the mid-twentieth century. After that, the nature of Inuit mobility changed dramatically.

This chapter is focused on government-supported or -directed relocations and migrations between 1950 and 1975. Some moves were coerced, and others were voluntary. The chapter draws on the archival record to describe many of the dates, policies, and objectives of government programs that expedited moves. The human dimension—the effects of these moves on peoples' lives—is told in the words of witnesses appearing before the QTC,

statements collected by the Qikiqtani Inuit Association (QIA), and from various research studies.

Moves between 1950 and 1975 affected all Qikiqtaalungmiut. Every Inuk who appeared before the QTC experienced a long separation from family members because of relocations, medical evacuations, or schooling. The QTC heard about the lingering effects of unexpected moves by a previous generation. Each move added to the harmful impact of individuals being separated from family and from the cultural practices that were central to a worldview rooted in their land and its resources.

This chapter examines three types of events: the moving of groups, the moving of individuals, and the closing of communities. Within each event type, the moves can be categorized in terms of motives. Relocation describes the planned movement of people to a location that has been chosen by an external agent. Migration refers to moves carried out by Inuit themselves in a manner that appeared to be voluntary or motivated by enticements. Dislocation refers to coerced moves undertaken by Inuit who felt pressure from Qallunaat, usually government representatives, to move either permanently or for a specific reason. Evacuation refers to the temporary movement of people by government in real or perceived emergencies.

Concepts

CONSENT

To consent means to agree to something. As a legal concept, consent can be either expressed or implied. However, it is real consent only if it is given voluntarily and with a full understanding of the proposed action and its possible effect—the greater the risks or impacts, the greater the need to obtain real consent.

Cross-cultural challenges affected consent, which explains why officials often thought a pressured "dislocation" was a voluntary "migration." Yet it is also clear that many Inuit chose to move off the land from their ilagiit nunagivaktangit because they believed life in the settlement would prove to be a positive experience, as they were repeatedly told by government and by some Inuit already working in settlements. In the words of Gene Rheaume, active as both a civil servant and a politician in the period, "It was [sometimes] a subtle pressure, but it was coming at you from everywhere." People on the move expected any sacrifices they made to benefit their families. Inuit were explicitly promised access to housing, health care, schools, and wage employment. The reality, however, was often much harsher than they could have imagined, especially during the first years in a settlement. Even over time, improvements were slow or not fully realized.

Southern agents, such as government staff, RCMP, missionaries, nurses, or ship stewards, involved in moves might have believed Inuit consented because they never said, "No, I will not go." Inuit sometimes expressed disagreement with silence or by withdrawing, and this may have been mistaken by Qallunaat as compliance. Inuit consent, however, was likely a culturally determined way of dealing with Qallunaat. To an Inuk, Qallunaat appeared to be demanding consent, not asking for it. During the QTC hearings, Commissioner Igloliorte asked Gordon Rennie, a former HBC Manager, "Did anybody ever question you personally or did anybody ever question the dog laws in those days at the time when the dogs were running loose?" Rennie replied, "They wouldn't dare." He went on to explain, "Nobody questioned me . . . I was a person in authority then." This obedience happened within an established power relationship and psychological context Inuit call "ilira." Ilira can be explained as powerful social fear or inhibition caused by inequality in power. In her 1993 essay, Rosemary Kuptana explained that a generation or two earlier "a challenge to the authority of the Qallunaat or defiance of their requests was almost unthinkable."

The capacity of government to obtain consent was complicated by ilira, other cross-cultural non-verbal factors, and by the difficulty of delivering services in Qikiqtaaluk. For a variety of reasons, administrators could not adequately predict all the possible outcomes of their plans. Instead, they usually made optimistic forecasts that failed to come true. Qikiqtaalungmiut were geographically isolated from decision-makers, and those who planned the moves neglected—or were ignorant of—Inuit cultural practices that would be harmed. Language barriers and other intercultural communication challenges also made it very hard to get valid consent before moves. After interviewing many Elders in 2008, anthropologist Ann McElroy explained that "it is difficult at times to reconstruct whether a family's move should be categorized as relocation or as voluntary migration." In addition, she noted, the reasons people moved to a town were often not the same as the reasons they stayed there.

KINSHIP AND PLACE

In order to understand how all types of moves affected Inuit, we need to first understand the importance of both kinship and place in their worldview. Inuit kinship systems are different from those in European/Western cultural traditions. As explained by Christopher Trott, the concept of ilagiit (kindred) is based on the root ila, which simply means "to be with" or "accompany." For Inuit, families are the combined result of birth, circumstance, and choice. Kinship has practical implications for security, psychological well-being, hunting, sharing food and material resources, intra- and intergroup relations, education of children, and leadership.

The interconnectedness of kinship and place is central to the Inuit worldview. Cultural geography professor Robert Williamson explained to the Royal Commission on Aboriginal Peoples (RCAP) how difficult it must be for an Inuk to leave the places associated with his or her kin:

> Every geographic feature . . . has names and the name is a metaphor for the totality of the group remembrance of all forms of land relatedness, of the successes and failures in hunting, it recalls births, deaths, childhood, marriage, death, adventure. It recalls the narrations and the ancient sanctified myths.

As Inuit travel across the land, sea, and ice, they strengthen their relationships with each other and deepen their understanding of their own pasts and kin.

Qallunaat often mistook and continue to mistake the semi-nomadic history of Inuit as evidence of a lack of attachment to place. In fact, the ability to move to follow game while also maintaining connections with kin who live over a wide geographic area is the result of an intimate experience of place. Williamson insisted, "The attention to this habitat is as strong as the attachment of kinship. It is a love of a very profound kind."

COMMUNITY AND MOBILITY

In 1950, Qikiqtaalungmiut inhabited over one hundred ilagiit nunagivaktangit seasonally. By 1975, almost all were concentrated in the present twelve hamlets and one city. This revolution in where and how Inuit lived has been called by various names, including relocation, in-gathering, settlement, and centralization. Inuit reasons for moving from a nomadic pattern that was a thousand years old to an experiment with modern living are often debated. Some observers argue that the change was necessary and beneficial, and was embraced willingly. Others emphasize the cultural loss, disappointment, and coercion that marked this period of disruption and tarnish its legacy.

Today, almost all Nunavummiut live in hamlets of 130 to 1,459 people. The city of Iqaluit has a current population of 6,699, and is growing by almost 300 each year. Even the smallest of these communities is more populous than the biggest year-round settlements before 1950. There are both local and external reasons for the locations of these communities. Ten of the thirteen present-day community sites in Qikiqtaaluk were chosen before 1950, mainly by RCMP, missionaries, and trading companies. These became administrative centres for regional management and delivery of services. Each place is on saltwater and is accessible by ships or large boats at least once a year. From 1909 onwards, the Hudson's Bay Company (HBC), with a near monopoly, aimed to have a single trading post in each productive hunting area. Inuit dispersed as widely as possible from each post, while leaving no gaps for competing traders to exploit. The RCMP and missions followed the HBC, so that when modern centralized communities emerged, they were reasonably convenient for both water transport and availability of game. Today game remains dispersed, but people are concentrated in a few places.

Before 1950, there were many different types of inhabited places. Official reports usually referred to "settlements" and "camps," but both terms are debatable. What Qallunaat called settlements were the places where outside agencies, always including the HBC, maintained a few small wooden buildings to provide lodging and storage space for the handful of Qallunaat who lived there. These settlements could more correctly be called enclaves. While a few employed Inuit and their families may have lived there, these enclaves were surrounded and heavily outnumbered by Inuit. Although dispersed, Inuit were much more permanent and continuous in their use and occupancy of the land than Qallunaat.

In 1944, a semi-official map of "Eskimo Camp Sites" by geographer J. Lewis Robinson, noted the "White Settlement" as his first category of inhabited places. The map outlined the different ways in which multi-family Inuit hunting groups lived on the land in "usual" or "occasional" summer ilagiit nunagivaktangit and winter ilagiit nunagivaktangit.

Robinson did not include weather stations and small defence establishments, where a handful of Inuit families settled temporarily and were paid for domestic labour and other chores. These were neither true settlements nor communities. However, they did sometimes provide a range of services coupled with hunting opportunities, and they did give some Inuit an experience of the cash economy for a limited time.

The rich expression ilagiit nunagivaktangat communicates the importance of kinship among people who share a community, and the permanent relationship they have with the land. Both of these values were threatened by centralization, which gathered into larger communities large numbers of people who were almost strangers to each other, far from the places to which they were most attached.

When Inuit moved into modern communities or hamlets, they also lost the flexibility and purposeful seasonal movements that were part of their culture until the middle of the twentieth century. Robinson's list of seasonal settlement types partially describes Inuit mobility and seasonal rounds. However, it does not illustrate the social dynamics within extended kin groups, which could form, dissolve, and re-form over time within their distinct but overlapping hunting territories. Movements in periods of disruption were also purposeful, though risky. A Scottish writer stated in 1841, early in the whaling era, that Inuit from Cumberland Sound migrated long distances to meet the ships, "impelled by curiosity, and animated by the hope of traffic [i.e. trade]." This was essentially the same explanation that an Iqaluit Elder offered for why her family came to Iqaluit in the 1950s: "When someone finds plentiful amounts of something, like work or food, they come to get it." Qallunaat in the twentieth century often misunderstood such Inuit movements. Their hasty observations suggested that Inuit were not especially attached to their local surroundings and that they were so adaptable they could easily move from a familiar place to a strange and distant one. These mistaken prejudices and beliefs gave rise to the government policy of moving Inuit around, which sometimes led to distress and injustice.

In this report, we use the conventional word "settlements" for the small enclaves around trading posts before centralization occurred. The term "community" is used more flexibly. Before centralization, it describes all the members of multi-family hunting groups in a region. After centralization, we use "community" to describe the places where pre-1950 "settlements" had grown into larger service centres with mostly Inuit populations. The relationship between present-day communities, the settlements where they were founded, and the people of the traditional territories that surround them, differs from place to place.

Moved Groups

THE DUNDAS HARBOUR RELOCATIONS

The Dundas Harbour relocations (1934–47) are early examples of government-directed moves of Inuit. While the relocations fall outside the QTC's time frame, they appear in this chapter because they demonstrate a pattern of government practice. Inuit were moved because the government generalized that all Inuit were semi-nomadic hunters who could live anywhere in the Arctic. It neglected the subtle nuances of regional identity, differing seasons, terrain, linguistics, wildlife, geography, food preferences, technological adaptations, and survival strategies. Despite the specialization of culture within specific regions, the government transferred Inuit to areas where they had inadequate knowledge of animal patterns or environmental conditions.

In 1934, Dundas Harbour was an abandoned RCMP post located on the southern shore of Devon Island, in the High Arctic. It lies within a region set aside in 1926 by the Canadian government as the Arctic Islands Game Preserve (AIGP) for sovereignty and wildlife preservation reasons. The HBC wished to establish trading posts in the southern parts of the Preserve, while the government wanted to experiment with inducing Inuit to occupy more northern areas, including Devon Island. The HBC agreed to operate a trading post at Dundas Harbour, importing Inuit to hunt and trap there, in exchange for government permission to re-open a post at Arctic Bay. The government's motives were complex. Reopening Dundas Harbour made a sovereignty statement at little or no expense to Canada, and also brought Inuit to an unpopulated area from more southerly locations that were considered to be overhunted. Crucially, the agreement made the HBC responsible for the welfare of any Inuit it relocated. Additionally, the agreement stipulated that "in the event of the company withdrawing from Devon Island the company agrees to return the natives to their homes at its own expense or to transfer them to such other trapping grounds as may be designated by the Department."

In August 1934, the HBC ship R.M.S. *Nascopie* picked up fifty-two people and one hundred and nine qimmiit from Cape Dorset, Pangnirtung, and Pond Inlet, along with a seasoned HBC clerk, Chesley Russell. The different parties were transferred together to Dundas Harbour, where they were expected to trap and trade for at least the next two years. The relocation was a failure. The harbour was choked with rough ice and proved exceptionally difficult to navigate in the small boats available. The HBC post closed after two years and the *Nascopie* returned to pick up the relocatees. The families from Pangnirtung were returned home (the last port of call for the homebound *Nascopie*), but the others were transferred to Admiralty Inlet. In 1937, some of these people were moved southwestward to the HBC's new Fort Ross post on Bellot Strait. This also proved difficult to resupply, and the group was moved yet again in 1947, south to Taloyoak on the Boothia Peninsula. In a dozen years, these people were relocated four times. Some eventually returned to Arctic Bay.

Years later, a senior official, R.A.J. Phillips, remarked that the "thirteen-year-long resettlement project was a heavy burden to the Hudson's Bay Company." Phillips called the whole experience a "tragedy" and said that the Inuit were in theory volunteers, but "the story of free will and Eskimo decision-making could not withstand careful examination." Ethnographer David Damas, using official HBC records, documented an unsuccessful effort by the Fort Ross hunters to migrate to Kimmirut in the 1940s, evidence that not all was entirely well on Somerset Island. These opinions (of an official and an academic) conflict with that of Ernie Lyall, who helped organize the 1934 migration for the HBC and married into one of the Cape Dorset migrant families. Lyall emphasized that people were very willing to go to Dundas Harbour and that they were generally satisfied with Arctic Bay, Fort Ross, and Taloyoak. With no agreement among those involved directly in the move and a researcher looking critically at the historic record, it is particularly important to consider the testimony of a survivor and of certain descendants.

Susan Singoorie of Pond Inlet, now living in Ottawa, is one of the still-living Dundas Harbour relocatees. She accompanied her parents to Dundas Harbour when she was eight years old. More than seventy-five years later, she shared her experiences with the QTC:

> We set camp on the other side. We experienced a lot of cold. We were just in a tent. There was no snow to build iglus there. It became very windy. Before the ice melted, we would move by dog team and my mother walked well. They were not hungry because there was lots of wildlife up there. Once, the tent was drooping from the cold. We used only qulliit for heat and light. Once it became very windy. We could not keep the camp because it was so windy in the tent. We started walking, my father tied up ropes around our waists. We would stand for a long time. It was very painful. I wanted to share my experience with you. When we got to the RCMP shed, we were brought to the HBC store and we all stayed in there. It was crowded. Once ice set in we started moving again. Once we got an iglu built, it seemed to be so much warmer.

Others testified about the Dundas Harbour relocation on behalf of deceased relatives. Rhoda Tunraq told the Commission about her parents' move to Dundas Harbour and about her mother's feelings for Devon Island:

> They were living in Arctic Bay when they were moved to Devon Island. Then they got used to Devon Island. After a while they were happy there as a family. When they moved back to Arctic Bay, the families were dying off even while they were living here. There is a saying in Inuktitut that they "cut off the life" so I feel that they were cut short in their life. My mother used to say that. [Interviewee too emotional to talk] My mother was never happy because she always spoke about being homesick for Devon Island.

Those who were moved and their descendants felt the effects of the relocations for generations. Some longed for the rest of their lives for their families and ancestral lands. Tagoona Qavavouq told the Commission that her mother-in-law Ajau went "insane" after the relocations and died prematurely. She explained to Commissioner Igloliorte:

> When the Elders are moved to a different area, when they return home, they can heal and feel better when they return home. Because they came from Cape Dorset, they were like orphans here. They were different, being different people from a different land, people did not really communicate with them in the same way. We always feel it, those of us who are the wives.

Others, like Pauloosie Kaujak, who spoke to their children and grandchildren about one day returning to Cape Dorset, have since passed away.

The Dundas Harbour relocations were the first example of a Canadian government relocation program. It is striking that the government partnered with a private company, putting all the risk on the HBC and the Inuit.

As a result of the relocations, the relocatees became increasingly dependent on the HBC. With no way home and no strong kinship support network in place, the relocatees had no choice but to adapt and accept their situation. The legacy of the relocations continues on both the northern and southern coasts of Baffin Island, especially in Cape Dorset, Arctic Bay, Grise Fiord, Pond Inlet, and Resolute. The children and grandchildren of those relocated, while closely connected to their current communities, want to learn more about family members living in other communities and experience the land that sustained their ancestors.

THE HIGH ARCTIC RELOCATIONS

While the QTC's mandate excludes investigation of the High Arctic Relocations, the events cannot be ignored in a report on the history of mobility and Inuit life. Inuit were expected to be adaptable, but insufficient resources provided for the relocation and poor planning created further hardships for the relocatees. Additionally, Inuit were insufficiently informed about the moves and the possible consequences.

Planning for the move started in 1950. The plan originally developed with the dual purpose of moving Inuit from regions thought by government to be short of game, especially in Nunavik, and strengthening Canada's claim in the Arctic Islands. Families from Nunavik would be relocated to the established present community of Grise Fiord on Ellesmere Island, where game conditions were thought to be better. The plan was also considered an experiment to determine whether Inuit could actually be induced to live on the northern islands. Throughout the planning stages, there was concern that the "experiment" might not work and that Inuit from Inukjuak might not be able to thrive so far north.

Alexander Stevenson, an experienced officer with the department responsible for northern affairs, sought to confirm that people had volunteered and that they were satisfied with the conditions. In her detailed study of the High Arctic Relocations titled *A Case of Compounded Error*, Shelagh D. Grant writes, "Arriving at Inukjuak long before the departure date, [Stevenson] sought reassurance that the Inuit fully understood the situation. He was only able to find 'two hunters,' but was satisfied that they were fully cognizant of the details." Grant's careful analysis of the relocations includes her important observation that "there is no mention of questioning women or children." It was assumed that the men could speak for everyone.

During the summer of 1953, seven families from Inukjuak, Nunavik, and three families from Pond Inlet on Baffin Island were sent to Cornwallis and Ellesmere Islands aboard the Arctic supply and hospital ship *C. D. Howe*. Upon arrival at Craig Harbour on Ellesmere Island, the groups were broken up. Some were to be offloaded at Craig Harbour, while others were to be moved to Alexandra Fiord or the military weather station at Resolute. The first warning that they would be forcibly separated came aboard the *C. D. Howe* when they were already in High Arctic waters. Samwillie Elijasialak, who was relocated to Grise Fiord in 1953, testified before RCAP about the forced separation. His "mother was told that her children were going to go to Alexandra Fiord. She was not happy at being told that her children would have to go where the government people told her they would go." Family members successfully resisted this splitting of a seventeen-year-old from his parents, but years later Elijasialak recalled feeling "that the separation of the people was as if the government people were separating dogs." The forced separation of families demonstrated to the relocatees that they were pawns in the government's relocation plans. The plan to distribute some at different points in the High Arctic shows that the welfare of Inuit was not the government's primary concern. Instead, the government was concerned with populating the High Arctic and providing workers to the base at Resolute.

After disembarking some passengers at Craig Harbour, the *C. D. Howe* met up with the icebreaker C. G. S. *D'Iberville*, which was to transfer some people to the RCMP post at Alexandra Fiord. However, ice prevented the vessel from reaching that harbour. Two families were dropped off at Craig Harbour to join the relocated group while the remaining families were delivered to Resolute.

By this point, the relocatees had been on board the ship for weeks in substandard living conditions. Martha Flaherty was eight years old when she and her family were relocated to Craig Harbour. She spoke to the Commissioner about her experiences on the *C. D. Howe*:

> I had nightmares for years because of the ship experience we had. It was dark and rainy. We wore life jackets. That was scary. I used to be picked up by an RCMP officer and he would hang me in the water. I kept that memory for years. I had nightmares about that. I fought so that they would not brush-cut my hair because they thought we had lice. I ran upstairs and locked myself with my mother and I don't remember after that.

From Craig Harbour, people soon moved approximately 60 kilometres west from the RCMP post to the Lindstrom Peninsula, on the west side of Grise Fiord. A government official said the move was to reduce the tendency to look for handouts. In 1956, the RCMP detachment moved to the site of the current community, where only two families lived at the time. The rest remained at the camp west of the fiord on the Lindstrom Peninsula, until the arrival of the federal day school in 1961.

Living conditions at both Resolute and the Lindstrom Peninsula were exceptionally harsh. It must be remembered how different the High Arctic was from Inukjuak, Nunavik. The distance between the two locations was approximately the same as between Toronto, Ontario and Miami, Florida. The High Arctic has a three-month period of darkness, much colder temperatures, completely different landscapes and ice formations, and different animal habits. Additionally, cultural and language differences created difficulties between the people of Pond Inlet and Inukjuak. Anthropologist Milton Freeman observed that "indifference, ridicule, and even hostility were not uncommon features of intergroup relations." At Resolute, Inuit received inadequate supplies, substandard housing, and a broken boat. The Craig Harbour Inuit had limited building supplies and no access to goods and services. In 1955, thirty-four more people were relocated from Inukjuak and Pond Inlet to Resolute, while another family of four was relocated from Inukjuak to Grise Fiord.

The High Arctic relocations also affected the families left behind, as well as succeeding generations born in the High Arctic. The RCAP final report, *The High Arctic Relocation: A Report of the 1953–55 Relocation*, discussed some of these effects:

> The relocation had an immediate impact on some people and a longer-term impact on others, leading to depression and despondency. Family relationships were disrupted in various ways. Families were broken up as a result of the initial departure from Inukjuak. There was further disruption when the families were unexpectedly separated onto different ships and sent to different places. These separations continued for years and were compounded by the departure of people to hospitals in the South for treatment of tuberculosis. Young people had great difficulty finding spouses.

RCAP condemned the government for its handling of the relocation in its report:

> The Department proceeded with the High Arctic Relocation without proper authority. The relocation was not voluntary. It proceeded without free and informed consent, there were material misrepresentations, and material information was not disclosed.

> The true nature of the relation—that is, a rehabilitation project—and the inherent risks were not disclosed ... Moreover, many Inuit were kept in the High Arctic for many years against their will when the government refused to respond to their requests to return.

Fundamentally, RCAP found in its final report that "the government was negligent in its planning and implementation of the relocation. It did not keep the promises made to the relocatees." Shortly after, on March 29, 1996, the government signed a memorandum of agreement with Makivik Corporation (working on behalf of individuals relocated to the High Arctic). The Memorandum acknowledged the contributions of the relocated Inuit to a "Canadian presence" in the High Arctic and the "hardship, suffering, and loss" encountered during the initial years. $10 million was awarded to the individuals, and Aboriginal Affairs Minister John Duncan gave an apology on August 18, 2010.

The High Arctic relocations stand out in the history of Qikiqtaaluk partly because of the recognition earned by the RCAP investigation, but also because of the sheer magnitude of the experiment and its lasting effects. Relocatees were moved to far-off and isolated locations, creating a dependency on government for the provision of services and travel. The moves stand out vividly in Inuit memory and history.

THE CUMBERLAND SOUND EVACUATIONS

In the winter of 1962, most of the inhabitants of a dozen ilagiit nunagivaktangit surrounding Pangnirtung were evacuated by federal authorities who feared they would starve during the course of a highly contagious disease among their qimmiit. The department responsible for northern affairs was concerned that Inuit would be unable to hunt, and believed that only two support options existed. One option was to fly or otherwise transport food and fuel to people in their familiar surroundings. The other option was to withdraw them temporarily to Pangnirtung, where shelter was not available but food and fuel could be found or brought by air until the qimmiit population recovered. The decision to evacuate could be interpreted as either a sound precaution or a sign of panic. Whatever the motives, officials soon found themselves administering a settlement of over four hundred people with an infrastructure designed for one-quarter that number. Other challenges included the wide dispersal of the many small settlements, poor weather, and a shortage of qimmiit to transport emergency supplies. Officials also fretted over the notion that providing Inuit with relief on the land would cause many people to lose interest in hunting. Harold Zukerman, the regional welfare chief said:

> Although several of the camps close to Pangnirtung are in no danger of starvation they have suffered seriously through the depletion of their dogs. This has reduced both their meat procurement and their cash income through the sales of the skins. This situation is going to last for several years until the dog population again approaches normal. During this time many of the camp members will be idle as their hunting activities are restricted. We could provide relief assistance to the camps, however, it is felt by the people at Pangnirtung that this would not be appreciated as relief during a crisis. There would most likely develop a dependence on relief assistance, which would be hard to terminate. Rather than have the camp members idle in their camp and receiving relief issued, we feel it is preferable that they move to Pangnirtung where they can take part in the work programme now in progress. They can also participate in the crafts programme, which is now getting under way. Such a programme, if successful, would enable them to return to their camps and supplement their hunting by the production of crafts.

Zukerman's explanation is confusing. The make-work program drew Inuit into an artificial and unsustainable cash economy. While the government supported dependency through a make-work project, it was not willing to support the ilagiit nunagivaktangit with emergency relief. The quote also demonstrates a lack of cultural understanding. Zukerman's concern about relief neglects the importance of hunting for Inuit—country food is nutritionally rich and culturally important. Additionally, the use of the term "idle" connotes unproductive time. It fails to acknowledge important cultural activities that were occurring during seemingly idle times, such as socialization, storytelling, and preparing skins. Despite the large number of qimmiit lost to disease, people could pool their remaining qimmiit to make teams, as others did a few years earlier around Kimmirut. In Cumberland Sound, some could have walked to nearby polynyas or the floe edge. Qimmiit disease was prevalent throughout the region during this period, but Inuit from the ilagiit nunagivaktangit in the Cumberland Sound area were the only ones evacuated. It is possible that the availability of a police aircraft in 1962 explains the more aggressive action.

The decision to evacuate anyone willing to move to Pangnirtung came in March 1962, and went ahead under the direction of Peter Murdock, Superintendent of the Rehabilitation Center at Iqaluit. Inuit living close to Pangnirtung were moved using the remaining dog teams; the ilagiit nunagivaktangit further afield were evacuated by aircraft. The authorities left rations behind for those who refused to move. By the end of April 1962, only eighty-three people remained on the land; four hundred and sixty had either been evacuated by the government or had voluntarily moved into the settlement. The three ilagiit nunagivaktangit that remained in May 1962, Kingmilksoon, Ikaloolik, and Avatuktoo, each still had enough qimmiit to make up a team. According to official records, almost a fifth of the population of Cumberland Sound decided to remain on the land.

Many Inuit at the QTC hearings in Pangnirtung spoke about the evacuations of 1962. In many cases, they stated there was no need to be evacuated.

Some qimmiit had survived, and a number of hunters could reach the floe edge on foot. The rushed evacuations resulted in the loss of personal property, such as boats, motors, skins, and clothing, which could not be replaced in the settlement. It also led to temporary separation of families. Norman Komoartuk was thirteen when he was taken ahead of his family from Illungayut (Bon Accord Harbour) to Pangnirtung. He was loaded on top of the cargo and flown to the settlement. Arriving in Pangnirtung without his parents, he recalled, "I had no relatives here then. I didn't know where I could stay because my mother was never picked up. I had no parents. I was going through a struggle because it was over a week and my parents were not here."

Pangnirtung did not have the needed infrastructure to accommodate the large influx of Inuit arriving from the ilagiit nunagivaktangit. While the Department of Native Affairs reportedly "worked out plans for housing, employment, community hunting, relief, welfare, etc.," the plans for housing were wholly inadequate. The government planned to house people in:

> Accommodation now occupied by the [Inuit] who reside permanently at Pangnirtung. Houses will be constructed for the new arrivals using a snow wall with a duck [canvas] roof. It is considered by the [Inuit] at Pangnirtung that this type of dwelling is mot [sic] suitable for March and April. When the warmer weather comes they will be moved to tents.

Inuit who agreed to be evacuated had to live in overcrowded houses and were cold in the temporary shelters. The organizers of the evacuation ignored the significant differences between a summer tent and a well-insulated qarmaq. Leah Evic shared with the QTC her memories of arriving in the settlement in March 1962:

> We had to leave in March. The weather was very cold. We arrived with just our bedding. We were told that we had to come here.

> The plane came and we had to pack very quickly. It was very hard. My older sister was living in Pangnirtung because we didn't have anywhere else to go. There was a lot of people staying there. We had to stay on the floor. Because there were so many people we had to get help from social services. We had to get canvas and to pitch our tents. In our camps, we had qarmaqs, but they're winterized. It was now hard to keep the children warm. There was only a Coleman stove. We put up a frame. We put some cardboard inside. It was very cold. We were brought here but back in our camp we had everything. We had food. But the only meat that was provided was Klik meat in cans...when you are not used to it, it wasn't easy to eat.

The government's primary concern was not shelter but work programs to lessen the likelihood of Inuit becoming reliant on relief. Some Inuit were employed to build houses and public works, while others produced carvings and handicrafts. The organized community hunting project transported men who were judged to be "better hunters" to the floe edge using the community's sole autoboggan or the remaining dog teams. The hunters were paid $20 per week with their catch distributed to Inuit gathered at Pangnirtung.

For most, the evacuation to Pangnirtung was temporary—most were back on the land in ilagiit nunagivaktangit within the year. The government did not initiate the Cumberland Sound evacuations to centralize Inuit in settlements, or to have them abandon traditional practices. Rather, the government undertook the evacuations to stave off threats of disaster. The government was anxious to avoid anything similar to the tragedies the Kivalliqmiut faced in the famine of 1957–58. Because it lacked confidence in its ability to provide services in ilagiit nunagivaktangit, the government temporarily intensified services in the settlement so that it could control conditions among the Inuit of Cumberland Sound. Inuit expected when they relocated that they would be adequately housed and fed, but in many cases, these expectations went unfulfilled.

Moving Individuals

The QTC heard from students and families moved for schooling and medical treatment, or simply because they wanted to live in a settlement. Because of the importance of kinship in Inuit culture, and the vital role each person played in ensuring survival of the group, every move had an impact on a family. While a more detailed history of government-sponsored health care and education is described in other QTC thematic reports, this report considers moves made for medical and educational reasons.

MEDICAL MOVES AND EVACUATIONS

Most communities in Qikiqtaaluk had negligible or substandard medical facilities during the 1950–75 period. Initially, the government relied on RCMP, missionaries, and traders to deliver first aid. Evacuations for medical care are emphasized in Inuit testimony, historical literature, and popular culture. Until air travel became more common in the late 1960s, a significant number of the sick were moved on the long, uncomfortable voyages of the *C.D. Howe*. After 1950, the annual patrol sailing aboard the *C.D. Howe* stepped up the battle against TB, conducted dental and medical surveys and immunization programs, and repatriated former patients. The majority of evacuations occurred in response to TB, which ravaged Qikiqtaaluk from the 1930s to the early 1960s. Between 1953 and 1964, almost five thousand Inuit from the Northwest Territories (almost half the Inuit population) had been institutionalized for varying periods. The majority of Inuit from Qikiqtaaluk went to southern sanatoriums, while some were treated in Pangnirtung at St. Luke's Mission Hospital.

The Eastern Arctic Patrol (EAP) patrolled to accessible points where Inuit had already been instructed to gather each summer during the 1950s and early 1960s. Each visit was short, but was looked upon with great trepidation by Inuit. Author Pat Grygier tells us, "Sometimes a priest would connive at hiding people who were afraid they would be sent south, and sometimes Inuit in outlying camps would flee when they saw the ship coming or when they heard the helicopter." In a case near Arctic Bay in 1958, a helicopter flew to an ilagiit nunagivaktangat where sick Inuit were trying to avoid evacuation. It picked them up and flew them to the ship.

Once on board, Inuit were hastily examined by teams of doctors, dentists, radiologists, and nurses. Those suspected of having tuberculosis were identified and marked. Gene Rheaume was aboard the *C. D. Howe* in 1958:

> It was so primitive even when I was on there. They marked a red arrow on his [an Inuk's] hand right after he had been X-rayed. That meant he wasn't allowed off the ship. So they got to learn. They tried to erase that ink because they knew. They took the parents—mother and father—and the ship would pull away and the kids were left standing on the beach.

Some evacuees had just a few hours to gather their belongings and to say goodbye to family before boarding the ship to the mainland. Others were given no time. They came aboard where they were tested, and the sick were immediately sent down into the hull of the ship. Walter Rudnicki, one-time head of the Welfare Division of the Department of Native Affairs, recounted to the QTC, "If it was a mother with a baby in the hood, the radiologist would pick the baby up and give it to whoever was standing closest." Robert Williamson also vividly described the conditions:

> The ship was deep in misery. It was terrible because it was the ship which carried the Inuit away from their homes to the sanatoria in the south. And they were herded together in the [bow], in the hold of the ship in three-tiered bunks, mass-fed, mass-accommodated. In

> the stormy seas they were sick, they were terrified, they were demoralized. They were frightened of what was happening to them, of what was likely to happen to them.

Patients were kept aboard for the remainder of the long journey and then transported by air or rail to a sanatorium in Manitoba, Ontario, or Quebec. Jonah Apak shared his childhood memories of the *C. D. Howe* with the QTC:

> I was one of the people sent out on the *C. D. Howe* for TB. I did not want to leave my parents behind but we had no choice but to go for medical purposes . . . There was a section up front where they segregated Inuit to the section where it was the bumpiest. It was like we were treated low class, were put there where there was a lot of movement.

Bryan Pearson, a long-time resident, business owner, and politician in Iqaluit, spoke to Commissioner Igloliorte about the coercive nature of the evacuations. When the *C. D. Howe* arrived in Iqaluit in the early 1950s, Phyllis Harrison (a social worker) was visiting the qarmaqs in Apex. In one of the houses, she visited Nutaraaluk and his wife. Their two-year-old son Aatami was sick with tuberculosis. Aatami's father refused to send his son aboard the *C. D. Howe* "because he knew he would never see him again." Harrison told Nutaraaluk and his wife "that it was compulsory, that he had no choice. The kid had to go. He had TB and that was it." Nutaraaluk still refused. Harrison then threatened that if Nutaraaluk refused she would fetch the RCMP. Eventually Nutaraaluk capitulated and Pearson carried Aatami out to the car.

Some witnesses who spoke before the Commission spoke of loved ones who had died in the South. Thomas Kublu spoke of his father's death. "It was the most emotional and difficult time for me. One of the major hardships

I've had in my life." His father had been sent to a hospital in Quebec for tuberculosis treatment. There, he was confined to a bed. "He was emotionally very unhappy being confined and with the loss of freedom of movement. It bothered him emotionally and he became very depressed. He died shortly after . . . in the spring of 1952." No one informed the family that he had died. When the *C.D. Howe* returned in August, Kublu and his family expected to welcome back their father but "there was no sight of [him] but [the] belongings [that] were handed over to [them]." Thomas explained that not being informed about his father's death was "disheartening and you feel minimized as a human being because they do not bother to follow up or inform you about death in the family, your own father especially." He went on:

> It makes me realize that we Inuit were not important enough to be given the courtesy [of being] informed about the death of our father. I began to realize that the authorities, the Qallunaat, did not value us as worthy human beings. This was very hurtful to us to be lied to and waiting my father's return home. The shock of learning about his death when we expected to welcome him home is one of my painful memories; it is one of the first experiences when the colonizers treated us very poorly as human beings. I began to see that there was no respect or concern for us as human beings.

Many evacuated Inuit eventually did return north, but some were too weak to ever return to the land. The Department of Native Affairs established rehabilitation centres at Iqaluit, Hall Beach, and Rankin Inlet to help Inuit adapt to post-sanatorium living, and specifically to become more self-sufficient in the modern economy. Trades, money management, home economics, sanitation, and business skills were taught. These centres played a necessary role in caring for returning patients, but they also tried to play an important role in integrating Inuit into the wage economy.

Other people who were returned to Qikiqtaaluk from southern sanatoriums were sent to the wrong communities instead of being sent home. Often the misplacement of Inuit was a result of language difficulties, haste, and even bungling. With Inuit who spoke little to no English and Qallunaat in hospitals and vessels who spoke no Inuktitut, there were many opportunities for things to go wrong. Inuit were labelled with tags that they could not read. So although their homes were in Cape Dorset they might have been tagged for delivery to Clyde River. They would have been unable to explain or protest their own misplacement. Grygier reported that one man committed suicide after being delivered to a place he did not know and with no way to get home.

The QTC has heard more stories about the misplacement of Inuit. Martha Flaherty was part of the High Arctic relocations. She and her family were moved to Grise Fiord while her sister, Lucy, was in a southern sanatorium receiving treatment for tuberculosis. Lucy was returned to Nunavik, but no one realized that her family was no longer there—they were in the High Arctic. Lucy was then shipped to Resolute. It was not until the following year that Lucy, Martha, and the rest of the family were finally reunited in Grise Fiord. These mistakes caused anguish for her father.

Temela Okpik's story is equally disturbing. Okpik told the QTC that he had been sent from his ilagiit nunagivaktangat near Kimmirut in 1956 to a southern hospital for treatment of tuberculosis. He spent the next three years down south before finally boarding the *C. D. Howe* to be sent home. A measles outbreak occurred in southern Qikiqtaaluk that year and passengers destined for Kimmirut, including Okpik, were diverted to Resolute, over 1,600 kilometres away. The following winter Okpik was again transferred, this time to Iqaluit. He was finally returned to his camp when an Inuk leaving Iqaluit by dog team agreed to bring Okpik home. Temela Okpik had been away almost six years—his journey home from the sanatorium alone had taken more than two.

SCHOOLING

By the early 1950s, the government abandoned earlier erratic attempts to provide schooling in the ilagiit nunagivaktangit and started building and staffing schools in the settlements. Some Inuit moved to the settlement so their children could attend school and work towards a job in the wage economy. To accommodate unaccompanied children in the settlements, the government built hostels. These were meant to be a gentler alternative to sending young children to far-off residential schools, and were sometimes supervised by Inuit.

Not every parent wanted their children to abandon traditional learning for western schooling; many were coerced into sending their children to settlement schools. This affected almost all Qikiqtaalungmiut, prompting one witness, Ruth Sangoya, to lament, "Our children were disappearing." Inuit felt they had no choice but to send their children into the settlements when the social worker, teacher, or RCMP officer came to their ilagiit nunagivaktangat and told them attendance was mandatory. Both the written record and Inuit testimony demonstrated that some Inuit were threatened with the loss of family allowance if they did not send their children to school. Gordon Rennie, long-time HBC post manager and a resident of Nunavut, told the QTC:

> When the Federal Government was here they encouraged all of the people in the camps. Or the word I had was that they were "encouraging" the people in the camps to move into town so that their children could go to school with the idea, I think, of learning English. You know, I don't have that word for word, but we assumed that. Then there was sort of an unspoken indication that if these people didn't follow directions well then they could have their family allowance rescinded.

Government records reveal that the threat of the suspension of family allowances was an accepted method of deterring truancy, albeit a largely unsuccessful one. In some cases where this did not work, people were threatened with prison. Annie Shappa's father was one of these people:

> When we were moved to Arctic Bay, we were picked up by Ski-Doo . . . I remember being taken to the community to go to school. My father was advised that if there was any social assistance, they would be charged or sent to jail, if he didn't comply with us going to school.

At Clyde River, Thomasie Panniluk told Commissioner Igloliorte how dislocations and evacuations tore his family apart. Panniluk and his stepfather were sent south for tuberculosis treatment in 1956. Although Panniluk was sent home a year later, his stepfather was not. Panniluk was too young to support the family at that point, so the government moved his family to another settlement where they would have easier access to social programs. Panniluk's mother was then evacuated in 1959 for medical reasons and Thomasie was sent to live in Qikiqtarjuaq so that he could attend school. The impact on his family was devastating:

> That was a hard time for me because I didn't have my parents with me. I had to go to school, stay in some sort of hotel. It was called residential school at the time. So, not too long after that there was another incident during which my brother and my step-brother Noah died in Cape Dyer. His place burned down. It was burned down with the fire of course. I was without my parents, my brother was gone. My real father had died. Those kinds of things . . . it was so hard.

On returning north, many Inuit found members of their family had been removed for schooling or for health reasons. The close kinship groups that defined many ilagiit nunagivaktangit were ravaged by the relentless removal of family and friends. Removing even one member of the small kin-based camp could be devastating for the whole family or ilagiit nunagivaktangat.

VOLUNTARY MOVES

Similar to other voluntary migrations that have occurred around the world, some moves were undertaken by Inuit searching for a better life for themselves or their children. They were attracted to settlements for a variety of reasons, including schools, family members who had already moved, employment, health services, and government offers of permanent housing. In many communities, promises were made to Inuit about what they could expect if they lived in the settlements. When Moses Kasarnak was asked by QIA interviewers if he was "forced" to move to a settlement he replied, "We were never told to move. Since we were coming back here often, we decided to stay here." He went on to say: "We were just very happy that we were going to get a house here . . . We were directly told that if we moved we would get a house and that it would have a table and dishes. It was like Christmas that we were going to get all these things."

For some Inuit, the relative ease of settlement life was appealing compared to the difficult conditions that could exist in ilagiit nunagivaktangit. On the land, periods of plenty were contrasted by times of hunger—the economy was dependent on the volatile fur markets, and health care was hard to access. Peter Akpalialuk told Commissioner Igloliorte about the challenges of subsistence living in camps. "When food was scarce it was stressful times worrying when the next food will come from and when. It was how we lived and it was a hard life but we did not know any other lifestyle so it was still a satisfactory life for us." People admit that ilagiit nunagivaktangat life could be hard, though they also recall the sense of belonging and connection to the land that was part of everyday life.

Some Inuit who voluntarily moved into the settlements might have initially believed their moves to be temporary, but they found themselves living there for more extended periods, and then permanently. When their qimmiit were killed or when they could not afford to maintain a snowmobile for long-distance hunting, a further barrier was placed between them and a return to the land. In the northern Foxe Basin, the number of year-round ilagiit nunagivaktangit had been reduced from eleven in 1950 to only five in 1970. There were, however, seven seasonal ilagiit nunagivaktangit, places where hunters who were not steadily employed in the settlements took their families to hunt and fish in the summer. For these Inuit, and almost everyone else, the decision to move into the settlement was not a choice to abandon traditional practices, but rather a way to relieve some of the pressures of life on the land by taking advantage of settlement services. Inuit did not accept or intend the impact that settlement life had on their culture, language, or nutritional intake.

Perhaps the greatest difference in the experience between those who voluntarily moved and those who were coerced or forced to move is the lingering feeling of powerlessness. One witness, Juda Taqtu, told the QTC, "The government had already prepared our future. That is why life is completely different from what life used to be."

Closing Communities

Occasionally the government withdrew services from places where Inuit were already established, and pressured people to migrate to another nearby community. Noteworthy examples of how communities ceased to exist come mainly from the south of Qikiqtaaluk. Killiniq (Port Burwell) was a substantial settlement on an island where the boundaries of Nunavut, Nunavik, and Nunatsiavut met. It was difficult to supply by air and lost its services and population in the 1970s. Inuit, whose kin connections were with Nunavik and not with Qikiqtaalungmiut, were relocated to nearby Nunavik communities. Further west on Nottingham Island, not far from Cape Dorset, closure of a weather station in 1970 led to the breakup of a small community of Inuit, mainly station employees, which had existed there since the 1940s.

Paallavvik (Padloping Island) and South Camp (Belcher Islands) were the sites of government-constructed schools and homes prior to the closings. The closing of these communities and the centralization of services in larger settlements eased the government's administrative burden and reduced the cost of delivering services. In the case of Paallavvik, the government had pressured people to move for several years, but finally made the decision for them by terminating all services there in 1968. In all closings, people's ties to places where they had deep connections, knowledge, and better access to the land's resources were severed or diminished.

PAALLAVVIK (PADLOPING ISLAND)

Inuit along the Cumberland Peninsula had been in contact with Qallunaat since 1824 when whaling vessels began to cruise the eastern shore of Davis Strait. A trading post operated at Kivitoo north of Qikiqtarjuaq from 1912 to 1927, and there was another, more poorly supplied post near Paallavvik about the same time. During the Second World War, the United States Air Force (USAF) established a weather station at Paallavvik, and it became a focal point for settlement by Inuit who hunted in the general area. Beginning in 1955, the Qallunaat presence and impact in the area greatly expanded with the construction of several DEW Line facilities along the Cumberland Peninsula. The biggest of these Inuit habitations was an auxiliary site at Qikiqtarjuaq. The government was anxious to prevent Inuit from becoming dependent on unreliable short-term employment in the area, so it actively discouraged "loitering" by any of the families except those directly employed on the DEW Line. On one hand, the policy of dispersal still encouraged Inuit to pursue traditional activities and to stay away from Qallunaat settlements. On the other hand, the DEW Line needed Inuit workers and the government helped identify suitable individuals.

The DEW Line site at Qikiqtarjuaq was a terminal for transportation to and from Iqaluit and became the administrative centre for the north coast of Cumberland Peninsula. The government erected a school there in 1960 and a school hostel in 1962. The HBC was a late arrival, opening its post on the island in 1962. From the police point of view, Qikiqtarjuaq was an isolated responsibility of the Pangnirtung detachment, but from this point forward, Qikiqtarjuaq developed as the administrative centre for the Davis Strait coast.

At this time, a small group of thirty-four Inuit lived at Paallavvik, 100 kilometres south of Qikiqtarjuaq. The community had a one-room schoolhouse, a generator, and seven low-cost houses. According to Kenn Harper, who arrived there as a teacher in 1967, the government had been intent on closing the community that year. A group of government representatives arrived in the spring of 1968 and met with the community to explain that the school was to be closed and the generator shut down. Residents were advised to move to Qikiqtarjuaq. According to the government representatives, they would have better housing, a store, better medical care, and easier transportation outside of the community. After the summer hunting season, the families moved to Qikiqtarjuaq. Harper described the moves as coerced, not voluntary, and people who spoke to the QTC agree. Jacopie Nuqingaq told Commissioner Igloliorte:

> They came in to ask us and pressure us to move. They used to have someone come from Qikiqtarjuaq to encourage us to move to Qikiqtarjuaq. They had an Inuit who was the middleman. He was there to encourage us to move on behalf of the Qallunaaq. I real-

> ize that we were passive. We were scared of Qallunaat so we did whatever they said. We are passive. We are not retaliating people. We were scared of the Qallunaaq. We didn't want to move because we had no plans to move here. When we got here, our dogs were slaughtered and we had no choice. My father had a Ski-Doo at a later time.

Joshua Alookie said his parents were promised running water, good housing, good schooling, and employment opportunities in Qikiqtarjuaq. Alookie's parents had to wait almost twenty years after relocating before they had indoor plumbing.

SOUTH CAMP IN THE BELCHER ISLANDS

Sanikiluaq (formerly known as North Camp) is located on Flaherty Island, one of the larger of the Belcher Islands. In 1959, a school opened at the southern end of Flaherty Island at the site that became South Camp. More than a dozen children were enrolled in the school by 1960–61, many of whom were moved to South Camp from ilagiit nunagivaktangit even though the government was uncertain about whether it wanted to continue providing services in the Belcher Islands or establish a single permanent settlement. At one point, in an effort to keep people away from enclaves, it proposed putting the school in one place and the HBC in another.

In 1967, a newly arrived area administrator encouraged members of his adult education group to meet to discuss local governance, including the controversial issue of centralizing services in one community. He reported that Inuit "unanimously" agreed that the "creation of one larger community from the present two would solve many problems and hasten progress." In 1968, Don Bissett, an area survey officer, reported that the existing school site, South Camp, lacked the abundance of marine mammals that a unified settlement would need. A meeting was held in Ottawa in March 1969 to determine whether the development of the Belcher Islands would occur at Sanikiluaq or at South Camp, and to identify the priorities for development. Without explanation, the memo concluded that the meeting decided, "All future expansion of facilities would be carried out in the northern settlement."

People in Sanikiluaq spoke to Commissioner Igloliorte about meetings held to determine which community would be developed. Sanikiluaq was preferred as a location by the government and more people lived near there than around South Camp. In 1969–70, the people near South Camp came under enormous pressure to move quickly to Sanikiluaq. Mina Eyaituq told the QTC, "The government officials came to us, social workers came to us. We were living in a tent. Every time I think about it, I shiver. He told us that we were being relocated to North Camp and that if we didn't the government was not going to assist us in any way."

People also recalled that the government provided no assistance for the relocations—people moved on their own by boat, snowmobile, and dog team. Some groups became separated while others became stuck in the ice or had to carry a boat over land. With no radios, limited rations, and crowded boats (including Elders and young children), the move was dangerous. Upon arrival in Sanikiluaq, promised housing had not arrived. Many of the relocatees had left what little possessions they had behind, expecting the necessities of life to be provided for them in Sanikiluaq. Lottie Arragutainaq told the Commission about her experience:

> I was almost the last one in South Camp. Everybody had moved here [to Sanikiluaq] but I refused to move. On the way here we ran out of supplies because of the fog during the day we tried to move here . . . We left our houses with only our clothes that we were wearing; we left everything else behind . . . thinking that we were coming back. When we moved here there was no assistance

> of any kind. We just walked out of our houses. It was a very sad event for me.

Other residents also testified about the inappropriate and insufficient number of houses in Sanikiluaq. Annie Appaqaq-Arragutainaq, who had already been moved to South Camp in 1962, was with the first group that was moved to North Camp. She told the Commission, "We were going to be boarding with other people when we came here it turns out . . . The houses had not been built yet."

Emily Takatak experienced great uncertainty and confusion about the details of the move.

> We didn't even know we were relocating here, we just thought we were coming here for a short time. We didn't take any belongings. Even my babies didn't have anything; nothing to comfort them. During the night, my children were cold. We thought we were going to go home right away and then we realized we were moving here. They didn't give us any sort of transportation to pick up our belongings. We were put in a homemade shack. In the evening, in that house, we didn't even have a pillow to sleep on, we didn't carry anything. All our belongings we left behind. We took only necessary clothing, changes for the children. We thought we were going back home right away, we didn't know how long we were going to be here, nobody informed us how long we were coming here or why. I felt very poor here. In the evening, when they realized we didn't have anything to sleep on, people gave us stuff to sleep on.

Appaqaq-Arragutainaq also recalled the sadness of seeing families with children arriving in Sanikiluaq:

Early spring they were coming here by boat and they got no assistance from anyone. And no wonder children were hungry and had no energy because of hunger. One infant was still being breastfed. One lady breastfeeding would breastfeed other children. They were surrounded by ice so they ended up walking here. I remember that, it was in 1970. They had gone through great hardship; children were hungry and had no more energy.

Paliisikkut

Policing in Qikiqtaaluk

This chapter examines the relationship between Royal Canadian Mounted Police (RCMP) and Inuit in Qikiqtaaluk, especially during the period from the 1940s to 1975. The first permanent police presence in Qikiqtaaluk came with the detachment set up in Pond Inlet in 1922, primarily for sovereignty purposes. Law enforcement and providing other services to about eleven thousand Inuit and the few Qallunaat scattered across the region was only a secondary consideration. Until the 1940s, a few scattered police detachments existed across the region, which endeavoured to deliver basic services to ilagiit nunagivaktangit.Almost all Inuit, with the exception of very few who were working directly for the Hudson's Bay Company (HBC) or the RCMP, still followed a semi-nomadic seasonal hunting and harvesting cycle. Some families visited the trading post a few times each year, where they would encounter the traders, and possibly a missionary and an RCMP officer. Even more rarely, the RCMP would make rounds to visit ilagiit nunagivaktangit, with either the support of an Inuit special constable or an Inuit guide. In both types of encounters, the RCMP spent time collecting information for annual patrol reports, as well as providing some medical services.

In almost every way, the relations between Inuit and RCMP paralleled the experiences of the RCMP with other First Peoples—they were promising at the start, but deteriorated with the arrival of newcomers. Tensions were aggravated by an imbalance of power, the lack of a coherent justice system, racism, and poor intercultural communications. In Western Canada, the new groups were permanent occupiers (rail workers, farmers, and city-builders). In Qikiqtaaluk, they were more likely to be transients—bureaucrats, military personnel, contractors, teachers, and welfare workers—congregating in settlements. In both regions, however, new government institutions, economic structures, and land-ownership patterns proved to be permanent fixtures on the social, political, and cultural landscape of Indigenous peoples.

Inuit also faced the reality that the policemen (and they were, without exception, male officers who were posted in Qikiqtaaluk before 1975) themselves were transient. Very few officers stayed in the Arctic for more than one or two postings. When combined with the fact that RCMP exercised considerable discretion in their work, Inuit found police to be unpredictable—one missionary complained that they were "involuntarily erratic, inconsistent, and even blundering." An action that might be ignored by one officer could be deemed by another officer as an offence warranting time in detachments. Further, Inuit were expected to help care for the RCMP in spite of the challenges that families were already facing. Elijah Panipakoocho of Pond Inlet told the Qikiqtani Truth Commission (QTC):

> Without the help of the Inuit, [RCMP] would not have survived, they would have been dead ... They tell stories of being heroic but they had to be housed, clothed, fed. It was [like] looking after a five- or a six-year-old. They ... would start suffering immediately

> when they were alone. Those Inuit really had a hard time, they had to look after themselves and the RCMP.

Inuit fully recognized the power that police and other Qallunaat authorities had in the north, which went well beyond making sure that specific laws were followed. RCMP were also responsible for doing the bidding of the government on a much wider range of powers. As examples, they ordered Inuit to relocate to other places, including the High Arctic, and they threatened families to send their children to school. In many cases, individual officers may not have been aware that Inuit were unhappy, angry, or confused. That is because of ilira, the Inukitut term to describe a sense of fear, intimidation, and embarrassment. In customary contexts, ilira was a positive method of social control, but in relationships between RCMP and Inuit the feeling of ilira stopped Inuit from speaking out against injustices. The police were the most intimidating of all Qallunaat with which they came into contact. If Inuit failed to listen to RCMP, or didn't adequately understand the police, they could be taken away and imprisoned. In explaining why his family relocated from Inukjuak, Quebec to Resolute, John Amagoalik explained:

> I think it's also important for people to understand that when the RCMP made a request to you in those days, it was seen as something like an order. You are ordered to do this. The RCMP officers had a lot of power. They could put you in jail. That's the way they were viewed in those days. A request from the police was taken very, very seriously.

Taissumani Nunamiutautilluta, 1920 to 1945

INUIT JUSTICE

Throughout the Arctic, all Inuit experienced a very long period in which the sea and the land provided almost everything people needed. The QTC reports call this period Taissumani Nunamiutautilluta. The RCMP did not bring policing or justice to the Arctic—it was already there. Since time immemorial, Inuit had their own means of exercising justice and encouraging social cohesion. As described by Inuit, interdependence with the natural world and with each other necessitated certain strong, but largely psychological, means of influencing behaviour to ensure survival and happiness. Inuit were cautious and respectful of nature. Trusted wisdom from previous generations was a framework for Inuit actions and rationales, with control and leadership localized in a kinship-based community. Each group had leaders "whose influence and authority equipped them to make decisions that affected both the community as a whole and their own families within it." Joshua Idlout told the QTC, "Each clan had its own land, a governance system, and Elders. Elders were the primary decision-makers of that camp." Social control was normally executed by the family and by the community more generally. Families placed a strong emphasis on self-control, since rash decisions or actions could endanger the entire community.

Mechanisms to control and punish all but the most serious of transgressions were psychological in nature, and included gossip, mockery, avoidance, and ostracism. Storytelling was central for teaching children about dangers, both in terms of the environment itself and behaviours. Humility was seen as a positive means of minimizing direct conflict. If problems persisted, leaders or shamans (called angakkuit in Inuktitut) could address them individually or during feasts or religious rites, and call upon those involved to reconcile with the community. In some places, conflict resolution could also take place through a singing duel (iviutit), or through physical challenges, where opponents took turns hitting each other (tigutijut). Banishment and execution were rare, almost always occurring in situations when a person was deemed to be too dangerous. Shelagh Grant describes various means of keeping individuals and groups from harm, including taboos and the importance of gaining control over emotions. She also highlights the rich language used to describe emotions and motivations that individuals could experience in relationships and actions associated with maintaining order and control in groups. She writes, for example, that "in North Baffin an adult was expected to refrain from showing anger and instead show isuma, meaning 'the capacity for a sense of reason.'" Taking a life without prior consent or provocation, inuaqsiniq, was the most serious crime "because of the adverse effect it would have on a group."

While Inuit were still living in ilagiit nunagivaktangit, the RCMP generally recognized Inuit as sets of autonomous groups for the purposes of law enforcement and justice within the groups. W.C.E. Rasing explains in the context of Igloolik, which was one of the last areas where Inuit moved into a government-sponsored settlement, "the Iglulingmiut [in the 1960s] were hardly affected by Canadian law enforcement . . . only [annual] police patrols reminded people of the presence of the law. Preserving order in the camps in fact remained in Iglulingmiut hands, although the Inuit were officially subjected to the laws of Canada."

Inuit methods of justice and control were challenged as soon as Inuit began interacting with and living among Qallunaat. Missionaries, traders, and police arrived first, and each of them played specific roles in undercutting customary Inuit beliefs and strategies regarding individual and group behaviour, punishment, and rewards. Further changes came when Inuit attended school and came into contact more regularly with nurses and social workers.

BACKGROUND: THE RCMP AND OTHER INDIGENOUS PEOPLES

The North-West Mounted Police (NWMP), which became the Royal Canadian Mounted Police in 1920 when it merged with the Dominion Police, was established in 1873 to impose a Victorian legal code onto the vast tracts of the Northwest Territories that had recently been sold to Canada by the Hudson's Bay Company. The government's failure to consult with Indigenous groups on this territorial transfer inspired mistrust and resistance. It was part of the Force's unofficial mandate to set these relationships right without compromising any government plans. As police, judge, jury, and jailer, as well as occasional postman and medic, the NWMP officer became a jack of all trades for the Dominion government in the Northwest Territories and held immensely concentrated power in his community. Historian Walter Hildebrandt points out that the entire "goal of the Mounties could eventually be described as a cultural one—to gain the trust of the Natives and then wean them from their customs and beliefs by enforcing laws intended to diminish the Native culture." In order to facilitate the establishment of the Force's jurisdiction in the area, First Nations and Métis men (and later Inuit) were hired as special constables, a role that combined the jobs of guide, interpreter, and cultural mediator. This was a subordinate and highly vulnerable role that could involve enabling in the arrest of one's own family members, and could lead to social ostracism of the constable and his family.

The Mounted Police also worked directly with predecessors of the federal department of Aboriginal Affairs and Northern Development Canada, beginning with treaty negotiations in the 1870s. Relations between the police and bureaucrats were at times tense, but they allied in support of the government for most of their institutional histories. Police helped Indian Agents enforce provisions of the Indian Act, scooped children up for residential schools, enforced liquor laws and restrictions on cultural practices, and ensured that settlers remained undisturbed by any actions, such as hunting or removing fences, that might have been done or contemplated by First Nations and Métis. The Mounted Police therefore acted in many ways as a force of cultural assimilation in themselves, as well as mediators between other forces and Indigenous peoples in the Northwest Territories.

Indigenous peoples' understanding of the purpose of the NWMP and then the RCMP fluctuated according to the level and nature of contact each community had with the Force. In the early years, during the treaty negotiations of the 1870s, the NWMP was probably seen as being a semi-autonomous mediator between First Nations, Métis, and the federal government. During treaty negotiations, the Police frequently accompanied bureaucrats on horseback, often armed and usually in uniform dress. First Nations and Métis felt intimidated and threatened by the presence of the Mounted Police, even aside from their experience during the Métis resistances.

Restrictive and humiliating government policies support by the RCMP, racism in words and deeds, limited recourse to unfair and illegal police actions, and other negative experiences with the RCMP and its paternalistic attitudes caused a multi-dimensional and intense distrust from many Indigenous people, in spite of the Force's highly publicized acts of heroism and support. During the 1970s, when the RCMP became embroiled in scandal for performing illegal activities, one national Aboriginal periodical wrote:

> The irony of the present outrage and scandal directed at the RCMP is painful. For a century the RCMP have been victimizing Native people ... Predictably, little attention was paid to the plight of the Native people who fell victim to the harsh brutality of the RCMP racism. The public can remain oblivious to the Native suffering for 100 years, but let the word get out that a few telephones have been tapped and a few offices broken into by the RCMP and the public

> is incensed. Suddenly the public feels the RCMP is out of control. To tens of thousands of Canada's Native people it has never been any other way.

Arrival of the RCMP in Qikiqtaaluk

The RCMP already had almost fifty years of experience policing among Indigenous peoples in Canada before its first criminal investigation occurred within Qikiqtaaluk. In 1920, following reports of a murder of an Inuk man the year before, two police were sent to the Belcher Islands to investigate, after Quebec reminded Ottawa that the Belchers were within the boundaries of the Northwest Territories. Following the investigation and a trial in front of a jury consisting of a police sergeant and the boat crew, no charges were laid. The jury determined that the victim "was killed for the common good and safety of the Band." The RCMP officers recommended, however, that "a responsible representative of the Government be sent amongst these people to instruct them in the laws of the country." A year later, while numerous discussions were taking place about ways to ensure Canadian sovereignty over the Arctic Islands, the government sent one officer to Bylot Island to investigate the murder of Newfoundland trader Robert Janes. Sergeant Joy held three Inuit at the new detachment at Pond Inlet while they waited for a trial that was eventually held in 1923.

Prior to this, the RCMP presence had been temporary and focused on sovereignty. In 1903, diplomatic considerations resulting from Norwegian and American interests in Canada's Arctic Islands led the federal government to set up a police post at Cape Fullerton, near Chesterfield Inlet on Hudson Bay. Between 1906 and 1911, expeditions were sent further north as far as Ellesmere Island under the direction of Captain Bernier as evidence of Canadian occupation of the area. For several years, there was much discussion but very little action concerning the addition of a government presence north of Hudson Strait.

In 1920 and 1921, however, the government began to take threats to its claim over Ellesmere and other Arctic islands more seriously—demonstrating the rule of law became more important. Measures proposed included more police posts, game laws, and relocation of Inuit families to the High Arctic. The government was also receiving more reports of violence involving qallunaat in the Arctic, which gave the RCMP additional reasons to increase its presence in the North. As historian William Morrison explains, "the Canadian government sent the police to bring law to the Inuit not out of concern for their welfare or a desire to regularize their society, but rather to demonstrate that these people and their land belonged to Canada." Those people consisted of eleven thousand Inuit and a few missionaries and traders. By 1922, through Eastern Arctic Patrol (EAP), the RCMP had a limited presence in Qikiqtaaluk through two detachments (Craig Harbour and Pond Inlet), annual EAP patrols, and patrols from the detachments.

RCMP DETACHMENTS IN QIKIQTAALUK BEFORE 1975

Detachment Name	Dates of Operation
Alexandra Fiord	1953–63
Cape Dorset	1965–
Clyde River	1970–
Craig Harbour	1922–26, 1933–56
Bache Peninsula	1926–32
Dundas Harbour	1924–33, 1945–51
Cape Christian	1954–70
Grise Fiord	1956–
Igloolik	1964–
Frobisher Bay (Iqaluit)	1945–
Lake Harbour	1927–
Pangnirtung	1923–
Pond Inlet	1922–
Resolute	1953–

Official policy dictated that law enforcement was the foremost concern of the RCMP, but the police were also tasked with collecting taxes and duties, delivering the mail, and distributing first-aid supplies and other necessities to Inuit and traders. The low numbers of police investigations meant that most members spent a significant portion of their time preparing for patrols, keeping their quarters tidy, and conducting interviews with Inuit coming into settlements to trade, participate in religious services, and meet the supply ships. The RCMP were also expected to send information back to Ottawa to help officials make decisions related to the well-being of people in the region. In practice, however, two types of concerns were top of mind among officials: keeping the cost of administration low and, related to this, keeping trading posts active to off-set the costs of administration and demonstrate a government presence in the area.

RCMP Recruits

The RCMP officers who served in Qikiqtaaluk were drawn from a select pool of individuals who were required to be British (later Canadian) citizens who met education and physical requirements, including a minimum height. The stories of RCMP living in the Arctic, travelling by dog team, and assisting with everything from first aid to mountain rescues, contributed greatly to both the myth of the Force and the attraction it held for potential recruits. The RCMP exploited the stories whenever it could, and many individual members published accounts of their years of service in the Arctic, in particular. In 1954, a member of the Force wrote that "young men volunteered for Northern Service with the idea that it was one phase of life in the Force that they should not miss. They all had visions of travel by dog team, canoe, and aeroplane, and in addition all the associations with Eskimos etc."

For almost the entire period under study, the RCMP received next to no training on northern work or Arctic conditions. As late as 1962, a recruit spent one hundred and forty hours learning to ride horses, another seventy hours taking care of the stables and only twenty-five hours on the criminal code, out of a total of over twelve hundred hours. In 1953 or 1954, the RCMP began to offer a short course in Edmonton that introduced recruits to northern conditions. It included lectures, which specialized in tuberculosis treatment for First Nations and Inuit, at the Camsell Hospital; lectures on acts and ordinances enforced in the Yukon and Northwest territories; and films about "police life at isolated places . . . members going on patrol by dog team, attending to dogs, handing out Family Allowance to Eskimos, and numerous views of isolated detachments." Recruits that ended up working in places like Whitehorse and Iqaluit, where most of the work was done physically within the community, and were likely to involve more non-Aboriginal transients and settlers, were disappointed.

The reason or motivation for a posting had bearing on the quality an officer provided and the relationship that developed between him and the community. An officer might anticipate that a posting in the North could lead to higher wages, adventure, promotions, opportunities to work independently, and a chance to see one of the most unique landscapes in Canada. Others went north to escape financial or personal problems in the south. They were often rotated out after their two years of service, sometimes sooner. Former RCMP officer Hugh Fagan in the film *Qimmit: Clash of Two Truths* recalled:

> Those guys didn't come back North when they went out. They served their time maybe or maybe just part of it and we weeded them out and got rid of them and they didn't come back. All the people around this table I'm sure were all repeaters. We were sent outside after a length of time and we volunteered to go back because we liked the north, we liked the people, we liked working with the people and we felt that we were doing something worthwhile.

Some men, such as Constable R. D. Van Norman, who served at Iqaluit and along the eastern section of the Distant Early Warning (DEW) Line in the 1950s, were very interested in Inuit perspectives and customs, and demonstrated respect for Inuit as individuals. In contrast, a few RCMP tended to write about Inuit in broad, racist strokes. In between, each community found that the majority of RCMP served their northern tours of duty with little or no interest in Inuit culture beyond collecting anecdotal stories as reflections of themselves.

The policy of keeping postings to two or three years, and of never serving the same community twice, stemmed from the belief that becoming too involved with a community weakened an officer's ability to maintain order. There was also a common feeling among officers interviewed that an officer's role was to "protect . . . the community . . . without trying to change or alter it." This perspective ignored the fact that simply by entering a community, let alone policing it using external laws and policies, a policeman was altering that community.

The most interesting part of RCMP life remained patrolling by dog team or boat with assistance from Inuit special constables. The patrols brought officers into close contact with Inuit. While special patrols were carried out to explore new regions, investigate allegations of crime, treat the sick, or provide food relief, the most common form of patrol was the annual rounds made to visit ilagiit nunagivaktangit to collect information for the annual "Conditions amongst the Eskimos" and "Game" reports. Both types of documents listed information under standardized headings, such as health, morale, clothing, general activities and pursuits, hunting equipment and dogs, population in relation to resources, percentage of males and females, intermarriage information, and suggestions for improving economic conditions. Some observations were routine, such as the number of qimmiit estimated to be healthy in an area, while others were insightful about conditions and critical of government management of programs and supplies.

The game laws caused hardship for Inuit and were a consistent point of friction between Inuit and RCMP for several reasons. The RCMP were required to work with other government agencies to enforce the laws, specifically the Northwest Game Act (1917) and the Migratory Bird Protection Act

(1932). The rules, especially as they applied to Inuit, made almost no sense in the Arctic context. The regulations were based on best guesses as much as on scientific fact. The authorities charged with enforcing them knew that they were unreasonable and inappropriate. The impacts on Inuit livelihoods, well-being, and cultural practices were profound and the RCMP took advantage of the laws to threaten Inuit with fines and even prison.

Roles of Inuit Special Constables

The capacity of RCMP to communicate with Inuit and to survive in Arctic conditions required help from Inuit, both as employees and simply as neighbours providing support in times of need. All regular police detachments were staffed by at least one Inuk employee, normally serving with his wife and children. Beginning in 1936 and continuing until at least 1970, patrol reports submitted to Ottawa officially referred to Inuit staff as "special constables," an official rank and employment status within the RCMP. Men sent north with the RCMP often received no special training on northern survival, navigation, or travelling; on patrol, they were entirely reliant on Inuit special constables who hunted food for qimmiit, built iglus, navigated, and translated. An officer is quoted in *Policing the Baffin Region* as stating, "There was nothing in the manual about how to use a dog sled. I learned from the special constable. He did all the travelling with me . . . It was a rare occasion when we travelled by ourselves." Inuit special constables also maintained equipment and did chores around the detachment. The families of the Inuit special constables also offered considerable and invaluable assistance to the RCMP, often without compensation. Women would make and mend the trail clothing, do household chores, and prepare meals.

Children were expected to help with the detachment chores. Inuit special constables were usually compensated with a salary, although some reports indicate that some Inuit were given accommodations and rations instead. By the 1960s, they were provided with housing that was of the same standard as the quarters provided to regular members, and at the same cost.

Testimonies to the QTC by RCMP and Inuit special constables described roles and relationships between RCMP and Inuit special constables. A former RCMP officer interviewed for the film *Qimmit: Clash of Two Truths* explained:

> You have to trust these guys explicitly, because you are putting your life in their hands. One accident at 45 below; if he can't make an iglu, you are dead in the water . . . He was the guy you could trust. He would whip up these iglus and we would sort of watch with amazement.

Another officer said, "I would depend upon him for my life and have . . . We were faced with a charging polar bear once and he killed it without a blink. Now, that was not an easy thing for him to do. He had no intention of wanting to kill that bear, but it was a 'have to' situation."

Inuit were fully aware that RCMP officers, especially new recruits, could not survive without Inuit assistance. Some Inuit special constables described the RCMP as childlike, clumsy, or unskilled. Mosha Akavak told the QTC, "I have never seen the police having their own dog team . . . they couldn't do it." In 1994, historian Shelagh Grant interviewed many Elders about the RCMP as part of her research for *Arctic Justice*. Sam Arnakallak told her:

> [RCMP officers] were just like kids, when they were having tea outside and they weren't able to grasp the cup with their hands, the cup would be held for them exactly like children because they were from a warm climate . . . The Inuit would have to dry their mitts and

> kamiks. Once they stopped for the night, the [guides] would have to hurry and build an iglu as if they had small children. Once they put them in, they'd have to light the stove to get them warm. Then [the guides] would have to stay outside to feed the dogs.

Timothy Kadloo explained to Grant:

> The RCMP told us that they weren't actually sure what to do, that they would need help. Like children, they would watch you before they actually knew what to do. But once they found out what to do, they would start helping out. They would end up helping a lot after that. They were a bit clumsy because they were qallunaat—because they were not used to this kind of activity. That's what we had to do, we had to help each other. We'd learn different things from them. They would help us sometimes.

As Kadloo points out, it took time for an officer to become competent in land-based skills, but some men eventually became proficient at handling dog teams and travelling over snow and ice.

There is little evidence that the RCMP anticipated that special constables might eventually chose to become full RCMP officers. Inuit staff members were not offered any training or duties that might have led to better pay or new positions. The RCMP's use of qimmiit was essentially finished in 1969; as soon as the RCMP no longer needed Inuit to help them travel by dog team, Inuit special constables were largely assigned to the role of interpreter.

Sangussaqtauliqtilluta, 1945 to 1960

The RCMP were key facilitators of the period called Sangussaqtauliqtilluta, meaning "when people started to be persuaded to change their ways." As the sole representatives of government in most places in the region, the RCMP were responsible for enforcing laws and promoting services in almost every sphere of life. They continued to register births and adoptions, collect people for medical checkups, inoculate qimmiit, and assist with medical emergencies. It was during this period, however, that the government set out to deliver national programs—family allowances and old-age pensions—and become more active in getting Inuit to send children to school.

The era includes the Second World War and the early portion of the Cold War that brought tumultuous change to Qikiqtaaluk as the Arctic gained a higher significance for Canada. Thousands of Americans arrived in Qikiqtaaluk to build the Frobisher Bay airfield in Iqaluit in the 1940s. The construction of the DEW Line in the mid-1950s was a major catalyst for changes in Inuit life and, in many ways, to the duties of the RCMP. DEW Line contracts brought thousands of Qallunaat military personnel and civilian engineers, as well as millions of tons of building materials, into the Canadian Arctic. All the activity also attracted Inuit to construction sites, where they might be able to get temporary employment and access discarded supplies. The attraction of building activity and the potential for work was particularly strong in Iqaluit.

Military police operated on the bases themselves, but the RCMP was responsible for the policing of all civilians, including contractors, suppliers, and Inuit. Terry Jenkin, a retired RCMP officer, told the QTC, "The military were not allowed fraternization. One of our duties was to monitor such activity to ensure that there was no collusion between airmen and young Inuit girls. If we did find that, we took the Inuit girl back home and reported the airmen to the authority." Sexual relations between military contractors and personnel were known to be taking place, some of which were certainly against the law, either because the girls were not of age or because they were sexual assaults. In 1958, for example, a Canadian worker at a military station (FOX-3 on the DEW Line) in Qikiqtaaluk felt compelled to write an anonymous letter to the Minister of Northern Affairs, saying:

> Eskimos are getting a raw deal on the Dew Line. In one instance a Federal Electric officer is currently taking advantage of his position as Station Chief of Fox-3 to rape Eskimo woman. This man should be banned from Northwest Territories if law and order are to be maintained in this country. Apparently Federal Electric is aware of this fact because it is known to everybody on the Line.

It is unknown if action was taken.

In 1959, RCMP officer Van Norman spoke out against what he saw as the sexual and emotional exploitation of Inuit women by DEW Line employees.

The Canadian government determined that an increased police presence was needed to maintain order in this quickly changing social atmosphere. The RCMP shifted its work to policing the increasing number of Qallunaat who were working and settling in Qikiqtaaluk while simultaneously being removed from having to deliver other types of services.

The end of the era came around 1960 when many of the tasks historically undertaken by the RCMP were fully taken over by civil servants, most notably area administrators and northern service officers. In between those years, almost all Inuit moved, often under pressure, into government-run settlements for schooling, medical services, and housing. The effect of life on Inuit was profound, as described in more detail in other QTC histories. The ways that Inuit governed themselves and chose options for the future changed, and the RCMP was a key player in the changes. In his autobiography, Inuit leader John Amagoalik succinctly explained:

> When Inuit families were out in their seasonal camps they were in control of their lives. But once they moved to communities where the RCMP, the missionaries, and the Hudson's Bay Company were, they had no more say. The qallunaat decided what was going to happen in those communities, and nobody else had any input.

RCMP DUTIES AND THE ARRIVAL OF THE NORTHERN SERVICE OFFICERS

Through most of the era, the RCMP spent a major portion of its time on duties that would have been the responsibility of other agencies in other parts of Canada. The Force did this work "not by choice or because they were trained to do so, but for the usual reason—because they were on the scene" and it was cheaper than creating a separate administrative unit. The variety and the tedium of the job are evident in the explanation of duties from the 1951 RCMP Annual Report:

> Nineteen federal departments alone depend on our assistance in the North in such things as the registering of vital statistics; the issuing of various licenses, destitute rations, family allowances, medical supplies, the collecting of Income Tax, Fur Export-, Crown Timber-, Fur farming-fees, Customs and Excise tariffs, meteorological data; the inspecting of drug stores, scales and weights, and licensed and unlicensed magazines containing explosives; and acting as agents for the Public Administrators in cases where persons have died intestate.

In 1954 the position of Northern Service Officer (NSO) was created to administer programmes, "improve economic, social, and cultural conditions," and "supervise and develop Eskimo participation" to "diversify the economic basis of Eskimo life." The tension between the Department of Northern Affairs and National Resources and RCMP in serving as the "authorities to whom they should look and listen" crept into much of their correspondence in the 1950s. Into the early 1960s, there were obvious overlaps in the responsibilities of various federal agents, to the extent that confusion about roles was common. Initially, NSOs were expected to travel widely to visit Inuit wherever they lived, leaving the RCMP at detachments to do minor administrative duties and law enforcement. Within a few years, however, NSOs were spending most of their time in settlements where most Inuit lived.

TWO VIEWS

RCMP and Inuit perceptions of the relations between police and Inuit during the patrols to ilagiit nunagivaktangit offer contrasting perspectives. Although some RCMP officers recalled feeling isolated and ostracized by Inuit, they generally recall positive experiences. Calvin Alexander, who served in Pangnirtung, described how communities went out of their way to welcome and honour RCMP officers:

> We would pull in to a camp and everybody would turn out. After you got done shaking hands with everybody from the camp boss to the baby on the mama's back the men unhitched the dogs for you. They fed them for you. It was protocol. You always stayed at the camp boss' home. Mama first kicks the kids out to go live with grandma or auntie. John and I were given the children's sleeping platform for the duration of our stay. We would feed the family while we were staying with them and leave them with what goodies

> we could spare, depending on what camp it was and how far we had to go yet. On the trail, Joanasie was the boss and I was the junior man. When you pulled in to a camp Mama took your furs, if you had to wear them that day, and beat the frost out of them and hung them up to dry. She took your kamiks and put them over the qulliq. In one instance, she patched the hole in my duffle socks.

Alexander took this special attention as a sign of affection and welcome, and assumed that the relationship was based on reciprocity and mutual aid:

> You never went in to a camp where you weren't welcomed with open arms and after you got settled and had a bite to eat, you went over to visit other homes and asked how the hunting was, how their health was. If anybody was sick you got told about it real quick when you got in to camp. In the joint society there were parameters that we did our best to look after the administration side (welfare, family allowance) for the people. We looked after things that were strange to them and when we got out on the land and it was relatively strange to me they looked after me.

Inuit often felt quite different about the relationship. For many, the warm greetings and hospitality expressed in the ilagiit nunagivaktangit masked their discomfort. Joe Tikivik told the QTC, "We were so scared of the police we couldn't even look at them." He continued to recount how Inuit reacted to news that RCMP would be arriving, saying "We used to check to see if we had done anything wrong just before the police came in, just thinking 'maybe I did something wrong' . . . because we didn't know any better." The RCMP and Inuit represented "two solitudes in a single land," and experienced a deep cultural disconnect that RCMP did not always even know existed.

HIGH ARCTIC RELOCATIONS

One of the critical episodes in the relations between Inuit and RCMP concerns the High Arctic Relocation, a subject that has been covered in previous studies that include information from Inuit about their experiences. While it fits into the era when the government was still uncertain about whether it should be finding ways to support Inuit living on the land or whether it should be preparing everyone for life in settlements, the decisions made by the government were part of a pattern that clearly spoke to its determination to exercise control over Inuit, no matter where they lived. Relevant histories describe the RCMP's role in the relocations in detail, including choosing the families who would move, choosing their destinations, gathering them for the move, accompanying them, acquiring goods for them, and even managing money on their behalf. Individual officers provided support to the families and "at times circumvented the illogical rules through their own initiative," but they were also clearly attached to the government and its objectives.

Nunalinnguqtitauliqtilluta, 1961 to 1975

In the 1960s, almost the whole population of Qikiqtaaluk lived in centralized settlements, with outside forces shaping them into the present thirteen communities. R. Quinn Duffy, in *The Road to Nunavut*, describes the Euro-Canadian political framework that was systematically installed in Qikiqtaaluk in the late 1950s and 1960s as a "total social system." It encompassed "the legal system, land tenure, resources ownership regulations, communications networks, military organization, and system of individual rights and privileges." This period of "Nunalinnguqtitauliqtilluta" was marked by increased specialization among government agencies, the pushing of the RCMP into a more traditional policing role, and the arrival of many more Qallunaat into the region.

Both police and Inuit were forced to adapt to a new relationship once RCMP officers' duties became increasingly focused on enforcing both new laws and laws previously unenforced. This led to confusion over the role of RCMP and Canadian law in communities, with no forum available for Inuit to speak their minds or contribute to solutions due to language and to the lack of democratic institutions in which their voices would matter. No evidence was found that would show that Inuit were told the limits of police power or their rights in the cases of arbitrary arrest, seizure of property, or perjury. Important English words had no equivalent in Inuktitut, including the word "guilty." In 1962 an official explained:

> [Inuit are] quite confused about many of the white man's ways and one of the spheres of misunderstanding particularly relative here is the white man's law . . . It was suggested to me from several quarters that considerable education "in the law" should accompany law enforcement.

Inuit were confused, but they also sought a solution. Cape Dorset petitioned for an RCMP detachment in that same year because "it [was] felt a representative of Law and Order should be present to assist and teach our young people about these matters."

During the whole era, Inuit never had an opportunity to adjust their own social and cultural beliefs and structures to the new system—as Duffy writes, it was just "grafted" onto them. The RCMP were only one part of the new system, but the most visible and powerful on the ground. When Inuit moved into settlements, they became part of a collective to which more laws and rules applied, such as ordinances concerning loose dogs and liquor consumption. More mechanisms were also in place to ensure that rules were not broken. Police exercised their powers of arrest, fined people, and held sway over potential employers and the distribution of social benefits. July Papatsie recalled that his father forced him to go to school after the RCMP warned his father, "If your son doesn't go to school, you are not going to get family allowances, and you are going to lose your job. And, also if you get sick, you will not be allowed to go to the hospital."

The Qallunaat who most commonly moved to these settlements were transportation engineers, nurses, teachers, government employees, and church officials. This meant that RCMP could relinquish their official social welfare duties to new administrators, narrowing their own set of responsibilities to strictly policing as much as possible.

The RCMP still maintained responsibility for delivering social services in some of the communities. The Force was very reluctant to give up these duties to other agencies, since it provided steady work for officers and allowed them to go into the community and speak to people for reasons other than crime. Detachments were very aware of the impact of the changes in their duties on their position in communities.

In 1971, the renewed Agreement for Policing the Northwest Territories dealt with significantly narrowing the range of duties the RCMP was to perform. The new agreement required the RCMP to perform "such duties and render such services as are ordinarily performed or rendered by peace officers in aiding the administration of justice and in carrying into effect the laws of the Northwest Territories." This no longer included issuing licenses, collecting taxes or fees associated with licenses, impounding dogs, carrying out inspections related to health, sanitation, or fire related bylaws, or any other "laws of a similar regulatory nature which . . . are not suitable for enforcement by the Force." This change was designed to keep a "policeman's role in its proper realm and generally restrict him from performing non-police duties." In 1976, the Force instituted a cross-cultural education course to be taken by new recruits. The course was designed to create "an awareness of cultural and individual differences existing in a multicultural country, with the Canadian natives being used as a focal group to sensitize the student to their desires, attitudes, and heritage." By 1977, the police were no longer responsible for prisoner transfers, runaway juveniles, collection of fines, collection of fur-export tax, enforcement of non-police orientated bylaws, mental patients, serving jury summons, or a wide range of other activities. The police were now only responsible for the duties expected of community police anywhere in Canada.

IQALUIT

The further growth of settlements in the 1960s added to the strains in the relationship between the RCMP and Inuit, as did the increasing amount of alcohol available in communities. The influx of Qallunaat as contractors, teachers, traders, prospectors, government administrators, and transport workers meant that RCMP officers were now responsible for maintaining order within and between Inuit and Qallunaat groups.

The impact was most acutely felt in the rapidly growing centre of Iqaluit, where the police presence was strengthened, rules were more strictly enforced, and fewer opportunities existed for informal cultural contacts between the RCMP and Inuit. As the regional transportation hub and administrative centre, it attracted a large population of Qallunaat and Inuit from all over the Arctic looking for work. Everyone (academics, Qallunaat, and Inuit) agreed that modernization forces in Iqaluit in the late 1950s and early 1960s were having a severe impact on Inuit residents. Anthropologist Toshio Yatsushiro, who conducted field work in Iqaluit in 1958 and 1959, wrote "The incidents of theft, marital discord, deviant sexual behavior . . . gambling, and drinking are causing considerable anxiety" to Inuit Elders. The police, now surrounded by more Qallunaat, more crime, and more Euro-Canadian amenities, stayed near their detachment rather than undertaking regular patrols. For Inuit, life in the settlement included more frequent contacts with Qallunaat and activities that could lead to legal infraction, including accusations of theft, charges under the Liquor Ordinance, and exposure to the effects of the Ordinance Respecting Dogs. At the same time, RCMP became less dependent on Inuit for survival, which meant that the job position of Inuit special constable was more closely aligned to the day-to-day activities of the police and other authorities.

In 1961, the head of the Frobisher Bay detachment described the impact on RCMP work:

> It would be well to mention that in the eyes of the local Eskimo the Force at this point is associated with the ills of the transition period of the Eskimos adapting to a new way of life. The active enforcement of liquor and criminal law, a departure from our traditional role of benefactor and protector as in smaller Eastern Arctic settlements, cannot be rationalized by the Eskimo. Consequently, there is no particular desire to associate themselves with the Police; Eskimos who actively aid the Police are viewed with disfavour among the Eskimos.

For detachments other than Iqaluit, the lack of criminal activities also made it increasingly difficult to justify keeping RCMP in many communities. T. E. R. Lysk, Inspector in Charge of the Criminal Investigations Branch, wrote in 1964: "It should be clear to our members that if we had to rely strictly on police work to justify our existence, then all our detachments would probably be closed with the exception of one or two." Officers continued to provide maintenance, plumbing, heating, and even tax help alongside their policing duties in communities into the late twentieth century.

INUIT SPECIAL CONSTABLES AND INTERCULTURAL INTERPRETATION

The duties of Inuit special constables in the era also narrowed from general guide and aide to the important role of translator and intercultural mediator. The goal of the RCMP was in many ways a cultural one, helping Inuit to shift from one cultural legal framework to another. Despite this, the force's central responsibility to accurately convey information between the government and Inuit was passed on to Inuit special constables because the RCMP did not deem learning Inuktitut to be necessary, and so it was acquired informally at the officer's discretion, if at all. In any case, pressure was placed on Inuit special constables to be translators, both linguistic and cultural, for the RCMP. As Mosha Akavak told the QTC, part of his father's role as a special constable was "to try to inform the people of Kimmirut about what the RCMP was doing in the area." Inuit special constables were vulnerable in the community because of this role as cultural intermediary, and sometimes ostracized for their involvement with RCMP.

The quality of translations provided by Inuit varied since they, too, received little formal training. Mosha Akavak spoke to the QTC about his father:

> [He] was not an official interpreter. He only spoke a little bit of English but he could understand. And I remember him doing that, interpreting. For more technical messages that were to be conveyed to the people they had interpreters like store clerks or ministers. When there was a good interpreter available, they would use interpreters. My father was not an official interpreter. My mother understood more English than my father . . . My mother used to help with interpretation.

Ejesiak Padluq told the QTC that one Inuit special constable he remembered from his youth was a "very bad interpreter and wouldn't really relay information." The quality of interpretation, translation, and therefore intercultural communication varied widely in different communities and over time, and translators were often faced with trying to translate terms that had no equivalent expressions in the other language. For example, even in 2012 there was no Inuktitut word or expression meaning "guilty" or "not guilty."

Lack of institutional support for translation training for either Inuit special constables or RCMP severely impeded the force's performance in Qikiqtaaluk, although individual RCMP officers did not always realize the extent of this impediment. Other times, the RCMP blamed their interpreters, whether trained or informal, for any miscommunications. The *RCMP and Inuit Sled Dogs* report states:

> Unfortunately, many members were not fluent in the Inuit languages and dialects, and therefore had to rely upon interpreters, who often were special constables. Many former members reported instances where they gave a lengthy explanation to the Inuit for a decision being made, only to witness the interpreter reduce it to several sentences. The assumption by the members was that the interpreter conveyed only the decision, not the explanation.

RCMP headquarters was aware of ineffective translation services, but did little to change it. In Iqaluit in 1961, for example, the position of Inuit special constable stayed vacant for almost a year because the RCMP was not willing to increase the salary for the position to be on par with other departments that were hiring translators and interpreters. In one case, an Inuk suspected of stealing a rug had been held for seventeen days before the police could get a statement from the accused because there was no interpreter available. This issue still had not been solved by 1973, when the officer commanding "G" Division reported:

> Several of the Eskimo leaders raised the matter of lack of direct communication between our members since very few of our people speak the Eskimo language. Our special constables act as interpreters but this is not always satisfactory since there is often a loss in the translation which leads to misinterpretation and misunderstanding . . . I feel that it is very important that more of our members learn to speak the Eskimo Language inasmuch as our role in the North is quickly changing . . . Our police role with all its manifestation is not clearly understood by the Eskimos because they do not understand the intricacies of the various laws and ordinances.

This sentiment was echoed by retired RCMP constable Terry Jenkin, who explained to the QTC the difficulties he faced in communicating with Inuit: "I got some basic understanding and ability to speak Inuktitut. You don't know how well you are communicating. It was with great difficulty."

Recognition of Inuit special constables has been scarce. One constable, Kyak, was appointed an Officer of the Order of Canada for his "service to his fellow Eskimos as a Special Constable in the Royal Canadian Mounted Police for nearly thirty years." Deceased special constables at Cambridge Bay have recently been recognized by the placing of RCMP markers at their grave sites. Inuit special constables, who contributed so much to the RCMP northern history, have yet to be recognized as a group. This omission seems particularly inappropriate since the RCMP chose to recognize in 1973 the contribution of qimmiit to the Force's northern work.

An RCMP report from 1961 complained that it was becoming very difficult to hire "competent Eskimo interpreters," especially in Iqaluit, because the pay for special constables was relatively low compared to the salaries offered by other federal, military, and private employers. The RCMP also admitted that they had reduced the number of people interested in the job due to its own actions, stating that a large group of potential bilingual candidates "[had] been involved with the Police—principally in infractions of the N.W.T. Liquor Ordinance." The detachment was so severely affected by the lack of interpreters that it even opened the possibility of using a female Qallunaat stenographer, noting that the potential candidate "[was] fluent in Eskimo and English, and [had] good experience in stenographic duties."

RCMP officers with experience in the Arctic expressed dismay over the many changes that affected the Force in the 1950s and into the 1960s. The emphasis on the enforcement of laws, without the benefits of a full justice system consisting of courts, lawyers, interpreters, and laws made by the people most affected by them, meant that many Inuit were even more likely to view the RCMP as threatening authority figures, a power dynamic that has permeated Inuit–RCMP relations ever since. In the process, ilira was replaced by resentment.

Game laws and related rules meant that the police could dictate to Inuit where to go, what to hunt, and how to behave. Repeatedly under the Liquor Ordinance the police imprisoned and punished people—under the Dog Ordinance they killed qimmiit. In numerous places, RCMP had sexual relationships with Inuit women that resulted in both anguish for the women and lingering hurt for children who never met their fathers and were physically different than others in their community.

Additionally, Inuit actions that had traditionally been acceptable were now coming into conflict with Canadian law, which had been in place for decades but which was now being more strongly enforced. For instance, with Regina v. Amak, Avinga, and Nangmalik (1963), three Inuit were charged with assisting in Arrak Qulitalik's suicide. Bob Pilot, the RCMP officer assigned to the case, was hesitant about proceeding but was told fthat this was a case worth prosecuting in order to demonstrate the "evolution" of the police and to show "that the police are not just givers of welfare." The three pleaded guilty, but their sentence was suspended by Judge Sissons on the advice of Pilot, who pointed out that punishing the men with incarceration would remove three important hunters from the ilagiit nunagivaktangit and their families.

Some RCMP, like Bob Pilot, attempted to bend the laws to conform to traditional Inuit practices, but in the 1960s in particular more laws were being introduced and police were increasingly being called upon to enforce them more vigorously. While Inuit had no option but to comply with laws, they did not accept these laws as their own. With respect to game laws, for example, Qanguk told Hugh Brody, "When we knew that the police were coming our way we knew that we were going to be asked all kinds of questions. And we began to get our answers ready." In some cases Inuit moved away from the police to avoid contact with them. Qanguk explained, "We knew that we were going to be asked about the animals we had killed . . . We were not allowed to kill too many. This was against their rules. So we decided to move farther away, and to go and live beyond the policemen's journeys, because we were scared."

A report to the Commission of the NWT in 1978 about new policing agreements provides a helpful summary of the RCMP's perceptions about the challenges that it faced in performing "non-police duties" over the previous decade. The duties addressed in the report included among others acting as prosecutors, collecting taxes, issuing licenses, impounding dogs, and enforcing municipal bylaws. The section on serving as prosecutors revealed the extent to which many officers were uncomfortable with the role. The report stated:

> One final tension point revolves around the fact that the RCMP are required to prosecute cases coming before the Justices of the Peace Courts. Mixed feelings were expressed to the Committee about the RCMP assuming this role. Some individuals thought that the conflict was so fundamental that they should restrict their role to traditional policing work; others enjoyed the experience;

> others felt they should receive more detailed training to handle such responsibilities. Few saw any real alternatives to the present system. This can and occasionally does have unfortunate results. Individual RCMP can be called upon to provide policing, prosecutorial, and defence counsel services and, in addition, to provide guidance to a lay Justice of the Peace on the laws. Such tripartite conflicts in a court situation can affect community perceptions of the role of the RCMP.

Dog Ordinance and the Killing of Qimmiit

As is discussed in other chapters, a recurring point of conflict between Inuit and RCMP was the handling of qimmiit. For decades, RCMP were entirely reliant on qimmiit for their work, especially for the multiple patrols they made each year to visit ilagiit nunagivaktangit or to check up on traders and missionaries where there was no detachment. RCMP were responsible for inoculating qimmiit against rabies and doing whatever was needed to stabilize qimmiit populations. As an example of RCMP actions to help keep qimmiit healthy, after the qimmit population in Cumberland Sound was almost destroyed by disease in 1959, the RCMP transported qimmiit from other regions into Pangnirtung—RCMP officers even tried to establish a qimmit breeding program in the community. In the same period, however, RCMP were invoking the Ordinance Respecting Dogs to kill loose qimmiit in places like Iqaluit where Inuit were likely to stay for extended periods of time and where many Qallunaat were also living.

As of 1950, all RCMP officers officially became dog officers and could and did shoot qimmiit not tied up or otherwise in violation of the Ordinance. In his autobiography, Inuit leader Paul Quassa of Igloolik described an incident in Igloolik:

> The RCMP said that the dogs had distemper or rabies or some kind of sickness, but they weren't sick at all. The community was growing but the dogs weren't everywhere. The dogs were in one place. Perhaps the RCMP constables were scared of them and they slaughtered them. Sometimes they didn't even tell the owners.

In effect, enforcement was both a result of the conditions of the time and place, and the inclination of specific officers. In some cases only a single qimmit was shot, while in other cases entire teams were destroyed. In two particularly excessive examples, the police shot more than two hundred and fifty qimmiit in both Iqaluit and Pangnirtung. Other authorities were allowed to shoot qimmiit, but in most cases, the shootings would have been done with RCMP knowledge and in many cases with RCMP involvement, either by officers or by Inuit special constables.

As is discussed elsewhere in this book, the manner in which qimmiit were killed proved very painful for Inuit. Jacopoosie Peter's family's qimmiit were killed by the RCMP in 1966. He told the QTC:

> That year in the summer, I had the fright of my life. I was nearing three years old. My mother shouted, "The police are shooting the dogs!" We all went outside. My mother went outside and was screaming and yelling. My grandfather chained the dogs . . . I remember shots being fired and an RCMP officer running. I was very scared that time. I always had nightmares over it.

For Mosesee Qiyuakjuk, the RCMP officers shooting qimmiit was representative of their broader disrespect for Inuit. He told the QTC:

> The RCMP used to mistreat us badly those days when they considered themselves superior to Inuit. The RCMP considered Inuit as though we meant nothing in their eyes. The mistreatment of Inuit and their actions were inconsiderate of Inuit welfare those days. They did not have the audacity to inform or warn us that they would shoot and kill off our dogs. The RCMP had no concern of Inuit rights then and they are more considerate now and inform the owners prior to killing dogs now. In those days the RCMP did their own thing without informing Inuit of any of their actions. In those days I remember their actions and what they did to Inuit were unforgiving and deliberate as if trying to scare the Inuit by their actions.

Witnesses who spoke to the QTC recalled that it was difficult for Inuit to kill qimmiit, but that they were compelled to do what they were told by the police while trying to keep Inuit safe from the mayhem. Joshie Teemotee Mitsima told the QTC about an incident during his childhood in the late 1960s when the RCMP were shooting qimmiit in Apex in Iqaluit. The Inuit special constable, Paul Idlout, "was ordered by the RCMP Constable, a white guy" to untie the family's qimmit. The dog immediately ran towards young Joshie, who described:

> [Paul Idlout] was yelling to the other policeman "Don't shoot!" Because I was in the way. The other policeman shot the dog anyway. Just as it was between me and the policeman he shot the dog. It looked like he was shooting right at me. It was like in slow motion I could almost see the bullet coming down and hitting the dog. It was so strange.

The perception that RCMP were largely responsible for the killings, and the poisonous relations that were being created, was captured by anthropologist Toshio Yatsushiro, who quoted an Inuk in 1958 as saying "Maybe the police will kill Eskimos then, just like the dogs."

RCMP and Inuit Women

The RCMP held a policy that condemned romantic or sexual interactions between officers and Inuit women, whether due to racist beliefs, a fear of compromised policing, or a concern for abandoned illegitimate children once officers returned South. Despite this policy, sexual interactions were well known, according to Inuit and historical records. The relationships were common enough that a cartoon about liaisons between Inuit women and RCMP made it into the magazine *RCMP Quarterly* in 1950 (Figure 1). Romantic relationships followed a spectrum of interaction, from brief, consensual relationship to longlasting marriages, but it is also certain that some RCMP used their position of authority to coerce Inuit women into sexual acts.

July Papatsie, from Pangnirtung, described the RCMP's power over women:

> With that much power, they could do anything they wanted to do.... The RCMP could do anything they wanted with any woman that was living up north. Anything. Now that woman who was forced sexually by this officer cannot talk back, has nowhere to go and complain. Her husband knows but cannot do anything, is powerless.

He also explained that the RCMP took advantage of Inuit customs:

> Inuit used to live a simple life. Adultery was not accepted but swap was allowed. RCMP exploited it to the extreme. Once they

found out they could trade husbands and wives freely . . . people were forced for sexual favours. If the DNA of RCMP officers were to be looked at, they would be found everywhere because people were forced for sexual favours. We Inuit know that. When they accepted, the child was told what happened in tradition but with the RCMP, the child would not be able to talk to the father.

Figure 1: *RCMP Quarterly*. Cartoon Supplement, 1950.

Papatsie linked the "negative energy" from RCMP relations with Inuit women to problems within families, including abuse.

Some Inuit told the QTC about their experiences as children of Inuit women and Qallunaat RCMP officers. Elisapee Ootoova told the QTC, "I have an RCMP father. I am different from my sister. I am an illegitimate child. And it is embarrassing. I was so close with my [non-biological] father and when I started learning that I have a white father, when I started going older, I was very agitated by it." Joshua Idlout told the QTC that his mother getting pregnant by his RCMP father had severe repercussions for his family: "My mother's husband . . . was out for TB recovery [and] came home to find his wife pregnant. This was one of the biggest painful experiences he went through. She had me for nine months although her husband tried to have me miscarried. I heard a lot of bad stories about it."

Inuit and RCMP share a history, in the sense that many of the events that shaped their pasts unfolded in the same time and place, even though the impacts and experiences were personal and singular. Both groups were being bombarded with messages that the North would be developed and that they needed to either move aside or take positions in support of new, comprehensive economic and political agendas. For the RCMP, this meant that officers were expected to focus on law enforcement near military bases and other places where Inuit were arriving in growing numbers. For Inuit, who found themselves suddenly living year-round in settlements, this meant continuous exposure, without any support, to dozens of laws in a justice system that was both new and complicated.

In their long history in Qikiqtaaluk, the RCMP viewed themselves as guardians of Inuit, enforcers of Canadian laws and values, and interpreters of a new political, economic, and cultural system that was always believed to be just around the corner. For Inuit, however, police in the local detachment or on patrol embodied an outside world that was imposing strange and inappropriate laws and practices on Inuit life. Individual officers, who rotated in and out of detachments every two or three years, could be sympathetic or mean, reliable or unpredictable. Some officers caused great distress in communities and families due to personal actions and behaviours. Inuit were unable—or afraid—to challenge the RCMP directly. Also, as the RCMP admitted in its report *RCMP and Inuit Sled Dogs*, many officers were paternalistic in their attitudes and behaviours—they acted as though they knew what was better for Inuit than Inuit themselves.

As document records and Inuit memories show, many RCMP officers shared a strong admiration for Inuit skills, knowledge, and culture, and in many instances individual officers lobbied the federal government on behalf of Inuit. Police officers requisitioned supplies, travelled great distances to get medical help, and stretched rules to issue relief. In general, however, paternalism, coupled with immense authority and the power to enforce laws that made no sense in the cultural and environmental context of Qikiqtaaluk, created an imbalance in the relationship between Inuit and RCMP. As a result, Inuit ended up doing things they did not want to do, or resisted and ignored laws. The RCMP found it very difficult, for example, to hire special constables when other jobs were available, noting that Inuit exhibited "some reluctance" to take jobs with the RCMP.

The RCMP has served as the longest-standing agent of the federal government in Qikiqtaaluk. For this reason alone, a more thorough examination of the shared history is called for. The history is needed both for the sake of RCMP serving in the North, so they can better understand how their predecessors' actions have affected Inuit, and for Qikiqtaalungmiut, to provide them a with a more balanced history about important issues, such as the enforcement of liquor laws and the treatment of Inuit women, than what has so far been made available.

Inuit outside the Hudson's Bay Company post, 1949

LIBRARY AND ARCHIVES CANADA

Inuit children playing in front of the R.C. Mission, September 1958
LIBRARY AND ARCHIVES CANADA

Inuit artist in the craft centre at Cape Dorset, hanging prints to dry
LIBRARY AND ARCHIVES CANADA

Inuit family and skin tent, Clyde River, August 26, 1932
LIBRARY AND ARCHIVES CANADA

Inuit children with supplies for the R.C. Mission, July 1951

LIBRARY AND ARCHIVES CANADA

In the Hudson's Bay Company store at Igloolik, 1952

LIBRARY AND ARCHIVES CANADA

Inuit unloading supplies from supply ship anchored off shore at Arctic Bay
LIBRARY AND ARCHIVES CANADA

Inuit women cleaning walrus hides
LIBRARY AND ARCHIVES CANADA

Loading furs for Montreal, at Arctic Bay, on the barge of the *C. D. Howe*, July 1951

LIBRARY AND ARCHIVES CANADA

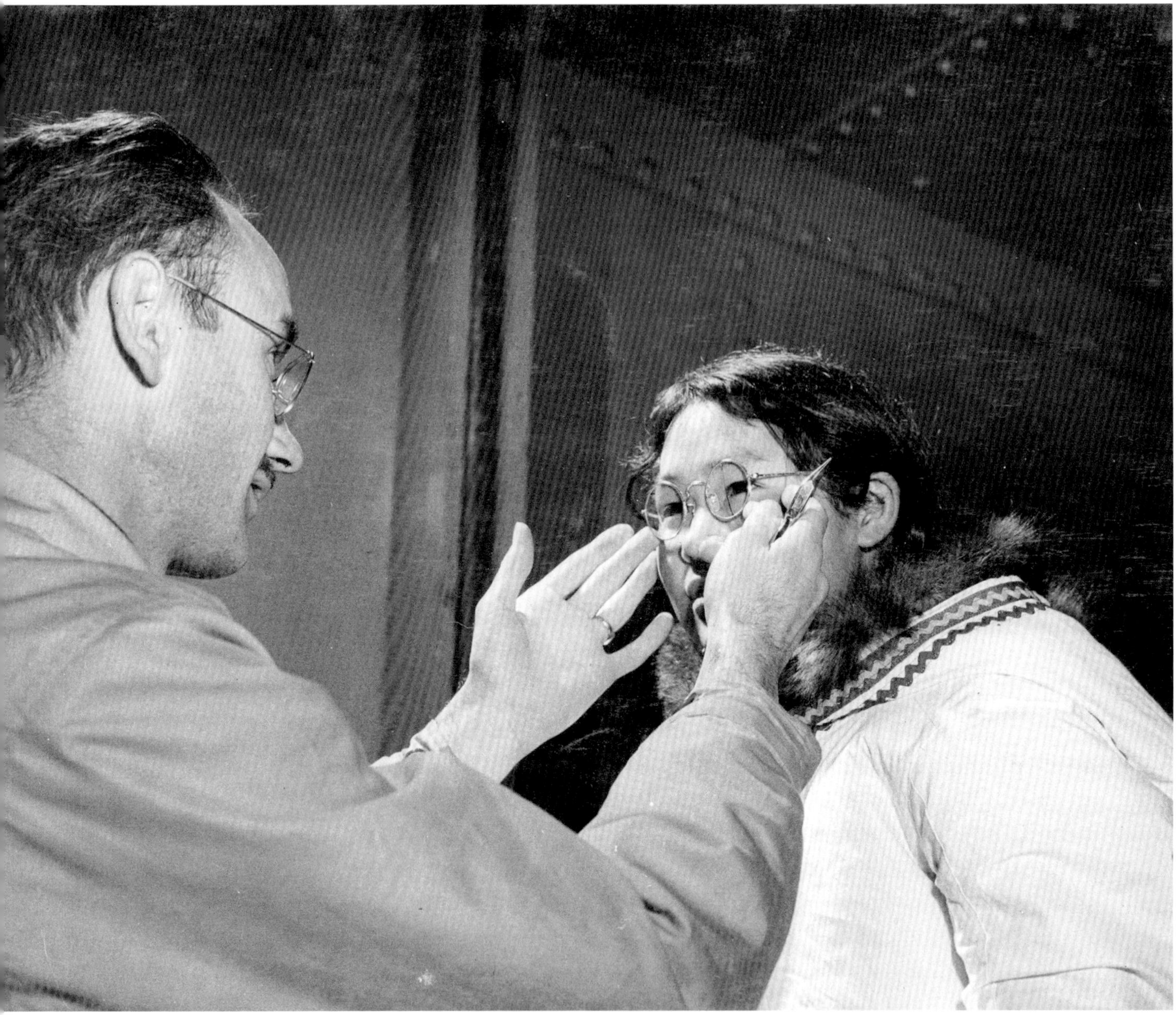

Inuk woman is fitted with a pair of glasses by W. J. Fostner, 1947
LIBRARY AND ARCHIVES CANADA

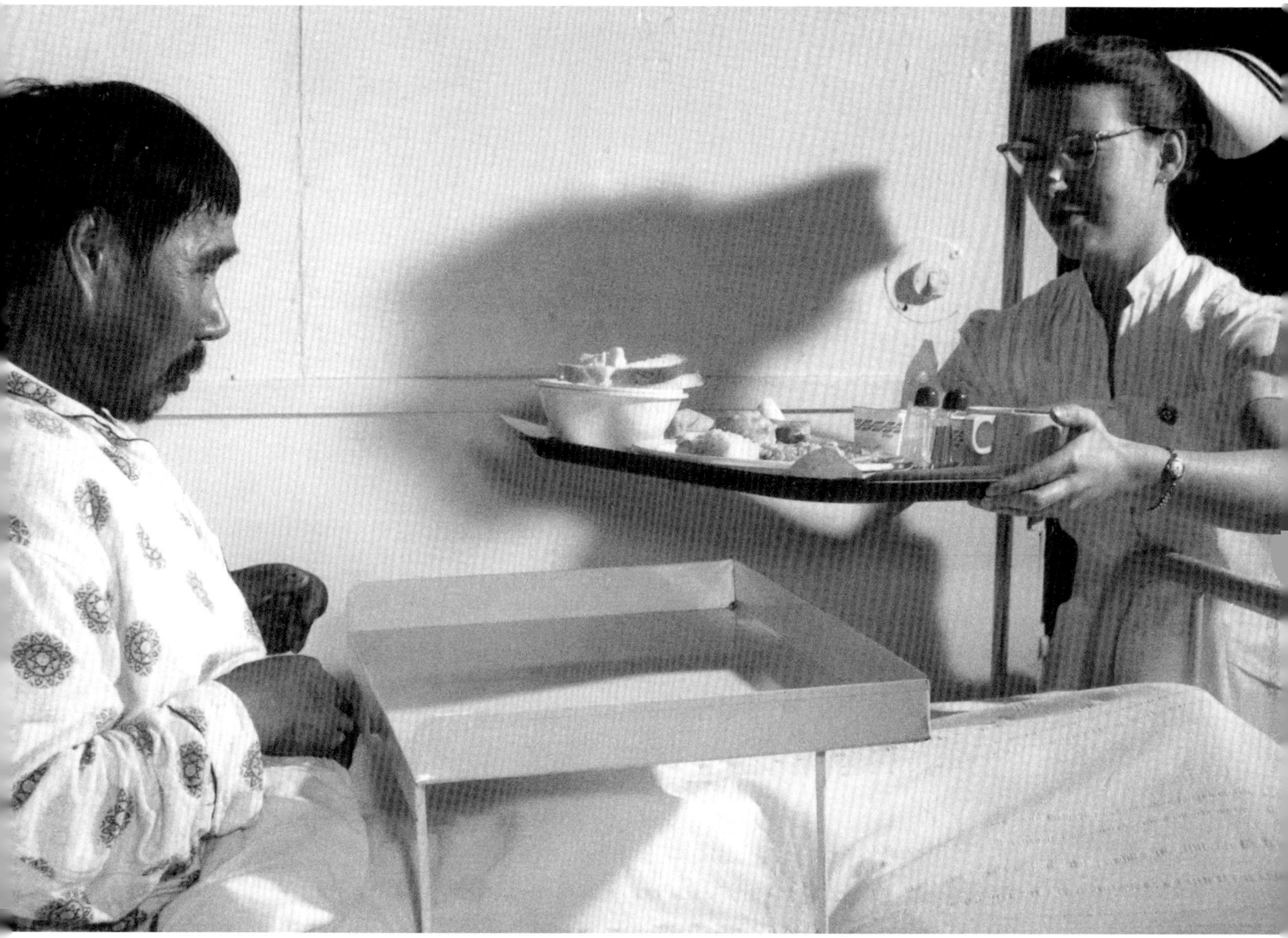

Nurse brings Inuk man food in hospital

LIBRARY AND ARCHIVES CANADA

Panikpakuttuk (centre) and Qajaaq (right) outside of the RCMP detachment

LIBRARY AND ARCHIVES CANADA

Preparing for the trip to Enukso Point

LIBRARY AND ARCHIVES CANADA

Stretcher case takes ambulance to airport for flight to Montreal hospital, July 1951
LIBRARY AND ARCHIVES CANADA

Still from the film *Land of the Long Day*—Inuit gathered in an iglu for their meal

LIBRARY AND ARCHIVES CANADA

Pivalliajuliriniq

Economic Development in Qikiqtaaluk

BACKGROUND AND APPROACH

Beginning in the 1950s, the Canadian government increased its investment and involvement in all parts of the North, including Qikiqtaaluk. The intended beneficiaries were not only the region's Inuit inhabitants, but also Canadians in the South. In official policy statements about its new interest in the North, the government tried to show respect for the importance of hunting to Inuit life, but its actions spoke differently. Modernization was pushing forward, especially through schooling, direct investments in local infrastructure, and an emphasis on moving people into Southern-style housing. The impact of the development was immediate and deep. In the 1950s, most Inuit lived in multi-family hunting groups in about one hundred flexible ilagiit nunagivaktangit that were mobile within traditional territories of considerable size. By the 1970s, almost all Inuit were living in twelve hamlets and a town, which is now a city. Despite this, Inuit have never abandoned hunting as a foundation for their local economy, even as technology evolves and operates in parallel to the cash economy, resource development, and access to consumer goods.

The various parties involved in development in Qikiqtaaluk have long understood that the region could not be developed as the south had been, through agriculture, forestry, and European immigration. The constraints are ecological, demographic, and cultural. The biomass is extremely low, and a very small human population is widely dispersed across a large area. The skills needed to feed people from the land are outside the market economy, and require knowledge, techniques, and work disciplines that do not fit well with southern employment routines. Differences in work patterns made it difficult to train people locally or to attract and retain qualified workers in the region. Additionally, the region is located far from centres of industrial production and potential markets for its goods. Isolation, prolonged periods of bad weather, and frozen seas make surface transport irregular and expensive. All communities rely heavily on the South for goods and services. In return, most of what Inuit produced for outside markets in the twentieth century were luxury goods—white fox furs, sealskins, and the artistic output of carvers, printmakers, and weavers, as well as memorable tourism experiences. Qikiqtaaluk also has had its own modest record of the boom-bust cycles typical of northern mining.

Broadly speaking, the publicly funded development strategy for the region has been to install infrastructure, such as schools, housing, diesel generators, landing strips, and navigation aids; to encourage local hiring for mining and other development projects where possible; and, as in the days of the fur trade, to organize production of other exports.

CULTURAL CONSTRAINTS—GOVERNMENT ASSUMPTIONS

Behind all government programs in the period from 1950 to 1975 were a set of questionable assumptions and external influences that shaped policies and the chances of any program's success. These are introduced here as background.

The first assumption was that the federal government had an unquestioned right to administer the North, without any need to consult its indigenous people. Administration was very limited and investment was all but absent before the Second World War. It was largely in the 1950s with defence-related projects, as well as the growth of Canada's universal welfare programs, that decisions were made about developing modern infrastructure in the north. Hall Beach and Qikiqtarjuaq, for example, were located at major Distant Early Warning (DEW) Line facilities, while Iqaluit was a major logistical centre for military initiatives by Americans and Canadians from 1944 onwards. The economic impact of these and other government installations was widespread and permanent.

The second assumption was that Inuit culture was of great value, but highly vulnerable. Initially, government and church observers recognized hunting as the most sustainable source of food and cultural rewards for Inuit. Yet outsiders were also naive. They considered hunting to be hard, risky work, and assumed that, if anything easier came along, Inuit would drop it and ultimately lose the necessary skills. Especially in the early 1950s, the federal government considered itself responsible for finding a path between two extremes. One extreme was excessive contact with Qallunaat, which officials imagined would lead to demoralization and dependence; the other was isolation, which officials believed would impoverish Inuit while southern Canadians took over the best in the North.

The inconsistent logic of the second assumption is well expressed in a formal statement of policy on economic and cultural change from 1956:

> Where [Inuit] in remote areas are relatively free from contact with white civilization, it is planned to leave their present economy as undisturbed as possible. In those areas where there is already permanent contact, integration with the white economy will be encouraged. Between these two extremes employment of Eskimos will be encouraged, provided it does not interfere unduly with their normal life. It is also planned to diversify the Eskimo economy and to continue to transfer families from unproductive areas to regions where game is more abundant or employment is available.

This vague and unrealistic policy was never really put into practice. With compulsory schooling and the concentration of services like health care at a handful of locations, the design of government services decisively affected the way practically all Inuit were drawn into settlements, in spite of cultural risks and lack of economic guarantees.

A third assumption was that most Inuit lacked the knowledge or skills to make informed choices in the Canadian economy. If this was true in any way, it was the result of government policy. In the nineteenth and early twentieth centuries, Inuit in many places participated in non-traditional ways in foreign-sponsored industries and trades, notably whaling and, on a small scale, mining and the sale of handicrafts. In 1924, a well-travelled government scientist remarked:

> The net result is that while [Inuit] have taken hold of a great many of the white man's ideas, they have [gotten] nowhere commercially. It is a fair statement that there is not one [Inuk] in Baffin Land who has any idea of the real value of his own products. Their position now is that they are in the best possible frame of mind to learn, and anxious to do so.

This sort of progress was thwarted for the next thirty years by the economic grip of the fur trade and the lack of an effective government presence. Defence construction projects in the mid-1950s made this sort of isolation untenable. In Iqaluit, dozens of families from surrounding regions reacted predictably, as Elder Naki Ekho told anthropologist Ann McElroy in 1999, "I came here by dog team from upland with the whole family [in 1957]... The reason we came here was when someone finds plentiful amounts of something, like work or food, they come to get it."

LONG-RANGE GOALS OF GOVERNMENT AND INUIT ORGANIZATIONS

Throughout the years from 1950 to 1975, the economic development goals of the federal government, and roles it assigned to Inuit, were explained to the public in official announcements, publications, and speeches. These covered the spectrum from support for dispersed hunting in the early 1950s through to strong statements boosting mining and petroleum industries in the 1970s. In 1970, the federal Cabinet approved seven vague "national objectives for the development of northern Canada." The seven objectives included constitutional evolution, sovereignty, and security, a rising standard of living in the North, and contributions to the national economy. Environmental protection was also mentioned.

The Department of Indian Affairs and Northern Development's intentions emerged two years later in a general statement included in a report published as *Canada's North, 1970–1980*, in English, French, and Inuktitut. Its central message to Indigenous people was that northerners could benefit from big changes driven from the South and that change was inevitable. The statement echoed the Department's discredited "White Paper on Indian Policy" (1969), asserting that, "An essential aim is therefore to prepare and assist [all] the native peoples to integrate into Canadian society... in such a way that they can maintain their pride and cultural heritage." This pride was not for everyone; the government would continue to relocate people en masse, and would encourage the best-educated and trained Inuit to relocate within the territories or to southern Canada. Finally, the statement emphasized, "The economic future of the North lies in the ground."

Government officials were accustomed to having the first and last word on questions about the future of Qikiqtaaluk. By the 1970s, however, strong voices were being heard from Aboriginal people across the North with their own traditions and visions for the future. In 1988, the Tungavik Federation of Nunavut (TFN) issued this expression of long-standing Inuit views about economic development:

> We will continue to adapt to changing circumstances, but this does not mean we are prepared to adopt all southern ways, mores, and values, and to cut ourselves off from our culture and our land. Instead, we want to design a society and economy that enables us to participate effectively in the old ways based on the land and its bounty, as well as in the new ways based on space-age technology and world-wide communication.

TFN insisted that the future could be made secure through the creation of better programs to support hunters.

> The animals we kill provide us with highly nutritious food, which is shared with other Inuit who cannot, or do not, go hunting. Inuit harvesters in Nunavut produce approximately $40 million worth of country food per year ... If, through the land claim settlement, we can help Inuit afford to stay on the land, we will ensure that Inuit remain a land-based culture.

Preparing Individuals for Economic Development

TRAINING

As early as 1953, before the public announcement of air-defence projects in the far North, the government invited select Qallunaat across the Arctic to survey "Eskimo potential" by identifying young men and boys who could be trained for employment as "radio operators, meteorological technicians, stationary engineers, mechanics, vehicle drivers, carpenters, cooks, maintenance men, teachers, hospital orderlies, [and] office workers." Training, especially in the territories where the federal government delivered provincial-type services, would not be criticized by Qallunaat as being a handout—it was an acceptable kind of transfer to individuals that would encourage independence, not dependence.

While planning crept ahead, sudden shocks brought small groups of Inuit face to face with training opportunities. One was the widespread evacuations after 1950 of tuberculosis patients to the South, where many learned to speak and write in English. The other was the flood of men and materials north to build the DEW Line in 1955. In the process, crisis management overtook planning. None of the planning supported the desires of many individuals and families who wanted to move back and forth flexibly between the wage and hunting sectors of their economy. This lack of coordination forcibly alienated some hunters from the land and, in extreme cases, led government officials to kill off qimmiit, sending a stark message about the difficulty of dividing time between traditional and contemporary economic activities.

A departmental statement in 1955 summarized the Government's attitude towards training in the North:

> As the opportunities for employment in the industries of the north and in defence establishments become more widespread and as educated and trained young people become available, those Eskimos and Indians who wish to enter wage employment should be able to do so in skilled and semi-skilled trades.

This statement shifted from an individual approach (jobs for some) to a universal one (integration for all):

> It will not be good enough for them to remain as untrained and largely uneducated labour engaged in the more menial tasks. These native Canadians will with training be able to develop their abilities and to make their full contribution to the nation's growth and to their own welfare. Integration into the national life and activities will follow progressively.

Most government efforts directed towards individuals did nothing to support hunting or reward the skills people already possessed. In 1966, an inventory of courses offered across Canada, including centres in many provinces and a special federal school in Churchill, Manitoba, boasted of courses in "fabric painting, fur grading, sawmill operation, boat building, and guide training" as well as "carpentry, heavy equipment operation, commercial art, commercial subjects, baking, marine mechanics, plumbing, equipment mechanics, and handicraft management." Not mentioned in this official publication were the numerous courses given in communities to prepare Inuit, primarily women, to use the appliances installed in the prefabricated houses that were proliferating in even the smallest communities. Some women also received training in secretarial skills, sewing, and translation. Also available was on-the-job training, though there was no assurance that new jobs would open up when the work at hand ended.

Muckpaloo of Arctic Bay explained the importance of this type of training through the 1960s and 1970s:

> Because more and more people are working for such companies as Panarctic and the mine, they are going south to take special courses to learn their jobs. I first went south in 1962 to study welding and electrical wiring in Victoria and Chilliwack. In 1972, I went back to learn carpentry, plumbing, and the responsibilities of a fire chief.

For some Inuit, training followed health treatments in the south. Founded in 1956, the Iqaluit Rehabilitation Centre was an ambitious effort by Welfare Chief Walter Rudnicki to get Inuit out of hospitals in the South without forcing them back onto the land while they were still weak. By starting with people who were vulnerable and infirm, Rudnicki sidestepped the government's usual scruples against "handouts." Rehabilitation would help former patients learn a trade or occupation consistent with their capabilities and type of disability, "instructing them in the handling of money, home economics, sanitation, operation of businesses, and many different skills and attributes necessary to fit into a different type of life." As authors John and Irma Honigmann pointed out from their research in Iqaluit in 1963, rehabilitation was part of a general practice of "tutelage," and far from being limited to physical rehabilitation, its "ambitious aim" was "guiding Eskimos' resocialization," including help for young people in trouble.

By 1960, the Rehabilitation Centre had grown to thirty-five buildings accommodating eight staff, forty-seven residents and sixteen transients. A handicraft program was generating $40,000 a year. Although the centre at one time housed a third of the population of Apex, the Honigmanns noticed that its people were not recruited to leadership positions in the Community Association, Community Council, or the Church. In 1962, the centre organized "back on the land" activities to remind vulnerable people how hard their life had been in the ilagiit nunagivaktangit, but some participants did quit and move back to the land. Overall, however, the centre's "graduates" were twice as likely to go into wage employment as to return to the land. In general, with its Inuktitut-speaking staff and efforts to respect Inuit work routines, the Honigmanns found "the Centre undeniably ranks highly compatible with Eskimo values and aspirations." Its reach, however, was limited to the few dozen people who passed through its long-term program, and to ex-patients in transit. Less formal rehabilitation programs served smaller populations in places like Hall Beach.

EMPLOYMENT

Before 1950, the communities always offered jobs for a few Inuit, hired for general labour, domestic service and for hunting meat for the dog teams of missionaries, RCMP, and traders. Seasonally, Inuit helped unload the annual supply ship wherever it called. The addition of teachers and civilian administrators to communities increased the need for such help. In Iqaluit, the United States Air Force (USAF) never built housing for its sizeable Inuit workforce, but in 1955, the Canadian government developed a new "civilian establishment" a few kilometres away at Apex Hill. Here it imported prefabricated housing and community buildings. Smaller versions of this kind of settlement sprang up around other communities, which gradually increased the number of local civilian jobs for Inuit.

Widespread employment was slow to get started. A 1960 estimate reported that only 6% of Inuit in all regions had ever experienced "steady wage employment." Others worked intermittently in jobs such as stevedoring, freighting supplies, and carpentering, for periods lasting from a few days to a few weeks. A list of employed Inuit prepared for the Minister in 1962 showed just over two hundred in ten Qikiqtaaluk communities, with more than half the jobs being in Iqaluit. However, growth of communities saw some corresponding need for unskilled and semi-skilled Inuit labour. Schools and houses demanded diesel electric generators, which needed mechanics to maintain them. Vehicles were imported for water and sewage services, requiring drivers and road crews. Nursing stations and schools needed janitors and secretaries. Construction jobs continued into the autumn after each season's sealift brought new buildings, though this work was temporary. Many Inuit preferred to combine seasonal or part-time work with hunting, but the low figures overall show how slowly government progressed with its policy of preparing Inuit for wage employment.

The importance of government jobs in an individual community is indicated by a survey taken in Pond Inlet in 1966. In 1956, the total wage bill for Inuit was estimated to be $6,000. Ten years later, there were three Inuit federal employees each earning more than that amount, and six earning between $1,110 and $3,900. About forty employed men and women worked, generally part-time, as hostel parents, classroom assistants, interpreters, and casual labourers, but specialists like teachers and nurses were almost exclusively recruited from outside. These sensitive posts went to people who might take years to understand Inuit culture, while the number of jobs, even at less-skilled levels, did not meet demand for work from the increasing number of people living year-round in the communities.

While most jobs were in communities, the isolated weather stations and air defence posts played a large part in hiring Inuit. Witnesses at Sanikiluaq mentioned looking for work or being offered jobs and training at Kuujuarpik. At Kimmirut, Henry Boaz described a childhood spent at isolated weather stations on Hudson Strait. He was born at Nottingham Island, where his father, Willy Unaalik, worked for the Department of Transport weather station. He grew up on Resolution Island among a rotating staff of four or five Qallunaat and two or three Inuit families. In the following exchange with Commissioner James Igloliorte, Boaz spoke about how his father's employment ended.

> Boaz: My parents had gotten tired of working for the weather station and we [kids] were getting old enough to go out on our own and that was the main reason.
>
> Commissioner: When they asked to move what did the weather station people do about that? Did they help them move or did they say that they had to find someone else to do that?
>
> Boaz: We were basically on our own. We were given large rations by the weather station people and we were moved by the RCMP but dumped quite far from Lake Harbour [Kimmirut], out in the wilderness.

Numerous employers, including government bodies, did not carefully follow employment law and employment conditions, such as who would bear the cost of returning workers to a previous community. Some Inuit would continue to be paid to use their land skills in new ways, guiding parties outside the settlements. As Manasie Amagoalik of Pond Inlet explained to the QTC, "Sometimes [Inuit] would work for RCMP, other times they would take out other explorers, other people, [who] wanted to go [to the] High Arctic, sports hunters, geologists." However, Amagoalik also noted that payment was uncertain, and work was often "voluntary." Ham Kudloo of Pond Inlet spoke about the unpaid work he did for the medical team at each community at which the *C.D. Howe* called, on his way home from a hospital in Quebec:

> I was acting as an interpreter, I had that role as an interpreter at every port of call both for the eye doctors and other medical personnel. At that time I was thinking, "Alright, at least I'll be making some money, and I'll have some money when I get to Pond Inlet." But only afterwards I found out it was a voluntary position, and

> basically it was charitable because I was not given even one dollar. And then the *C.D. Howe* left, and the doctors, and the nurses, the eye doctor and everybody left on the *C.D. Howe* and they did not even give me a thank-you note or even a dollar for my services. That's what stood out in my recollection. And as I got older and I could start thinking more or reflecting more, I was thinking, "Boy, I must have been very patient," and I could not understand how I let these things pass when I was a young person.

Employment, as well as underemployment, affected Inuit in different ways. There were changes in the relationships between youth and Elders, between the best hunters and others, between those who spoke English and those who did not. Change also affected men and women differently. George Wenzel told the QTC that following centralization, nostalgia for life on the land was more common among men than among women. Some observers have suggested that Inuit women's traditional skills were more easily transferred to modern life than men's were. A study by Abraham Tagalik and Archie Angnakak in 2008 identified problems in men's and women's different communication styles and skills, expectations, and roles. It suggested that girls were usually put to work on household chores, and therefore developed skills in setting priorities and coping with problems, while some traditional skills that boys learned as hunters directly conflicted with how they were supposed to behave in the classroom or workplace.

Similarly, Elders pointed to differences in men's opportunities to develop interpersonal skills and relationships. For example, in discussing suicide prevention and resilience, one group of Elders noted:

> Previously men did not have to relate in larger groups as they were out hunting, and perhaps girls had learned how to live in groups better. The move to living in settlements and communities meant men were constantly exposed to more complex relationships in

> their new environment, yet they lacked previous experience in this regard. On the other hand, women had ... coping skills and strategies that aided them in adapting to newer, more complicated, and busier circumstances.

Community-Focused Development

Economic development provided a major motive for the government to concentrate the inhabitants at a dozen communities between 1950 and 1970. In addition, the government looked for savings by deploying at only a few places the high-cost imported specialists (teachers, nurses, and administrators) who were considered necessary, and their supporting infrastructure of buildings, generators, landing strips, and other tools of centralization. The result was that Inuit were drawn or pushed into unfamiliar settings, moving in a single generation from being one of the most dispersed populations in Canada to one of the most concentrated.

Centralization was almost complete by the 1970s, but the decade opened with uncertainty about how community development would work in practice. The Government of the Northwest Territories tried to develop a policy of funnelling investment to the most promising "growth centres." "There is a natural tendency for economic activities to congregate in a major centre and for other activities and services to follow. The Government merely has to work with these natural forces in a planned way." One skeptical official wrote in the margin, "Seems like a lot of people will have to stay on the land." However, in Qikiqtaaluk, almost all families had already left the land. The same document stated, "It is mandatory that no move be made until suitable jobs were available to absorb them and that they could make the inevitable social adjustment." Documents like this one summarized the ambitions of politicians and bureaucrats, but their doubts and warnings were rarely heeded. Government and private investors almost never found the right balance of centralization with employment.

INFRASTRUCTURE

Steadily, following the arrival of the first DEW Line materials in 1955, the external view of Qikiqtaaluk's economy shifted from the land towards government services and commodities for export. The trading economy was only connected to world markets via a minimal infrastructure of a dozen tiny settled places. Each was accessible by sea, with just enough wooden buildings to warehouse a year's trade goods and house a transient population of between five and twenty non-Inuit. The transformation that occurred in the period from 1950 to 1975 moved the region's economy from one conducted under Inuit customs primarily for local benefit towards one designed by southern planners with the interests of the South in mind and with little distinction made between the roles of Inuit and other Canadian citizens.

It is important to note how the placement of Qikiqtaaluk's communities generally follows the siting of commercial, RCMP, or military establishments at the end of the Second World War. Access to good hunting terrain was of secondary importance, though many of the early trading posts were located along coastlines where people already lived. Most of the settlements have a harbour or anchoring place that could be reached by the kinds of vessels used in the Arctic in the 1940s and 1950s. There are five exceptions. Two are in the High Arctic, where the relocations of 1953 created Resolute and Grise Fiord; two are former DEW Line sites, Hall Beach and Qikiqtarjuaq; and one is Sanikiluaq in the Belcher Islands, where there were no year-round Qallunaat establishments until 1959. At the other eight communities, the service centres and municipal infrastructure of today are strongly influenced by the distribution of government and trading activity before 1945.

Qikiqtaaluk saw two waves of airfield construction, one driven by defence and the second by community development. Iqaluit owes its existence to the broad, level site of a Second World War airfield, which was revived as a marshalling point during work on the DEW Line. It is the least favoured of the communities in terms of access to game but it survived and grew by maintaining the original momentum from the airfield. Similarly, airports at Hall Beach and Resolute handled significant military traffic, and this affected development. Air travel came slowly to the rest of Qikiqtaaluk, beginning with occasional visits from aircraft equipped with floats or skis. By the mid-1960s, most communities had chosen a place that could be levelled for year-round scheduled flights. By 1975, all thirteen communities were linked to each other and a few to the South by air. This focus on air travel between communities resulted in the neglect of unloading facilities at the many points served by the annual "sealift." Even Iqaluit has no wharf for ocean-going vessels—cargo is winched off sealift vessels into barges and then unloaded directly onto beaches.

As communities grew, they had numerous infrastructure needs, and in the early 1960s, the northern administration began to receive the financial resources to address them. Tank farms for diesel and other fuel were set up relatively early and enlarged as time went on. Community freezers encouraged hunters to cache meat and fish for later distribution within the community. Nursing stations began to spread in the late 1950s, and local radio in the early 1970s, with a small paycheque and local celebrity status for announcers. The housing boom of the 1960s brought a rush of construction—bigger schools, community halls, municipal garages, welding shops, and sewage lagoons all provided a sharp contrast to the former trading enclaves where Inuit were not supposed to "loiter." Housing was the biggest investment and, along with schools, the driver of other changes: the introduction of a housing program for employed Inuit in communities in 1956; low-cost houses for purchase after 1959; and the universal rental housing program of 1965–66 were other landmarks. By 1970, Inuit community leaders were generally calling for an increase in municipal infrastructure, while keeping a critical eye on the planning, quality, and operation of what was sent.

MUNICIPAL INSTITUTIONS

As the northern administration gained experience, larger budgets, and agents in the field, its priorities in communities included the development of elected civic government. The elected bodies were sometimes ineffective, but most communities saw a federal effort to develop community organizations that would help prepare Inuit to deal with bureaucratic processes related to self-government. This trend was slow to develop; while Inuit were often eager to take up new challenges and opportunities and participated eagerly when consulted, officials were afraid to give unilingual local populations political power. It was feared they would be numerically swamped, culturally corrupted, and economically exploited by wealthy incomers. By this, they did not mean government employees but newcomers, such as the hundreds of young men without wives at the DEW Line sites, or—even worse—the thousand imaginary miners who were rumoured to be on their way to the Belcher Islands in 1956. Today the solutions that administrators proposed sound extremely paternalistic, but they reflected real concerns about the lack of formally schooled leaders in communities exposed to sudden change. These disparities were regularly exaggerated, for, as M. P. Gene Rheaume observed in 1964, Inuit might not be ready to vote in territorial elections, but "they will be ready for the vote the day after they get it."

The creation of councils and co-operatives under the tutelage of the Department of Indian Affairs and Northern Development intentionally undermined the authority of the churches, the Hudson's Bay Company (HBC), and the police. Through these various councils and committees, the federal government, at a slow pace and with many doubts, set out to prepare Inuit to lead the transformation of their own society and economy. The transformation also sharpened existing divisions over spheres of influence within Inuit society. In the 1960s, Qallunaat tended to identify four different groups of Inuit. First were the "camp bosses" and other inumariit who excelled as hunters and leaders. Second were the settlement-based employees of the HBC, RCMP, and churches, as well as skilled hunters and travellers who generally spoke some English. Third were other families, the majority of the Inuit population, who did not fit into the previous categories. Fourth was a small number, mostly widows and invalids, who lived at the settlements and relied on social transfers. At first, most opportunities for leadership were offered to the second group. By 1975, bilingual young men with a high school or college education were challenging them.

At Iqaluit in the early 1960s, anthropologists John and Irma Honigmann proposed a different division of urban Inuit society into three groups: a new commercial or administrative class who wore business suits, a group of more traditional hunters, and others who lacked a distinctive identity. These alignments undermined established systems of leadership and status. In particular, the Inuit who worked for Qallunaat were acquiring prestige at the expense of the traditional hunting leaders.

The template for community development in Qikiqtaaluk was set in the 1950s at Iqaluit. The Honigmanns devoted an entire chapter to "Community Organization." This focused on a few formal institutions with elected leaders: the Community Council, Community Association, Church Council (an all-Inuit body), and the Sisi Housing Co-op. In the Honigmanns' view, the non-Inuit members were quite tolerant of increased Inuit involvement in local affairs, which was occurring with "considerable success." The success was due largely to strengths in Inuit culture:

> including their curiosity, resourcefulness, a readiness to "try it," intelligence to benefit from experience, and ... other characterological

> traits acquired in early life . . . [Inuit] are given to testing their ability to master some new experiences and in doing so may even venture beyond the bounds envisaged by Eurocanadian tutors. Change is probably aided by the fact that [Inuit] participate in many areas of town life as if they were fully entitled to those resources of the town.

Once established in Iqaluit, community organizations appeared in smaller, remoter communities. In the 1967–72 period, for example, Arctic Bay had a Housing Association, a Community Council, a Health Committee, a Recreation Committee, and—a vital institution everywhere—the Hunters' and Trappers' Association. The first chairperson of the Community Council wryly noted the acculturative influence of such bodies. "When the Community Council first started, we really didn't know exactly what to do and how to make it work. But we've kept trying and we know now." Although Qallunaat tutelage was still powerful, the communities' capacity to manage themselves grew through institutions like these.

CO-OPERATIVES

Creating openings for janitors, mechanics, and secretaries was not in itself a strategy for economic development, and only by creating skilled cohorts of administrative workers and entrepreneurs could the government expect to promote the social changes it wanted. Thus, any skills fostered through volunteer or elected office would prepare more individuals for jobs in sectors such as local retailing, trading in renewable resources (e.g., exporting Arctic char), production and sale of carvings, prints, weaving, and sewing, and tourism. Many Inuit had an aptitude for this sort of change and wanted to take part in it. The most significant way they found to encourage this was, unquestionably, the co-operative movement.

Co-operatives were eased into existence by a program called the Eskimo Loan Fund, established in 1953. This fund served Inuit in a region that lacked banks or other sources of capital for small businesses, without having to explain individual projects to Parliament. At first, a few Arctic co-operatives were set up in Quebec under provincial legislation that already existed. New legislation was created in the Northwest Territories in 1958, and five Qikiqtaaluk communities established co-operatives between 1959 and 1963, followed by four more in 1968, and another four in 1973–74.

The pioneer co-operative in Qikiqtaaluk was the West Baffin Eskimo Co-operative at Cape Dorset. Here, a northern service officer had encouraged carvers during the 1950s. With government and private capital, the project continued to thrive when reorganized in 1959 as a co-operative. Two High Arctic communities quickly followed Cape Dorset's example, and the experiments became a movement after a successful multi-community meeting at Apex in 1963. Soon the combination of Inuit talent and Qallunaat marketing created a new industry, giving prominence to both individuals and their communities.

Carvings, sewn goods, and other artistic works provided an economic base for co-operatives, which later allowed them to branch into other enterprises. Co-operatives also moved into other services relevant to their members, as well as to the external economy. At various times since the 1970s, they have ranged in scope from single-purpose wholesale/retail co-ops to the fully diversified bodies whose services (including contracting to municipalities) covered wholesale/retail, operation of a hotel, fuel distribution, cable TV, hardware, arts and crafts, rental, and leasing.

The political importance of the movement was explored in a provocative study by Marybelle Mitchell (1996), who portrayed co-ops as a tool for entrenching Inuit identity, though also as a source of class distinction among Nunavummiut. She felt it important to study the transformation of practices and relationships. In her analysis, co-operatives provided "the vehicle by which the state exported capitalism to the Inuit." This was because

Canadian policy-makers in the 1950s were undecided whether to assimilate Inuit or to let them continue hunting. The co-operative was the ideal development instrument because it left both the Inuit and the state with a foot in each way of life. For Inuit in particular, co-operatives offered a way both to "modernize" but also to continue to promote egalitarianism and "the buttressing of non-capitalist practices." She added, "Skills which Inuit acquired by managing co-operatives gave strength and focus to the land claim movement and to Nunavut itself."

LUXURY PRODUCTS AND SPECIAL INVESTMENTS

Government initiative, planning, and seed money for the co-ops were not the only government contributions to economic development. Beginning in 1958, and lasting for a decade, almost every populated Arctic area was the subject of an "area economic survey." Scientists whom the Department of Indian Affairs and Northern Development had engaged to conduct a literature review and field surveys covering development opportunities in the regions, carried out the work. For most regions, these were the first comprehensive, published surveys of game resources and patterns of Inuit hunting.

The area surveys added little to the existing knowledge of development opportunities, and in a period when the government was losing faith in the land-based economy, the knowledge collected through these surveys was not put to great use. Instead, some well-known attributes of Qikiqtaaluk and some new ones were exploited at local levels. Art and handicrafts were the most profitable of these, but adventure travel and the beginning of community-based tourism date to this period as well. Cape Dorset had a fishing camp for visitors for a time, and at Pangnirtung there were fishing camps and, after 1972, a national park near the Penny Ice Cap, where alpinists had been scaling cliffs and walking immense glaciers since the early

1950s. Although Auyuittuq National Park, Qikiqtaaluk's first, generated fewer than a dozen jobs in Pangnirtung, it helped cement the community's longstanding reputation as a place of outstanding natural beauty. While all these activities improved southern Canadians' awareness and positive image of Qikiqtaaluk, they did relatively little to cover the increased costs and expectations that Inuit encountered with settlement life.

Mining, Oil, and Gas

Until the 1970s, discussions of economic development in the Canadian north began with a mention of agriculture and forestry, because hopes were pinned firmly on the southern Yukon and the Mackenzie District, where those activities were technically possible. Such economic forecasts lost focus but gained enthusiasm as they approached Qikiqtaaluk and its unknown, untapped mineral wealth. During the 1950s, exploration on a limited scale provided some Inuit with infrequent and widely scattered opportunities to apply their skills on the land. In this role, they helped geologists and mining developers, from the iron deposits of Sanikiluaq to the oil and gas exploration of the High Arctic. In the 1960s, more intensive projects developed, notably in north Baffin, while the 1970s saw two produtive mines north of 70, both using Inuit labour for reasons of policy and convenience.

GOVERNMENT AND PRIVATE SECTOR

By 1950, the Geological Survey of Canada had completed preliminary surveys of the entire Canadian Arctic and offered hope that the North might be very rich in oil and gas, and the eastern Arctic a valuable possession to Canada. Theories about Inuit as a potential workforce for mining were first tested in Kivalliq, at the North Rankin Inlet Nickel Mines, 400 kilometres north of Churchill on Hudson Bay. A few Inuit worked underground, and on the surface, they made up roughly half the workforce and were, according to one observer, "adaptable, productive, and interested." These Inuit had no trouble learning aboveground techniques and some of the dangerous underground skills, but they disliked working on a rigid schedule that limited access to country food, something the managers only partially succeeded in addressing with flexible working arrangements. When the ore ran out in 1962 a community of just over five hundred people was suddenly out of work. Half went on social assistance, and relocation to other Canadian mining towns was tried with little success. The gradual replacement of mining with arts and crafts and a regional government service role allowed Rankin Inlet to recover.

Fortunately, a fall in the cost of air travel soon rescued Qikiqtaaluk from the "company town" model of mining. The new fly-in, fly-out practices meant that Inuit who wanted to work in mining did not have to move their entire families to a distant company town and relocate again when the boom ended. In 1977, when the Science Council of Canada had called for "an assessment of commuting from urban centres to northern mines by air" to encourage Inuit to work for wages, the idea had been "several years behind the action."

Commercial extraction of minerals was already familiar to Inuit in Qikiqtaaluk. There was exploration and small-scale exploitation around Pond Inlet, Cumberland Sound, Kimmirut, and the Belcher Islands intermittently since 1870. In the 1960s and 1970s, four prospects dominated planning: High Arctic oil and gas exploration by Panarctic, two separate lead-zinc deposits near Resolute and Arctic Bay, and the Mary River iron deposit south of Arctic Bay. The Panarctic Oil consortium did not go into production but spent at least a billion dollars on exploration, some of it employing Inuit labourers from northern Baffin Island. The Mary River deposit is likewise not yet producing, but exploration led to extensive hiring in the sixties. The Polaris mine near Resolute operated from 1981 to 2002, while Nanisivik shipped ore from 1977 to 2002 and employed Inuit, especially from Arctic Bay, throughout the period.

These four projects had impacts far beyond the several hundred individual Inuit who worked on them. Qikiqtaaluk communities, especially Resolute, Arctic Bay, and Pond Inlet, experienced first-hand the prolonged discussions and constant economic re-evaluations that marked the behaviour of private-sector mining companies and the Department of Indian Affairs and Northern Development, which regulated land-based activities and was a potential source of subsidies. Inuit learned that these bodies would not consult either early or consistently, nor explain key points clearly or fully to Inuit.

The first of five new actors on the scene was the Government of the Northwest Territories, whose 1972 "Hire North" program encouraged companies to include local residents in their workforces—first from the communities closest to a projected mine, and later through employment meetings up to 700 kilometres away.

A second stakeholder was the newly formed Inuit Tapirisat of Canada (now Inuit Tapiriit Kanatami, or ITK). Because one of ITK's goals was Inuit control of land-use planning, the ITK used community meetings to fight for recognition at every stage of development. In 1982, the ITK's official publication, *Inuit Today*, printed an assessment by Cape Dorset community leaders of recent projects in their area. The focus was on the dangers that prospecting activities, notably helicopter over-flights and abandonment of toxic wastes, posed to game animals and as a result to the traditional economy. They did not refer to employment opportunities, and called for settlement of their land claim, including Inuit control of land use, before development could go ahead.

Third, communities near the mines insisted on a place at the table, especially in Arctic Bay where planning for Nanisivik produced a range of controversial options. One was to be a self-contained company town at

Nanisivik, segregated from Arctic Bay just 34 kilometres away. Another scheme was to relocate the whole population of Arctic Bay to Nanisivik, even though the area had little game and no small-craft sea landings. The chosen option was to link Arctic Bay by road to the new mining town, creating a workforce of local commuters mixed with a fly-in, fly-out population of Qallunaat and non-local Inuit living in bunkhouses.

A fourth player was a new environmental bureaucracy. In the 1970s, it became clear that Polaris and Nanisivik needed a more thorough evaluation than the required quick hearing by the NWT Water Resources Board. This was also the era of Thomas Berger's Mackenzie Valley Pipeline Inquiry. It raised concerns about hazards to wildlife and built a constituency in the south for treating Arctic territories as homelands needing protection, not frontiers calling for exploitation.

Finally, the potential workforce had to be consulted throughout the development, to adjust the social aspects of work routines, notably establishing a culturally appropriate balance of shift rotations. Fortunately, the fly-in, fly-out approach encouraged non-Aboriginal workers to make similar demands. All these interests came into play against a background of economic uncertainties and the new regulatory challenges of bringing proven ore bodies into production.

INUIT RESPONSES

Predictably, Inuit did not migrate en masse from one mining prospect to another. They made choices based on strategies for their extended families and their communities as well as for themselves individually. A total of twenty-four communities eventually supplied Inuit labour to the Nanisivik mine. Sociologist C. W. Hobart interviewed 31% of the people who had worked at the mine. He found that Inuit objected to working at least six weeks before being allowed to return home. The industry standard for imported workers was twelve weeks, but Inuit disliked both the separation from family and the loss of opportunity to hunt.

Following Hobart, anthropologist George Wenzel intensively surveyed thirteen workers from Clyde River who worked in mining between 1975 and 1979. Wenzel found the men less likely to work at Nanisivik during periods of high prices for ringed seal skins and for polar bear skins, which rose as high as $1,000 a hide. As such, most of the movement occurred when sealskin prices were low, and stopped when prices rebounded in 1978. Altogether Clyde River sent three different groups to Nanisivik. The first party were men in their early twenties, the second set were older, and the third group were four married men, one of whom had worked on Western Arctic oil rigs. Most claimed that curiosity was a major reason for enlisting. All the experienced hunters would have preferred to stay in Clyde River to hunt, only to be employed when short of cash, but they needed the extra earnings from the mines.

Wenzel's informants brought about $16,400 into the hamlet over the four years and spent it in ways that reflected Inuit traditions. One man bought a new snowmobile and then gave his old one to a son for hunting. Others bought a freighter canoe, a snowmobile, and high-powered rifles. Another helped his father and brothers buy an outboard motor, which all shared, and another gave two rifles as gifts to a brother-in-law. As Wenzel noted, these examples "demonstrate the adaptability of the Inuit resource-sharing system itself. Over time, this system has expanded to include access to the actual materials of the hunt, as well as the product of the hunting effort." Looking at a larger population, Hobart was puzzled by the findings. "There is a striking conflict in the findings of this study, between the general excellence of work performance of the Inuit workers, and their need for wage employment on the one hand, and their disinterest in working at the Nanisivik mine on the other." Wenzel explained this by understanding that the main motive for working at the mines was to acquire and share equipment for hunting.

The current state of economic development in Nunavut results from a distinctive geography, an old and resilient culture, and six decades of public policy, which tried, with uneven intentions and results, to find a balance between the traditional use of renewable resources and the pursuit of cash incomes. Carving, sewing, and printmaking, for example, provide a source of earnings that merges the advantages of the traditional and market sectors. Many Inuit find that cash earnings do make it easier to bring a steady supply of country food into the settlements. Employment in tourism as outfitters and guides also gives hunters and their family members valuable time on the land. Those who do not wish to hunt but are committed to staying in Qikiqtaaluk can work for the administrative bodies created in the recent past at the municipal, territorial, and federal levels. They also benefit from opportunities in offices, boards, and NGOs created under the Nunavut Land Claim Agreement. Negotiation of this agreement was a major goal of Inuit organizations in 1994, and it has helped to shape Inuit involvement in directing economic choices.

Through settlement of their land claim, Inuit acquired access to revenues, as well as jobs, in a sector of the economy whose profitability (minerals, oil, and gas) and environmental safety had been debated for much of the period since 1950. To many Canadians, extractive industries seem to offer the best opportunity to create jobs in the international economy, jobs which can be rewarding in themselves and may help sustain harvesting activities into the future. This tentatively better view of the future came at the cost of much political struggle. The view endorsed in recent documents such as the Nunavut Economic Strategy is that a relationship with the land is essential and that other economic development will help sustain it. This approach reverses a long-standing government perspective, and is faithful to views that Inuit have expressed all along.

Igluliriniq

Housing in Qikiqtaaluk

This chapter examines Inuit experience with the provision of government-supplied housing (single- and multi-family dwellings) in Qikiqtaaluk between 1950 and 1975. A dwelling, whether a qarmaq, an apartment, or a castle, is much more than a human necessity—it is both a reflection and product of culture, social organization, and environment. It marks the boundaries of relationships, creates spaces for family intimacy, exposes connections and separations in the spheres of daily life, and defines the spaces where gender and generational roles can be performed.

The chapter tries to show that the expression "home" is dynamic. A "home" is the place where someone feels they belong, but its geography is not always fixed in time or space—it can expand, contract, move, and change shape according to cultural and personal experiences. Inuit homes had a specific relationship to the land—they came from it and they were part of it. Nobody in particular owned the land or its resources, but they could achieve a measure of status from understanding it. In the new settlements, and in new houses, outsiders with almost no knowledge of the environment set out

to completely redefine the relationship between Inuit and the land. In this way, colonization became very real.

Before whalers and fur traders arrived, "home" for Inuit families was a broad geography where they were able to find or build everything needed to survive. By the middle of the twentieth century, however, Inuit were expected to become part of an economic, political, and cultural system brought from the South that viewed shelter as a commodity that could be bought and sold.

In 1959, when the federal government outlined the Eskimo Housing Loan Program, the speed at which change was about to occur in Qikiqtaaluk could not be anticipated. Housing was not a stand-alone issue for Inuit or governments. It was completely intertwined with other factors related to the in-gathering of Inuit into settlements. Surrounded by new technologies, business practices, social organizations, and political processes, Inuit had almost no opportunities to influence housing programs or the design of settlements. The federal government did not set out to harm Inuit, but it took advantage of the confusion by implementing programs that met their own objectives first. It was only in the 1970s that Inuit were able to take more control over their communities and housing. During the intervening period, with the limited information available to them, they tried to choose the options that would be best for their families, both in terms of where they lived and the type of shelter they used.

Many Inuit did not feel "at home" for many years after moving into the government-sanctioned settlements and into permanent housing, but they never fully released themselves from the land they knew well, nor from the cultural practices that were performed inside houses. Anthropologist Hugh Brody noted that even after most Inuit had moved into settlements in the 1970s, they continued, as they often do today, to live on the land for at least part of the year.

> However much they may depend on rental housing in a government village, whatever their problems of isolation as the last to

stay on the land, such men as the Inummariit still keep many or most of their possessions in the camp and try to spend as much time there as possible.

Inuit also continued to live in multigenerational families, and to share food, chores, stories, and laughter together in a single room.

Inuit Housing

For thousands of years, Inuit built permanent all-season houses and semi-permanent winter and summer shelters. Permanent all-season qarmaq were often semi-subterranean and made of stone, whale bone, and sod, sometimes insulated on the outside with snow. Summer shelters consisted of tupiq made of skin, duck, or later canvas, sometimes lined with moss. In some instances, wood obtained from whalers and traders was integrated into more traditional forms. In winter, igluvigaq were used only on hunting trips, since they were quick to construct. European observers (explorers, naturalists, and ethnographers) were impressed by Inuit structures. Franz Boas, in his description of snow houses, described them as "ingenious" because they afforded "the possibility of building a vault without a scaffold." Both qarmait and igluvigait could be lined with a tupiq, which kept the insulating snow cold and the inside of the house dry. These houses usually included a porch, constructed either as a place to store food or as a shelter for qimmiit. A communal sleeping platform was usually constructed at the back of the house. Furnishings were generally limited to a few benches. Igluvigait could house multiple family groups, with a large main room attached to smaller rooms for individual families.

Across Qikiqtaaluk, regional variations existed in the sizes, materials, and groupings of houses, but the house units were all quick to construct using harvested materials. When the interior of igluvigait or qarmait became blackened with soot from the qulliq, the walls could be scraped clean. If a house was structurally unsound, a new one was built. Furthermore, Inuit houses could be adapted easily to the size of a family, the conditions of the weather, and the location where they settled for one or many seasons.

Even as Inuit engaged in the fur trade in the early twentieth century, they continued customary house forms, while also taking advantage of access to canvas, ropes, and salvaged wood to simplify the process of erecting and moving qarmait and tupiq. The alternative was a more permanent type of structure, known as an iglurjuaq, constructed of wood, concrete, or metal that could be heated, cleaned, and ventilated over a period of many years without being deconstructed and moved. Qallunaat RCMP, traders, missionaries, and teachers were normally provided with permanent wooden buildings, but Inuit coming into the new settlements to socialize or trade would set up a tupiq or build an igluvigaq. An Inuit family wanting to move to an enclave for any reason would have found it very difficult to build an iglurjuaq because everything had to be salvaged or ordered in advance—wood, furniture, appliances, shingles, and hardware.

Government Involvement in Qikiqtammiut Housing

During the second half of the twentieth century, the Canadian government increased its presence in Qikiqtaaluk to meet three key objectives: to demonstrate its sovereignty in the region; to prepare the North for the development of natural resources; and to address the wide differences in the kinds of services that were available to residents in northern and southern Canada. Inuit were enticed, and often coerced, to move to government-supported settlements—the thirteen communities in Qikiqtaaluk today—for employment, schooling, and health services. Promises made by the government about the quality and cost of housing was an important factor in convincing families that it might be worthwhile to move into a settlement to be closer to children in school, to have access to potential employment opportunities, and to get more regular access to medical services.

Bringing people closer to services was only part of the government's rationale for supplying houses. The linking of new housing to both health and education remained central to the rhetoric of housing policy and programs throughout the period, although the government itself put people at risk through inadequate preparation for housing. In one example, Inuit who had been relocated to Grise Fiord and Resolute were obliged to live in a tent in bitter cold because the snow was not suitable for building igluvigait. Sarah Amagoalik spoke in 1990 to the House of Commons standing committee investigating the relocations. She explained, "When spring came, we gathered wood scraps from the dump, the dump of the Qallunaat . . . Then when summer came around, they started to build houses from the wood from the dump." People also gathered coal as their only source of heat, but they had no light. When the Canadian Broadcasting Corporation (CBC) went to film people in Resolute, Inuit had to go to the military base where it was possible to get electricity and light for filming.

By the early 1950s, in all parts of Qikiqtaaluk where military or government officials were to be found in any numbers, Qallunaat were consistently reporting that Inuit were winterizing tents by using scrap lumber for floors and reinforcing walls with wood, cardboard, and paper. Kerosene heating of homes left a residue of soot on the inside of houses and on clothes and bedding. When houses were crowded together, often near military bases, government officials and military personnel were quick to point out that health and sanitary conditions were being compromised. Good ventilation, low levels of humidity, and warm rooms were also noted as being essential to good health, and numerous sources advocated that houses equipped with both electricity and natural light were a necessity for families with school-aged children.

The precedent of providing housing to other groups of Canadians also played a role. During World War II, the federal government introduced a wide-scale housing program, commonly known as the Wartime Housing program, to accommodate the workers flooding into urban centres to work in factories. The prefabricated houses were small and designed with inexpensive materials so that they could be constructed quickly and cheaply. At the time, these designs were believed to be suitable for construction anywhere in Canada. Wartime housing, which was also adapted for postwar programs, ranged in size from 600 to 800 square feet, included two entranceways and large windows.

While government agencies touted the benefits to Inuit of living in new houses, the historical record and the material evidence show that programs were created to meet one government goal, namely to ensure that the costs of administering the North were as low as possible. With Inuit living year-round in one location, it was easier to provide public services, especially schooling, and to bring Inuit into the wage economy. Housing programs also served as a convenient way to teach construction and business skills, while also justifying investments in power and transportation infrastructure. The government discovered very quickly, however, that it was not simply a matter of building houses where services were available. "All the extras—medical services, welfare, social services, the wage economy, community conveniences—go with a house."

Some Inuit welcomed and sought out opportunities to live in new houses. When anthropologist Toshio Yatsushiro interviewed Inuit in Iqaluit in 1958, after the first prefabricated bungalows or "matchbox houses" had been introduced, he reported that 75% of the interviewees said they wanted to live in one. Other families were less interested in government-provided housing, but felt pressured to move. Gamalie Kilukshak of Pond Inlet told the QIA, "They wanted us to have houses that were matchbox houses. Some of us didn't want to get a house but they insisted... We were being pressured to get into a house so we complied. That's what I remember. So we agreed to get into a house." The comfort of new houses, especially models that were larger and better constructed than matchbox houses, appealed to Inuit, of course. Peter Awa told the QIA, "We were told that we were going to live in houses, warm houses."

In 1958, the Department of Northern Affairs and National Resources (NANR) said that it wanted to "design homes to suit [Inuit] budgets at the various stages of economic independence starting with a more healthful substitute for the iglu and tent." A decade later, the government used similar terminology, stating that the delivery of houses in northern communities would provide "a warm, dry, sanitary environment, [which] is of major importance during this critical transition from isolation to active participation in northern development."

The rhetoric was backed by policies and programs that were implemented on the ground by the RCMP, nurses, teachers, and Northern Services Officers to move Inuit into settlements where houses were supposed to be available. Alicee Joamie, who moved from Pangnirtung to Apex as an adult, told the QTC that health concerns were cited as the reasoning behind the bulldozing of her family's qarmaq and their moving into a rigid-frame house:

> The nurse that first came to us was with a teacher. We were not allowed to stay in the hut anymore because [my children] would get a cold at school. That is what we were told. They told us we would get housing. We didn't know who the government was but we weren't given any house. They took our house away [by bulldozing the qarmaq]. We had to go to our father-in-law to stay.

Initial Government Housing Programs, 1955 to 1959

The federal government entered housing programs very tentatively, in part because it was uncertain about how much it wanted to encourage Inuit to engage fully in a wage-based economy. While some Inuit had been provided with housing or given access to building supplies on military bases and in some settlements, there was no formal program to address the difficulties that Inuit who were staying in settlements without permanent housing were facing. The confusion can be seen in the government's reactive approach to two separate situations. In 1955, three "temporary" dwellings for Inuit staff were sent to the new subdivision of Apex Hill in Iqaluit. In the next year, houses were sent directly to ilagiit nunagivaktangit in other places as a way of encouraging Inuit to remain on the land. Almost a decade later, in reference to Igloolik, an RCMP officer recommended that:

> [Inuit] should be encouraged to remain in the camps. If the long-range plan is to provide every Eskimo family with a house, then they should be built in the camps where this is applicable. If a closer relationship between the Eskimo and the administrator is desired, then the administrator should visit the Eskimo in his camp. This not only applies to the administrator but to any other white person who has an occupation dealing with the people. The idea of keeping the people on the land would benefit them both in the area[s] of morale and economic[s].

Officials recognized from the outset that government support would be needed to get materials into the north and to supply houses for staff, both Qallunaat and Inuit, but it also intended to use housing to ameliorate what it perceived to be substandard living conditions contributing to poor health outcomes.

Iqaluit proved to be an important catalyst for a federal housing initiative. In 1955, the community was divided into three distinct parts—the military base and airport, an informal and unserviced Inuit neighbourhood called Ikhaluit where families lived in houses made from a combination of traditional and salvaged materials, and the newly planned Inuit village at Apex Hill built by the government. In this latter area, the government supplied several houses in 1955 and 1956 for government employees and people returning from southern medical facilities.

In the mid-1950s, the government also began examining options for permanent housing in the North more seriously through the National Research Council (NRC) and the Canada Mortgage and Housing Corporation (CMHC). It began experimenting with housing that combined Inuit and Euro-Canadian designs and materials—prototypes included a styrofoam igluvigaq built at Cape Dorset and Igloolik, and aluminum houses insulated with caribou moss. Although these models, estimated to cost between $1,200 and $1,800 in 1957, were expected to be significantly less expensive to produce than southern-style homes, they were soon discarded in favour of the prefabricated plywood bungalows. Wooden houses made of prefabricated members and standard-sized materials could be reconfigured into different sizes with various amenities, such as indoor water basins, heaters, and stoves.

The second catalyst was the building of the Distant Early Warning (DEW) Line, a series of radar stations that stretched from Alaska to Greenland, with major stations at Hall Beach and Cape Dyer. As per an agreement with the United States, which was the primary funder and operator of the DEW Line, Canada planned to supply housing for Inuit employees. The first houses, scheduled to arrive in the summer of 1958, were only delivered at the beginning of the winter. A second batch arrived in 1959, consisting of flexible-walled Atwells and rigid-framed duplex units. Changes in the rules about who would receive housing and how much it would cost were difficult for anyone, bureaucrats or Inuit, to understand and monitor. The major private-sector employer, Federal Electric, provided housing free of charge to employees and criticized the federal government for charging rent for its houses at $78 per month, about 30% of the salary of an Inuit DEW Line employee. Government inspectors also found that the houses were deteriorating due to a lack of maintenance.

Eskimo Housing Loan Program, 1959 to 1965

The first major housing initiative open to all eligible Inuit, whether employed by the government or not, was the Eskimo Housing Loan Program, launched in 1959. Bureaucrats feared that a fully subsidized housing program would make Inuit dependent on the government; as an alternative they developed a rent-to-own scheme that sought to encourage Inuit home ownership. In effect, they sought to insert southern real estate concepts into the North and to continue the "ideological construction that assumed [that] relief creates dependency."

The program never accounted for multi-generational Inuit families, the instability of Inuit income, or the mixed economic system that existed in the North due to the heavy subsidization of most Qallunaat working there. The idea of paying for a house was neither intuitive nor rational in the context of Inuit life in the 1960s. As a government official stated in 1960, "many [Inuit], and particularly Easterners, have not yet swung around to the view that housing is something for which one pays money." Inuit also found the idea of purchasing property from the government to be illogical—many Inuit held that "those with less have a right to share in the bounty of those with apparent plenty." For Inuit, then, "the government's wealth seemed enormous and therefore the need to compensate that government was initially incomprehensible."

It is also clear from comparing government documents and QTC testimonies that government officials and Inuit had very different priorities concerning housing. Government reports, for instance, discuss at length the buy-back program, an initiative whereby Inuit could upgrade their housing after paying off most of their loan or mortgage. In effect, the government expected Inuit to "want more," as suburban Canadians did. The QTC testimonies and anecdotal evidence show that Inuit (at least in the 1960s and 1970s) rarely moved within communities. Static incomes and high building costs limited options for moving, but cultural factors might have also been important.

A contemporary lack of investment in communications was another important factor affecting the success of housing programs from all perspectives. Meaningful consultation to ensure that Inuit choices, expectations, and knowledge were considered in decision-making never happened. No one took time to explain to women and men how a housing program might be structured, what trade-offs could be made to keep house prices within the means of both government and Inuit, and how many houses would be needed in any settlement. Inuit were seldom informed about even basic government plans. As Emily Takatak told the QTC, "They didn't inform us that they were building houses here for us to live in." Once provided with housing, poor intercultural communication, as well as a general reluctance to complain to government officials who appeared to hold so much discretionary power in the community, impeded Inuit from expressing dissatisfaction with their homes.

The Eskimo Housing Loan Program was not the first government initiative that attempted to provide inexpensive housing to a large population in a short period of time with limited supplies. The rigid-frame houses shipped to the North by the government in the late 1950s and 1960s, however, were even smaller and cheaper than the wartime houses. The Department bought and built twelve hundred basic one-room "matchbox" houses, also known as Style 370 (as it measured 370 square feet), across the Northwest Territories, and re-sold them to Inuit between 1959 and 1965. There was also a two-bedroom model used by both Inuit and Qallunaat called Style 512. Government administrators designed these units with the objective of keeping construction and heating costs as low as possible. Housing dimensions followed multiples of standard four-by-eight-foot plywood sheets so that construction was simple, with the exception of the angle cuts on the end walls for the gable roofs. By minimizing the square footage, less fuel would be required to heat the houses.

Different communities received these new houses at different times. The prefabricated houses were made largely from plywood, and were hailed as costing only 25% of conventional construction. There were also rigid-frame A-roofed plywood houses, which some government officials believed were good transition homes for Inuit used to living on the land, since they felt like big tents and were very simply designed, not even including bathrooms. Initially the government also budgeted $500 to furnish each house—the furnishings were then to be rented to Inuit as part of their mortgage. These houses were constructed either by Inuit or by Qallunaat crews. It was difficult, however, for Inuit who were working long hours during the day to find time to construct their own homes.

Regardless of the government's attempts to keep housing costs low, the Eskimo Housing Loan Program failed to recognize the irregularity of employment for most Inuit. Wage employment was primarily seasonal and dependent on development activities related to government and the military. A 1960 estimate reported that only 6% of Inuit in all regions had ever experienced steady wage employment. Without consistent wages, Inuit could not be expected to make regular payments towards their housing.

Government officials appear to have assumed or hoped that Inuit would be absorbed into an ever-expanding northern economy of high-paying permanent jobs. An RCMP memo from 1961 cited the following wages for Inuit working for the government as: $4,000–$5,000 for labourers, $5,000 for interpreters, $6,000 for truck drivers, $6,400 for technical officers, and $7,000 for foremen. For most Inuit, however, jobs paying this well were mostly available in Iqaluit or near military bases. In 1961 the NANR and the Department of Transport collectively employed approximately one hundred and thirty-eight of the approximately eight hundred Inuit residents in Iqaluit. In the Northwest Territories as a whole, however, the average per capita income of Inuit was estimated at $400 for 1965.

The Eskimo Housing Loan Program was unaffordable to most Inuit who subsisted on hunting and seasonal employment. The fact that the amount of money needed to purchase a house kept increasing was also problematic. Initially, houses had cost $400 to $500; later matchbox houses cost $1,500 for the model without a bathroom and $1,800 for the model with a bathroom. Even with the limited income of many Inuit, it was conceivable to economists and bureaucrats that a family could purchase a house in small annual payments within a ten-year period. However, in the mid-1960s, policy-makers shifted their plans "away from the so-called 'primitive' housing of early experiments towards housing more comparable to what could be found in a middle-class southern neighbourhood." Prices rose accordingly. Three-bedroom units, which became the norm for new construction, cost $3,500 to own after a $1,000 government subsidy, but were hardly in the same architectural category of typical "middle-class" houses found in the South.

The expense of owning a house was not limited to purchase price. Ancillary costs also increased; the fuel costs were higher than many Inuit could pay, even with heavy government subsidies. Indeed, many Inuit felt that the government had not been clear about the associated costs of fuel and other amenities when renting or buying a house. Elizabeth Kyak told the QTC, "The government promised [my family] housing but they didn't get housing. Then they got housing and then they were told that they would never pay for power, utilities ... The government made promises and didn't keep these promises." Juda Taqtu told the QIA, "At the time heating fuel cost only $20 per 45-gallon barrel. At first, prices . . . were low just at the time we started living in the community but then started getting higher before long."

Housing Co-operatives

Inuit did not necessarily have to shoulder the cost of buying and constructing a house alone—there was also the option of housing co-ops. The first housing co-op was formed in Iqaluit in 1961, when fifteen families came together to share the cost of acquiring three-bedroom houses, applying for the government subsidy of $1,000 per house. The houses arrived in the fall of 1962, and the families built them that fall and winter, sharing labour. Accordingly the co-op was considered a success, and two more Iqaluit-based housing co-ops were formed in 1963. This co-op housing was only available to those who could afford a monthly cost of $120 for mortgage and utilities. This was much higher than costs associated with government housing, and only families with steady employment could seriously consider joining. Other co-ops formed later in other communities.

For much of the study period, Qallunaat held most of the administrative and logistic control concerning the design, size, and location of houses. Within the Iqaluit housing co-op, for instance, construction could only take place on areas levelled and prepared by NANR, and thus determined by the government. In effect, permanent housing allowed the government to see, literally, where and how Inuit lived. This was true of non–co-op housing as well. Houses were set along streets laid out by the government on sites where construction equipment could manoeuvre over the land. Unlike the traditionally small groupings of dwellings that accommodated dozens of people, government officials planned for hundreds of people to live in communities. Houses were set side-by-side on roads laid out in patterns similar to those in suburban developments. Often the roads radiated away from the water, inhibiting access to it for many residents. Inuit valued the water, especially as a means of transportation, and traditionally would have selected a site near the water for their dwelling.

Inuit were sometimes able to, and did, make suggestions for improving the government's initial housing designs, which in one case allowed Inuit to apply for loans for garage construction. Theoretically the various housing programs would provide the mechanisms for the desired transition for Inuit to better health and improved living conditions, but in practice the results were not so simple or successful.

Eskimo Rental Housing Program, 1965 to 1968

The year 1964 "marked a critical point in the development of northern housing. By then everyone was aware that the previous policy, the Eskimo Housing Loan Program, had failed nurses, doctors, policemen, administrators, parliamentarians, and the Inuit themselves." Inuit in Qikiqtaaluk did not have access to sufficient wages and savings to purchase houses, which were becoming larger and closer in amenities to southern housing. By 1965, 90% of Inuit who had been contracted to buy houses under the Eskimo Housing Loan Program failed to make payments. Government officials also noted that housing was not improving Inuit health as promised, but merely changing the form of the problem due to overcrowding, poor ventilation, and indirectly, to bringing more people into settlements where they often had less access to nutritious food.

As an alternative, the government set up a social housing program known as the Eskimo Rental Housing Program in 1965. It followed changes to the National Housing Act in 1964 that extended federal government assistance for public housing. The rental program shipped about 1,500 houses north and had the added effect of adding to the presence of government in Inuit lives by literally opening the doors of Inuit homes to officials.

Monthly rent for a one-room house was initially set at around $25, $5 for furniture rental and $10 for services like water and fuel. The government determined the rental price by employing a complex system based on income and housing type, with rent paid to the commuity's housing authority, later named the Housing Association. In this new system, the area administrator sorted Inuit in his jurisdiction into three categories. Category A was made up of families with steady, full-time employment income who did not rely on family allowance or social assistance; these families paid either 20% of their monthly income as rent, or the maximum rent for the house type, whichever was lower. Category B consisted of people in need of social assistance, whether for health or other reasons. These people received housing through a social assistance scheme and paid rent of $2 per month. Category C was made up of those not permanently employed, usually seasonal hunters and part-time employees for the government. The government devised a special formula to adjust rent for people who fell into this category.

The federal government intended the local housing authorities to "give a real voice" to Inuit, although this intention often carried paternalistic overtones. As one government report stated, "We see these local housing authorities as possible embryos for municipal governments and therefore wish to encourage the transfer of real authority and responsibility to this group as quickly as they can demonstrate the ability to handle it." Elijah Padluq told the QTC that housing associations held considerable power in the community: The association was "a group of people who wanted some control over the units and [to] design the units ... They controlled the way the budget was being managed, how they were going to manage rent payments, and how to reconcile rent payments and budget."

A report in the late 1960s by the Department of Indian Affairs and Northern Development (DIAND) outlined the bylaw template for local housing authorities. They stated that members were to be elected to the housing association, composed of all renters in a community, but that the area administrator could choose the chairman and secretary. Decisions concerning the types of houses that would be available and the distribution of supplies remained under the control of Ottawa officials. This system meant that the government held de facto control of the group and its decisions. Inuit did become increasingly involved in housing issues in the 1970s.

Many Inuit who provided testimony to QIA or to the QTC rented houses under Category B. People said they were told that rent would not increase, but found out that this was not true. Ham Kudloo told the QIA, "the government said that they were going to help us and we were happy . . . but apparently we were cheated on—the rents [were] going higher and higher and it became very upsetting." Johanasie Apak told the QIA, "We started renting at $2 per month. Later on, after the community [of Clyde River] was moved to the present location, three-bedroom housing cost $15 per month."

Each family's position within the income-based system was to be re-evaluated annually by the area administrator, but it is unclear who did the calculations and how families were notified. The government also intended for the maximum rent for Inuit rentals to rise in proportion to increases in rental costs for employee housing. Both of these factors could have contributed to the increase in rent that was experienced in the communities. However, it is evident from the testimonies that rules, as well as the equation that government used to determine rent, were not adequately explained to Inuit.

This lack of communication was acknowledged in the South, as was the need to resolve it. In a letter sent to NANR on May 11, 1966, Anglican Bishop Donald Marsh concluded, "There is a need of a written statement of policy of the Department on the question of housing, and this statement should lay down very clearly the responsibility of the Eskimo people and Government." He added, "Misunderstandings are increasing in the North."

It is important to note that despite widespread dissatisfaction, some people were content with government-provided housing. Julia Amaroalik told the QTC that she moved to Igloolik in 1969 and stayed with her parents. Moving into her own house was a relief. "When the buildings were built, they gave us housing . . . I liked the house that was given to us. I got tired of being with my parents. My children made too much noise . . . I wanted a house for so long. It was a good time when we got our own."

Elijah Padluq told the QTC: "We moved into the matchboxes . . . It seemed so beautiful and so warm—I liked it. Yes, when they started establishing the housing association, we were moved to a larger unit with three bedrooms. It was a huge house. What a difference!"

Mary Battye told the QTC that she found her new house in Pangnirtung very large. "[At first] I got a slanted matchbox through social services . . . When they started building houses, they moved me to the other houses, to a three-bedroom house . . . I could hear an echo it was so big." Moses Kasarnak told the QIA that he was pleased with his new house. "We were just very happy that we were going to get a house here . . . We were directly told that if we moved we would get a house and that it would have a table and dishes. It was like Christmas that we were going to get all these." He continued, however: "After we had [the] house for quite a while, problems started to come up—we had to do everything ourselves."

Yet problems persisted even with new initiatives. Housing distribution, for instance, remained uneven within and between communities in Qikiqtaaluk. Between 1965 and 1969, Inuit living in Qikiqtaaluk and Keewatin received a total of six hundred and fifty-five houses; one hundred of these went to Iqaluit, seventy-nine to Baker Lake, and the rest distributed among the other communities. More houses were scheduled to arrive over the next decade. Housing was largely allocated by the government during this period based on need and order of arrival into the community as well as income. Consequently, as housing types improved over the study period, people arriving in communities later often received bigger houses with more amenities.

Continuing Challenges

Major challenges in the provision of government housing in Qikiqtaaluk were the inter-related problems of logistics and affordability—technical issues related to cold, wind, and even permafrost presented less significant difficulties. The government did not want to give the houses away to anyone, which meant that it was always trying to make them as cheap as possible to match the limited income of Inuit for rent and heating. All supplies—wood, nails, shingles, concrete forms, etc.—needed to come from the South. The materials needed for a three-bedroom house, for instance, weighed ten tonnes and cost about $1,400 for shipping alone in the 1960s. The government's demand to build and heat homes cheaply, coupled with the sheer volume of houses needed, drove down the quality of construction materials and the size of the houses. Meanwhile, other problems arose beyond volume and materials. Housing kits sometimes arrived with parts missing, in the wrong size, broken, or in some cases all three, as occurred with a shipment to Iqaluit in 1962. There were also problems with harsh working conditions and short construction seasons. The chronic shortage of materials also meant that Inuit trying to improve their homes by building porches, sheds, or garages, or by improving interior features were restricted to either materials ordered from the South at great expense, or to what they could find at the dump left over from other construction projects. Supplies for housing were sometimes scarce even in larger, more concentrated settlements. Elisapee Arreak told the QIA, "My husband built a small building for us to live in . . . There was hardly any wood to build a house so it was very small."

A common theme expressed in QTC testimonies was the frequent delay in the government's provision of prefabricated housing once a family moved to a community. While waiting for permanent housing, Inuit constructed houses with the materials available to them. Some people from ilagiit nunagivaktangit brought their one-room houses from campsites and erected them pending construction of new dwellings. Some constructed qarmait or tents, while others used scrap material left over from the prefabricated houses, such as wood, canvas, and cardboard, to construct framed houses. These temporary houses were not always solidly constructed and did not resist the elements well. The effects that these living conditions had on Inuit health were dire and contributed to their mortality.

In many cases, Inuit spent months or even years living in tents, qarmaqs, and other temporary dwellings after they moved to permanent settlements. In testimony to the QTC, Leah Okadlak described the one-room house in Arctic Bay where she lived with her children and a large extended family until the mid-1960s as being "full of snow." She added, "I think about the house sometimes and I cry . . . we were living in a house that was not healthy. We were able to get some fuel for the Primus stove. The floor was all wet. The inside became ice."

Inuit were confused and hurt when they were told to move to a community with the promise of housing, and arrived to find nothing available for them. Elijah Padluq told the QTC, "There were some people who were asked to move [to Kimmirut] without housing [being] available . . . I think that this was the hardest part for people. There was no ready-made housing when we moved here." Isaac Eyaituk told the QTC, "We didn't get a house right away. I don't remember who gave us a canvas tent but I remember it being erected by the church. [We waited to get a house for] almost a year, a whole year." Alooloo Kautuk told the QTC that his parents moved to Hall Beach in May one year and "they lived in a tent even though it was very cold. They lived in a tent for eight months until Christmas. [My mother's] leg was broken. She was staying in a tent with a broken leg. They . . . didn't get a house until December."

Heating these homes was a serious challenge. Markosie Sowdluapik told the QTC, "It was very cold when we pitched our tent. I had to stay up all night because I was worried that one of my children would freeze."

Apphia Killiktee explained that a teacher came to her family's ilagiit nunagivaktangat near Pond Inlet and told her family that they were to send the children to school in the settlement. The family made the move, but found themselves without a place to live.

> We ended up in a tent near the river. The whole winter we stayed in the tent. It was so difficult for us. We didn't have any food to eat. Every morning we woke up to everything frozen. It was so difficult for our parents and for us. At that time, I was in kindergarten . . . Our grandpa in the winter would try to pick up some cardboard boxes and put them in around and inside the tent, and when we had enough snow, he would build an iglu around the tent to keep us warm. It was difficult for us, not knowing, coming to the community like that and not having housing.

Leah Evic told the QTC:

> We had to leave in March. The weather was very cold. We arrived with just our bedding . . . It was very hard. My older sister was living in Pangnirtung [and so we went there] because we didn't have any other place to go . . . In our camps, we had qarmait, but they're winterized. It was now hard to keep the children warm. There was only a Coleman stove. We put up a frame. We put some cardboard inside. It was very cold . . . Because we pitched our tent in a bad place we had to move our tent. It hurt us because we came from a qarmaq that was winterized to living in a tent . . . It was hurtful. We were hurt.

Overcrowding was a fundamental problem that continued as Inuit moved into permanent communities in the 1950s and 1960s. In Iqaluit, for example, the Inuit population quickly increased from two hundred and fifty in 1956 to eight hundred in 1960. Delivery of housing was delayed, in large part due to bureaucratic programs and complex shipping and construction schedules. Overcrowding was noted as a major factor in high rates of tuberculosis, infant mortality, and even excessive alcohol consumption, although other factors were likely important as well. Quppirualuk Padluq noted that eighteen people lived in her house at one time, and Apphia Killiktee remembers there being around the same number in her matchbox house.

The government was aware that Inuit with permanent houses were disappointed with their homes. A 1966 report revealed veiled self-criticism about government delays, stating, "Many [Inuit] voiced their pleasure that the government was taking the trouble to explain things to them" and "When this was followed also by the houses actually arriving when we said they would, the effect in the settlements was electric. That the formulation of a different government image was in process was quite clear to everyone. Interestingly, government officials were also disappointed in the houses they inspected. In a 1967 survey by CMHC, inspectors recorded that "it was extremely uncomfortable to sit near an outside wall in which windows were located," and that ventilation through chimneys caused a vacuum, sucking in snow from any crevice. They also reported a critical lack of storage space. Other government inspections found substandard stoves and pipes, and an "outstanding deficiency" in roof construction leading to widespread leaks. Official reports, with their use of technical and clinical terminology such as "deficiencies" and "discomfort," only touched the edges of the truths experienced by Inuit.

New styles of houses were introduced to alleviate these problems. The one-room, slope-walled Angirraq style emphasized simplicity and low cost, although it appears that the structures were sent to the Arctic without sufficient testing of the stability of plastic elements in cold conditions. Other new styles included row houses, called Style 130, and three-bedroom houses. In the mid-1960s the federal government's housing administration developed standards for the allocation of houses by family size: matchbox houses were for single adults or for couples without children, while two-bedroom houses were for one or two couples with up to one infant each, or for parents with two young children. Three-bedroom houses went to larger families and extended families.

Still, the chronic shortage of houses continued. In 1965, the federal government reported that there were over twelve hundred people living in Qikiqtaaluk in qarmait or tupiit, with an average of more than six people per house, mostly in one-room or one-bedroom dwellings. A government report concluded that it would take thirteen years at the current pace of construction to house everyone, not factoring in population increases. The federal government aimed to fill a sixteen-hundred-house gap across the Arctic by 1967 in a massive production boost, but it only managed to ship two hundred homes to nine communities in Qikiqtaaluk. Cultural differences concerning housing needs were not resolved. The permanent houses then being introduced, for example, still did not take into account peoples' needs to cut and store meat or fix equipment.

Gender Issues

Conventional housing also reinforced divisions in the roles of men, women, and children through distinct spaces that supported separate spheres of activity. When living on the land, Inuit women determined the location of the tupiq, qarmaq, or igluvigaq, and took care of the home while the family stayed there. This role changed when government officials began controlling the location of prefabricated houses, while at the same time encouraging Inuit women, once established in a permanent home, to fit the Qallunaat definition of a homemaker.

In southern suburbs, the three-bedroom bungalow mirrored expectations about domestic roles. The woman was expected to be responsible for the whole house, but especially the kitchen. The man ate in the dining room and retired to the living room after dinner. Children, girls in one bedroom and boys in the other, stayed in their well-lit rooms to read books and study, unless they were outside playing. And, perhaps most importantly, a mother and father slept together in the same bedroom by themselves.

While the government did not describe the relationship between cultural norms and three-bedroom houses so starkly or honestly, it came close. In the *Q-Book, Quajivaallirutissat,* published by NANR in 1964, Inuit living in conventional houses in settlements were told that "many wives also enjoy being good housekeepers" and that a clean house would make women proud. Home economists, often wives of Qallunaat men working in Qikiqtaaluk, taught courses for Inuit women with varying degrees of cultural sensitivity and dedication. Among other duties, home economists taught women how to prepare meals using stoves and packaged or canned foods available at the HBC store. Some aspects of these new responsibilities clashed with traditional Inuit gender and social roles and were less likely to be adopted. For example, in discussing how to incorporate and prepare new foods, teachers overlooked the fact that men were traditionally in charge of bringing home food, including goods from the HBC store. Men, not women, determined which new foods, if any, would become part of the family's diet. Lengthy, intensive food preparation also hindered a woman from engaging in other tasks, such as child-rearing and giving proper attention to visitors.

In other respects, such as in keeping houses clean or in developing personal styles and colour palettes, home economics teachers were more successful. In their book *Eskimo Townsmen,* a report on a 1950s study of Iqaluit, anthropologists John J. and Irma Honigmann indicated that Inuit women were in charge of choosing paint for co-op housing in Iqaluit in 1962. Women in co-op housing had electricity, a kitchen stove, and often a steady income in the family that they could invest in Qallunaat-style housing culture.

Still, many Inuit women were disappointed with the conditions of their permanent housing. Often the houses came with few amenities and no furniture, and were of poor construction, cold, and cramped. Alicee Joamie told the QIA that her prefabricated house came without any of the promised furniture:

> We lived in a very nice qarmaq in Apex. When the Government didn't want us to live in a qarmaq anymore, we had to move to a small house . . . There was no bed, and no furniture, only an oven. We slept there that night and we were given blankets. We slept there on the floor, my children and my husband, near the oven because there wasn't anything in there.

Emily Takatak had a similar experience. She told the QTC: "When the house was finished, the house had nothing in it, except an aluminum tub. That was the only thing that we had when we moved into that house . . . It consisted of a few plates and cups." Iqaluk Juralak told the QTC how disappointed she was with the state of her new house:

> They took us to Apex to our house, a place where we were going to stay. When we went in to the place I was hurt to see what I entered because I was told that we were going to get a brand-new place or a house. That place had no furniture whatsoever–not one thing in it. The only thing that was in there was one of those wooden things that you use to do carpentry and a whole bunch of leftover wood from building the place or fixing up the place. There was leftover wood and sawdust in the house and that was about it. I have been waiting to express that for the longest time we were sure we were going to be put in to a place that was brand new and nice. But I was so hurt by what I saw. When we started living here there was no mattress—nothing to sleep on. We were fortunate enough to get some blankets and sleeping material from other families.

Leah Okadlak told the QTC:

> After three years, my parents got their house. It was one of those little square ones, a Qallunaat house. It had a little stove. It had no furnace, and no bedroom, just one room. We lived there. My father had twelve kids and we were all living in there . . . My husband was also here. We were all together in this little square house, which had no bedrooms . . . I was looking after my sister's children and we were living in a house that was not healthy . . . The floor was all wet. The inside became ice. It was very hard to dry it up.

For these women, who were in charge of taking care of their homes, these inadequacies in housing presented significant and often insurmountable problems in their lives.

Housing Differences

Some of the same officials who were advocating that Inuit should be content with their small houses were expecting much more for themselves. A January 1963 internal report to the Minister of Northern Affairs and Natural Resources about conditions in Resolute noted, "There is a house built by the Department for a Northern-Service officer at an alleged price of $75,000. The house has been heated since October 6th, and is still to be lived in." While this house was likely an extreme example of the difference in housing available to Inuit and Qallunaat in Qikiqtaaluk in the 1960s, the differences were regularly noted by observers. It is perhaps noteworthy that in the same report, the Minister was told that DEW Line employees "also feel that [Inuit] are not being given adequate care, especially in relation to housing facilities." Staff wrote in the margin of the report, "Let them [presumably

Inuit] know about our housing program," but it is unclear how or why single Inuit men or families temporarily employed at a DEW Line site for a few years could have used the housing program.

A very thorough critique of housing in the North was published as *Eskimo Housing as Planned Culture Change* in 1972. D. K. Thomas and C. T. Thompson pointed to numerous deficiencies and a lack of cultural sensitivity in the provision of housing. Anthropologist David Damas, who spent many years studying changes in Inuit communities, pointed out in his book *Arctic Migrants/Arctic Villagers* that it was important to "be aware that perceptions of what constituted adequate housing for the Inuit changed profoundly" in the 1960s. "While there were errors in planning, the evaluation of thinking regarding housing in the North was rapid as the decade advanced." It can also be noted that more Inuit became involved in the administration of housing in the 1970s, in particular.

Northern Rental Purchase Program

Government housing for Inuit improved in the 1960s and early 70s in concert with improvements to community infrastructure, such as water supplies, generators, and fuel services, and with greater involvement of Inuit. The Eskimo Housing Loan Program was replaced in 1968 with the Northern Rental Purchase Program, an initiative that once again treated rental payments as mortgage payments. A year later, the housing program was transferred to the Government of the Northwest Territories.

By 1972 the Inuit population in communities had risen to the point that the federal bureaucrats recommended increasing the number of proposed new houses to be built by 1978 by over a hundred, just to try to keep up with demand. In 1973 the territorial government set up the Northwest Territories Housing Corporation (NTHC) to manage public housing construction and operations. The following year, it built twenty-four new houses in Qikiqtaaluk, but this was far less than was needed. NWT councillor Leda Peterson decried the housing conditions for Inuit in Qikiqtaaluk and Central Arctic, while fellow councillor Bryan Pearson noted that most houses were still constructed in the South, imported to the North and assembled by Qallunaat, instead of capitalizing on local initiative and labour. Pearson argued that houses should at least be constructed from northern trees in the Western and Central Arctic, to encourage northern industry.

Inuit and Qallunaat held fundamentally different expectations concerning housing and wealth. This in turn affected the process of implementing the government's housing initiatives. Inuit were very pragmatic—throughout their lives, they had been engaged in a trading economy that they understood very well. They had seen the value of their primary trading resource, fox furs, fluctuate wildly, and also understood the concept of debt. At any time, they either owed the HBC furs or a portion of their social benefits, or the HBC owed them goods. They supported themselves using earnings from trade and jobs to buy what they needed to make hunting more efficient, by conserving resources and constructing their dwellings with materials that were available to them without cost.

In 1958, in response to public comments about the lack of good housing in the North, the federal government had reported internally, and perhaps in preparation for media consumption, that:

> It is the ambition of the Department of Northern Affairs and National Resources to make living in Northern Canada attractive. Accordingly, for its servants it attempts to provide a standard of housing reasonably close to that which they would occupy in the more settled parts of Canada. For those it serves, the Eskimos, it endeavours to design homes to suit their budgets at various stages

> of economic independence, starting with a more healthful substitute for the iglu and tent.

In effect, the government was stating that socio-economic differences in access to housing that were so obvious in the South should be repeated in the North and that Inuit, no matter what their reasons for living in settlements, should begin with a house that was merely a "substitute" for a snowhouse or a canvas tent. Where a Qallunaat family might expect to be provided with a three-bedroom house, an Inuit family would only be provided with a one- or two-room structure. As late as 1975, Inuit in Iqaluit represented 70% of the population, but occupied only 35% of the housing. Qallunaat government employees, representing 30% of the population, lived in 65% of the housing, and the best housing at that. The health problems and cramped, damp living conditions persisted because many plywood prefabricated houses were still in use well into the 1970s. As many people told the QTC, frustrations continue about housing to this day.

Today, Qikiqtaaluk communities bear witness to contradictory conclusions that can be drawn from an examination of the history of pre-1975 housing programs. On one hand, houses in all communities provide evidence about an inferior building stock that was designed without input from the people who understood the environment and were destined to occupy the buildings. On the other, a substantial portion of everything that can be seen in the hamlets and city that make up Qikiqtaaluk today is the result of the labour of a generation of Inuit who took advantage of anything that was available to them to create permanent places where they could live, work, and raise families.

Aaniajurliriniq
Health Care in Qikiqtaaluk

Inuit health knowledge is holistic in its approach and upholds that all aspects of a person's needs, including the psychological, physical, and social, are connected. For Inuit, healing injuries and sickness goes hand in hand with developing a strong mind and resilient body; for this reason, health is closely tied to personal identity. Adults are expected to act independently with the interests of themselves and their families in mind. Sick people are treated with love and care, and satisfying the patient's needs and desires is considered paramount for recovery. Inuit health knowledge also refers to more than general healing techniques—it concerns knowledge of the body and its social environment.

In almost every sense, Inuit ideas about health are consistent with the widely accepted definition put forth by the World Health Organization (WHO): "Health is a state of complete physical, mental, and social well-being, not merely the absence of disease or infirmity." To date, no comprehensive history of health ideas, needs, and services in present-day Nunavut has been published, although a number of excellent studies of institutions and medical conditions exist. A full history would require a careful examination of connections between a range of diverse topics, such as cultural practices, language, colonialism, legal history, and medical knowledge. This short history about health care in Qikiqtaaluk is focused on medical practices and policies as delivered by government agencies. It is hoped that others will continue an examination of broader issues in Inuit health history.

One of the few histories to look at broad issues related to the history of Aboriginal health in the twentieth century is *Colonizing Bodies: Aboriginal Health and Healing in British Columbia, 1900–1950*. Historian Mary-Ellen Kelm based her work on oral evidence provided to her by First Nations informants, as well as on many archival, published, and oral sources. The study's analysis and conclusions have parallels in the health history in Qikiqtaaluk, although it places more emphasis on church-run residential schools and less on health evacuations than is relevant to Inuit history. Kelm describes how Euro-Canadian policies and programs introduced poverty and greater susceptibility to disease, while simultaneously displacing Aboriginal knowledge about health with medical treatments that were intended, in large part, to prove the benefits of assimilation. She also shows how improvements to Aboriginal health were recast as being in the "national interest" in the 1940s, especially over fears about epidemics that were perceived to be spreading from, rather than to, Aboriginal populations. Finally she considers how First Nations set out to reclaim control over their bodies by demanding better health services from government, addressing connections between health and social conditions, and by sharing and applying indigenous knowledge in treatments.

This chapter looks at Inuit experiences with medical services established in Qikiqtaaluk by the federal and territorial governments in the 1950 to 1975 period by focusing on issues raised in interviews for the Qikiqtani Inuit Association (QIA) and the Qikiqtani Truth Commission (QTC). It does not address the histories of St. Luke's hospital in Pangnirtung, the Eastern Arctic Patrols (EAPs) of the 1920s and 1930s, or services provided in other parts of present-day Nunavut, such as Coral Harbour and Cambridge Bay, in detail.

The history is divided into three periods, beginning with the early twentieth century. During the period of Taissumani Nunamiutautilluta, when the sea and land provided almost everything Inuit needed, Inuit needing advice or treatment for health matters relied almost entirely on their own health knowledge, supplemented by a small Anglican hospital at Pangnirtung, medical teams visiting trading centres annually by ship, and very limited treatments provided by the Royal Canadian Mounted Police (RCMP), missionaries, and Hudson's Bay Company (HBC) traders.

Taissumani Nunamiutautilluta was followed by several years of disruptions caused by the influx of Qallunaat who were tasked with ensuring that Canada's North and its inhabitants would be subject to southern Canadian ideas, laws, and institutions. This period is called Sangussaqtauliqtilluta, when people were more or less forced to change their ways. Improvements in health services in the region, such as the staffing of nursing stations, were both a belated response to long-standing complaints made by missionaries, researchers, bureaucrats, and American military personnel about high mortality rates and chronic conditions, such as respiratory illnesses, and a result of more government involvement in the provision of health services to Canadians. Some actions intended to improve Inuit health added to suffering by patients and their families. This was particularly true with respect to the removal of Inuit for diagnosis and treatment in the south, for tuberculosis and other diseases. People who were infected or sick were removed without notice for indefinite stays in southern hospitals. Inuit who refused screening or were known to be ill were sometimes tracked down at their ilagiit nunagivaktangat by the ship's helicopter. Inuit sent south for treatment often endured weeks on board the ship even before they spent many months or years in treatment, far away from their families. A number of those people were returned to Iqaluit for observation or to attend the rehabilitation centre and never found their way home.

Inuit patients sent south were sometimes treated with exceptional kindness, but others were left alone without companionship in very unfamiliar and unpleasant conditions for months or years. Miluqtituttuq Akesuk recalled being sent to Toronto for tuberculosis treatment in 1964 when she was ten years old. She told the QTC, "I thought I was lost. I thought I would never come back here to my parents when I first went down. I really thought I was lost." Children were particularly vulnerable to the loss of cultural knowledge and language and to lasting psychological impacts. Poor record-keeping led to the return of some patients to the wrong communities, and to tragic circumstances in which families waited for their children and parents to return, not knowing that they had died at the hospital.

By the period of Nunalinnguqtitauliqtilluta, the time when we were actively (by outside force) formed into communities, almost the whole population of Qikiqtaaluk lived in centralized settlements where they were provided with low-quality services that were intermittent and limited in scope. Geographer and historian George Wenzel argues that "few, if any, Inuit, presently living in a government village or settlement, would dispute the importance and benefits represented by the availability of Western-type health care," but they also knew that the quality and availability of care had not been ideal. Inuit access to medical services during this period was not on par with the care available in southern Canada, and Inuit were not involved in important decisions about how health outcomes could be improved.

In all three eras, bureaucrats, health professionals, and Inuit understood that there were important connections between a healthy body and related health factors, such as nutrition, housing, education, and feelings of self-worth. There is little evidence, if any, that Inuit were asked to provide input into options that could have made their lives better while also addressing grim statistics related to infant mortality, cardiovascular disease, and growing incidences of addiction.

Taissumani Nunamiutautilluta

INUIT HEALTH KNOWLEDGE

Knowledge was typically passed down orally by Elders to everyone who needed it—it did not belong to specific individuals. While someone with special healing powers, such as a shaman, could be sought out in times of need, everyone regularly kept medicines and first-aid equipment in their households. Typical materials would include bearded seal oil and blubber to stop infections and allow wounds to heal, and caribou membranes, Arctic fireweed, lichens, willow leaves, and other natural materials for treating other injuries and sicknesses. These medical supplies were often gathered during the summer and stored for future use. Kudjuarjuk describes one particularly important plant in John Bennett and Susan Rowley's *Uqalurait: An Oral History of Nunavut*:

> There are not too many Eskimo medicines but there is one, which is very good: it is called [pujualuk] and is a little plant that grows in damp mossy areas. They are white on top and brown inside [puffballs]. In the summertime, we used to collect all the [pujualuit] from the moss for the winter and wrap them and store them in a dry area. These [pujualuit] have a dry powder in them and on the big cuts we would put on [pujualuit] as medicine and a bandage to stop the bleeding and heal the wound.

Contact with Europeans, especially whalers, in the nineteenth and early twentieth centuries introduced Inuit to many new infectious diseases. Customary approaches did not work against these diseases, resulting in the deaths of many Inuit, possibly hundreds in the 1850s alone.

GOVERNMENT AND MISSIONARY MEDICAL SERVICES

St. Luke's Hospital and the Outpost Nursing Program

The first permanent clinic and hospital to be built in Qikiqtaaluk was St. Luke's Hospital in Pangnirtung. It was opened in 1931 by the Anglican mission with the encouragement and support of a government doctor, Dr. Leslie Livingstone. Anglican Bishop Archibald Lang Fleming had been arguing for a hospital in Kimmirut, since the settlement was on the regular supply routes and was accessible to the large number of Inuit residing in southern Baffin Island. The Anglican Church eventually conceded to operating a hospital in Pangnirtung in the hope that a second hospital would be built at Kimmirut. The latter was never constructed, and the government chose to build a nursing station there in January 1946.

St. Luke's was initially funded by the Anglican Church and private benefactors in England and Canada; government funds were limited to shipping supplies and covering the costs of some drugs. Once the hospital was opened, the Canadian government covered the salaries of hospital staff, mainly female nurses. In fact, the hospital relied heavily on nurses rather than doctors, as they were more likely to live and work in the North. Nurses were generally single women of British descent, sent north on one-year contracts. They were also expected to serve as government representatives in their interactions with Inuit. The support staff was generally Inuit. They included, at times, a receptionist, dental therapist, interpreter, and community health representative. While at St. Luke's, patients were treated for all kinds of medical conditions, with most of the time spent treating influenza, typhoid and "shiptime fever," or performing surgeries. From the outset, beds were allocated to tuberculosis patients, a need that increased in later years.

During the Second World War, St. Luke's faced financial and staffing challenges. In some years, such as 1944, there were no doctors, only nurses. Nurses were often capable of providing a wide range of medical services, from standard curative measures to preventative care, immunizations, emergency treatments, assisting with childbirth, identifying tuberculosis cases, and treating other infections. When the hospital had no doctor, the female nurses had to defer to the authority of a council composed of male RCMP officers and the HBC manager.

At the same time, the government often advocated a policy of hospitalizing as few Inuit as possible. The nurses, for their part, were often critical of this policy, which seemed more concerned with budgetary concerns then the health of Inuit. One example can be seen in Edith Prudence Hockin's letter to the bishop, dated October 6, 1943, in which she conveys her concerns:

> The *Nascopie* arrived on the 4th in the midst of a snowstorm ... We were a little disappointed not to get patients this year as we had heard there were several. The people from *Resolution* were left at [Kimmirut] by the McLean and are *still* there. There were also patients at Wolstenholm, [Kimmirut], and Pond. No very good reason seems to be forthcoming for not bringing any. Looks like a straight case of "saving on the Hospital bills" to me. Dr. Collins from the Dept. is on the *Nascopie* and of the *Resolution* people he said it would be a pity to clutter this place up with them, they are all sick.

At this time, the EAP was responsible for transporting patients to and from the hospital as well as providing hospital supplies. As such, hospital staff often had to anticipate what supplies would be required a year at a time. If patients missed the ship, they also had to wait a year for the next one. At these times, the hospital was responsible for accommodating them while they waited. In order to do so, the upper floor of St. Luke's was converted into a residence.

Eastern Arctic Patrol

Through the 1920s, and into the early 1930s, Inuit across the Arctic had been provided with relief from time to time by the Department of the Interior. The EAP was the first unofficially government-directed health care program in the North. Anxiety over sovereignty, fed by the presence of American whalers in Hudson Bay and Denmark's potential claim to Ellesmere Island, resulted in the government adopting an approach of "effective occupation" in the Canadian Arctic in the early twentieth century. The establishment of RCMP posts throughout the Arctic to be serviced by the EAP vessels *Arctic* (1922–25), and *Beothic* (1926–31), was a product of this approach. While the initial aim of the EAP was to provide support to the RCMP, the ship's doctor occasionally provided basic medical care to Inuit encountered along its route. However, it is important to note that much of the medical assistance provided was limited, and the only point where the EAP met a concentrated amount of Inuit was at Pangnirtung.

By 1926, the Canadian government was feeling more secure about its jurisdiction over the North and more inclined to help northern inhabitants. Unfortunately, the onset of the Great Depression resulted in the government having to cut back on services. In order to save on costs, in 1932, the EAP began conducting its patrols via the HBC supply ship, the *Nascopie* (1932–47). At this time, EAP services expanded to include general inspections of Inuit and game, as well as the transportation of missionaries, RCMP officers, medical personnel, and Inuit going to or from Southern hospitals for medical treatment. During the interwar years, concerns of diabetes, cancer, and heart disease were receiving more attention and some doctors began accompanying the patrol in order to conduct research among populations in the North. The addition of Dr. Charles Williams of the University Of Toronto Faculty of Dentistry to the 1939 charter also raised concerns over the oral health of Inuit in light of the new white-flour diet, and soon after a dentist joined the wartime EAP medical staff. Nevertheless, health care services, including dental care, which was often restricted to extractions that could be done quickly at ship stops, remained minimal and sporadic.

The federal government's decision to develop more medical services in Qikiqtaaluk was not the result of a simple evolution of thinking on the part of bureaucrats. It flowed from the Supreme Court of Canada's ruling in 1939 (in a decision commonly referenced as "Re: Eskimos") that Inuit were to be treated as Indians under the Indian Act. Prior to this decision, the federal government took advantage of the confusion about its responsibilities for Inuit. Since the 1880s, the government had provided services for "destitute" Inuit in parts of the Arctic through mission schools and medical attention. With an obvious need to deal with infectious diseases in the Arctic, especially TB, the government amended the Indian Act in 1924 to give the Department of Indian Affairs responsibility for "Eskimo Affairs." The meaning of the term "Eskimo Affairs" remained undefined, and the government continued to back away from any interpretation that meant that it was responsible for the people themselves. Even after the government transferred responsibility for Inuit affairs to the Northwest Territories Council, the Indian Act made no reference to Inuit.

A dispute between the governments of Canada and Quebec (the only province with an Inuit population) about which body should be responsible for the costs of assisting destitute Inuit finally reached the Supreme Court of Canada, and led to the 1939 "Re: Eskimo" ruling, which determined federal responsibility. The federal government immediately appealed to the Privy Council in London, but the start of the Second World War delayed the case. While the 1939 ruling effectively became law, the federal government carried on delivering a minimal level of services (specifically health, education, and welfare) to Inuit through various agencies, without the benefit of a policy or legislative framework specific to Inuit.

Sangussaqtauliqtilluta

WAR TIME

From 1939 to 1945, the Second World War focused the government's attention on sovereignty issues, rather than social ones, and the "Re: Eskimo" decision had little effect on the delivery of government services or programs for Inuit. However, concurrent international pressures would increase the demand for improved Canadian health care in the North. During the Second World War and the beginning of the Cold War, the Canadian and American governments worked together on a number of defence projects in the North, resulting in a substantial influx of US military personnel to the Arctic. This had a tremendous effect on the infection rates of communicable diseases, with far more serious implications for the Qikiqtaalungmiut than for Qallunaat. The 1940s saw a high mortality rate among Inuit resulting from epidemics of influenza, pneumonia, meningitis, typhoid fever, scabies, and tuberculosis.

The Canadian government had asked the US military to provide medical services to all staff, including employed Inuit. The situation was confused by the lack of a clear definition of the meaning of the term "employed" and the reality that Inuit men travelled with their families to bases and weather stations looking for work. When someone living temporarily nearby was in need of medical attention, the local military medic would feel obliged to do what was possible, especially in the absence of Canadian civilian health clinics and services.

Not surprisingly, US military personnel, as well as foreign journalists visiting the military bases, began calling attention to the lack of medical services in the region. Their criticism often concerned the lack of treatment for tuberculosis and treatable infections, such as scabies. At one point, the US military flew medicine into Southampton Island after expressing shock at the lack of response to a meningitis epidemic. In order to avoid international embarrassment, the Canadian government determined they would have to be seen as helping the Inuit. While the Northwest Territories government largely dismissed the international concern regarding the medical services in the North, the federal government did move to investigate. A 1943 federally commissioned report concluded that the general lack of proper medical care for Inuit was attributable to the distance and isolation of the North and problems associated with transportation. Despite recommendations provided in the report, government officials remained in disagreement over what measures should be taken to remedy the situation and to what extent the government was obliged to provide medical services.

AFTER 1945

In 1945, with only two hospitals operating in the geographic area that is present-day Nunavut, there were only forty-eight beds for just a little under four thousand people. In that year, however, the responsibility for the health of First Nations and Inuit was transferred to the Department of National Health and Welfare (DNHW). The transfer of responsibility for medical programs to the DNHW contributed to the development of a clear mandate to tackle tuberculosis in Aboriginal populations, including Inuit. In 1939, the government figures show the tuberculosis death rate for Inuit was three hundred and fourteen out of one hundred thousand, compared with fifty-three out of one hundred thousand for the rest of Canada. Figures had continued to rise, and finally peaked in the early 1940s. In 1946, tuberculosis was the leading cause of mortality and morbidity in the North. Even though tuberculosis had been a national concern since the First World War, nothing had been done to address tuberculosis among Inuit. Strained government funds and the effects of the Depression most certainly played a role as well. In 1945, the government created an Advisory Committee for the Control and Prevention of Tuberculosis among Indians. Its purpose was to look into existing efforts to identify, treat, and provide after-care to sufferers, and to recommend improved and efficient means of accomplishing these objectives in the fight against the disease. The Committee's origins were rooted in the government's approach to tuberculosis as a problem to be overcome by medical professionals, rather than a broader socio-economic issue.

In 1946, the DNHW established Indian and Northern Health Services (INHS) and appointed Dr. Percy Moore to the office of Director. This reform happened for a number of reasons, including sovereignty concerns stemming from the heightened US presence in the Arctic, embarrassment resulting from international concerns over the state of Inuit health, and increased pressure from Canadian medical personnel in the Arctic arguing for the centralization of services. While the reorganization alluded to change in overall policy, in reality, the INHS inherited the position of the previous administrators, which was characterized by inaction, indecision, and limited funding.

In its first year, the INHS spent $28,620 on Inuit health in the Eastern Arctic. With an Inuit population of roughly six thousand, this amounted to $4.77 per person, a very small amount by any standards during this period. From the outset, the INHS also actively worked to limit the perception among Inuit that they had a right to free and unlimited medical and hospital services and that governmental funds were unlimited. In a letter to the Director of the Northern Administration and Lands Branch, Northern Affairs and National Resources, Dr. Moore wrote, "Medical and hospital care at public expense is not something [Inuit] can demand as a right . . . [O]ur funds are not unlimited and must be distributed to the greatest possible advantage for those genuinely in need." There is no evidence, however, that Inuit had high expectations about the types of medical services that would or could be offered. The rhetoric appears to have been intended to reconfirm that staff would take fiscal limitations seriously.

The government decided against building hospitals in Qikiqtaaluk in favour of outpost nursing stations in Cape Dorset and Kimmirut under the care of the INHS. If staff at the nursing station determined specialized treatment was required, Inuit were flown out to southern hospitals, often to Quebec. Over time, the chain of INHS nursing stations offered more sophisticated care and grew to include stations in Iqaluit (1955), Hall Beach (1957), Cambridge Bay (1958), and Kuujjuarapik (1962). Generally, two or three nurses staffed the stations, though at times a local priest or RCMP officer operated them. In remote areas in particular, nurses performed a variety of care, including some dentistry, mental health care, counselling, pre- and postnatal care, local public health inspections, and laboratory technician work, including X-rays. In more populated communities, nurses would screen patients and perform diagnostic tests, and visiting specialists would consult. For example, the nurses at the public health clinic in Iqaluit often conducted preliminary screenings for eye health concerns on a request basis, and had the authority to order prescription glasses. Health specialists then followed up as needed.

Nurses were also tasked with public health education focused on reducing preventable diseases and encouraging better infant health. A Royal Commission presentation at the WHO on "Disease and Death in Canada's North" explained:

> The first line of defence under these circumstances, particularly for those who live at some distance from sources of professional care, must surely be the arming of all residents with at least some of the knowledge and the means to prevent disease by the preservation of health, and with knowledge of first aid and home nursing.

The language reflected an underlying belief held by most medical workers that Inuit knew little about health and medicine.

Early on, public health education was greatly informed by the perspectives of the churches. The nurses interacted very little with Inuit, and did not attempt to incorporate traditional Inuit practices or knowledge into their work as health care professionals. One Elder described the conceptual and practical distance inherent in the nurse-patient relationship when she recalled, "the nurse told me whenever one of my children was sick, or when I thought a child might get sick, I was to bring it to the nursing station right away. She would take the child and return it to me when it was better." She added, "I never know what she does."

By the 1950s, various private agencies and government bodies were involved in providing a range of limited health care initiatives in the Arctic, resulting in a slow pace of improvement to health services in the region. Even in 1952, the only full-time medical officer working in the region, aside from doctors working for the military or private contractors, was the doctor at St. Luke's in Pangnirtung. Funds were neither "unlimited," nor adequate for the population and geography. A memo to the Advisory Committee on Northern Development stated in 1954 that "medical and health services in the Yukon and Northwest Territories often fall seriously below the standards generally acceptable in Canada." In that same year, in an effort to deal with the issues of inefficiency, the Northern Health Services Division was formed within the DNHW to administer all public health functions as established in the Canadian North. At the same time, a Permanent Advisory Committee on Northern Health was established to "serve as a co-ordinating body" between the federal department and the territorial governments. Medical facilities were now paid for in conjunction with the INHS and Territorial Governments, and beginning in the mid-1950s, the Department of Northern Affairs and Natural Resources (NANR) began sending permanent northern service officers, later referred to as area administrators, to assume the welfare functions.

C. D. HOWE

With the transfer of responsibility for Inuit health to the Canadian government in 1945, and in light of the burgeoning tuberculosis epidemic, the EAP and its medical facilities also became crucial to carrying out the government's policy for treating tuberculosis among Inuit populations. Treatment in the South generally involved isolating people in hospitals. In 1925, Quebec and Ontario each had eight sanatoria specifically for the treatment of tuberculosis, in addition to a number of general hospitals set aside for tuberculosis patients. Ultimately, the same treatment policy was adopted for patients in the North, but Inuit were transported thousands of kilometres away from their homes for treatment. Beginning in 1946, X-rays were conducted by the EAP at each stop; anyone diagnosed as being tubercular had to immediately board the ship to be sent south. The ship was crowded with patients, crew, supplies, government employees, and traders. It was almost as much a source of disease as a method of prevention. It was soon realized that a better-equipped ship was required to bring all active tuberculosis cases to southern sanatoria.

Following the sinking of the S.S. *Nascopie* in 1947, the government purchased and outfitted its successor, the Canadian Coast Guard ship *C.D. Howe*, as a medical and supply ship. The new ship could accommodate a crew of fifty-eight, as well as up to thirty Inuit passengers, and came equipped with radar, echo sounding, and a helicopter for personnel transfers. The medical wing had a surgery room, dispensary, X-ray room, dental office, and six patient beds. Its immediate medical goals were to reduce the incidence of tuberculosis, conduct dental and medical surveys, immunize people, evacuate patients south, and return them to their communities from southern sanatoria.

Since the EAP's inception, Inuit had grown accustomed to gathering at Qallunaat enclaves where the ships stopped for trade or temporary employment. These stopping points were often dictated by the location of HBC or RCMP posts, or other Qallunaat agencies. The insistence on the part of the government to ship people south for treatment centred on the argument that it was the least expensive available measure. However, it was also very likely the least humane, and the protocol used to identify and evacuate infected Inuit often caused widespread confusion and emotional hardship. Where in the past Inuit had gathered in anticipation of shiptime, the new tuberculosis-screening policies began generating great fear among Inuit. People were rightly worried they would be taken away from their families and sent to a foreign location. A situation that repeated itself all too often was for a family to watch one or more members board the *C. D. Howe* for medical tests, and then watch the ship sail away with the family members still on board, without any goodbyes, and without explanation. Elijah Padluq shared his experiences of his mother's evacuation with the QTC:

> [You] didn't have any choice but to go on the ship. You had to see the doctor ... [The] patients were not to get off the ship. They stayed on the ship because they had TB ... They would leave in July ... My mother finally came back a year later, in the following spring.

During his testimony to the QTC in 2008, Walter Rudnicki, a retired social worker, explained that this strict policy of removing infected persons went so far as to separate mothers from their children. "The baby was sent to the person [standing closest] to the mother and she was sent off," he explained, "No concern was given to who would take care of the child. I saw this going on." Similarly, dangerous practices were performed upon the return of people to their communities after treatment. According to Rudnicki, "In winter, they were discharged with their summer clothing. It never occurred to the medical personnel that you don't wear summer clothes in the dead of winter in Pang."

Fear of being sent south became widespread because many people often did not return, having died while being treated away from their homes. In 1955, RCMP reported that Inuit in the Kimmirut area were now avoiding the settlement at shiptime because they had no desire of "being evacuated to the Land of No Return." Pat Grygier, author of *A Long Way Home: The Tuberculosis Epidemic Among the Inuit*, described, "Sometimes a priest would connive at hiding people who were afraid they would be sent south, and sometimes Inuit in outlying camps would flee when they saw the ship coming or when they heard the helicopter." The helicopter was often used to seek out Inuit who had not gathered at the port and bring them to the ship for examination. RCMP officers were also asked to help medical officers organize the examinations, but many disliked having to persuade Inuit to board the ship. In an attempt to alleviate some of the fear associated with the evacuations, the NANR instituted a public relations campaign that included distributing photographs, motion pictures, and messages of recovering tuberculosis patients to awaiting family members. The success of this campaign in relieving anxiety among Inuit is not documented.

By 1955, almost one thousand Inuit had been evacuated to Southern sanatoria. Treatment generally averaged twenty months. This meant that in 1956, one in seven Inuit were in hospitals in the South. Frank Tester, Paule McNicoll and Peter Irniq, in an analysis of Inuit accounts from these hospitals, tell us that Inuit patients generally suffered from homesickness, cross-cultural misunderstanding, loss of control over their own health, and irreparable damage to their self-esteem. While the effects of this process on individuals and their communities is discussed later in this chapter, the following quote from a patient letter shows the extent to which a person's individual autonomy was lost, especially in the case of the sanatoria program:

> I really do want to go home. I do want to stay outside. I cannot tell you about my health, as I am not able to understand English ... I am

> obeying the medical staff. I take aspirins . . . It is hard to tell . . . Also, I cannot cure myself . . . I very, very much want to speak English. I am just trying to obey the directions of the medical people. I want to get home too. Sometimes I appear not to be listening . . . I want to follow the wishes of the medical people. I, however, do not understand.

The archival record also shows that the government was aware that the policy of evacuation was very upsetting to Inuit and that many people wanted treatment centres to be established in the North. RCMP Inspector H. A. Larsen wrote in 1951 that the impact of this policy on Inuit was "not good," and that "the period of recovery and convalescence might be much shorter if the Eskimos went under treatment in the environment to which they belong." Correspondence between Dr. Moore at the INHS and Anglican Bishop Marsh also serves to demonstrate the degree to which the government was informed about the negative effects of this policy on the well-being of the people to whom they were tasked with administering health care. In one exchange, the Bishop exclaimed in a letter to Minister Jean LeSage, "I have come to the conclusion that the Department of Health and Welfare are not concerned with the true meaning of the two words (as far as the Eskimos are concerned) which make up the title of the Department."

In addition to being torn from their families and homes, once on the ship, Inuit faced further challenges. Despite the presence of qualified staff, there were many complaints of disorganization, dirty and unsanitary conditions, a lack of effort in providing adequate information for Inuit passengers, and no emergency instructions provided in Inuktitut. Other criticisms described "deplorable service given by the health authorities" and heavy drinking among personnel. Rudnicki told the QTC that he was forced to arrest a captain one year because the man was drunk and putting the lives of everyone on the ship in danger.

Even those who remained behind were affected, as rates of communicable disease infection in the ilagiit nunagivaktangit, small communities, and enclaves increased as a result of the EAP visits. Cold viruses, influenza, and other respiratory infections were regularly transmitted from crew members to Inuit working as guides or moving cargo. These infections, sometimes referred to as "shiptime fever," were often passed on to entire communities and could result in secondary complications like TB. In an effort to curb the infection rates, physicians recommended patients and ship crews be vaccinated and that any sick staff be quarantined during calls at port. Unfortunately, the recommendations do not appear to have been implemented. Indeed, evidence suggests that infection rates continued to climb during the annual port calls, especially at places like Pangnirtung.

CENTRALIZATION

Almost all medical services in Qikiqtaaluk in the 1950s were delivered by nurses. There was never more than one resident physician and only an ad hoc approach to improving services where people lived. From a nurse's perspective, it was not easy to ensure the effective delivery of health care to Inuit living on the land. Personnel and supply shortages, a lack of adequate equipment, and communication issues were only some of the challenges nurses faced. The Northern Health Services Division tackled these issues in part through a policy of centralizing services in selected areas. The massive construction projects and resulting infrastructure developed in association with joint US-Canada military projects, especially the Distant Early Warning (DEW) Line.

The policy of centralizing services, which began in the 1950s and continued through the early 1960s, was in contrast to the Canadian government's previous policy of keeping Inuit engaged directly in hunting and trapping. The growth of the outpost-nursing program and greater investment in hospital services over the years were some of the main outcomes of this policy, and continued during the transition to centralization, whereby almost all Inuit lived in government-supported settlement.

Ethnocentric assumptions and colonial and paternalistic governmental attitudes towards health care in the North were captured clearly when the DNHW asked, "How much public money should be spent trying to save the lives of infants born in hovels to parents who choose to live miles from civilization over rough terrain in one of the toughest climates in the world?" Nevertheless, by 1963, plans were underway for an extension of health care provision to additional outposts by way of medical circuits. The plan called for medical personnel to be transported by aircraft to ilagiit nunagivaktangit outside the reach of nursing stations. In addition, Inuit health workers were trained as interpreters and assistants. In Cape Dorset, for example, Inuit workers were employed to help ensure that local families were being screened for tuberculosis and taking their medicine.

In the following years, the government developed additional tools in an attempt to overcome challenges presented by distance and terrain. The health station, the lay dispenser, and the "Eskimo medicine chest" were implemented by the early 1960s to supplement care extended by the nursing station program. Health stations were smaller than nursing stations, and were generally used as medical facilities by visiting personnel or as layovers for patients awaiting air transportation to hospitals. Lay dispensers referred patients to an individual—often a missionary, trader, RCMP officer, or teacher—who was given supplies and a radio in order to tend to the health needs of accident victims or common illnesses, and an "Eskimo medicine chest" was a first-aid kit given to Inuit families for their own use.

With Inuit moving to settlements, nursing stations found it easier to diagnose, treat, and follow patients. More airports made it possible to evacuate people south and to return them north. With that said, it is highly feasible that improvements in health services could have been made sooner. When contrasted with the medical services provided to military personnel in the North, for example, it is obvious that the capacity for improvements existed long before the 1960s and that the delay cannot be solely blamed on distance, transportation, or difficult terrain.

As was normally the case in the history of Qikiqtaaluk, Iqaluit presented a special situation in the region's history. The development of Iqaluit and the establishment of health services there in the form of a hospital and rehabilitation centre brought about a shift in the administrative hub of medical services from St. Luke's in Pangnirtung to Iqaluit.

Requests for a hospital in Iqaluit stretch as far back as the establishment of the INHS in 1946. The primary reason for constructing a hospital at Iqaluit centred on the argument that flying patients to southern hospitals for specialized medical care was harmful to Inuit and their families. In 1951, RCMP Inspector H. A. Larsen suggested that it would be easier for Inuit to be closer to their home environments during treatment. He also argued that it would be less costly for the government, as there was an opportunity to develop pre-existing infrastructure in the settlement using abandoned US Air Force (USAF) buildings. Larson noted that, while functional, the hospital at Pangnirtung was a "disease trap" and "unfit for human habitation." Unfortunately, it would be many more years before such health care facilities were constructed at Iqaluit.

A rehabilitation centre was eventually opened at Apex Hill (in Iqaluit) in 1956, and a hospital opened in 1964. The construction of the two facilities was a response to the rapid development of the region and the rising associated health concerns for Inuit and Qallunaat. The rehabilitation centre accommodated the large number of Inuit returning from southern sanatoria by ship through Iqaluit.

The massive centralization of Inuit at Iqaluit placed strain on the settlement's resources, and by the late 1950s, threatened public health. The threats were largely due to the overcrowding and unsanitary living conditions in the settlement. Despite the fact that the federal Committee on Eskimo Affairs formally acknowledged in 1961 that "the inadequate housing in which Eskimos were living" was directly tied to high mortality rates and the spread of disease, the government moved relatively slowly to build more houses. Rather, priority was given to the construction of medical facilities, a school, and an apartment building. The lack of response by the government to the housing crisis persisted in tandem with the undisputed recognition of the link between poor housing conditions and very high rates of infant mortality and tuberculosis. It was three years before the government acknowledged the health "disaster" the housing crisis had caused by exacerbating infectious diseases, but even then, new housing arrived slowly.

Eskimo Rehabilitation Centre

As discussed previously, large numbers of Inuit were evacuated each year for treatment in southern hospitals. After treatment, many of these people were sent home with little consideration given for the problems of reintegration into their communities. This created problems for patients when they returned, as many had trouble adapting to the lives they had left behind, often a few years prior to heading south. These problems were well known by the government by the 1950s, and while efforts by government doctors and prominent missionaries to convince the INHS to build sanatorium facilities in the North were not fruitful, the government did try to introduce ways for patients to establish better communication with families while they were being treated. One of these methods was the putting in place of a letter-writing campaign, so that patients could remain in communication with their families.

The problems incurred from the sanatoria program went well beyond an individual's loss of self-esteem to contribute to the ill health of interpersonal and familial relationships, and those within the broader community. A former young patient wrote while in a sanatoria in the South:

> My parents have not written in a long time. They forgot about me. No wonder, they do not love me. They forgot! ... I am forgotten about by my mother. I am scared now. Whenever I get home, I wonder what my mother and my older sister will be like. They will not love me...it is not a wonder I am scared of my fellow Inuit now.

In 1950, an article in *Canada's Health and Welfare* explained that the fear and lack of trust felt upon returning home was mutual, as ex-patients were often looked upon "as foreign, with suspicion."

In recognition of the need to manage the care and repatriation of Inuit returning from southern sanatoria, Rudnicki convinced the government of the need for an "Eskimo Rehabilitation Centre," which eventually opened in 1956. The centre was run by the NANR, which was in part convinced of its utility due to the knowledge that 25% of patients brought to sanatoria were readmissions. It was believed that this number and associated costs could be lowered with institutionalized rehabilitation. By the time it opened, Apex Hill had already been transformed into a town site around the Centre, which also operated a number of services for nearby inhabitants, such as a coffee shop, bakery, and movie house.

This was different in concept from transit centres, although one building often served both purposes. Transit centres were facilities set up at points between southern hospitals and Inuit communities in the North. It was felt that the development of a transit centre in Iqaluit, and a few other places, would lower an individual's wait time in the hospital, and thus cut down on costs. Government officials felt that this time could be used "constructively" by Inuit while they stayed and slowly adjusted to life in the North again.

In addition to its primary aim of patient rehabilitation, the centre soon became a facility for dealing with what were regarded as behavioural problems stemming from the rapid development of Iqaluit, and the presence of a large Qallunaat population and associated facilities and opportunities for "getting into trouble." The social problems associated with the opening of the rehabilitation centre were characterized by the *Edmonton Journal* as "the most expensive experiment in race rehabilitation ever attempted."

Many Qikiqtaalungmiut remained in Iqaluit due to their stay in the rehabilitation centre. Jonah Kelly from Iqaluit told the QTC that:

> [People] who went for medical in Quebec City and Hamilton . . . had to travel back to their communities by plane . . . Before they went home, they were treated at the Rehab centre . . . Abe Okpik used to tell me all these things through his travels through the airline and anyone who could travel on the plane was sent to the rehabilitation centre. That is how some stayed in Iqaluit.

Tuberculosis often resulted in permanent health ailments, making it impossible for some people to return to life on the land, or continue with jobs that required physical labour. Many needed continued physical as well as social or financial support, which kept many living in settlements with close access to health care and/or family allowance distribution. Census notes reveal that many of the centre's patients were youth and children. As a result of their stay in the centre, many have grown up in Iqaluit when they may have otherwise desired to live elsewhere. Sytukie Joamie from Iqaluit talked to the QTC about his mother's relocation to Apex for admission to the rehabilitation centre there.

> Some people do not have resources and they end up living in Iqaluit and Apex because they had no means to return home. It is in the same picture of any relocatee from any other area. They were dumped for medical reasons or so-called health reasons, when in reality, they themselves, younger generations have endured unhealthy lifestyle because of that. Some people's healthy lifestyle is not the same. There are a lot of people living today, descendants who are stuck where they may not want to live.

Inuit Women and Health

There was some acknowledgement by health care providers stationed in the Arctic of the gendered nature of the changes facing Inuit during this period, specifically those facing women returning from southern hospitals. An article by Irene Baird published in *The Beaver* discusses the shift in lifestyle that occurred when women made the transition to life in the settlements. Baird offered, "Many of us [Qallunaat women], if the roles were reversed, would spend at least part of our time fighting off (or submitting to) a sense of instability and confusion." Robert Collins agrees that the changes Inuit women faced were likely quite difficult. He laments that the circumstances of the era had Inuit women doubting their worth. "In illness, in education, in the incessant foraging for food, she used to be essential." Despite the empathetic tone, Baird and Collins reveal the colonial attitudes directed at women and Inuit culture in general. Baird, referring to Inuit customary pre-contact lifestyles, described the "old days" as "evil" and saw the breakdown of Inuit culture as inevitable. Bob Green, a social worker at the Iqaluit rehabilitation centre, remarked, "[T]his assimilation will not be easy. I am absolutely sure there is no painless way for Eskimos to make the transition." To assist with the "transition" into the role of housewife, in 1959, the rehabilitation centre at Iqaluit began offering classes to women in cooking, clothes making, childcare, and family economics.

Distribution of Services

Literature produced by the DNHW clearly documents that Inuit who needed health care were told to relocate to areas where nursing stations were available. This was often accompanied by promises of housing, family allowance payments, and other services. Many people testified that when encouraged to move by a Qallunaat agent, they listened. Unfortunately, as with other enticements used by the government, promises related to health care went unfulfilled. Geosah Uniusargaq told the QTC he originally moved to Iqaluit for health reasons, believing the promises that Inuit "would not be deprived of anything," and that they "would receive cheques every month." In this case no cheques were received.

The concentration of Inuit in settlements, the establishment of nursing stations in the region, and the building of a hospital at Iqaluit in 1964 lessened the demand for EAP services. Historian C. S. Mackinnon attributes government institutional momentum to the continuation of the EAP and its medical services in the 1960s. Over the years, the number of beds on board was increased from twelve to thirty-six, interpreters and nursing assistants were added to the staff, and racial segregation was ended. With the majority of people living in fixed settlements, and significant developments in air transportation in the Arctic allowing for easier and more efficient access to remote areas, the EAP's final charter was completed in 1969.

While centralization had obvious benefits for the administration of health care, the increase in concentration of Inuit migrating to sites overwhelmed resources. When DEW Line construction ended, there were about five hundred Inuit living at Iqaluit, half of this number living in homes supplied by the government in Apex and the other half living in a beach community east of the airstrip, for the most part in shack housing built from discarded military waste materials. Concerns began to arise over the conditions of Inuit families living near the bases and the potential impacts on health. Based on his observations and extensive interviews with Inuit, Frank Tester told the QTC that the shack housing being constructed from the waste materials of DEW Line stations and other military activities was "grossly inadequate for both the climate and culture . . . They were a disaster for human health." The case of Iqaluit, the location of an American air base and hub of related activity, is perhaps the most glaring example of the sort of public health concerns that accompanied the concentration of families near bases and defence stations. Increased alcohol consumption, conflict between Qallunaat and Inuit, and poor housing and diet are a few of the related consequences, which defined the following decades.

In the end, the government continued to depend on the little service available for providing care to Inuit well into the 1970s, often citing the lack of developed transportation infrastructure and communication capabilities as the reason for the discrepancy in care between northern and southern Canada.

Nunalinnguqtitauliqtilluta

CHANGING NATURE OF RISK FACTORS

Through the dominance of much of the political, social, and economic aspects of Qikiqtaaluk life, all aspects of health and well-being were touched by non-Inuit administration, culture, and expectations. In light of this, a discussion of risk factors is necessarily complex. This era was characterized by shifts in mortality rates as medical epidemics became less common, and by an increase in health problems stemming from colonial policies, socio-economic realities in settlement life, and the effects of modernity. Mental health problems grew both in number and character, and common health issues persisted.

By the 1960s, tuberculosis was no longer a primary cause of death. By the end of the decade, mortality rates were more likely to be due to accident, injury, or violence than disease. This shift speaks in part to the efficacy of the government's overall approach to containing epidemics but also about the impact of decades of policies of assimilation with regards to social organization, culture, and mental health. The socio-economic realities of the time exacerbated health concerns. R. Quinn Duffy, author of *Road to Nuna-*

vut, refers to a study undertaken in 1958 by the University of Alberta and the DNHW that found "low family income, alcohol, and poor housing, water supply, sewage, nutrition, and education" factored more prominently in infant death rates than circumstances surrounding the provision of medical services. Infants in particular succumbed to disease rapidly, especially in circumstances where parents were also sick and unable to provide the required care.

Accidents, injuries, and violence remained the main cause of death through the 1960s and into the 1970s and included suicide, drowning, crib death, gunshot wounds, asphyxia, motor vehicle accidents, falling through the ice, and homicide. It is estimated that alcohol was associated with 40 to 50% of the incidents. It is worth noting that drugs were not prevalent during this period. In the decades between 1950 and 1970, alcohol consumption had increased among Inuit populations as a result of contact with Qallunaat and colonial policies, giving way to cycles of abuse and self-harm. Alcohol was often mentioned in the QTC and QIA testimonies. Jeetaloo Kakee told the QTC:

> After the people got together in Pang, the adults were not looking at the children. The older children were looking for the younger children. They gambled and drank because they got too many people together in one place. The alcohol in 1965 started coming and it didn't come from the Inuit. The Pang social worker planned for alcohol for Christmas, this is when it started pouring in.

Martha Idlout also spoke to the QTC about the impact that alcohol had on her and her family. When asked about her parents' experience with alcohol, Martha responded, "I begged them not to go drinking. Other people were controlling their lives. [My parents] were nice people. They did what other people told them to." In the community, she recalled, "I guess not too many people had too much food because people were falling into alcoholism . . . There was a bar here too, military too. The whole time they would get drunk and us children would have to find a place to stay . . . we would be ignored." Child neglect, sexual abuse, and domestic violence were often directly related to binge and persistent drinking, and to the trauma experienced by the children of drinkers, some of whom became alcoholics themselves. In spite of this, some testimonies reflected a sense of resiliency in the face of this cycle of abuse and dependence. Martha also talked about the changes that she wanted to make for the sake of her grandchildren:

> The past has an impact on our lives, some is bad and some is good . . . Everyone was hurting inside, not living as they should. People were growing up with a lot of pain. I don't want my grandchildren to grow up with that kind of pain and end up like us. We know that we took all the substances, alcohol and drugs because of our pain . . . No one wants to go back to those days, no not at all.

Other people told the QTC that alcohol had not been a significant concern in their communities. Levi Evic told the QTC about life in Pangnirtung in the 1960s. He recalled, "We would occasionally see drunk people but not very many . . . They were not in high number but we used to see drunk people on the street passed out, on the ground."

At the same time, an increase in sexually transmitted infections during this period was viewed by the government as being a social problem associated with "the excessive use of alcohol" and degradation of "morals." Medical practitioners, on the other hand, were of the opinion that STIs existed primarily among youth, and despite the government's claim that infection was linked to alcohol consumption, rates in the North were not exceeding the rates reported in the South. Despite the conflicting views, in 1965, the rate of contracted gonorrhoea was legitimately quite high, reporting as just over two thousand five hundred per one hundred thousand people in the Northwest Territories alone in 1965. This was in comparison to approximately one hundred per one hundred thousand in Canada. By 1971, in Qikiqtaaluk, the rate rose to over five thousand per one hundred thousand. The figure for the rest of Canada increased only to two hundred per one hundred thousand. While syphilis was also present, there are no indications of serious outbreaks during the 1960–1970 period.

While major epidemics diminished, incidences of cold and flu persisted through this period. Eye diseases were also quite common, as were skin diseases and conditions such as eczema, boils, impetigo, lice, and scabies. In the book *Saqiyuk*, Apphia Agalakti Awa recalled traditional treatments for skin infections:

> At that time people used to get big boils inside their skin. You would put a lemming skin on top to get the boil out. If there was tobacco around, we would use the tobacco pouch . . . the boils wouldn't always burst by themselves. They would have to be cut to get the pus out . . . that was our way of doing medicine.

Government policies that on the surface had little to do with health at times also affected the care and well-being of Inuit. Many families were told that their children had to attend school, and in many cases, this meant that they had to leave their homes. For some families, this meant that children were no longer able to help care for ailing family members or help out around the home. Leah Otak spoke about being forced to attend school. "We left our mother despite her condition—she was disabled—even though we would have helped her in her many tasks, but we were forced to attend school."

NUTRITION, FOOD SECURITY, AND DIET

Due to a number of factors, Inuit relationship to food was in great transition throughout the period of 1945–75. As a result of sustained Qallunaat contact, access to food changed, hunting patterns were affected, and transformations in diet and the nutritional content had major effects on the health and well-being of individuals. Rhoda Kokiapik, who was born near Igloolik in 1931, explains the sort of customary roles that food played in Inuit society:

> My ancestors hunted with their own tools, made of stone and animal bone. Pots, oil lamps, and needles were also made of animal bones and stone. For weeks Inuit hunted in hopes of finding game. Sometimes they would come home with no luck. Some days my ancestors drank only melted snow to stave off their hunger. But, if they were in luck, they ate what they caught and shared the meat with other people in their group. Back then Inuit wore clothing made from caribou skin, fox fur, and seal skin. If an animal was killed, nothing was wasted. Inuit ate the meat, made clothing from the skin, and tools from the bone.

When most Inuit lived in ilagiit nunagivaktangit and hunted regularly, their diet "ranged from game to marine mammals . . . supplemented by a variety of land and sea vegetables, such as berries, willow buds, herbs, and some roots." It centred on the ingestion of meat and fat, consumed raw, frozen, or aged, and understood to be nutritionally complete. It had been long known, and evidenced in 1944 by a nutrition services report, that Inuit who lived long distances from trading posts were healthier than those living in settlements, due to their sustenance on a country food diet. Throughout the 1940s, the link between poor nutrition and morbidity grew clearer. By 1948, as more Inuit were beginning to live in settlements where they purchased Qallunaat food, some nurses expressed concern about nutrition.

The transition from a diet consisting mainly of country food to that of imported southern food was helped along by rather naive presumptions about health and diet within the visiting medical community. Literature produced during this period often said that meat-rich diets lead to vitamin deficiencies, which would, in turn, lead to a "weakness to germs." Inuit were compelled to accept heavily processed and sugary Qallunaat foods, such as white flour, tea, sugar, and biscuits through relief programs. Family allowance payments were traded at HBC stores for certain foods, and trapping income was used to purchase food at the stores. Inuit were also unable to hunt country food regularly, and were thus drawn in by the convenient availability of store-purchased food. These means by which Inuit became accustomed to Qallunaat food left many communities vulnerable to fluctuations in availability and costs of food at HBC stores, and the prices of furs, which greatly declined following the Second World War. Living in settlements, as well as steady employment and regular school hours, reduced the time available for hunting.

Inuit were discouraged from customary practices related to food, diet, and food security. Dr. G. E. Gaulton, working in Pangnirtung, displayed an all-too-common assumption that Inuit needed to be coached to eat properly, in spite of centuries of living successfully by hunting: "[T]he fact that most of the deaths occur at the poor camps show that nutrition plays a very important part . . . Camp sanitation is very bad. This, of course, is a matter of education, as is also the proper feeding of children." Inuit women were dissuaded from breastfeeding, for instance, and encouraged to use baby formula. The payment of family allowances often came in the form of items deemed by the Government to nutritionally benefit the children. The authorized list included canned milk, Pablum, cereals, egg powder, flour, and sugar. As R. Quinn Duffy explained, medical research has uncovered that through the late 1940s and the early 1950s, death of children due to infectious diseases, such as tuberculosis, actually increased. A reduction in the proportion of mothers breastfeeding (as in the rest of Canada), due to access to promoted store-bought items, resulted in markedly higher infant mortality. Although it has decreased substantially since the 1950s, the rate remains about five times higher than the Canadian average.

The issue of food poisoning is another example of government interference in nutrition. This had always been a concern for Inuit. David Kalluk from Arctic Bay told the QTC, "A lot of people got sick after eating contaminated walrus, people were dying from food poisoning. If the seal was not healthy, if you eat a sick animal, that is what apparently happened." In disregard for customary practices regarding Inuit handling of this issue, nurses created public health campaigns that dictated how they should handle related problems. Nurses tackled botulism in part through the distribution of a letter, drafted in 1971, cautioning Cape Dorset residents against leaving dead seals on the beach.

Access to animals from communities was always an issue. The killing of qimmiit had an impact as well. Shorty Shoo told the QTC, "When there were no more dogs and there was no snowmobiles introduced yet, we would get hungry. I wasn't the only one, but as a family we would crave to eat." Solomonie Qiyutaq in Pangnirtung talked to the QTC about her experience with changes in food security.

> Dogs were an important source for providing food . . . we would use the dogs to travel long distances to hunt caribou or seals inland or on sea ice . . . It seemed as though I became disabled with no transportation available for subsistence hunting. After my dogs got killed, we stopped hunting altogether and stopped consuming seal meat and only ate store-bought foods that was provided, especially during the winter months . . . We struggled to survive and seal meat was not part of our diets after the dogs were gone, we only survived on luncheon meat that was provided for us.

The transitions to Qallunaat food also had serious implications for dental health. Dr. Curson, a dentist who pioneered a topical fluoride program in 1950, was astonished at the amount of tooth decay among young children, noting, "Today I see children of four who need every tooth in their head extracted." He attributes this to a practice whereby mothers add sweetener to milk bottles for their children to suck from for eight or nine hours a day, a practice he also saw in Britain. Prior to the introduction of a Qallunaat diet, however, his study of one hundred and sixty Inuit skulls at a British museum uncovered only seven cavities, and no missing teeth.

Arguments about the superiority of imported foods over Inuit diets disappeared rather quickly. In 1941, a medical officer at Pangnirtung, Dr. J.A. Bildfell, wrote that "native foods alone" protected Inuit "from any dangers of starvation." He described the quality of imported foods as "very unsatisfactory," adding that these foods did harm when they were not supplemented by country food. During the 1970s, increased co-operation between intergovernmental bodies and other stakeholders led to a coherent and widely distributed set of infant nutrition guidelines, put in use by those responsible for the delivery of community health programs. Along with better living conditions and improved medical services, a renewed emphasis on the importance of breastfeeding was considered to be an important factor in the reduction of the infant mortality rate, which still remained very high.

The motivation to assimilate Inuit populations informed and coloured many of the policies surrounding nutrition, as did matters of administrative convenience. According to Duffy, the administration was long aware of the negative effects that imported foods were having on Inuit health, although little attention was paid to determining which foods were causing the problem. As well, the prospect of receiving imported foods when the EAP docked each year drew Inuit into the settlements to work on the supply ship, and according to RCMP officer Major McKeand, if imported foods were no longer distributed, at this point "some substitute or other form of entertainment would have to be provided otherwise the independence of the natives would assert itself and many would refuse to come to the settlement. In this event discharge of the ship would be seriously hampered." The government did nothing substantial by way of policy changes and by 1971,

90% of Inuit were living in communities where the source of food was the local supermarket.

An important relationship exists between epidemics, social issues, and food security. Government correspondence reveals that it recognized that epidemics left Inuit vulnerable to "mental and physical depression." The toll that high death rates took went further than individual physical suffering, to a wider impact on the families and communities, which had intergenerational consequences. Relocation of family members often occurred as a result of a death in the family, and many were unprepared for trapping season, or were not caching food in the fall. Relief offered by the government was then often a means of feeding the family.

The concentration of Inuit into settlements and the increased capacity for surveillance made it easier for government and independent Qallunaat researchers to undertake their work on and among Inuit populations. The 1960s and early 1970s were in fact marked by what Helle Moller referred to as "extensive" biomedical examinations.

Rhoda Katsak recalls Qallunaat researchers visiting Pond Inlet in 1972 to transplant skin grafts from children's arms to those of their siblings:

> In Igloolik there was lots of research going on about the "Eskimo." There was study after study about us . . . It was like they couldn't get enough! Sometimes I wonder why people agreed all the time when they didn't want to. I guess what it comes down to is that Qallunaat have always been the people with authority . . . the grafts didn't heal into my skin. Jake's and Oopah's skin fell off, and the holes healed over . . . I have had the scars ever since.

Research for the QTC did not reveal more context about the reasons why specific experiments were done or the number of people affected.

MENTAL HEALTH

The period covered in this report saw widespread transformation in mental health. It is theorized that this was due to the various impacts from socio-economic changes brought about by policies of assimilation, sustained contact with non-Inuit, and treatment practices of shipping patients to southern hospitals. A form of mental illness referred to as "pibloktoq" is said to have already been prevalent in many parts of the Arctic. This condition involved convulsive behaviour, such as seizures, and was occasionally followed by amnesia or in rare cases symptoms of conversion, a disorder where psychological stress is expressed physically. According to Frank Vallee, author of a study on Inuit theories of mental health, conditions of mental illness other than "pibloktoq," including manic depression or self-directed aggression, were rare or non-existent among Inuit prior to sustained Qallunaat contact.

For historian and social worker Frank Tester, the rise of social problems in the 1970s was linked to a rise in mental illness. He explained to the QTC that, from his experience as a social worker in the Arctic, "mental health is cultural health," and that when "people were in charge of their own lives . . . people were much better off." Several people testified to the QTC about the existence of mental illness among their family members. Often it was attributed to the inability to take charge of their own lives, poor nutrition, the lack of ability to participate in important cultural practices like hunting, and feelings of worthlessness, often resulting from assimilationist policies and the consequences of government decision-making.

Many of the above triggers were often caused by the loss of one's qimmiit. Beginning in the 1950s, and continuing through the 1960s and in some cases into the 1970s, many Qikiqtaalungmiut reported their qimmiit being shot by RCMP and other Qallunaat agents. These shootings were often associated, in part, with the Ordinance Respecting Dogs, which required qimmiit be tied up at all times within settlements. Qimmiit had long held an important role in Inuit culture and day-to-day life. Their destruction often left Inuit to have feelings of terrible loss and helplessness as they were, for a time, a person's only means of transportation. Many Qikiqtaalungmiut spoke at length with the QTC and QIA about how the loss of qimmiit impacted their lives. Laimiki Innuaraq explained how he felt after his qimmiit were killed: "I am never satisfied with things. I started noticing, 'Why do I look for things all the time?' I realized that it was from losing my dogs. It impacted me psychologically to such a degree that I became psychologically disturbed."

Many people also spoke about the pain of watching a family member suffer after their qimmiit were killed. Alicee Joamie remembered:

> We could hear the moaning and growling of the dogs . . . I was trying to soothe my husband. I wondered, "How am I going to help my husband?" He was quiet for such a long time. He held the whip in his hand for the longest time. He was gripping the whip so much that his knuckles turned white . . . My in-law had to take care of my kids because my husband was moving around. I was trying to soothe him. I didn't know how to care for him or how to make him feel better. He almost uttered things to me but he shut his mouth before he said anything . . . My son cried for the longest time because his father was the most important person to him.

Memories such as this were so traumatic for Alicee, as for many Inuit, that she noted, "It was only when I started going to healing groups that I started to get these memories back."

For many people, schooling also played an important role in poor mental health. The removal of children from their families and homes had a tremendously negative impact on both the individuals who attended schools and their families. Thomas Kublu described the impact on his siblings of receiving a Qallunaat education as "poison." He explained:

> My younger brother Paul Quuliit attended the residential school in Chesterfield Inlet from 1955 for three years until 1958. He forgot the family values, Inuit culture, and family ties and responsibilities in the family system. He was a stranger by then. He was detached and had no sense of family or Inuit values ... He no longer had a clear identity or a sense of belonging. Being caught up in the two cultures, neither of which he was comfortable in or could call his own, he became an alcoholic. He died of a massive heart attack in September 1987 ... The three younger ones went through the educational system and the colonizers' attempts to kill the Inuk in them and make them like the Qallunaat was too difficult for them emotionally, mentally and spiritually. Physical illnesses in the end killed them when they too should have enjoyed living longer, like me. I would be alive with them today had they not been forced into the school system ... I regret that my younger siblings died so early in life; the educational system killed them.

In addition to the effects of loss of language and identification with Inuit culture and values, the trauma of having been a victim of physical and sexual abuse at the schools also had implications for health, self-esteem, and well-being well into adulthood. Many Qikiqtaalungmiut told the QTC about the abuse they experienced while attending school and the effects it had and still has on them. Annie Shappa explained how the abuse children suffered often affected their intimate relationships. She shared the following:

> I can say for a fact that when we were young teenagers and we moved to Arctic Bay, those students were sexually and physically abused. It became a fact of life. It was part of that system in the community ... Those of us who had husbands, those who were abused at residential schools, were not the only ones affected because of our experience. It seems as though they forgot about us

> and disregarded us. Those of us who experienced that abuse . . . I don't know if it was because of us that it happened.

Certain health care policies contributed to the increased incidence of mental illness. As mentioned earlier in this report, the large numbers of Inuit who were sent south to be treated for tuberculosis in sanatoria often suffered in ways unrelated to tuberculosis. Culture shock and homesickness left individuals feeling isolated and confused about identity, and communication between family members was often strained or non-existent. Mental health was affected in the sanatoria, and the strain on individuals when reintroduced to their home communities also affected their well-being.

Inuit suicide is closely linked with the problems discussed in this section. When considered in light of corresponding trends and within historical context, like mental health overall, Inuit suicide throughout this period has its roots in colonialism and the effects of aggressive assimilationist and paternalistic policies. Tester and McNicoll demonstrate this by pointing out the marked decline in suicide rates during the period covering the move to settlements, where there was initial and sudden access to medical care and comforts such as electricity, water, and housing. A survey of seventy-nine Inuit conducted by John J. and Irma Honigmann in Iqaluit in 1963 revealed that "with few exceptions, informants who answered said they were content."

Over time, however, the initial sense of opportunity and community associated with settlement life dampened with the children leaving to go to school, the slaughter of qimmiit, the gradual loss of relative autonomy, and the constant surveillance of settlement life. Honigmann and Honigmann put it:

> True, parents, camp leaders with authority, and strong shamans exerted some power, but there was nothing like the subordination of nine hundred people to the laws of Canada and the Northwest

> Territories and to the power exerted by administrators, doctors, school principals, police, and traders. The Eskimos today must perform to meet relatively "foreign" standards. They must satisfy people whose values often diverge radically from their own. An Eskimo's happiness depends on such performance. He may hunt game birds only in season, must send his children to school, must go to the hospital if he is tubercular, must control himself from drunkenness, dare not trespass on forbidden property, must report for work on time, may use his car only with due propriety, etc.

In the 1970s, suicide rates in the Eastern Arctic greatly surpassed those of the national average. Tester and McNicoll also believe that the manner in which historical experiences of shame, abuse, and anger as a result of colonial practices and policies have been communicated through generations of Inuit have led to internalization of emotions, fostering the potential for self-harm.

IQALUIT

The doors of the new hospital at Iqaluit, with the current institutional name of Qikiqtani Hospital, opened in November 1964. It had twenty adult beds, eight children's beds, an operating suite, a maternity and nursing station, an outpatient department, an X-ray unit, a dispensary, a dental suite, and a public health lecture and demonstration area. It was staffed by a small number of doctors, nurses, visiting specialists, and a few rotating residents from the Montréal General Hospital and the Montréal Children's Hospital. McGill University allowed medical staff to undertake research in Iqaluit on general health issues and on topics more specific to Inuit, such as respiratory diseases. One chronic disease resulting from repeated exposure to cold air became commonly known as "Eskimo lung."

INHS director Dr. Moore had been reluctant for years to sign off on the construction of the hospital at Iqaluit for practical and budgetary reasons, but also because he felt staffing the hospital would pose a challenge. In reality, finding doctors to work at the hospital did not prove nearly as difficult. Rather, other staffing issues, such as dissension, resignations, and in-fighting between coworkers caused the most problems. It seems the problems stemmed from poor administration, and, in at least two cases, frustration with the inconsistent delivery of health care to Inuit in Qikiqtaaluk. Two physicians wrote in their resignation letter:

> We were ostensibly hired to provide medical care for the [Baffin] Zone; however, in fact, continuous medical care was provided only to the inhabitants of Frobisher Bay. The remainder of the population would see a doctor only when critically ill or when visiting the *C.D. Howe*. Each year the *C.D. Howe* was staffed by different physicians, and each year it passed by some of the settlements.

Responsibility for delivering medical services in Qikiqtaaluk was beyond the resources of one hospital alone. Even before the EAP was cancelled in 1969, some communities never saw a doctor from one year to the next. Proposals for improvement were regularly sent to Ottawa, but were always rejected. This resulted in constant frustration among medical staff in Iqaluit.

The growing importance of Iqaluit for health services had impacts elsewhere, especially in Pangnirtung. In 1972, the Anglican Church abruptly closed St. Luke's Hospital in Pangnirtung to the surprise of the government. The hospital had largely become a treatment facility for tuberculosis patients, and since incidences of infection had declined, the per-patient costs had increased greatly. In its place, a temporary nursing station was constructed by INHS to service the needs of the seven hundred Inuit in the area who were left without a local medical facility—a permanent station was only planned for 1975.

By the early 1970s, Canada's Eastern Arctic was experiencing a dramatic increase in population. According to medical practitioners working in the area, Inuit had the highest birth rate in the world, three times higher than in southern Canada, in 1971. In the smaller communities, Inuit midwives were still delivering 70% of babies. In response to a questionnaire distributed to Inuit that included questions on the topic of childbirth, an unknown respondent stated with regard to childbirth, "Some Eskimo women come [and] help. Usually women. Maybe wife's mother, husband's mother, and friends." Another respondent points out, "Certain women do better than others. Usually the older ones ... But if it is a difficult birth they ... call a doctor." A third respondent indicates that the "husband tells people of birth of baby ... they tell police of the birth of the baby five days afterwards." In the mid-1970s women were sent to southern hospitals for delivery, sometimes for the last six weeks of their pregnancies. Only later would this role pass to the hospital at Iqaluit.

The RCMP raised concerns over the availability of birth control, and during the NWT Council Debates session in 1970, Dr. Barber presented a motion that was carried concerning family planning in the North. The motion stated that current employment opportunities and resources were incapable of sustaining the population if it continued to grow as it was. Action was required in order to develop appropriate family-planning education and "devices." Dr. Barber continued to press the NWT Commissioner in June 1969 and January 1970 regarding the government's progress on the matter. The Commissioner responded by referring to the existing birth control information available at health centres across the NWT. He simply offered that any new development would be a lot of "hard work," and that the matter is under review.

The history of access to birth control in the North is complicated by the experiences of women who were convinced or forced to undergo sterilization. Roman Catholic priests called attention to the issue, which received national coverage. Father Lechat estimated that 23% of women in Igloolik had been sterilized; nationally, the Minister of National Health and Welfare said that four hundred and seventy Inuit and Aboriginal women had been sterilized in 1972 alone. Similar procedures also occurred at the hospital at Iqaluit, in addition to male vasectomies. Barry Gunn, a former regional administrator in Iqaluit, claimed women agreed to the sterilization procedures and signed forms to that effect. However, due to language issues, they may not have realized what they were agreeing to. Medical personnel have argued that the policy was not rooted in malice and the women were not forced. Discussions about birth control and the reports of sterilization were revealing about Qallunaat and government attitudes towards the role and future of Inuit. J. R. Lotz, who had worked for the NANR, wrote an article in 1968 about "northern development" that set out in stark terms the way in which racial factors influenced policy. He wrote:

> Despite the demand by the government for people to go north and develop the area, the same government manages to give the impression that there are too many Eskimos and Indians. At their Spring 1968 Session, the Council of the Northwest Territories noted high infant mortality in the North, squalid living conditions, reduced health services, and came up with the inevitable statement that birth control services were needed. If Eskimo women keep losing children—a source of wealth and comfort to them—then no amount of propaganda about birth control will convince them of the need to keep the population down. The Northwest Territories showed a curious paradox in 1968—all the official talk was of boom and economic expansion and the need for labour in the North, whereas the Territorial Council endeavoured to keep the native people from reproducing.

The analysis hit many points, including the reality that medicine, just like economics, religion, and art, is a product of culture as well as science.

Canada's national Inuit organization, Inuit Tapiriit Kanatami (ITK), believes that "health and the environment are interconnected and a holistic approach is essential to Inuit well-being." The history of health services and experiences in Qikiqtaaluk in the 1950–75 period demonstrates that institutional approaches pursued by government rarely, if ever, considered the value of the "Inuit model," as described by George Wenzel in 1981, in which illness was always to be connected to social and environmental relationships.

The nurses, doctors, and dentists who delivered medical services on behalf of government focused on treating Inuit bodies alone, albeit with some references to the impact of poor nutrition, housing, and sanitation. Inuit themselves, as well as medical practitioners, sought options that could bridge the gap between the desire to have access to new medical treatments that were only available through professional staff and facilities and their need to sustain cultural values that placed great emphasis on individual choice and on maintaining family relationships. They faced a bureaucracy that could not or would not establish a forum where fulsome discussions about health could take place. One of the first tasks of the new Northern Health Services branch in 1954, for example, was to meet with other bureaucrats to sort out funding responsibilities, not to understand health issues.

Generally, bureaucrats, even more than politicians, evoked images of a remote, isolated, and indomitable Arctic landscape in which language and cultural barriers were too high to allow the delivery of appropriate medical services. They also tended to ignore the impact of poverty on health even though it was often at the root of the problems they were paid to address. In 1951, Inspector Henry Larsen of the RCMP estimated that the value of a month's family allowance for a child in an Arctic community would only cover two or three days' worth of food for that child. Bureaucrats often blamed the HBC for limiting food options in settlements, but offering better food could only make sense if it was affordable.

Over the period of study, medical practitioners in the region increasingly tried to refocus government efforts from the fear of contagion, especially tuberculosis, to even more serious issues. As one example, physician John S. Willis pointed out in 1959 that tuberculosis rates were dropping, but that statistics from 1957 showed that 23% of all Inuit infants died before they reached the age of one year; the figure for the rest of Canada was only 3%. Very few people, including the medical community, were impressed with the results of the health programs in Canada's eastern Arctic. In 1967, a year when Canada was celebrating its achievements, a leading bureaucrat, Gordon Robertson, wrote: "We could take no pride ten years ago at the condition of most of the people of the North, and we can take little now, despite the efforts that have been made."

This dramatic difference in mortality rates has persisted to the present day and was always visible to Inuit when they looked at the Qallunaat in their midst. As a result, health care remains a very serious issue in Qikiqtaaluk. Of particular importance are high suicide and violent death rates, as well as infant mortality rates.

John D. O'Neil, the author of a health study conducted in 1985 in the Keewatin District, almost two decades after most Inuit had moved from the land into settlements, found that Inuit were "ambivalent" about medical institutions and their dependence on nursing stations. They found their encounters to be "stressful and humiliating." Even the nurses and doctors "expressed comparable sentiments." Typically, medical staff were frustrated at being unable to communicate, especially when so many people who went north were "instilled with egalitarian ideals and cross-cultural interests." Patients objectified them as The Nurse or The Doctor and they were very discouraged by the "inertia of the medical system." He concluded that cross-cultural understanding was not enough; decolonization was required whereby Inuit would have more or complete control over the medical system in their communities.

The complexity of the history of health services in Qikiqtaaluk is clear in the words of Mary Iqaluk, as told to the QTC in Sanikiluaq:

> I was moved to Hamilton because I had tuberculosis. It was hard to understand their language at first. We were being assisted very well. I remember one person who was not doing so well. They had to send him back here for a while because he really needed to come back. I had been using headphones just before we ate and the nurse hit me because I had not been prepared just before meal time. I was young and that was a bad experience for me in some areas but I am very grateful that they helped us get better. I remember some of the patients down there with me being sent away. They said they would come back sometime but I don't recall them coming back so those are just some main things that are imprinted in my mind.

Like those of so many people who spoke to the QTC, Mary Iqaluk's words acknowledge that Inuit appreciated that there were people—doctors, nurses, and police—who repaired broken bones, healed damaged lungs, and saved children's lives, even though government institutions and rules could have been more responsive and helpful to Inuit.

Qimmiliriniq

Inuit Sled Dogs in Qikiqtaaluk

For uncounted generations, Inuit and their qimmiit lived and hunted together in Qikiqtaaluk. During that time, qimmiit—sled dogs—provided the only means of winter transportation. The practical uses for qimmiit were enormous: They pulled sleds in winter, carried packs in summer, sniffed out seal holes, avoided ice cracks in fog and darkness, and warded off polar bears or surrounded them and held them for the hunter's harpoon or rifle. Qimmiit were the only animals Inuit gave individual names, and were constant companions even in childhood. Children were given puppies to raise, and young Inuk boys, once they had a small team of their own, were taken seriously as men. Pauloosie Veevee spoke to Qikiqtani Inuit Association (QIA) researchers about the importance of qimmiit:

> If one has a dog team with many dogs, not hungry, content dogs and able to go for miles, now at that point the owners' masculinity is heightened. Now his extent of his masculinity is interpreted

> by how healthy and fast his dogs are. That is how much the dog teams were important to our lives as Inuit. For instance, if an Inuk man cannot keep dogs in his team, he has to walk everywhere he goes. Not all Inuit men living in traditional camps had dog teams. If an Inuk man does not have a team of his own, it is interpreted that he is yet not quite a man. This is how much the dogs were important to us. An Inuk was judged in accordance to the dogs' performance, appearance, health, and endurance. If the dogs looked well-fed and well-mannered, the owner was seen as a great hunter and admired by others. If an Inuk man's dog team were notably happy and well-fed, they would be able to take him long distances, aiding his independence and masculinity.

These patterns, along with a way of life, were shattered less than three generations ago.

Understanding Qimmiit

ORIGIN AND DESCRIPTION

Qimmiit are Inuit sled dogs—this is the plural form of the word qimmiq. Qimmiit appeared in Alaska among the Thule, ancestors of the Inuit, and migrated towards Arctic Canada around one thousand years ago. The qimmiq is one of four North American Arctic dog breeds, along with the Siberian husky, the Samoyed, and the malamute.

Qimmiit are pack animals. Because the status of each qimmiq within the pack is determined by its physical strength, fights occur. This is especially true when new animals are introduced to a pack. Once the status of each qimmiq is set, however, fights are rare, except when the status of one is challenged or when a female is in heat. Usually, but not always, the alpha dog (angajuqqaaqtaq) is also the leader of the dog team (isuraqtujuq).

QIMMIIT IN THE TRADITIONAL INUIT ECONOMY

Until the late 1960s, qimmiit played a fundamental role in the daily economic activities of most Qikiqtaalungmiut. They were primarily used for transportation and as hunting companions, but they could also be a source of food in times of famine and their hide could even be used to make clothing. On snow and ice, Qikiqtaalungmiut harnessed qimmiit to qammutiik through a fan-hitch, with each qimmiq having its own trace. During storms or blizzards, qimmiit could track scents to follow paths. Isaac Shooyook of Arctic Bay mentioned that during blizzards, qimmiit "could lead [him] home without giving commands." Qimmiit were also able to recognize dangerous areas on ice and could walk long distances with saddlebags for hunting caribou inland. During the summer, qimmiit were generally left to fend for themselves near the ilagiit nunagivaktangit.

As hunting companions, qimmiit were used in winter to find the agluit (seal breathing holes in the sea ice). During late winter and early spring, qimmiit participated in the seal hunt. Peter Akpalialuk of Pangnirtung explained in an interview with the QIA:

> Since time began, the dogs have been the most important possession of Inuit, such as for searching wildlife, and have been a testament for our survival as human beings. The dogs can sense seal holes even when they are covered in snow and not visible at all, due to thick ice. When the hunters were preparing to wait for the seals to pop up, the dogs would start sniffing for non-visible breathing holes for seal and with their help—we were always usually successful in our hunts.

Pauloosie Ekidlak of Sanikiluaq expressed some of the joys of travelling with a well-trained team:

> The dogs used to be really helpful, they used to know and obey when they realized where they are going. Then they would get really fast to reach their destination as they would know where they were going and seem to understand the Inuit language. Just by talking to them one could steer them ... Also if I stopped to wait for a seal at the seal hole then they would just leave me alone and wait. They had a mind of their own and would wait for their master. If I had stopped to brew some tea, my dogs would wait till I finished ... They would hear me putting my teacup down than all my dogs would get up and prepare to be on the road again ... If you stop using the dogs then, yes, sure their manner will change in short time.

Qimmiit were good polar bear hunters. When they smelled a polar bear track, they followed it. When they got close to the bear, the hunter uncoupled the toggles, the buckle between the line and the harness, and the qimmiit dashed towards it. When the bear was weak from the qimmiit attacks, it was harpooned or shot by the hunter. Qimmiit still protect travellers in polar bear territory. Peter Akpalialuk described the importance of qimmiit to QIA interviewers:

> Owning a dog team was very crucial to our survival. The dogs were the only transportation when searching for wildlife and for transporting meat to other camps far away that needed food to avoid starvation. It was still the same during the summer and one would always be accompanied by dogs wherever they travelled, and with dogs' help we would bring back a lot of meat for consumption. The dogs were like people and they were treated as such. When

> we went hunting and came empty-handed, as an owner you would feel badly for the hunger they were experiencing and that was a fact of life for us. It is quite different today but there is still a need to have the dogs around, especially when travelling to the polar bear country. We start missing having dogs for safety purposes, especially at night when one cannot see what is approaching our camp. The dogs would alert us if a polar bear was near since the bears like to roam at dark searching for game. It is easier when it is daylight. The dogs are still very useful today as they were yesterday.

Isaac Shooyook of Arctic Bay reinforced this in his testimony to the QTC:

> They also protect their owners. If any vicious animals such as polar bears came unexpectedly, the dogs would notify the owner. That way they protected their owner.
>
> I just want to say again how knowledgeable the dogs were. My father was a polar bear hunter, and I will tell you the truth of how knowledgeable the dogs were. He was using binoculars and told me there was a polar bear. The dogs who cannot speak knew what "nanuq" means; they sat down and started looking for a polar bear. I tried to keep them calm, and they started looking. That is how knowledgeable they were.

Qikiqtaalungmiut only ate qimmiit under tragic and exceptional circumstances, when there was absolutely nothing else to eat. Eating a qimmiq was the last step before eating leather from clothing, tents, or qamutiik lines. Qikiqtaalungmiut rarely bred qimmiit for their hides. However, if a qimmiq happened to die, its hide could be used to make clothing. In Mittimatalik, qimmiq fur was used to make kamikpait, the socks that were worn between the inner socks and the kamik [the boot]. Similarly, Cumberland Sound Inuit use qimmiq skin to make mitts because it does not freeze. In southern Qikiqtaaluk, qimmiq fur was used around hood collars to protect the face from the wind. Around Kangiqtugaapik, the hide was used to make parkas.

MYTHS AND SYMBOLIC CULTURE

Qimmiit play a central role in several Inuit myths. One of these explains the origins of the Qallunaat. It began when a young woman married a qimmiq and gave birth to qimmiit. Because she was poor and could not take care of them, she "made a boat for the young dogs, setting up two sticks for masts in the soles of her boots, and sent puppies across the ocean . . . They arrived in the land beyond the sea and became the ancestors of the Europeans." In other versions, this myth also explains the origin of Inuit. Qimmiit also play a prominent role in the story of Sedna or Nuliajuk. In a version collected by Rasmussen among the Ammiturmiut, the woman who eventually became Sedna married two men. She first married a qimmiq and had children and qimmiq-children who respectively became the Allait (First Nations people) and Qallunaat.

Another myth is similar to the one recounted above, except for the fact that after sending her offspring away, she went back to her home village where another man married her and took her to an island where his ilagiit nunagivaktangat was established. She realized too late that the man was in fact a petrel whom she despised. Her father decided to bring her back home on his qajaq. This made the petrel angry, and to prevent both from reaching the shore, he created a storm. To save his own life, the father threw his daughter overboard but she tried to hold on. Her father then cut off her fingers and toes, which fell in the water and became sea mammals. She drowned and became Sedna, the Inua of the sea mammals. She was later joined by her first husband, the qimmiq, who became guardian of her home, and her father who had died of grief.

The importance of qimmiit is not limited to traditional stories. They also have special significance in Inuit culture, as seen in naming and the centrality of qimmiit in daily life. They are the only animals to which Inuit give names or atiit. Often they were named for their appearance. Qimmiit were also named in the same way as children, being given the atiq of a deceased person. In that case, qimmiit would integrate the atiq's social attributes because atiit are autonomous entities with their own attributes and kinship relations. Hence, qimmiit could be fathers, grandfathers, mothers, grandmothers, uncles, aunts, and so forth to their Inuit families. Jimmy "Flash" Kilabuk (Nowdluk) of Iqaluit confirmed this when he said, "The dogs were like a member of our team as a family unit as well as our companions." He added that his "father would treat his dogs like he would treat individuals." This explains the extremely tight bond that unified Inuit with their qimmiit. It also explains why, during the QTC and QIA hearings, some simply explained that qimmiit were "everything."

Laws Affecting Qimmiit

Across Canada, laws at the provincial and territorial level had long been in place to protect dogs from random or unjustified harm, and to protect people and their animals from dangerous or diseased dogs. The Ordinance Respecting Dogs was one such law, and it was enacted without information or advice from Inuit and with little understanding of traditional practices in Inuit Nunangat. All Inuit in Qikiqtaaluk felt its impact.

The Ordinance was modelled on southern Canadian laws. It was first introduced in 1928, thoroughly revised in 1949, and has remained in force, with amendments, ever since. While earlier discussions had brought forward options for an ordinance to address sick and abused dogs, the 1928 ordinance focused on preventing dogs from hurting people. It arose from an incident described by the Health Officer and Indian Agent at Fort Resolution. He wrote a letter to the Council of the Northwest Territories (NWT) about the killing of the young daughter of the local trader by two loose dogs belonging to the RCMP. The letters prompted the Council to enact the Ordinance Respecting Dogs, which became effective on October 1, 1928.

The new law made it illegal for dogs to run loose in prescribed areas. Dog owners who violated the Ordinance could be prosecuted and fined up to $25 or jailed for up to thirty days. The ordinance was to be enforced by dog officers appointed by the Commissioner of the NWT, who were required to "take in charge" roaming dogs and keep them for a period of five days. Owners could get their dogs back if they paid the expense of catching and feeding them—otherwise the dog officer could hold an auction for the dogs and unclaimed dogs would be destroyed. On May 31, 1929, all RCMP members in the NWT were appointed ex officio as dog officers.

The federal Department of the Interior and the RCMP had different opinions about how the Ordinance should be implemented and whether it should apply equally to settlements and to smaller places where people lived on the land. Some understood that a strict implementation of the ordinance could cause undue hardship for Dene and Inuit. This was especially true for people in Qikiqtaaluk, where very few Inuit lived at settlements. In February 1930, the Ordinance was put in effect in twenty-three NWT settlements, almost all of them in the Mackenzie District. In November 1930, Kimmirut became the first Qikiqtaaluk settlement to come under the Ordinance; in May 1938, Pangnirtung became the second. In both of these places, the presence of Qallunaat women may have been an important factor. In 1930, Kimmirut had an Anglican mission and a government scientist and his wife took up residence in a new house there; by 1938, Pangnirtung had a small hospital with a married doctor and four Qallunaat nurses. In 1946, the ordinance was extended to the US Army

Air Force (USAF) base at Iqaluit, though not to surrounding places where Inuit were living on the land.

The government continued to monitor dog incidents in the western Arctic, noting an attack on an eighteen-month-old baby by tethered dogs in Yellowknife in 1942, and the injury of a six-year-old girl by sled dogs driven by an older child near Fort Smith in April 1945. In both cases, the owners had been complying with the Ordinance. A set of amendments were then proposed by Ottawa officials to strengthen the Ordinance by requiring that dogs be kept muzzled when working and setting a minimum age for the person controlling the dogs.

In 1949, the Ordinance was thoroughly revised to add these new requirements, along with an exemption (as requested by Aklavik) that allowed municipal governments to enact local bylaws with similar requirements. The 1949 ordinance also introduced Section 9(6), which stated:

> Where, in the opinion of the officer, a dog seized under this section is injured or should be destroyed without delay for humane reasons or for reasons of safety, the officer may destroy the dog as soon after seizure as he thinks fit without permitting any person to reclaim the dog or without offering it for sale by public auction and no damages or compensation may be recovered on account of its destruction by the officer.

Almost as soon as this passed, amendments were requested to deal with complaints that dogs were still being left loose in Aklavik. The RCMP also explained that they were only succeeding in catching sick or young dogs. It was also noted that some RCMP suffered severe dog bites and were mocked by trappers for their failures. In November 1950, an amendment passed to allow officers to kill loose dogs that they were unable to seize. The amendment stated, "Where an officer is unable to seize a dog that is running at large contrary to the provisions of this Ordinance, or of any order, rule, and regulation made hereunder, he may destroy the dog." In 1951, another amendment allowed magistrates or justices of the peace to order the destruction of any dog belonging to an owner convicted under the Ordinance. Until then, convicted owners could recover their dogs after they had paid their fine.

In 1950, two orders extended the geographical scope of the Ordinance beyond prescribed settlements, including Kimmirut, Iqaluit, and Pangnirtung, to "within a radius of one quarter of a mile from any dwelling." The geographical scope received a decisive extension again in 1955 during activation of the Distant Early Warning (DEW) Line, after which it included the entire Mackenzie District and the immediate locality of all other settlements and military stations in the NWT. This order forced dog owners at these places to tie up their dogs at all times. Qimmiit owners in Qikiqtaaluk who lived in ilagiit nunagivaktangit were still exempt, except when they approached or stayed near a DEW Line station or one of the settlements.

In 1966, Simonie Michael of Iqaluit, one of the first Inuit appointed to the Council of the NWT, introduced new amendments that greatly increased the freedom of the police under the Ordinance. The most significant amendment concerned Section 10, which was originally designed to protect farm animals. It allowed almost anyone to kill any roaming qimmiit. It read:

> A person may kill any dog that is running at large and in the act of pursuing, attacking, injuring, damaging, killing, or destroying: (a) a person; (b) another dog that is tethered; (c) a food cache, harness, or other equipment, or (d) cattle, horses, sheep, pigs, poultry, or animals on a fur farm.

The Ordinance was rarely amended after 1966, and no amendments were substantive. A consolidation of the Ordinance in 1974 introduced no new amendments, and was replicated almost word for word in the Nunavut Dog Act of 1999.

The Ordinance had tremendous impacts on the life of Qikiqtaaluk Inuit. It had been designed for the Mackenzie District, and before 1955, was amended in answer to events that occurred there. In fact, initially the Ordinance was only applied in the settlements of the Mackenzie District, where there was a significant non-Aboriginal population. Amendments to the Ordinance, and particularly the orders extending its geographical range, accurately reflect the changing geography of the Qallunaat presence in the Arctic.

Qimmiq Diseases

TYPES OF DISEASES

At times qimmiit were vulnerable to contagious diseases that existed in their Arctic environment. Inuit who testified to the QTC or were interviewed by the QIA were well aware of the existence of separate diseases that others have labelled "rabies" and "distemper." Inuit explain that rabid qimmiit have runny mouths, are not scared of anyone, and act as if they have lost their minds. Simonie Michael of Iqaluit explained that qimmiit do not catch rabies every year, but that "after so many years, every so often someone would lose their dogs to rabies but maybe it would happen every five, six, seven years." According to many Inuit witnesses, qimmiit catch rabies from sick foxes. Rabies is feared because it causes whole teams to die off and because sick qimmiit represent a threat to Inuit. As Jacobie Iqalukjuak of Clyde River explained, "A lot of dogs died in a short period when they had rabies. I witnessed it more than once."

In reviewing records from the time, it is possible that rabies was being named while a different disease—distemper or canine hepatitis—was being described. Translation may also be a factor in interpreting oral evidence, but the written record may also be confusing. Rabies was a fatal disease when transmitted to people, and it seems that the RCMP applied the term rabies generally to all seriously ill qimmiit. Frank Tester has documented two episodes in 1961 that raised awareness and fear of rabies in the Arctic—a qimmiq at far-off Mould Bay (a weather station on the Arctic Ocean) caught rabies from a fox and at Chesterfield Inlet an Inuk trapped a fox that turned out to be rabid. In both cases personnel had the disease confirmed by sending the animal's head south for laboratory analysis. By making people more aware of rabies, these incidents also made them less tolerant of distemper and canine hepatitis, two diseases that were not transmitted to people but had similar symptoms.

Distemper is described by Inuit as a head sickness and is called niaqqirilutik or niaqunngujuq, terms that literally mean, "He has a headache." According to Neomi Panipakutuuk of Hall Beach/Igloolik, "Dogs with head sickness would just lie down, trickling saliva and not get up." Ipeelie Koonoo of Arctic Bay also mentions the two diseases:

> At certain times, dogs would get rabies or become sick with a head illness. When dogs had a head illness, they would salivate but they wouldn't become aggressive. They were in so much pain that they would salivate. They would probably feel a lot of pain in their head. People would lose their dogs through that kind of sickness as well as rabies. Foxes get rabies. Dogs may have caught rabies from them. Not all dogs would get it though. Just a few dogs would get either rabies or a head illness. Sometimes when a lot of dogs are sick, some people would lose a lot of dogs.

Distemper frequently infected qimmiit in Qikiqtaaluk, temporarily reducing the size of teams so that hunting became difficult, though not impossible. Inuit managed these diseases mainly by observing and culling sick animals when necessary. Although Inuit knew they could survive disasters of this kind, Qallunaat took a different view. Epidemics sometimes interrupted their plans for trade or long-distance travel. They attacked most of the severe diseases as a threat to public health, and saw eradication as a scientific challenge. As a result, qimmiit were immunized; when this failed, they killed all infected animals and sometimes all qimmiit in affected teams. Based on public health grounds, and on the assumption that a sick qimmiq was a dangerous qimmiq, the RCMP have since defended officials who shot qimmiit during the 1950s and 1960s. These killings were usually done without considering whether the approaches used in earlier generations would work.

Generally, Inuit used the experience gained from long observation of qimmiit to decide how to manage sick ones. Some were recognized as dangerous or certain to die, and were quickly dispatched. In others, the disease was allowed to run its course in the expectation that most would die, but enough would survive for rebuilding teams. This view distinguished between "rabid" qimmiit and those with the more prevalent but contagious forms of distemper or canine hepatitis. The southern view, at least by the 1950s, was that every sick qimmiq was a public health risk and should be shot.

Qallunaat and Inuit hunters alike experienced the inconvenience of cyclical qimmiq diseases. In one well-documented early case, the German geographer and anthropologist Franz Boas had to scrap a planned sledge trip in 1883 when his qimmiit died. In his work on "The Central Eskimo," he stated:

> The Eskimo of all these regions are very much troubled with the well-known dog's disease of the Arctic regions. The only places where it seems to be unknown are Davis Strait and Aggo [North Baffin]. Here every man has a team of from six to twelve dogs, while in Cumberland Sound, in some winters, scarcely any have been left.

In a footnote, he said he had since learned that the disease had spread to Davis Strait as well.

In 1932, Canadian researchers for the Department of Agriculture found evidence of distemper among qimmiit along both shores of Hudson Strait. Helped by long-term residents of the region, they wrote a detailed survey of the incidence and severity of recent epidemics. The report is not entirely useful, because there is some confusion between the diseases being described. The report references both distemper and "an entirely different disease" described by the local term, "fox encephalitis." The two main points were that diseases were cyclical, and that they could move through districts leaving some places untouched.

The 1932 research was aimed at prevention, but it also documented the process of natural recovery, usually within a year or two, that allowed the breed to survive. Typically, in even the worst-hit locations, two or three qimmiit would survive from teams of up to fifteen. It was consistently reported that the best-fed and healthiest qimmiit were likely to survive, and those that survived "the disease" were immune to it afterwards. This explains the reluctance of Inuit to kill sick qimmiit, since enough would survive to maintain a minimal ability to travel and the capacity to re-establish the teams within a few years.

MANAGING QIMMIIT DURING PERIODS OF SICKNESS

Inuit say that qimmiit suffering from rabies have to be killed right away, and that these sick qimmiit rarely recover. They also knew that some sick qimmiit posed a danger to people around them. This is especially true of rabid qimmiit who become wild and try to bite every qimmiq and person they can catch.

For other diseases, some Inuit also believed it was important to kill sick qimmiit to protect the people around them. Neomi Panipakutuuk of

Hall Beach/Igloolik recalled, "It was said that if a sick dog is not killed, that sickness will go to human beings and they will die instead of the dog. I think this still stands today. I can still recall when one of your uncle's dogs was sick. I advised that it be killed." The uncle did not follow this traditional belief, and "did not kill it. Shortly afterwards, their young son died. The dog got well." Also on Melville Peninsula, the term for a qimmiq that is falling ill is "qimmiijaqtuq," which literally means "he deprived himself" or "he disposes of his dogs." This term highlights a strong connection that exists for some people between a qimmiq's illness and the need to get rid of it. This appears to have been an old belief, but one that agreed with Qallunaat preferences for killing sick qimmiit without allowing time for some to recover.

Attacks by Qimmiit

ATTACKS IN QALLUNAAT CULTURE AND MEMORY

The reported dangers of keeping qimmiit in settlements played a major role in the long discussion of Inuit, qimmiit, and the law. The fact that many of the attacks were on white children or women indicates how unprepared many of those people were for life in Inuit Nunangat. Inuit who had been raised with qimmiit were simply not at risk in the same way as newcomers. To make matters worse, the new communities around the trading centres and police posts were much larger than most ilagiit nunagivaktangit, with a resulting increase in the number of qimmiit who were facing new and unfamiliar people and dogs. Most Qallunaat were probably not aware of these new developments. They just assumed that qimmiit were dangerous and should be tied up when not actually working, or shot when they got loose.

The result was that great pressure was put on Inuit to accept all the costs and burdens of managing qimmiit in a new social setting where people and qimmiit were more numerous and Qallunaat were a much larger presence than before. Officials appear to have assumed that Inuit would tolerate changes in their practices in exchange for the presumed benefits that would come with a Qallunaat presence.

No detailed list of attacks by qimmiit in Qikiqtaaluk exists. The general view is that serious maulings were very rare, but any attacks that were reported were so severe that southerners believed that qimmiit were unnecessarily putting people at risk. Dangerous qimmiit became a standard part of Qallunaat beliefs about the North, and stories of maulings and the rare cases of deaths, especially those of children, were told repeatedly. Pond Inlet resident Rosie Katsak told the QTC about an experience her father Ishmael had. An RCMP officer destroyed his dog team when Ishmael moved his family into the settlement, probably in the late 1960s.

> [A]ll of his dogs were killed by RCMP. He told me that an RCMP's wife was attacked by a dog team and then that the police [were] shocked, so he asked the police to shoot all the dog teams—that is what he told me. All of his dogs were killed by police. Somewhere in Nunavut, a police's wife was killed by the dog team.
>
> ...I think it was when they [were] starting to move people to a larger community when that lady was killed.

The story told to Rosie Katsak's father had some truth to it, but the police officer's wife did not die in the 1960s. Maggie Agnes Clay died of her wounds more than thirty years before and 1,200 kilometres away. Nevertheless, her tragedy became a vital part of the oral and written culture of Qallunaat in the North, sensationalist evidence that qimmiit can be lethal. Maggie Clay was possibly the only adult killed in Nunavut by qimmiit in the past century, but her story lives on, reinforced by other evidence of the dangers of misunderstanding qimmiit. In 1960, members of the RCMP were shocked by an attack at Arviat, when a family's pet husky, a bitch with pups, savaged a missionary's small son. Senior officers turned this into a widespread warning against dogs in general. The attack was turned into a stern warning to Inuit about the need to control their qimmiit. The following year an improvement was noted:

> Particularly gratifying is the fact that during the past year there was a reduction in attacks by vicious dogs [across the whole territorial North]...Only two children were attacked resulting in one death in comparison to the previous year when six such incidents resulted in two deaths.

In the late 1960s, anthropologist Milton Freeman was under contract to study qimmiit in Qikiqtaaluk. He met with some skepticism when surveying maulings. He told a QTC interviewer in 2009:

> I know I tried to look into this when I was doing this research because ... it was a contract, and I had to look at certain things and that was one of the things that I certainly looked into. I can't honestly remember if I got the feeling there were some people, some Mounties, who would tell me it's very rare, it's not a problem, I don't know why you're doing research on this, more people break their arms, there are other accidents, this is a non-issue. But it is an issue when children are injured, perhaps severely, or killed. It doesn't have to be a high incidence ... I mean the opportunity to get them to hospital if they're bleeding, if serious arteries have been severed and they need surgery, that's not available. So they die in the community or on a plane. So ... there was a real reason to be concerned.

Not all incomers regarded qimmiit as a complete danger and liability. Anthropologists Frank and Anita Vallee wrote in 1963 during fieldwork in Puvirnituk:

> We have written about the development during recent years of relatively large settlements in the Arctic, settlements to which hundreds of Eskimos are now attracted. Among the problems of daily living in such settlements, none is more serious than dog control. To the Eskimos who continue to trap and hunt, a large and strong dog team is a much more important possession than is, say, a wooden house, and many Eskimos expend more energy and money on feeding their dogs than [they do] on feeding themselves and their families. Dog health is a much more vital matter here than it is where dogs are kept only as pets.

Few southerners in the North showed this sensitivity to the cultural issues at stake, but the rest of the article was not complacent; the rabies virus was already believed to be present at the time, and seventy of the town's four hundred qimmiit had already been shot to slow the spread of the disease. The qimmiit, so important when people were living on the land, became a source of anxiety and risk in larger settlements.

ATTACKS DURING THE 1950s AND 1960s

A few particular incidents crystallized the official view that there was a dog crisis requiring strict management. This came to a head from 1959 to 1961, not coincidently at the same time as the Qallunaat population of the North was booming with the appointment of teachers and area administrators. A. P. Wight, an area administrator at a number of places, including Igloolik and later Inukjuak, was notoriously hostile to loose qimmiit, and began shooting them even before his own daughter was mauled at Igloolik in the late 1950s. A fatal incident at Apex in 1959 had a particular impact, because the victim's mother was a well-known government employee and health worker. While the immediate official reaction was to demand stricter enforcement of the Ordinance Respecting Dogs, the impact on public opinion was also significant. Gordon Rennie, an HBC manager, witnessed the Apex attack and told the QTC many years later:

> Then I heard this terrible racket down on the beach there and I went out. There was a pack. The dogs ran in packs then, six, eight. You know you didn't bother counting them, you just knew it was a pack of dogs.
>
> Unfortunate thing was they had got this little boy and they tore him apart, they went right up inside his body and made a terrible mess of him. And I know because I had to go on the coroner's inquest after that as a witness, and look at the body. It was scary. My love affair with dogs ended then.

Frank Tester documented a similar case at Pangnirtung about the same time, in 1961–62. In this case, a missionary's five-year-old daughter was attacked while playing outside her parents' home. This led to a series of dramatic airplane and helicopter flights to reach medical care that saved her life.

A seasoned Arctic administrator, W. G. "Moose" Kerr, observed in 1960 that maulings were part of a general pattern of avoidable risk in the Arctic:

> From experience in the North I personally do not think that "Wandering" dogs create any greater hazard than does the normal automobile traffic of southern Canada. In the South we warn our children of the necessary safeguards and there is no reason why we can't do the same in the North. It is also my experience that a

> tied-up dog, if approached by children, is more dangerous than a "Wandering" one.

Modern communications meant that incidents anywhere in the Arctic made newcomers very fearful, without giving them adequate preparation or training for the very real dangers they faced. Frank Tester concluded his passage on the Pangnirtung event by linking it to larger events in the communities:

> At the same time, undergoing phenomenal social and cultural change not of their making, and being experts at dealing with matters in camps and with camp life, it is not difficult to understand the confusion and problems created by trying to adapt to another living environment where conditions and resources were not always conducive to successful adaptation. For Inuit, these were hard times, made all the more difficult by the colonial attitude of many northern administrators and the lack of resources directed at meeting rapidly changing Inuit needs.

The Killings

The history of the killing of qimmiit is not a simple story. Over the course of twenty years, qimmiit were killed at many different times and by different people, mostly RCMP. There was a range of different motives for the killings, but the main effect was to prevent Inuit from keeping qimmiit if they were living at places where there were many Qallunaat. Most Inuit felt acute pain and loss, although some were more accepting of what happened. Some of the witnesses who testified to the QTC recounted deeply upsetting experiences connected to the killing of their families' qimmiit in the 1960s and 1970s. Eventually qimmiit were eliminated everywhere, though the major incidents always happened close to a trading centre or military station.

Generally, RCMP monitored the killing of qimmiit, even when it was not clear who actually killed them. For example, a report from Pond Inlet described events in 1954:

> Eleven dogs had to be destroyed in the Pond Inlet area due to some disease [that] was thought to be distemper. At the first sign of this disease, the dog was shot in order to save the rest of the team. As these eleven dogs were shot over a period of one year and at widely scattered camps, an epidemic was not considered, therefore specimens were not forwarded for examination by the responsible department. Twenty-four other dogs had to be destroyed in this area for other various reasons.

Throughout the period 1950–75, qimmiit were killed in the larger communities when they were deemed sick or a nuisance, or posed a threat to public safety. Shooting qimmiit that escaped from harnesses, ropes, chains, or pounds was widespread and was considered by the authorities to be a justified way of enforcing the Ordinance and educating Inuit about it. At times other methods were used to convince Inuit to tie up their qimmiit. Pauloosie Veevee told the QIA of a common practice at Pangnirtung, which was probably seen wherever the RCMP managed the post office:

> At that time we did not have a post office so even then children's welfare cheques [i.e., family allowance] were handled by the RCMP post. They were the only officials living here then, so we would pick the child welfare cheques from them. The last official RCMP officer was posted here before the government administrators were located. It was not a priority of the police; they would

> not even make an effort to hand them out to the families. Every time the cheques arrived we always had to approach and request the cheques. Every time before he handed [out] the cheques, he would ask every one of us that arrived if our dogs were tied up. That became a normal reaction. I believed he would not hand us our children's welfare cheques if we responded that they were loose and not tied up. His main concern was always whether our dogs were tied up during our stopover. Every single time we saw him, his first question and concern [was] whether or not the dogs were tied up.

This was not limited to specific occasions. Mosesee Qiyuakjuk described a general situation at Pangnirtung both before and after the population began to relocate there during a distemper epidemic in 1962:

> The RCMP started killing off Inuit dogs way before the dog distemper epidemic. The RCMP shot dogs all of the time. Even when the Inuit came to trade here and were planning to go back to their camp, the RCMP would quickly kill off their dogs that were waiting for their owner to come back from the trading post. And whenever the dogs got loose, even when they were behaving, the RCMP would shoot and kill them as if for no reason.

TIMING

The timing of the killings was not random, but was determined by external factors, notably the arrival of Qallunaat at the settlements. It is also important to note that at first, Inuit replaced their qimmiit that were destroyed. A government policy at the time encouraged most Inuit to stay on the land where they needed dog teams, but also to limit the numbers of their qimmiit and to give up their qimmiit once they had homes in a settlement. This explains why the RCMP took great efforts to keep qimmiit healthy through immunizations, but also led the campaign to rid communities of loose qimmiit. Jobs, houses, and schools all worked against the keeping of qimmiit. However, because employment was unreliable, the authorities also saw value in qimmiit. The snowmobile was a complicating factor as well. For many years, qimmiit were being shot when there were no viable snowmobiles to replace them. After about 1966, snowmobiles were more reliable, though very expensive to buy, run, and maintain.

The reduction of the number of qimmiit to almost zero in twenty years moved at the same pace as the growth of the Qallunaat presence. The government tolerated customary Inuit ways of managing qimmiit until there were large numbers of American and Canadian servicemen in Iqaluit.

The killings did not happen all at once. The first systematic killing of loose qimmiit occurred at Iqaluit during the period after 1956. This was at the same time as large numbers of Inuit were attracted to the area by opportunities to work at the airport and radar stations. A small town, Apex, was built at Niaqunngut to provide them with services and housing.

The second major episode of killings took place in the ilagiit nunagivaktangit around Cumberland Sound in 1962. The RCMP responded to a serious epidemic of canine distemper or hepatitis by systematically killing almost the entire canine population in the region.

The third major episode occurred piecemeal after the construction of schools and the resulting relocation of almost the entire population into thirteen communities. This wave of killings is the hardest to document because it started earlier in some communities (such as Cape Dorset); involved many different people firing the shots, including Inuit who were compelled to shoot their own qimmiit before relocating; and was generally carried out in stages, except at Pangnirtung where more than four hundred qimmiit were shot around the settlement in 1966–67.

Finally, there is some evidence that qimmiit were deliberately harmed to intimidate their owners. For example, Levi Evic of Pangnirtung recalled travelling from Illunguyat to Pangnirtung with his parents to trade in 1955 or 1956. While camping near his aunt's qammaq in the settlement, they were warned by the HBC manager:

> Someone came over and told my father that they were going to shoot his dogs tomorrow, kill all his dogs. It was winter at that time. In the middle of the night when it was dark, really cold, we left this community. He did not want his dogs to be shot. So in the middle of the night they took off, towards our home.

The HBC manager was accompanying a police officer and acting as his translator. Considering the date and the circumstances, it seems that the RCMP had decided that Jaco Evic (Levi's father) had stayed too long at the trading centre and needed to be pressured to return to Illunguyat.

Some shootings were also designed to intimidate people and warn others, as in the case of an incident at Igloolik around 1961–62. Louis Uttak told QIA researchers about a particular memory. "Lucian Ukkalianuk's dogs being killed by the 'Boss' all in one day. He arrived to the community of Igloolik by dog team, when he got his dogs off the harnesses they went all over the community. Without hesitation the 'Boss' shot them all with a rifle."

LOCATIONS

By the mid-1970s, almost every team of qimmiit in Qikiqtaaluk had been destroyed. The killings, however, did not occur in the same manner everywhere. Most of the killings occurred at town dumps, near DEW Line sites where mess-hall waste was dumped, on beaches, or on the fringes of settlements. Many Inuit remember qimmiit being hunted and killed among the settlement buildings or even in spaces under houses. These events were traumatic, but they must have also been very confusing. When the RCMP visited people in their ilagiit nunagivaktangit, they did not harass the qimmiit, and when people visited settlements, the killing of qimmiit was sporadic and not always preceded by warnings.

This section contains a brief survey of some examples of how qimmiit were killed in different communities. In many cases, an exact knowledge of community history and the personalities involved would provide a richer understanding, but in general, the differences between communities were minor and were due to the different pace of two kinds of events—the installation of government and commercial services, especially schools, and the pace of centralization of the population. Justice Jean-Jacques Croteau's inquiry found similar patterns in Nunavik.

Cape Dorset

Cape Dorset had a Northern Service Officer by the early 1950s, and most of its population centralized quite early around the activities of the artists' co-op. Killings are recorded from a time before there was a resident RCMP. Ejetsiak Peter told the QTC about qimmiq control in the 1960s, and linked it to the growing numbers of incomers:

> RCMP officers were not the only ones who slaughtered dogs. I saw that the social workers would help them out, maybe they assigned them. I am sure they were asked to do that. And it was very sad to lose the dogs because I looked after the dog team for a long time . . . After they shot the dogs you were left with nothing. I wasn't able to get a snowmobile right away when they shot my dogs so I was left with nothing. When I was a Board member, I was assigned to shoot dogs when non-Inuit started to come in more.

Nuna Parr had a similarly emotional experience during the period between 1958 and 1964:

> The RCMP killed the dogs tied up by the beach. One of my dogs was right beside me. I tied him up beside the hut. I heard a shot, so I ran up towards where the shooting was. When I reached my dog, it was dead beside the hut. I went to the police because I was really mad . . . When the dogs were slaughtered, the police were not telling the truth. They were shooting dogs right under the houses, breaking the laws. I witnessed them. They shot them with a shotgun. . . . The RCMP used to shoot dogs anywhere around the houses. And I wanted to bring that up because I remember those things.

Here as in other communities, the growth of the settlement and adoption of snowmobiles created more trouble for people who were not ready to give up their qimmiit. RCMP member Al Bunn told an RCMP questioner in 2005, "There were no dog teams in Cape Dorset, but lots of dogs in Cape Dorset." During his time there in 1970–72, Bunn "shot many loose dogs."

Kimmirut

The QTC received testimony from five people who witnessed qimmiq killings in Kimmirut or on the land near it. During the 1950s, the population of Kimmirut fell substantially because of migration to Iqaluit, and the qimmiq population suffered very badly from disease in the late fifties. By the early 1960s, these situations had both stabilized, with Kimmirut recognized as the trading centre of a small region with enough game to feed the people. This was also the decade when the school opened (1963) and was enlarged (1968). Pressure mounted on people to send their children to school, which led many to leave the land. Predictably, not everyone came in enthusiastically. Their accounts show that people were forced to give up their qimmiit in order to be accepted in the community. For the QIA, Taqialuk Temela recalled:

> When we moved to Kimmirut, the police started coming back and forth again wanting to kill the dogs while they were tied up near a small hill. I didn't want to let them go because they were my only source of transportation in the winter time. Again, I never said "Yes" for a while, but the police interpreters kept coming back so I finally said "Yes" when they were coming in every day. They said that they would be replaced by better things, not dogs. They said that they would give us Ski-Doos and that we should kill the dogs. They were all killed by the police and I was never given anything for them, not even a Ski-Doo.

Iqaluit

Iqaluit was the first place in Qikiqtaaluk to have a serious confrontation between government and Inuit over qimmiit. The situation here was exceptional because, from the early 1950s onwards, there were literally hundreds of Qallunaat living under semi-military discipline at the air base and weather station, and employment opportunities were a magnet for Inuit from as far away as Kimmirut and the southern shores of Cumberland Sound. The federal government fostered the movement of Inuit into Iqaluit by building a separate town site for them at Niaqunngut (Apex Hill), with housing and a school. Here, as at Kuujuarapik on Hudson Bay, the combination of a military presence with a growing Inuit settlement led to a conflict over the qimmiit that people needed when they returned to the land, either on short trips, or seasonally, when jobs were scarce in winter.

In the 1940s, fifty-three Inuit moved to Iqaluit to work as labourers during construction of the military airfield. The RCMP soon began reporting problems with qimmiit in the predominantly Qallunaat community. The USAF commander complained to the RCMP that qimmiit running around the base were becoming a nuisance; he warned that in the future all loose qimmiit would be shot. Safety was not cited as the concern; it was the nuisance caused by qimmiit tipping garbage cans and congregating in packs around the rear of the mess hall. In response, the US airport was designated an area in which no qimmiit were allowed "to run at large unless muzzled."

Iqaluit's Inuit population grew from just over fifty in 1950 to almost six hundred and fifty by 1956. Iqaluit's later qimmiq problems became apparent in this decade—qimmiit roaming loose were a problem for Qallunaat residents, Qallunaat in positions of authority were shooting qimmiit, and the solutions proposed by Qallunaat were impractical.

While there are crucial gaps in the written record collected to date, there is little doubt that the events here were a template for what happened on a smaller scale elsewhere. Qallunaat tried to apply the rules, and many Inuit tried to comply, but efforts to keep qimmiit tied or impounded generally failed. This led to wide-scale shooting, often without warnings to individual owners, and embittered relations between Qallunaat and the permanent residents of the region.

In Iqaluit, as in other communities, dog teams were being replaced by snowmobiles in the second half of the 1960s. There were fifty snowmobiles and only nine dog teams in the community in 1965. By 1967, the RCMP reported that "the days of the dog team are about gone in this area and the majority of hunting is done by Ski-Doo." An Inuk was hired as dogcatcher in 1968, but the position was difficult to keep filled. In later years, when it was vacant, the task of shooting loose qimmiit was once again left to the RCMP.

The Settlement Council often discussed the problems posed by loose qimmiit, the shooting of qimmiit, and the disposal of their remains.

Throughout the 1970s, local newspapers frequently carried letters to the editor and articles about the Ordinance and the shooting of qimmiit. A new bylaw was passed around 1973. It required the owners to license, water, and feed their qimmiit, and prohibited them from running loose in the community. Qimmiit would only be shot "when necessary, such as packs that cannot be caught." Notices were posted in a local newspaper in both English and Inuktitut advising owners that unless they tied up their qimmiit they would be impounded and the fines to get the qimmiq back could be as high as $200. The notice went on to instruct qimmiq owners in the proper care of their animals. Qimmiit, it said, were to be walked daily.

In 1976, the town's dogcatcher bought a tranquilizer gun to use on qimmiit that could not be caught. However, qimmiit were still being shot. On a single day in January 1977, the dogcatcher shot thirty-five qimmiit. The RCMP accompanied him for protection, but did not participate in the shooting of any qimmiit. As late as 1973, it does not appear that a dog pound was set up. By 1976, however, there was a pound, but it was reportedly in very poor condition.

Pangnirtung

Pangnirtung residents remember two particularly traumatic incidents involving qimmiit, towards the beginning and end of the 1960s. The first was the government's reaction to an epidemic of distemper that swept through the South Baffin region in 1957–62. The second occurred in 1966, when Constable Jack Grabowski decided to crack down on qimmiit in the settlement. He reported:

> The dog population decreased rapidly over the past year. Some Eskimos disposed of their own dogs when they were able to purchase Ski-Doos, while a good number were destroyed in contravention

> to [*sic*] the Ordinance. Referring to the latter, numerous requests were made by myself and members of this Detachment to the Eskimos to keep their dogs adequately tied, or penned. When these requests went unheeded I gave instructions that all dogs at large were to be shot, and in the period of slightly over one year, I would estimate that some two hundred and fifty dogs have been shot. This too, does not seem to have the desired effect, as almost daily dogs are still seen at large. A new approach to the apparent passive resistance of the Eskimo has been taken, whereby the owner will be sought out, and he will be prosecuted.

While both episodes are remembered with clarity in the region, the earlier one had a more profound impact. As Frank Tester described, "What happened in Cumberland Sound in this period is highly significant and, with respect to the history of sled dogs, likely the most significant event in the history of the Qikiqtani region. It is central to understanding the history and formation of Pangnirtung as a community."

While the hunters and trappers around Kimmirut had dealt with epidemics in customary ways by sharing qimmiit and building up their teams after disease passed, the situation at Pangnirtung was very different. Using a new RCMP aircraft and all the resources of a much larger bureaucracy than most other settlements possessed, the epidemic unfolded differently here than anywhere else. The RCMP visited many of the ilagiit nunagivaktangit by aircraft, concluding essentially that it would be hopeless for hunters to try to rely on qimmiit in the near future, and made plans to evacuate as many people to the trading centre as wanted to or could be persuaded to go.

In a very short time, more than half the people from around Cumberland Sound were evacuated to Pangnirtung, leaving behind their homes and property and crowding into tents in a community that lacked the supplies to feed them. As Levi Evic told the QTC, his family felt worse off in Pangnirtung than when living at Illunguyat and hunting on foot in the nearby tide cracks:

> Looking back today, that has affected me a lot, and also to my parents. When they moved us there were changes in us, even in myself, I changed . . . Our hunting practices were disrupted, looking for food by our fathers, they even lost some of that and experienced hunger when we were living in this community, whereas in the camps we never experienced hunger . . . The written and oral records, taken together, suggest that the police might have killed more qimmiit than necessary and might have overreacted when they brought almost everyone off the land. People who remained did not starve, and those who were evacuated were almost entirely cut off from country food and were hungrier, colder, and more demoralized than those who stayed behind in their qarmat. Two of the more isolated and independent inhabited places were never re-occupied.

The second crisis affecting qimmiit in Pangnirtung occurred in 1967 when, with the new amendments to the Ordinance giving police a freer hand against loose qimmiit, Constable Jack Grabowski set out to eliminate them altogether. In 1967, he reported to Ottawa that he had killed two hundred and fifty qimmiit in 1966 belonging to hunters who had left the land to live in the settlement, and that he planned to do the same thing in 1967. Although he was criticized by his superiors for overreacting, the number of qimmiit dropped dramatically. People remember that not all the qimmiit shot in Pangnirtung in the 1960s were loose. Adamie Veevee told the QTC in 2008:

> When we were here in Pangnirtung, they didn't want the dogs to be alive. There used to be a dog pound over there. When they were inside the cage, they were shot inside the cage. My father's dogs were shot inside the cage. They were used for transportation. We had no Ski-Doo. That was all we had for transportation. And I

> was getting to be a young man. The RCMP were getting to be my enemy. I hated them. Yes. We were watching when our dogs were being shot inside the cage. The three men's dogs were shot. That was what I really remember. That was our only means of transportation. I was learning to use my own dogs.

Asked if any reason was given for the shootings, he replied: "They tried to give us a reason. They said that they were too skinny, that they were too hungry. But they weren't like that. But in that time, even the dogs that were tied up were shot. It seems that they didn't want to see any more dogs alive."

That trend continued. In 1968, only three hunters were reported to be using dog teams, and the settlement and two remaining ilagiit nunagivaktangit had seventy snowmobiles altogether. In 1968, the RCMP switched to snowmobiles and disposed of their own dog team. This led them to abandon the annual fall walrus hunt at the mouth of Cumberland Sound that had been an important source of meat for the qimmiit of the area.

Qikiqtarjuaq

There was no year-round settlement on Broughton Island before 1960, but the place was seasonally useful to Inuit. In 1955, DEW Line stations were set up there and nearby at the traditional dwelling place of Kivitoo. A third good hunting centre, Paallavvik, had been the site of weather stations since the Second World War. Many years later, a former Marconi operator at the Kivitoo site recalled how qimmiit were poisoned in the 1950s:

> Loss of dogs could mean famine for all concerned. Such was the situation that faced one of the families at Kivitoo when its dogs,

> allowed to roam freely at the construction camp, were fed raw meat laced with Gillettes Lye. We then witnessed several victims in ghastly distress, wandering aimlessly with froth and frozen drool hanging from their mouth. This senseless, cruel act arose from frustration at failed appeals to the family to tether their dogs. That a member of the catering staff left FOX-D on the next available aircraft was no coincidence. RCMP were never contacted and those of us who observed this barbaric act and failed in our duty, have had to live with our conscience.

However, around the same time the American chief of the Broughton Island station boasted of having shot qimmiit that belonged to Inuit who were camped near his radar installation. A visiting federal official wrote:

> The Station Chief, Mr. Al. Watson, said that there was a dog problem in the area because the dogs were breaking into the food supplies. He had warned the Eskimos to tie up their dogs or else he would have to shoot them. He had already shot several and received no complaints from the Eskimos.

In the context of the time and place, it would have been pointless and difficult for Inuit to complain to anybody.

In this period, there was no trading centre or police post at Qikiqtarjuaq, only the DEW Line auxiliary station. In short order, the HBC, school, Northern Affairs, and RCMP arrived, and people came under pressure to centralize. In many cases, Qikiqtarjuarmiut testified that their qimmiit were slaughtered in order to tie their owners forcibly to the settlement. Jacopie Nuqingaq talked of this kind of experience:

> After re-supplies [in Qikiqtarjuaq] we would go back [home], when we still had our route to go back on our team, planning to

> go back before the ice broke up, then they slaughtered our dogs. I grieved for them, they were our only means of transportation. If I [knew] what I know then, I would never have agreed to come here. They made it impossible for us to go, we were stuck.

Leah, Jacopie's wife, also spoke about her experience:

> When we were starting to go, [the Qallunaat] told Jacopie our dogs are going to be shot [because] no dogs [are] allowed in Qikiqtarjuaq. Our dogs were tied out on the ice. We were getting ready to go back home, back to [Paallavvik] . . . We didn't want to talk back . . . Our dogs were slaughtered. We had no choice but to stay here.

Kakudluk, a member of one of the seven families relocated from Paallavvik recalled how strictly the Ordinance was interpreted in Qikiqtarjuaq. She had travelled to the area by dog team with her family. "Once they got there, the dogs were shot, she said, because dogs were not allowed in Qikiqtarjuaq." These killings occurred quite close to the time when the epidemic passed through the Davis Straits region, and the two things together made it hard for Inuit to re-establish their teams. By this time, snowmobiles were available for those who could afford them, but they represented a cultural loss. As Jacopie Koosiaq wrote in a local newspaper while re-establishing himself at Paallavvik, "This year, 1974, I'm living in my old home of Padloping [Paallavvik]. I have known this place since I was a child . . . I have discovered that children are forgetting our ways. I am trying to be an Eskimo, but I have no dogs."

Clyde River

There were several ilagiit nunagivaktangit in the region of Clyde River, some stretching along the coast to the north and a few further south, towards Home Bay. There were some employment opportunities at the DEW Line sites, and those places are mentioned by witnesses who spoke to the QTC about qimmiq killings. Other instances of killings involved qimmiit belonging to people who were just visiting the community to trade, as recounted by Jason Palluq:

> There was a person who came in at one time. His dogs were slaughtered. He did not have a Ski-Doo. The RCMP came up right there and then three dogs were killed. I saw that. I thought, "Ho my God, how is he going to get back home? He probably has family waiting for him at the camp." I did not know which camp he was from. I assumed he was from a southern camp because I did not know him. I saw it myself. He came in and he [hadn't] even unharnessed his dogs. They shot three of his dogs.

The police might have stopped at three because the owner argued forcefully with what they were doing. "I know that the Inuk was verbally trying to fight back or say something to him to stop it. That is what I saw." Joanasie Illauq spoke of a problem that was probably common throughout the region. In about 1966, his qimmiit got free after being tied up for the night on a visit from Igluaqtuuq to trade at Clyde River:

> When we arrived in Clyde River, we were told that our dogs were to be tied up. The community was right across from here. We used pieces of rope to tie them down on the sea ice … As soon as we got our supplies we were going to head right back. We had to buy lots

> of things, not just for our family, but for everyone in our camp. We bought lots of supplies and loaded them on our sled. We had to overnight. When we woke up in the morning, I went to check on the dogs because they were to be tied down. As soon as I went to our qamutik, I realized that some of them were missing. Our lead dog and some of the middle dogs had chewed off their rope and gotten loose. We were missing them. I ran back to my brother to tell [him] that they were missing. When we started looking around, we couldn't find them. We finally found them right in front of the store and they were all dead. Apparently, the RCMP and the store employee killed them. And right there and then, it was almost impossible for us to go back to our camp.

The trip home with only six qimmiit took three days.

Pond Inlet

Pond Inlet was a major point of contact between Inuit and Qallunaat in northern Baffin Island for the whole of the twentieth century, but only developed as a centralized community quite rapidly in the 1960s. In 1962, the settlement had a one-room school and most people still lived on the land. A bigger school, with hostels, brought a rush of people to the settlement a couple years later. In 1965, half the people of the area lived at the trading centre. By 1970, almost everybody had made the move. As a result, the authorities had become very conscious of qimmiit, and conflicts resulted.

Frank Tester described events in the late 1960s. By 1967, there was a persistent problem with loose qimmiit, and the authorities hired an Inuk as dog officer. At a meeting of the Pond Inlet Council in May 1967, Councillor Jimmy Muckpah complained that the new dog officer, Komangapik, was overzealous "about his job and on occasion was not warning dog owners before shooting. It was also suggested that certain dogs owned by white people lead charmed live[s]." A discussion followed in which it was decided that strict enforcement of the Ordinance was necessary, but that owners should be given one warning before any qimmiit were shot and that the Ordinance should apply to all qimmiit, regardless of who owned them.

As usual, the main burden fell on Inuit, and particularly those who were newly arrived in the settlement and who did not have snowmobiles. Paomee Komangapik moved with her husband and two children directly from Igloolik to Pond Inlet in 1966. In 2008, she told the QTC about her husband's team:

> I am a widow and I would like to speak about the dog slaughter.
>
> In 1969, my late husband's dogs were shot. Eventually, every one of them was shot. In those days, my husband's dogs were killed off. We had no means of transportation and we were put in an untenable position. We [could not] catch a seal. That is my permanent story about dogs.

Also in 2008, Rosie Katsak shared with the commission a story her father had told her before passing away. Ishmael Katsak moved with his family into Pond Inlet where an RCMP member promptly shot his qimmiit. "When they came to Pond Inlet, he had a dog team. All of his dogs were killed by the RCMP . . . He was sad. He couldn't go out hunting. He had no snowmobile so he had to walk on the ice to go out hunt for us to have food." The shooting seems to have been a pre-emptive move. "My father's dogs weren't sick. They were killed by the RCMP."

Arctic Bay

The QIA and QTC received twenty-nine statements from Inuit at Arctic Bay, many of whom had spent their lives in the immediate area surrounding the community. Several spoke of qimmiq killings, mainly late in the period. One of the most informative of these was Mucktar Akumalik, whose deep knowledge of qimmiit is revealed in his testimony about the time he spent as the community dogcatcher.

> When we moved here in 1966, everybody had a dog team, at least all the hunters did. They were all required to keep their dogs tied up. When the RCMP came in, I was selected by the Council to be the dogcatcher. I signed up at the RCMP station. When the RCMP came in each year, he would ask me how many dogs I had shot, how I was treated by the local people, and names of people who didn't like me as a result of my shooting their dogs. That's how well I was treated by the RCMP. They would ask me questions. We wanted everything to be done in a responsible manner. The Council would advise the public to be responsible for their dogs. When a dog became loose I would be responsible for notifying the owner. I was a dogcatcher for five years.

Mucktar Akumalik drew the same conclusion about qimmiit and schooling as Judge Croteau found across Nunavik.

> It was the school system that seemed to be the reason for all dogs getting killed. After we had arrived here in Arctic Bay, they didn't want the dogs getting stray and hanging out in the community. The community was just starting out and they didn't want dogs getting into people's food.

In an important and revealing remark, he stated that the Ordinance was not in effect in Arctic Bay until the time of his appointment, in 1967.

A review of documentary sources produced no reports of specific events related to qimmiit in Arctic Bay, with the exception of a reference in the RCMP's 2006 report noting that in 1965 about ten to fifteen qimmiit in Arctic Bay were lost to what was suspected to be rabies.

Grise Fiord

There are no recorded instances of conflict between Inuit and Qallunaat authorities in Grise Fiord over qimmiit. If there was any conflict over dogs during their replacement with snowmobiles in Grise Fiord, Frank Tester (2008), the RCMP research team (2006) and the witnesses at the QTC hearings in Grise Fiord did not bring these events to light.

Resolute

Resolute, like Grise Fiord, was one of the new communities created in 1953 by relocating Inuit from Nunavik and Pond Inlet. It had a relatively small population (less than one hundred and seventy in 1981), but it experienced the same problems as larger centres with the police reaction to qimmiit. Simon Idlout was a young adult when he saw qimmiit being shot around the community:

> I used to see the police officer. He just opened his window and he would shoot the dogs with his pistol as if he was just having fun. These dogs were owned by people. The police were just playing around with them. He just opened his window and just shot the dogs. The owners weren't around and were never asked or told, "Your dogs have been loose for too long." They started shooting

> any dog they saw. I didn't like that at all. We used to travel long distances by dog team and that is the only thing we had for survival. When the dogs were shot, it was very painful for me. They were just playing around, maybe they were target practicing. That is what it seems like. Here we were growing the dogs to use them in the future.

Frank Tester's survey of qimmiit described the situation here as similar to what was found at Grise Fiord:

> In 1954, the Officer in Charge suggested that he had interested relocated Inuit in improving the dog strain by bringing in dogs from Eureka, Greenland.
>
> By 1960, Inuit at Resolute Bay were reported to have teams of eight to twelve dogs in good condition.
>
> The following year (1961) the Officer in Charge reported that: There are about one hundred and ten dogs in the settlement. Each family has its own team of about eight to ten dogs. These dogs are well-fed all year round and seem to be of better disposition then [*sic*] some of the dogs the writer has seen in other settlements.

In 2008, Ludy Padluk testified to the QTC about the loss of his qimmiit in 1964, when he had an accident and lost his toes while working for Polar Shelf. While he was in hospital in Edmonton, he decided that he would give his dog team to his brother. However, when he recuperated enough to come back to Resolute he found his qimmiit had all been shot. He made an interesting observation about ownership of qimmiit, "They were family dogs. My wife and my kids owned the dogs. One person doesn't own those dogs. If I talk to my brother today, he has a dog-team; he would say 'our dogs.' If I say 'my dog,' a lot of people say 'our dogs.'"

Igloolik

In 1965, there were twenty-one dog teams and just seven snowmobiles in the settlement itself. By 1968, the RCMP reported that there were almost as many snowmobiles as dog teams, but unlike other settlements, people were keeping their qimmiit even while they were buying snowmobiles. The ability to store walrus and the supplies of dog food in a designated warehouse may also have led Inuit to retain teams. Well into the 1970s, many Iglulingmiut preferred the dog teams to machines for safety reasons. The use of qimmiit at Igloolik has never been completely abandoned, although now the main use is to earn revenue from tourists, with outfitters keeping dog-team skills alive.

Neither the RCMP (2006) nor Frank Tester's report for the QTC offered much documentation relating to qimmiit around Igloolik. It was clear that once people began to come into the settlement in large numbers with their qimmiit, the situation was little different from other settlements. Thomas Kublu spoke to the QTC about his troubles with his employers when he began working for the community in 1967:

> A by-law had been imposed in the community to chain all dogs in Igloolik. All loose dogs were shot, not that we wanted our dogs shot. We were vigilant about keeping our dogs tied up. My dog team began to decrease in numbers, and at this time we had the police and the government overseeing and controlling our lives. What they ordered us to do, we had to listen. I may not have worked as much as the agent wanted me to; I still had to hunt to feed my family and dogs. As a wage earner I could not do it without supplementing the food source as a hunter. Eventually my dog team dwindled to six and I still hunted. If dogs accidentally became loose, they were shot. Six dogs made a slow journey. This was not an easy

> task when my hunting was reduced to weekends and evenings. I arrived in Igloolik with thirteen dogs ... In the spring of 1965 while I was at work, all my dogs which were chained up were shot. I was not around when this happened. I saw the government agent after that, he did not say anything but was very embarrassed and red in the face. I was informed later on that the police had shot all the dogs, possibly as instructed by the government agent. I never understood why they were shot.

Thomas Kublu's experience suggested that his qimmiit would not have been shot if the government official had realized who owned them. Many of the other reported shootings seem to have been similarly random, and carried out without warning and without considering the consequences for qimmiq owners. Eugene Ipkamaq spoke with feeling about the number of people in the community—trading-post staff and civilian government officials—who kept their rifles handy and killed many qimmiit, a few at a time, over several years. The legacy of loss and mistrust remains strong in Igloolik.

Hall Beach

There does not seem to have been a major sweep of qimmiit, loose or otherwise, in Hall Beach, but several Inuit testified to having their qimmiit killed without their permission. Jake Ikeperiar also testified to being made to kill qimmiit under orders from a Qallunaaq. The experience of Jake Ikeperiar showed how accepting government employment could make difficulties:

> There were seven dogs that were together ... They would go to the dump or other locations. The owners didn't know that this was happening. The owner of the dogs was out of town. I am not a dogcatcher, I was not appointed. I knew that they were running

> around . . . There was no area administrator here. There was a power corporation engineer who was the boss. I know this because I was here to work with the government. He told us to come over because the dogs were bothering [him]. He asked what kind of a gun we had. We had .222 and .22. He asked how many bullets were needed to fill up a .222. We gave him a box. We were young. We were asked to deal with the dogs. He was told to do this by the area administrator . . . The person who told us to kill the dogs put aside some gas. When he came over to us, he told us to kill the dogs and burn the dogs. We didn't really want to do it but we had to.

One Elder, Moses Allianaq, described the loss of his eight dogs on the orders of an Inuk who was employed by the territorial government. The order came from the RCMP. The result was an almost total loss of mobility, a dependence on others for transportation, and a lack of meat in winter. "It was very difficult after the dogs were killed. We had to stay in one place. It was hard. It was good before the dogs were killed. And it cost a lot . . . [how would I] provide country food to my family members?"

Sanikiluaq

Inuit in the Belcher Islands had a different experience from many other places in Qikiqtaaluk. The islanders had no RCMP detachment until the 1970s. Teachers at the South Camp School (1960) seemed to have a good relationship with Inuit, and if any qimmiit were killed during the regular winter trading excursions to Kuujuarapik, this information has not been handed down. What really stands out is how qimmiit were treated when people were obliged to abandon South Camp for relocation to the slightly larger North Camp.

A detailed and moving statement was given to the QIA in 2004 by Pauloosie Ekidlak:

> I know first-hand about this issue of dogs being killed, we keep hearing about this issue for a long time now. I was told that better mode[s] of transportation [were] being made so it [was] okay to kill the dogs even though I did not want to do this, they were the only way for me to hunt to look for food ... I killed my dogs but the government was saying that they would provide better mode of transportation and I did not feel that it was up to me whether I wanted to do it or not. I felt pressured to kill my dogs by the government saying they have better mode of transportation. My dogs were the only way for me to hunt and to this day this hurts me. There was nobody to kill the dogs like the police so the Inuit were told to kill their own dogs.

The killing was carried out as the people were preparing, very reluctantly, to leave South Camp (which had a school, hostel, generating station, and tank farm) and resettle in North Camp. "I killed my dogs at the South Camp," said Ekidlak, "I couldn't leave them behind so I had to kill them ... I killed my dogs with a gun. I shot my dogs maybe two days before we were relocated to North Camp. Because I realized I couldn't come back for them."

The order to kill the qimmiit was passed from an unnamed government official through an Inuk, Joe Kumarluk. No order came directly from an official, but Ekidlak knew he had no choice. The same was true for everybody else at South Camp awaiting relocation by boat. As Ekidlak continued:

> Everybody was shooting their own dogs and knew that this had to be done because the government was telling them to kill the dogs. As you can imagine, killing all those dogs, shots going off all around and people knowing what is going on. All those dead

dogs. I covered my dead dogs with rocks; it was the only thing I could do.

MOTIVES

Qimmiit were killed mainly by Qallunaat or by Inuit acting under orders from Qallunaat for only a few reasons. The principal reasons were described as public health and public safety. Since rabies was difficult to diagnose and extremely dangerous to people, sick animals were likely to be shot without waiting for confirmation that they had this frightening disease. The public safety issue was more complex. Certainly when large packs of qimmiit ran through a settlement, they were extremely frightening and occasionally harmful. However, they were usually found foraging around a dump or breaking into storage areas, more a danger to property than to people. The "public safety" argument was often used to justify shooting qimmiit more for what they might do in the future than for what they were actually doing at the time.

Inuit found these arguments unconvincing, especially since they had lived with qimmiit for centuries. To some, it appeared that qimmiit were being killed to reduce people's mobility and force them to leave the land and live year-round in settlements under the control of officials. That seemed plausible, especially before snowmobiles offered an alternative, but in fact compulsory school attendance and threats to cut off family allowance seem to have been the main forms of coercion. There were also some potentially positive attractions to settlement life, including health care, housing, and the possibility of employment. One Inuk also suggested that there was a commercial motive behind the shootings, telling researcher Lorne Smith in 1969–70 that police were shooting stray qimmiit so that people would have to buy Ski-Doos.

A few Inuit agreed that there might be some truth in the official explanation that qimmiit were being killed in the name of health or safety. A more common view was that the killings were part of the government's ambition to control Inuit and to bring about rapid change. At Igloolik in 2008, sixty-two-year-old Abraham Ulayuruluk told Commissioner Igloliorte, "It was a form of manipulation by the government so that we would be less independent and so that we would rely on its resources." He contrasted this with the period when there were still qimmiit, explaining, "My father had a boat or a canoe and we traveled everywhere. We never experienced starvation. Dogs helped us hunt fish or caribou. They were well-mannered and well-behaved. They listened to us when we scolded them. The only diet we had was country food."

While these perspectives were expressed in public and to the QTC, what struck Inuit was not just the strange motives, but the sheer wastefulness and cruelty of killing qimmiit. At the time of many of the killings, qimmiit were absolutely necessary for families wanting to return to the land to hunt. Without qimmiit, people found themselves struggling with half a dog team or tied to a settlement, often without work or any other kind of productive activity, and unable to feed their families with nutritious country food.

WHO KILLED THE QIMMIIT?

Between 1955 and 1975, RCMP, who were ex officio dog officers under the Ordinance, killed a large number of qimmiit. This would include qimmiit shot by Inuit special constables. In communities where there was no police detachment, a settlement manager, HBC trader, or other Qallunaaq with a particular concern about loose qimmiit usually carried out these shootings. A lot of Qallunaat, including RCMP officers, avoided shooting qimmiit themselves and would try to pass the task on to someone else. On the other hand, even fewer wanted to go through all the legal steps of warning owners and trying to catch qimmiit and impound them before shooting.

Before the appointment of the QTC in Qikiqtaaluk and the Croteau Commission in Nunavik, many RCMP members angrily denied having shot qimmiit. Those who admitted to the shootings insisted that they only shot them when they were a danger to people, or when they acted under the authority of the Ordinance. However, a great deal of other evidence suggests that loose qimmiit were shot when they were not a danger to anyone, and that the warnings required by the Ordinance were often not given. Because of this, and a lack of written records of such local matters, it is difficult to estimate how many qimmiit were actually shot by police officers.

With the increasing concentration of people into settlements, municipal officers were appointed, and these often included a dogcatcher. This was a difficult and unpopular task because owners understood that qimmiit kept tied up did not travel as well as those who were constantly exercising. Despite the difficulties, Mucktar Akumalik of Arctic Bay, who worked as a dogcatcher, believed that Inuit respected him for doing his job in a sensitive way. He explained, "Because they were well-informed by the police, nobody was against me. They would probably have been angry if they had not been informed. They didn't get angry at me because they were informed." Akumalik once shot as many as thirty-two qimmiit in a single day. He gave up the job when he moved to another community. He told the QTC that he was not paid for this work, but did it as a service to the community.

Anthropologist George Wenzel also gave the QTC his perspective on his brief term as a dog officer at Clyde River in the 1970s:

> [George Wenzel]: In Clyde, loose dogs by and large were shot…We would give a warning. But if a dog was seen as constantly being loose it was shot. One summer I was asked to be the dog catcher and I shot a couple of dogs after giving warning…

> [Interviewer]: How did they take the warnings?
>
> [Wenzel]: They would say OK, but if I saw the dog the next day and it wasn't tied up then I shot it . . . There was an awful lot of rancour if somebody shot somebody's dog. I can understand. Even though the dog should have been tied up and was stealing the meat and so on and so forth. That was the summer I was one of the few Qallunaat around . . . After about three weeks, that was it, I was never doing that again. It was like being the guard at the jail. I am never doing that again.

Some of the saddest or most upsetting incidents are those in which people were coerced into shooting their own qimmiit. This seems to have happened more towards the end of the period, when, as previously mentioned, the inhabitants of South Camp were ordered to kill all their qimmiit as part of their relocation to North Camp (now Sanikiluaq) in 1970. In 1968, Goteleak Judea of Kimmirut also recalled that the uncle who was raising him was pressured to move into Kimmirut to retain family allowance benefits, and was ordered to shoot his qimmiit before making the move. What stands out in these accounts is the sense of Inuit being powerless against a high wall of bureaucratic and legal resolve.

INUIT PERSPECTIVES

Inuit unquestionably believed that when they lived in their own traditional territories they had the right to look after their own economic interests and to live according to their own customs. At a time of rapid change, Inuit might be convinced or coerced into changing their ways, but they did not recognize the validity of laws that were made elsewhere and made no practical sense. There was an opposite Qallunaat belief that Canadian sovereignty included the right of administrators in Ottawa to make laws for places they had never visited. These conflicting beliefs influenced how Inuit listened to instructions about handling their qimmiit and the resulting demoralization that came with having armed strangers behave as they wished.

Inuit knew that qimmiit needed constant exercise; tying them up weakened them. Qimmiit should be allowed to run loose when they were not working, as they did when on the land, because to pen or chain them—even if this were possible—was dangerous to their well-being and the well-being of Inuit who depended on them for transportation. It was also very hard to keep qimmiit restrained, whether the owners lived in the communities or were just visiting for a few hours to trade. There are many reports of dog pounds or compounds being built in communities, especially after 1960, but often these reports describe their poor condition and the tendency of qimmiit to escape. Qimmiit that were chained or tied also frequently escaped by chewing through their harnesses or by pulling at weak chains. In some communities, notably Arctic Bay, the hunters who kept qimmiit near the settlement during the summer often tried to keep them in secluded areas. As Ikey Kugitikakjuk explained:

> We tried to put our dogs in a secluded area where there were no people because there were about fifteen dogs. We just go and feed them so that they won't be loose around the community and they couldn't stay near our houses anymore, so we had to put them in a place where people wouldn't be walking about.

There may also have been a political side to the decision by many Inuit to stick to their old ways. One police officer thought he saw "passive resistance" in the decision of some Pangnirtormiut not to tie their qimmiit, and an Inuk in Iqaluit spoke frankly to anthropologist Toshio Yatsushiro about the evident desire of the authorities not just to control qimmiit, but to dominate Inuit as well: "First I thought of killing the policemen . . . Maybe afterwards there won't be so many dogs, since the police are shooting them. In five years, there may be none at all. Maybe the police will kill Eskimos then, just like the dogs."

Simon Idlout of Resolute was forthright in comparing traditional Inuit practice with the questionable aspects of the Ordinance:

> The puppies were not allowed to be tied up because of the muscles in their legs. If you tie them up they would become very weak. According to the way Inuit used to feel, they would never tie up dogs in the camp. They need to exercise. No puppies were ever to be tied up. That was the law of the Inuit. We get new laws from the federal government and because it doesn't make any sense, we don't agree with it but we have to follow it.
>
> That law is not coming from the community, it is southern law. This law is not right in Nunavut. These laws were made down South. It is very different in Nunavut . . . Am I going to follow that law from [England] in the High Arctic, is that right? No it is not right! It should be made in the Arctic.

Until 1966, the Ordinance set out a list of requirements that had to be met before loose qimmiit could be killed. These requirements involved warning owners, rounding up and impounding the qimmiit unless they were an immediate threat, and releasing them if their owners paid a fine. In practice, most of the qimmiit that were killed were shot with little or no individual warning and with little or no effort to catch rather than shoot them. The crucial change in 1966 was to remove many of the protections for qimmiit and their owners, protections that were not being applied anyway.

The important change was allowing people to kill, without trying to capture, qimmiit that were simply acting in a threatening manner or destroying "a food cache . . . or other equipment." With these much looser rules, the authorities moved more quickly to reduce the number of qimmiit. Many Inuit recall seeing qimmiit that were tied or impounded also being shot, a clear violation of the Ordinance.

The official record and other written records show that Inuit were rarely consulted and believed it was not feasible to change traditional ways of keeping qimmiit. Records also show that Inuit had no influence with government administrators on this issue, and that administrators knew that their policies and regulations would cause hardship, yet nevertheless thought it was necessary and justified to apply them. Furthermore, the Ordinance did not apply where the majority of Inuit lived before the mid-1960s. Even where it was in force, it was erratically applied, causing considerable confusion among Inuit. The government offered very little support to help Inuit change their ways of controlling their qimmiit.

MANAGING QIMMIIT AROUND PEOPLE

There were a few bitter, open conflicts between Inuit and Qallunaat in Qikiqtaaluk; the worst of these generally involved qimmiit. In fact, a local politician, speaking in the mid-1970s, traced much of the prevailing mistrust between Inuit and Qallunaat to the Ordinance. Speaking about the late 1950s, Member of the Legislative Assembly (MLA) Bryan Pearson told the NWT Legislature:

> And then this conflict went on for many, many years, because the hunters who were then the Eskimo people were coming into the community and bringing their families in from the camps. They were coming in with their dogs and dog teams and these regulations were being enforced in all of these communities. Regulations said, "Tie up your dogs or we will shoot them," to

> which they would reply, "Well, we cannot tie them up, they have nothing to eat, they have got to scavenge around to get food." That is where one of the greatest conflicts that ever happened in the North began when the Eskimo people, I do not know if the same applies here, but the Eskimo people in the Eastern Arctic then began to wonder about the wonderful white man and his wonderful system.

The conflict over qimmiit went far beyond a question of food—there was a complete difference of experience and views about how to handle qimmiit when they were not working. Although qimmiit sometimes ran away and occasionally bit people, mainly children, the safest and simplest way to keep them was to leave them to run free except when they were in harness. One practical reason for this was the ability of qimmiit to warn of approaching polar bears. An everyday reason was that qimmiit were more even-tempered when allowed to move around, forage for food, and socialize among themselves.

This aspect of managing qimmiit was based on the well-being of the qimmiit themselves. A great deal of evidence came out on this subject during early efforts by the RCMP and settlement authorities to negotiate a truce in the battle over loose qimmiit. Many Inuit were willing to try to tie up their qimmiit, though some were not.

The first of many qimmiq restraint initiatives began in 1957. It soon proved impractical, as the primary means of restraining qimmiit that were caught was with chains. Northern Service Officer Flucke reported:

> The Eskimos have pointed out that the chains do not give the dog enough room to exercise, and this is a pertinent point since presumably they will be tied up three hundred and sixty-five days a year, except when actually in team. Chains do not allow them to seek sheltered spots nor huddle together for warmth. The heavy ruff around their necks allows them to work their collars over their

> heads and escape. Moreover, on a large scale it is difficult to feed them, as each dog must be fed separately.

The chaining of the qimmiit was completely impractical. Flucke reported that Inuit who did comply with the rules to tie their qimmiit often lost them to freezing. Additionally, qimmiit that were allowed to forage were reported to be fat and sleek while the tied animals were poor and thin.

CONSEQUENCES FOR INUIT

The killing of qimmiit was one of the most traumatic elements of the changes that happened as the Canadian government tightened its hold on the everyday life of Inuit. The killings deepened the mistrust many Inuit were already feeling towards the government. Senior officials clearly understood this, but gradually lost control of the situation in the late 1950s.

The loss of qimmiit generally, especially in the years before snowmobiles could replace them, disrupted traditional values and routines. It also changed the social hierarchy. If ownership of large teams was a sign of full manhood and superior competence, loss of qimmiit made those relationships uncertain.

Joined to other aspects of settlement life, the loss of qimmiit fed harmful trends and practices. As the Commissioner of the QTC said in his final report:

> Those Inuit who lacked qimmiit or snowmobiles to access the land felt that life in the settlements was a form of imprisonment. For many people, alcohol and gambling provided a temporary, but often unhealthy, distraction from boredom and worries about life in general. By the end of this period, illegal drugs were also entering settlements.

The effects were also economic. Although keeping a team of qimmiit demanded time, effort, and money for rifles and ammunition, the cost of buying, fuelling, and maintaining a snowmobile was beyond the resources of many Inuit. Hunting became linked much more closely to the wage economy, as the people with money, rather than time, to run a snowmobile were primarily the ones with long-term employment. In addition, especially in the earlier years, snow machines often broke down and were less useful than qimmiit in many aspects of the hunt, especially navigation, working across thin or broken ice, and scenting seal holes and bears. Overall, it seems clear that over time Inuit would have converted from qimmiit to snowmobiles, as a handful did very willingly as soon as reliable machines were available. However, the transition, especially before there were reliable snowmobiles, and when qimmiit were shot without the owners' consent, was cruel and unnecessarily disruptive.

Snowmobiles

As government policies and settlement conditions made it difficult or impossible for people to keep qimmiit in communities, certain hunters were able to replace their teams with snowmobiles. For many families the transition was very hard, because the killing of hunters' qimmiit began about six or seven years before reliable snow machines became available in Qikiqtaaluk. Many others lost their qimmiit unexpectedly, could not plan for the purchase of a snowmobile to replace them, and were forced to spend two or three years, at least, with no means of winter transportation of their own. At Pond Inlet, Jaykolasie Killiktee told the QTC:

> Even up to today, when I do not go to Guys Bight, if it has been a fairly long period, I get the pang of homesickness. After a number

> of years here, my dogs were shot off, prior to being able to purchase snow machines. Other people had bought snow machines. It was distressing as it was the only mode of transportation and it was shot off. You are left with nothing.

Mary Iqaqrialuk told how her husband's and son's qimmiit were shot by police at Clyde River before they could afford to replace them with a snowmobile: "We were not told why. They were our only form of transportation. It was very hard on my husband. He had the responsibility to feed us, but he did not have the means of transportation ... It was a lot later that my husband was able to get a snowmobile."

Government and industry purchased the earliest tracked vehicles. Early versions of the one-person tracked vehicle were sent to the Arctic in the late 1950s, but only limited numbers were manufactured and even fewer saw use. The vehicles provided transportation within and to near settlements. Hunting and long-distance travel still required dog teams.

Advantages and disadvantages of each type of travel—snowmobiles and dog teams—were recognized and debated. The greatest advantage of the snowmobile was its speed. The first models were able to travel at speeds up to 20–25 miles per hour, five times the speed of a dog team, and faster than caribou and polar bears. Hunters could check traplines more often using snowmobiles, thereby reducing the loss of pelts to ravens and owls. Above all, hunters could spend less time hunting for dog food and more time on other things, such as wage employment.

Throughout the 1960s and most of the 1970s, however, snowmobiles were not entirely reliable for Arctic use. Mechanical failures were common, parts were expensive, stock of parts was limited, and snowmobile manuals, directed at southern recreational users, failed to provide information useful for trailside repairs. The manuals were also exclusively available in English and French until 1972, when the first Inuktitut translation appeared. In addition, snowmobiles could travel faster, but not as far, as dog teams, and the machines made noise that could alert seals and bears of an approaching hunter. Inuit also noted that qimmiit were integrated into hunting by assisting with the location of seal holes in the ice, providing advance warning of cracks in the ice and of polar bears, guiding hunters towards home in whiteouts, and helping with polar bear hunting. As a last resort, qimmiit could also be eaten by hunters when supplies ran out.

The introduction of snowmobiles altered hunting patterns. Speed triumphed over stealth when hunting polar bear and caribou. The need to hunt for dog food gave way to the need to hunt for ivory and skins that Inuit traded for cash, which in turn was spent on gasoline, parts, and replacement snowmobiles. Travelling by snowmobile necessitated travelling with a partner for safety reasons in case one of the machines broke down. Traditionally Inuit hunters were free to travel on their own. The noise of the snowmobiles also caused health risks. A team of researchers from Montreal discovered in one Eastern Arctic Community, six out of ten people had suffered partial hearing loss because of the constant use of snowmobiles. Almost 83% of men in the community suffered from at least partial hearing loss by the early 1970s.

Inuit Inquiries

The shooting of large numbers of qimmiit began in Qikiqtaaluk no later than 1957, and it was never a secret in the region. Inuit at Iqaluit spoke candidly about their losses to anthropologist Toshio Yatsushiro, who published their words in a national magazine in 1962. Local politician Bryan Pearson was vocal too, sharing his thoughts with the mass-circulation *Star Weekly* in 1966, and again in the NWT's Legislative Assembly in 1973. By then very few dog teams were left. The killings were not prominently discussed during the decades when major events such as the Nunavut Land Claim and the creation of Nunavut were consuming public attention. Yet individuals guarded their memories. Often, as witnesses told the QTC, those memories were silenced by feelings of shame and hurt.

Public discussion resumed in February 1999, at a meeting in Iqaluit of community members with senior RCMP officials. A month later, at a Makivik Corporation meeting, Nunavimmiut brought their memories forward and called for an inquiry, an apology, and compensation. The QIA quickly repeated this call on behalf of Nunavummiut. The QIA also considered bringing charges against the RCMP and federal government for the negligence and general harm done by limiting people's mobility. However, the Iqaluit meeting in February was already stirring a backlash among retired RCMP members, who vigorously denied reports of misbehaviour in the 1950s and 1960s.

Over the next five years, major Inuit organizations in Nunavik and Qikiqtaaluk interviewed Elders, interpreted the evidence surrounding the "dog slaughter," and developed strategies for redress for the harm caused by the government's past failures to consult or to respect its own fiduciary obligations to Inuit. In 2000, the campaign became national: Organizations wrote to federal and Quebec Ministers and to Members of Parliament. By the end of that year, leaders of Inuit organizations were convinced that the killings had been centrally organized and all parties involved took their respective positions. The Canadian Government admitted that some qimmiit had been killed, but insisted this was always justified on the grounds of public health and safety. Inuit insisted that healthy qimmiit were killed, that the government had recklessly disregarded the importance of qimmiit to Inuit culture, and that the documentary record had been tampered with to conceal government wrongdoing.

The following years were spent on research, interviews, and quiet efforts to gather support for a public inquiry. The Inuit Circumpolar Conference supported this call in 2002. Research, interviews, and analysis continued. Increasingly close attention was given to linkages between the qimmiq shootings and the general government policy of moving people into centralized settlements. In 2005, Makivik Corporation brought the subject back to public prominence, releasing its video treatment of the period, *Echo of the Last Howl*. In short order, this caught the attention of the national press and was aired in Parliament.

In March 2005, the House of Commons Standing Committee on Aboriginal Affairs and Northern Development heard numerous Inuit witnesses describe the killing of qimmiit in the two regions between 1950 and 1970. The Standing Committee called for a public inquiry by a superior court judge "to get to the bottom of the matter." *The Nunatsiaq News* was calling for an independent inquiry as early as August 30, 2002, and on June 17, 2005 reported the generally unfavourable reaction to the government's decision to conduct an internal inquiry.

The Government of Canada did not set up the requested inquiry. Instead, it asked the RCMP to review its own actions regarding qimmiit. The Force presented a preliminary report later in 2005 and a twenty-six-page "final" report to the Minister of Public Safety in 2006. At the same time, the Force collected media reports and letters from many different sources, and carried out intensive research, gathering these into a much longer compilation of research and interviews printed the same year. The reports were concerned with issues of law enforcement and the needs of the growing non-Inuit populations, and did not consider the effect of the Ordinance on cultural practices of Inuit or the rules of Inuit society during the period of greatest disruption. Inuit recognized that the RCMP's investigation of itself was part of a badly flawed process, and only a handful of individuals provided information. Instead, in 2007, QIA created a more open process, the QTC, to hear witnesses and investigate records of the times, seeking a more inclusive social purpose than the RCMP report. There has been little response from federal officials.

Makivik Corporation and Quebec took a similar direction, commissioning a retired superior court judge, the Honourable Jean-Jacques Croteau, to inquire into the dog killings in Quebec. Judge Croteau's findings mirrored those of the QTC: Reports of widespread killings were substantially true, the killings began around military establishments, and elsewhere they were linked to the establishment of schools and the sedentarization of the people. The main difference was the overlap between federal and provincial government roles, with the Sureté Québec taking a lead in shooting qimmiit between 1963 and 1965. Judge Croteau found that the concentration of people in fewer and fewer settlements made the number of loose qimmiit problematic, but that the government's process of getting rid of them was cruel and violated the rights of Inuit. Makivik Corporation and the province of Quebec signed a redress agreement on August 8, 2011.

Inuit have always understood the killing of qimmiit within a pattern of government domination and interference with Inuit decision-making. This was evident from the 1999 Iqaluit meeting, and, though often missing from headlines, from the framework for the QTC's work. The importance of the broader picture is therefore made clear in both the mandate and the Final Report of the QTC Commissioner, who recommended that:

> The Government of Canada formally acknowledge that the high rates of suicide, substance abuse, incarceration, and social dysfunction among Inuit are in part symptoms of intergenerational trauma caused by historical wrongs. This symbolic first step will clearly signal its commitment to help correct the mistakes it made over many decades.

QTC Final Report

Achieving Saimaqatigiingniq

Editor's Note: This final report has been preserved in its entirety in order to provide the fullest possible picture of the work undertaken by the Commission. Readers may notice some repetition of material presented in other chapters. This report has not been abridged from what was presented to the QIA Board of Directors in 2010. For this reason, too, the footnotes have been preserved in the text, as they were originally presented.

About This Report

From 2007 to 2010, the Qikiqtani Truth Commission (QTC) interviewed almost three hundred and fifty witnesses during public hearings, reviewed one hundred and thirty interviews taped by the Qikiqtani Inuit Association (QIA) between 2004 and 2006, and amassed an authoritative collection of historical documentation about the relationships among Inuit and governments from 1950 to 1975. Through this work, it documented in detail many of the decisions, actions, and consequences that led to the social and economic transformation of the Baffin Region.

The primary product of the QTC is this report, written by the Commissioner James Igloliorte. *QTC Final Report: Achieving Saimaqatigiingniq* was formally presented to the QIA at its 2010 Annual General Meeting on October 20, 2010. Other products from the QTC's work, including a video version of *Achieving Saimaqatigiingniq*, digitized collections of archival materials, and supplementary reports, will be made available as records are processed and reports are finalized.

Acknowledgements

The Qikiqtani Truth Commission (QTC) is indebted to the many men and women who attended our meetings and opened their homes to give their testimonies. People welcomed us warmly into their communities and spoke freely and honestly about their lives. Without their testimonies we would not have been able to fully appreciate what happened to Inuit during this period of immense transition. They also provided us with very thoughtful and constructive feedback and suggestions regarding the kind of recommendations that would promote reconciliation between Inuit and government.

The executive and board members of the Qikiqtani Inuit Association (QIA) were both responsive to the QIA membership and visionary in deciding to establish and fund this Commission. We are grateful for their consistent support over the past three years. In particular, we would like to thank Terry Audla, the late Thomasie Alikatuktuk, Joe Attagutaluk, and Pilipuusi Paneak, who all took a personal interest in our work and actively encouraged the QIA Board to make our goals achievable. The Board's decision to commission an independent and comprehensive analysis of the recent history of the Qikiqtani Inuit, as well as recommendations for future action, is to us a true demonstration of Inuit self-governance in action. I would also like to thank Nunavut Tunngavik Incorporated for its generous financial support, which was indispensable to the Commission's work.

I take great pleasure in giving due credit for the Commission's success to Madeleine Redfern, the Executive Director of the QTC. This Inuk, whom I taught so tentatively in her first course at the Akitsiraq Law School, and who subsequently articled with Madam Justice Charron of the Supreme Court of Canada, has developed into a first-rate professional and has been successful in all that she has undertaken in her career. Her meticulous attention to detail, prodigious mind, high moral standards, and passionate stance on Inuit governance issues have made my job as Commissioner an easy one to fulfill. Thank you, Madeleine, for all that you have done.

Our consultants at Contentworks supplied us with their historical research and report-writing expertise, as well as invaluable administrative support. They were sounding boards for our ideas, and partners in discussions of what we learned from our hearings and research. Truly, they were "the mouse that roared"—small in size but mighty in results, with a commitment to excellence. To Julie Harris and her staff—Ryan Shackleton, Joan Bard Miller, Philip Goldring, Carole Cancel, Teresa Iacobelli, and Gail Cummings—we are eternally thankful for and appreciative of your excellent work.

Paul Crowley, special legal advisor for the Commission and legal counsel for QIA, assisted us in our first year with his intimate knowledge and histories of QIA and Nunavut Tunngavik Incorporated. His attention to detail as well as his guidance on the big picture of the work of the Commission cannot be overstated. His decisive and confident manner allowed us to carry on despite his premature departure to other work opportunities in the Mediterranean.

The Community Liaison Officers under the guidance of Joanasie Akumalik, our executive assistant, ensured that we were met, transported, and guided in each community, and that the necessary public service announcements were made prior to and during our visits. Joanasie had the additional task of being the Commissioner's Inuk voice as he detailed the work and duties of the Commission in each community.

Our team of professional Inuit translators and interpreters from the QIA office as well as the freelance community showed to us the respect for language and its nuances and the amazing mental dexterity that interpreters and translators possess. We personally thank Jay Arnakak, Julia Demcheson, Mali Curley, Leetia Janes, Suzie Napayok, and Elisapee Ikkidulak for their invaluable service.

We decided, quite correctly, that we needed a clear, professional voice to gather the diverse perspectives of the Commission's testimonies and historical reports in the Final Report. Brian Cameron was brought on board to help me take on this monumental and important task, and we have not been disappointed. His empathetic manner, depth of experience, and quick mind, and the quality of the final product, have proven the wisdom of adding him to the Commission team.

We would also like to thank Maureen van Dreumel, exchange communications. Her ability to translate our extensive work on this pivotal time of transition into plain language helped us clearly communicate the Commission's work, findings, and recommendations to our stakeholders and to the public.

We employed SHOK media to produce high-quality public service announcements for our return into the communities for our consultations and our video report. The videographers, technical wizards, and travelling companions—Mark Poirier, David Poisey, Joelie Sanguya, and others—were an unobtrusive yet professional presence at our hearings, which allowed the true words and emotions of witnesses to be preserved for all time. Their work was ably complemented by the skills of script writer Stewart Dudley, Stiff Sentences.

Staff at numerous archives and libraries provided our research team with expert guidance, research support, and copyright permissions. In particular, the diligent efforts of the staff at Library and Archives Canada, the NWT Archives, the RCMP Archives Management Section, the Anglican Archives, and Archives Deschâtelets were indispensable to the Commission's research.

We very much appreciated the support provided by the RCMP and Commissioner William J. S. Elliott. This included granting the Commission access to RCMP archives and the right to publish documents and images. The RCMP has expressed its desire for a better, more co-operative, and mutually supportive relationship with Inuit, and I look forward to its future efforts towards achieving saimaqatigiingniq.

All research materials, as well as community testimony files, were compiled in a research database. This collection, which will provide future access and use of the materials by all Inuit and other Canadians, would not have been possible without the work of Tim Wayne, Xist Inc. who acted as its architect and provided ongoing technical support.

During the course of the interviews and throughout the research conducted in support of the Commission, many individuals have generously contributed their time and knowledge. These individuals have provided the QTC with a special insight into government, academic, and HBC involvement in the Qikiqtani region's past. The QTC would like to thank all of those individual contributors.

The Walter and Duncan Gordon Foundation provided the Commission with a substantial grant over a two-year period. This funding enabled the Commission to film the public hearings and private interviews, and to conduct archival research for the production of the final report.

The Inuit business community assisted the work of the Commission through generous discounts for all our travel from First Air, Air Inuit, and Unaalik Aviation/Kenn Borek Aviation. The support and professionalism of their staff made our work all the more enjoyable.

James Igloliorte
Commissioner

About this Commission

The QTC was established by the QIA to create a more accurate and balanced history of the decisions and events that affected Inuit living in the Qikiqtani region in the decades following 1950, and to document the impacts on Inuit life. Some of the changes imposed on Inuit in these years were relocations from ilagiit nunagivaktangat[1] to permanent settlements; the deaths of qimmiit,[2] which reduced their ability to hunt and support their families; the removal of Inuit children from families for extended periods of time; and the tragic separation of families due to the lack of medical services in the North. The QTC's mandate specifically excluded the High Arctic relocations and residential schools issues. The relocations were examined by the Royal Commission on Aboriginal Peoples and the schools are the subject of the ongoing Truth and Reconciliation Commission of Canada.[3]

In addition to the historical component of its mandate, the Commission was charged to begin a broader truth and reconciliation process that will promote healing for those who suffered historic wrongs, and heal relations between Inuit and governments by providing an opportunity for acknowledgement and forgiveness. Qikiqtani Inuit are seeking saimaqatigiingniq,

---

1 For the purposes of the QTC reports, the English term "camp" has been dropped in favour of the Inuktitut term ilagiit nunagivaktangat (plural: nunagivaktangit), which means "a place used regularly or seasonally by Inuit for hunting, harvesting, and/or gathering." It also includes special places, such as burial sites of loved ones, or sites with abundant game.

2 For the purposes of the QTC reports, the English term "Inuit sled dogs" has been dropped in favour of the Inuktitut term qimmiit.

3 I refer to relocations outside the scope of RCAP's studies and to all types of schools in the larger context of Inuit education.

which means a new relationship "when past opponents get back together, meet in the middle, and are at peace."

Our investigation had two closely related activities. The first was to gather testimonies about events between 1950 and 1975 from Inuit who had lived through this difficult period, as well as from their children, who continue to remember the suffering of their parents and other relatives. To that end, I, with QTC staff, travelled to all thirteen communities in the Qikiqtani region between January 2008 and May 2009, and invited all interested residents to share their memories and feelings about how their lives had changed. We also held hearings for the Inuit community in Ottawa, and paid return visits to all communities in early 2010 to report on our findings and ask for comments on our proposed recommendations. Including interviews that the QIA had already conducted in 2004, we had testimonies from approximately three hundred and fifty individuals.[4] Our hearings were conducted with more flexibility than normal legal proceedings, but to emphasize the seriousness of our task, I asked all witnesses to affirm that they would tell the truth to the best of their knowledge. I also respected the decision made by a few individuals to keep their experiences private.[5]

In addition to learning about events and impacts through Inuit testimonies, we also completed an extensive archival research program and interviewed Qallunaat[6] who worked in the region during this period. Among the people interviewed were several retired RCMP officers, government officials, and academic researchers.

---

4 The QTC accessed one hundred and forty-four transcripts and/or tapes of QIA interviews.

5 All of these testimonies had to do with sexual abuse, often during childhood, at residential schools, sanatoria, or in communities. Whenever possible these testimonies are included in the database, but the identities of the individuals have been protected by the use of pseudonyms.

6 Qallunaat is an Inuktitut term that describes anyone who is not of Inuit ancestry.

The testimonies and historical investigations have been used to write histories of each of the thirteen Qikiqtani communities (most have not previously been the subject of such detailed histories), and histories of twelve topics of importance to the QIA and the Commission, including relocations, alcohol, development, education, housing, the RCMP, and qimmiit.

The Commission has also developed a database to catalogue all the archival and oral history information collected. Information to be made available in the database includes transcripts and translations, as well as audio and video materials. Once completed, the database will be accessible through the QIA until a final repository and format are determined.

This report is divided into two parts. The first summarizes what I and my QTC colleagues learned from listening to Inuit testimonies, and from the Commission's archival research. It also presents an overview of my main recommendations. The second part is a detailed discussion of opportunities for change that will help heal the wounds that remain from this period of cultural, social, and economic transformation, promote recognition of the worth of Inuit culture and reconciliation with Qallunaat institutions, and contribute to numerous efforts being made by Inuit to take control of their futures from now on.

What We Learned

For many years now, Inuit elders in the Qikiqtani region have been haunted by a deep sense of loss, shame, and puzzlement as they remember how their lives changed in the decades after 1950, when Qallunaat began arriving in large numbers. Before then, most Inuit families lived on the land in dynamic and tightly knit kinship groups ranging from five to thirty people. They moved between ilagiit nunagivaktangit by dog team or boat, depending on the season, in pursuit of wildlife that supplied them with most of their needs—food, clothing, and shelter. From the time of their first contacts with explorers and whalers, and increasingly after the establishment of the Hudson's Bay Company, Inuit hunted animals—primarily fox and seal—to trade for rifles, ammunition, and other southern goods. They came into the year-round settlements established by traders, the RCMP, or the churches one or two times each year to trade, socialize, and participate in religious services and holiday festivities.

By 1975, all but a few Inuit families lived in government-created permanent settlements, and many of them felt that their lives had become worse, not better. The decision to give up the traditional way of life was almost never an easy one, and once made, it proved to be irreversible. Inuit made enormous sacrifices by moving into settlements, living in permanent housing, giving up their qimmiit, sending their children to school, or accepting wage employment. Once they had made their decision, they discovered that government assurances of a sufficient number of jobs and better living conditions were illusory in many cases. Looking around, Inuit often felt and saw despair as they, their family members, and their neighbours struggled to adjust to circumstances beyond their control, even though some received benefits from living in settlements, such as less risk in daily life, better health care, and options to work for wages rather than hunt. Settlement life often imposed a new form of poverty,[7] and hindered access to the land and the country food[8] that nourished them.

As I visited their communities over the last two years, Qikiqtani Inuit spoke to me in honest and straightforward terms about the day-to-day challenges and satisfactions of living as hunters and gatherers. Their deep

7 The term "poverty" should be considered in the context of the period. It was possible for Inuit families in ilagiit nunagivaktangit to feel they were living comfortably, even though they had very little income and would be considered extremely "poor" by western standards. Inuit in settlements, however, needed cash income from wage employment or social benefits to meet daily needs.

8 Country food is locally available and produced food by Inuit (e.g., seal, caribou, berries, polar bear, fish, etc.)

connections to each other and to the land sustained a rich culture and language. Extensive and specialized Inuit knowledge and skills passed down from generation to generation ensured their survival in the Arctic environment. While life on the land was never easy, they remembered the autonomy and self-sufficiency that were lost when families moved into settlements. They also spoke passionately and eloquently about the ties of kinship that united members of each ilagiit nunagivaktangat. Each person within a kinship group was valued for his or her contribution to the group's well-being and success. Excellence was highly respected, whether it was in hunting, problem-solving, leadership or sewing. At the same time, a tradition of humility dictated that gifted individuals should not boast or otherwise demonstrate pride. While conflicts were inevitable, they were minimized or resolved as quickly as possible, since they had the potential to put the group at risk.

In times of real hardship, knowledge that the hard times would pass and that the game would return gave people the will to continue, and find comfort and familiarity in the changing seasons. As Pauloosie Veevee of Pangnirtung explained:

> At times during winter months we would occasionally go hungry but not starve... It seemed like a happy life as long as we had food in our mouths and warm clothing to wear, we were content with it. Our standards today are much bigger now compared to what we had then. Today we have excessive possessions and we are not happy with our lives and we struggle with life when we have all the conveniences now.[9]

The Inuit who spoke to us wanted to tell us and all Canadians how their lives had changed dramatically, but they also wanted explanations for the changes that continue to affect them and their families today. How can

9 Pauloosie Veevee. Interview with the Qikiqtani Inuit Association. (July 1, 2006) Pangnirtung. [QIPA14].

a hunter who witnesses his qimmiit destroyed by government authorities cope with a loss of his self-worth? How can his wife and children cope with his loss? How do you deal with the interpersonal animosities that arise when you live in a settlement with ten or twenty times the number of people who lived in your ilagiit nunagivaktangat, and with many of whom you have no ties of kinship? Does the removal without a decent leave-taking of a loved one from your family outweigh the cure of a deadly disease? Was this the only choice Inuit had? Is it possible that one official could have exerted such awe and fear that people followed life-altering orders?

These are just some of the profound questions and observations presented to the QTC by Qikiqtani Inuit. Some were moved to tears by the memories of this traumatic period in their lives—tears that sprang from reliving grief and loss, or from a sense of relief at finally telling their history or giving a voice to the experiences of their parents and grandparents.

The depth of emotion also came from feelings of failure and guilt for mistakes that they believed that they had made as parents, husbands, and wives. Time and again, we were told the value of having accounts of events shared for the first time to an official Inuit-led body, which greatly aided in unburdening a heavy heart. There was also visible evidence that many of the speakers were at peace after testifying, or on their way towards healing.

In the words of Jaykolasie Killiktee of Pond Inlet:

> [We] were forced to undergo a forceful and traumatic period in our lives. I am grateful that the Commission was able to come to Pond Inlet and that this process has been well thought out. This very painful experience that we've held close to our bosom for many years is very difficult to speak of but I am so happy for the opportunity to talk about it. Thank you for giving Inuit that opportunity, and especially thank you for giving me the opportunity.[10]

10 Jaykolasie Killiktee. Testimony before the Qikiqtani Truth Commission. (10 December 2008) Pond Inlet. [QTPI10].

Inuit knew that this was probably a once-in-a-lifetime chance to ensure that their experiences became part of the historical narrative. They expressed great faith that the Commission's reports would provide a more balanced account of what had happened and how Inuit were affected.

THE FRAMEWORK OF CHANGE: GOVERNMENT AND INUIT

The Canadian government was the primary agent of the changes that swept the Qikiqtani region between 1950 and 1975. Government officials who planned and implemented these changes were part of a generation that believed the future would be better than the past, that Canada was a decent and progressive country, that education and training were keys to a better life, and that what they considered to be the "primitive" life and cultural traditions of Canada's Aboriginal groups were likely to end due to forces beyond the control of governments. With this cast of mind, government policy was to make the North more like the South and Inuit more like southern Canadians. While most officials convinced themselves that they were acting in the best interests of Inuit, their plans were frequently mismanaged or underfunded, and were designed and implemented without consulting Inuit. All too often their careers, the needs of southern Canadians, and the goal of government efficiency came first.

Before the Second World War, government had a very limited interest or presence in the region. In most localities, RCMP officers were the only year-round government representatives. In addition to law-enforcement duties, they were expected to keep official records of the Inuit population, to visit and report on conditions in ilagiit nunagivaktangit at least once a year, and, when necessary, to deliver relief supplies to people in distress or long-term poverty. The police presence was also intended to assert Canadian sovereignty over the region.

During the war, American military personnel moved into the region to develop and operate bases for transporting aircraft to Britain. Their reports on poor living conditions and lack of medical services among Inuit near the bases were a national and international embarrassment to the Canadian Government, and helped focus the attention of officials on the area. The development of DEW (Distant Early Warning) Line stations in the 1950s increased the government's stake in the region and directly resulted in the establishment of a year-round settlement at Hall Beach, the concentration of services at Qikiqtarjuaq, and the remarkable growth of Iqaluit (then Frobisher Bay) as an American and Canadian military base, and later as a government administrative centre.

Government also began taking a greater interest in the Qikiqtani region for its resource potential. Before the early 1950s, the federal government undertook extensive aerial mapping and mineral resource surveys, which covered most of the Arctic. In addition to developing services at Iqaluit, it built runways and weather stations at selected Arctic locations. These investments were expected to provide new jobs to replace the traditional land-based economy for a portion of the Inuit population, to reduce social assistance costs, and to generate wealth for the whole country.

In keeping with a new belief in an expanded role for the state in improving the lives of all Canadians, Ottawa increased its involvement in almost all aspects of Inuit life, including housing, education, health care, and employment. Early in this period, one high-ranking official wrote that his job was "to hasten the day when in every respect the Eskimos can take their own places in the new kind of civilization which we—and they—are building in their country."[11] The "new kind of civilization" never emerged—instead, the imperfect institutions of southern Canada were transplanted to the North, without due consideration of the different needs and traditions of those who lived

11 Northwest Territories Archives, Alexander Stevenson fonds, N-1992-023, Box 17, File 7, Policy—Inuit 1935–1959, item: letter from R.A.J. Phillips, Chief of the Arctic Division, Canada to Bishop (Anglican) Donald Marsh, 16 December 1957.

there. In the process, however, some opportunities opened that allowed Inuit to adapt their own styles of leadership and coordination to the new situation.

The changes imposed on Inuit by the Government of Canada in order to achieve this goal were rapid and dramatic—this was not a gradual progression from a traditional to a modern way of life, but a complete transformation. Inuit were not consulted about these changes, and many never knew why they were imposed on them, and in such a short period of time. For their part, the agencies of the Government of Canada that were responsible for the transformation—primarily Indian and Northern Affairs Canada and the RCMP—are still not fully aware of their own history in the Arctic or the effects of their decisions and actions.

FROM ILAGIIT NUNAGIVAKTANGIT TO YEAR-ROUND SETTLEMENTS

In 1950, the population of over two thousand Inuit lived mostly in small, kin-based groups in over one hundred locations across the Baffin region. These ilagiit nunagivaktangit were chosen for the access they gave, seasonally or year-round, to favourable sites for hunting and harvesting. In 1981, four times as many people lived in just thirteen permanent settlements. A few settlements were located near good hunting and harvesting areas because they had originated as trading posts. Most, however, did not provide good access to game because the single most important criterion for government was that they were accessible by sea or would fit into planned air routes. Inuit have suffered, and continue to suffer, from this lack of attention to their hunting needs.

The creation and growth of the settlements was tied to Ottawa's plan to educate Inuit children, provide medical treatment for the aged and infirm, and distribute social transfers, especially Family Allowances, welfare, and Old Age Pensions. In 1947 Ottawa created the position of "welfare teacher" which, as the name implied, combined the delivery of diverse social services with instruction of children in day schools. In 1955 the government also placed Northern Service Officers in two communities—Iqaluit and Cape Dorset—with another for the DEW Line. The Northern Service Officers developed economic projects, took over welfare programs from the school teachers, and reported back to Ottawa on general social and economic conditions. In some localities, before the appointment of a Northern Service Officer, the teacher might be responsible for individual and community welfare.

Between 1958 and 1963, government agencies rapidly appeared in all Qikiqtani region communities. Schools were set up in Resolute (1958); Igloolik, Qikiqtarjuaq, Pond Inlet, Clyde River, and Sanikiluaq (1960); and Grise Fiord and Arctic Bay (1962). With support from the federal government's Eskimo Loan Program, co-operatives were established in Cape Dorset (1959); Grise Fiord and Resolute (1960); and Igloolik (1963).

At first, government policy-makers expected that Inuit hunters from the ilagiit nunagivaktangit would visit settlements for short periods to trade, receive services, or drop off their children at school hostels, before returning to the land. By the early 1960s, however, more Inuit were effectively living in settlements, even if they arrived with the intention of remaining only as long as necessary for a child to complete schooling or for a relative to return from health treatment in the South.

Every Inuk remembers when he or she moved to a settlement. Those born in settlements know the stories of their parents. These moves and the consequences were a central theme in Inuit testimonies to this Commission.

Some Inuit families moved voluntarily to the settlements, often for employment or access to health care, or because the government was offering housing at very low rents. As Moses Kasarnak of Pond Inlet explained, "We were directly told that if we moved we would get a house and that it would have a table and dishes. It was like Christmas that we were going to get all these."[12]

---

12 Moses Kasarnak. Interview with the Qikiqtani Inuit Association. (February 17, 2005) Pond Inlet [QIPI21].

Many other Inuit moved to avoid being separated from children attending school, or to be with other family members who had moved for any of the above reasons.

However, other families moved because they felt coerced by government authorities. Thomas Kublu of Igloolik was one of many witnesses who remembered moving because he was ordered to do so:

> In the winter of 1962, the police travelling by dog team coming from Arctic Bay passed by our camp and told us that we have to move to Pond Inlet to enable the children to attend school. I believe the school in Pond Inlet had been operating since 1958. When the authorities like the police and Social and Family Services officials ordered us to move to Pond Inlet, we had no say and we had to comply with the orders from the authorities. We feared going against their orders and were scared of the authorities. This was the case with all Qallunaat who held the power and positions in the new settlement life. So we moved to Pond Inlet in April 1962.[13]

Many witnesses also told me that they were evacuated or relocated with little or no notice, and as result, they did not have the chance to pack and bring their belongings into the settlements. While Inuit had few possessions, those they did have were extremely important to them, and took a long time to procure or make. Without these items, it was difficult to resume hunting from settlements. Angawasha Poisey, who lived at Kivitoo, recalled the anguish caused by the government when her entire community[14] of about thirty people was evacuated with no warning to Qikiqtarjuaq. Government officials had previously argued that the community was no longer sustainable, but Inuit leaders would not give in to repeated pressures to

13 Thomas Kublu. Testimony read before the Qikiqtani Truth Commission. (January 26, 2009) Igloolik [QTIG19].

14 Kivitoo was a community, not an ilagiit nunagivaktangat.

move to Qikiqtarjuaq. Shortly after the tragic deaths of three prominent hunters, however, the government forcibly relocated remaining individuals, even while the families were still in mourning.

> Three days after my in-law, my uncle, died of hypothermia by accident on the sea ice, a plane came in. They didn't even warn us . . . They told us that we would have something to eat and a place to stay. They asked us to bring our cups and bedding. They did not even tell us to bring food because there would be enough to feed us. My in-law hid some tea and some food in the bedding. I was pregnant. They told us that there would be plenty of food and a place to stay . . . perhaps they should have given us some time to grieve and to accept the fact that we were moving. They should have told us in advance and let us prepare what to bring.[15]

Angawasha and others believed they would be returning home, so they stored all their belongings in their qarmaqs. When they came back to collect them, the qarmaqs had been bulldozed and/or burned with all their contents, including their personal items and essential hunting gear.

A few years after the closing of Kivitoo, the nearby community of Padloping was also closed and the thirty-four Inuit living there moved to Qikiqtarjuaq. A school teacher at Padloping at the time has written that the government was determined to close the community in the interests of administrative efficiency, and that the residents were coerced into the move. People who spoke to the QTC agree. Jacopie Nuqingaq told me: "They came in to ask us and pressure us to move . . . We were scared of Qallunaat so we did whatever they said . . . When we got here, our dogs were slaughtered and we had no choice."[16]

---

15 Angawasha Poisey. Testimony before the Qikiqtani Truth Commission. (September 8, 2008) Clyde River [QTCR02].

16 Jacopie Nuqingaq. Testimony before the Qikiqtani Truth Commission [QTQK02].

Another witness, Joshua Alookie, said his parents were promised running water, good housing, good schooling, and employment opportunities in Qikiqtarjuaq. Mr. Alookie's parents had to wait almost twenty years after relocating before they had indoor plumbing.

According to archival records, administrative efficiency was also the reason for the closing of a third community, South Camp on Belcher Island, and the relocation of its inhabitants to North Camp (Sanikiluaq) in 1969–70. Witnesses who testified to the QTC told me they felt enormous pressure to move quickly to Sanikiluaq. No assistance was offered by the government. People remember that some groups became separated, while others became stuck in the ice or had to carry a boat over land. With no radios, limited food rations, and boats laden with relocatees (including Elders and young children), the move was dangerous. Upon arrival in Sanikiluaq, the promised housing was not available. Many of the relocatees had left what little possessions they had behind, expecting the necessities of life to be provided for them in Sanikiluaq. Many also believed that the move would be temporary. All relocatees felt that they had not been properly informed or prepared for a permanent move.

Lottie Arratutainaq told me: "We moved here with our clothes and left everything behind ... as if we were coming back. When we moved here there was no assistance of any kind ... So it was a very sad event for me."[17]

The circumstances of relocations varied, but sadness and regret were expressed by virtually all Inuit who testified about their experiences of moving during this period.

HOUSING IN THE SETTLEMENTS

Whether or not they moved voluntarily, many Inuit told me that the promises about a "better life" that had been made to them were not kept. Some

17 Testimony in Inuktitut.

Inuit who moved into settlements, giving up their life on the land on the basis of those promises and assurances, especially for "free" or low-cost housing. Housing was a frequent source of disappointment: An insufficient number of houses were built, and these were often of poor quality and unsuitable for the Arctic environment. Beginning in the 1950s, government officials had identified poor housing as a leading cause of the extraordinary rates of illness and poor chances of recovery. Reports of "slum conditions" by visitors to the Arctic were an embarrassment to the government, and helped to spur efforts to develop well-built and affordable houses. However, while housing was the target of the largest government investment directed at Inuit from 1959 to 1975, the resulting programs were poorly planned and implemented, with little consultation with Inuit.

Some Inuit who spoke to us said that they appreciated the chance to live in permanent frame houses. Many others said that when they moved to a settlement, no housing was available, and they had to board with friends or family in already crowded houses, live in tents, or hastily build shacks from scraps left over from the building of government buildings. Apphia Kiliktee of Pond Inlet told me about one such experience of living in a dwelling that was not appropriate for life in the Arctic and feeling poor:

> I don't know exactly what the year was but I was about 6–7 years old. We had to move to Pond Inlet from Mount Herodier. A teacher came down to our camp and told us that we had to go to school . . . Knowing there was no housing in Pond Inlet, we ended up in a tent near the river. The whole winter we stayed in the tent. It was so difficult for us. We didn't have any food to eat. Every morning we woke up to everything frozen . . . We left everything at our camp. We didn't have anything in the tent except for sleeping bags, pot, cups. All I remember is my grandmother trying to use a tea pot to cook with. And that was for the whole winter. Our grandpa in the winter would try to pick up some cardboard boxes

> and put them in around and inside the tent, and when we had enough snow, he would build an iglu around the tent to keep us warm. It was difficult for us, not knowing, coming to the community like that and not having housing.[18]

Apphia and her family finally got what was known as a matchbox house, after about two years in the tent. Twenty family members lived in that one-room, twelve-by-twenty-four-foot house, sleeping on the floor.

In most of the Qikiqtani communities I visited, Inuit testified that they were promised housing free or at very low rents, and that these promises were not kept. In many cases, witnesses told me they had been promised they would pay only between $2 and $6 a month in rent, but that the rent was subsequently increased. Rental contracts, legal terminology, and financial concepts such as mortgages and cost-of-living increases were unfamiliar to Inuit. Various attempts were made to explain aspects of the housing program, such as the benefits, responsibilities, and true costs of occupying housing. However, nobody in the federal or territorial bureaucracies appears to have been given responsibility for explaining the entire program directly to Inuit in Inuktitut, from the delivery and construction of housing to payments, rents, maintenance, and ownership options.[19]

---

18 Testimony in Inuktitut.

19 Explanations about the rules concerning the terms and cost of housing were confusing to everyone—bureaucrats and Inuit. Until the 1970s, most Inuit had little if any disposable income. Those on social welfare were effectively given "free" or fixed low-rent housing, since government provided sufficient income to cover the monthly housing cost. Inuit also saw discrepancies between their housing and those of government workers, especially in Iqaluit. Officials acknowledged that concepts about ownership, renting, subsidies, and costs were inadequately conveyed during training sessions with Inuit in the 1960s. Compounding normal linguistic challenges was the reality that many terms, such as "regular employment" and "market value," were almost irrelevant in the Qikiqtani region. Similarly, the distinction between cost-of-living increases and rent

SETTLEMENT LIFE AND SUBSTANCE ABUSE

The settlements, especially Iqaluit, brought people from many parts of the Qikiqtani region together. These government-created entities, controlled by Qallunaat, left Inuit utterly dependent on outside institutions. This produced—and continues to produce—unbalanced and unhealthy power relations between Inuit and government, including Qallunaat officials. Qallunaat usually limited their relations with Inuit, working and socializing mainly amongst themselves.

All aspects of Inuit daily life and social relations changed in the settlements. Traditional marriage practices and adoptions were challenged by many officials. Settlements seemed crowded because many neighbours were also strangers—a situation that was completely new for Inuit. As Annie Shappa of Arctic Bay remembered: "When we were in the outpost camp, we had this tradition: We ate together, lived together in one place. The family system that was harmonious was lost when we moved to the community."[20]

Even within kinship groups, uneven access to Qallunaat officials and to jobs, with associated benefits such as housing, created divisions between Inuit. Some families were able to move into larger houses and receive benefits more quickly than others. Ironically, families led by the best hunters could be the poorest in a settlement because they had waited longer to enter wage employment or to accept benefits. Some Elders recalled feeling "useless" when they arrived in a settlement and women said that their husbands and sons, in particular, were unable to reconcile their cultural beliefs and values with their desire to provide for their families with settlement life. As I discuss below, many men were unable to hunt after their qimmiit were killed because they were simply stuck in the settlement. Others were fortunate

---

increases, the effect of changes in employment status in determining rents, and obligations concerning maintenance and repair, were not fully appreciated by lease-holders.

20 Testimony in Inuktitut.

enough to be able to share dog teams with close family members and, by the late 1960s, some people were using snowmobiles. Those Inuit who lacked qimmiit or snowmobiles to access the land felt that life in the settlements was a form of imprisonment. For many people, alcohol and gambling provided a temporary, but often unhealthy, distraction from boredom and worries about life in general. By the end of this period, illegal drugs were also entering settlements.

Settlement life brought many Inuit into regular contact with alcohol for the first time. Prior to this, an Inuk living on the land had limited access to alcohol, which was controlled entirely by Qallunaat. From the time of their arrival in the Arctic in the 1920s, RCMP officers applied provisions of the Indian Act to Inuit, making it illegal to give or sell alcohol to Inuit. A legal ruling in 1959 clarified that Inuit were not subject to the alcohol provisions of the Indian Act and that laws concerning alcohol in the Northwest Territories applied equally to Inuit and all individuals not subject to the Act.

Not surprisingly, most Inuit who had access to liquor enjoyed beer and spirits on occasion. The social and cultural context of drinking, however, was completely new to Inuit. The day-to-day messages they received about alcohol and underlying issues such as boredom and a feeling of displacement contributed to the number of incidents of excessive drinking. As examples, there were few places where Inuit could drink safely and comfortably in groups. Houses were small and military bars were restricted to base personnel. Inuit generally saw Qallunaat drinking heavily to get drunk, not as part of relaxed social situations. Drunkenness was often a legitimate defense for bad behaviour. In addition, the social controls that existed in tightly knit ilagiit nunagivaktangit were weakened and were difficult to apply in the settlement context. For all these reasons and more, some Inuit began drinking too much and too often, endangering their own health and compromising the health and happiness of their families. The response from officials was often moralistic and racist. In 1962, for instance, an official suggested that drunkenness among Inuit was the result of flaws in personality, rather than a symptom of changing social conditions or cultural experience. He asserted that the "trouble is not with recognizing or even acknowledging drinking as a problem but rather with finding within themselves the power to control their drinking."[21] Many officials ignored the equally devastating consequences of Qallunaat drunkenness on Inuit and did little to control the importation of alcohol (and later drugs) into the settlements.

No matter what the cause of drinking, however, by the 1970s, when almost all Inuit were living in settlements and most had access to liquor and even drugs, many families were experiencing first-hand the devastating consequences of substance abuse, including alcoholism, addiction, physical and sexual abuse, neglect of children, poverty, and death. In Iqaluit, Cape Dorset, and Resolute, in particular, drunkenness brought Inuit into increasing conflict with Qallunaat authorities, including Royal Canadian Mounted Police (RCMP) and welfare officials.

Martha Idlout of Resolute told us how her parents drank to dull the pain of their lives, and how their children suffered in turn:

> Everyone was hurting inside, not living as they should. People growing up with a lot of pain. I don't want my grandchildren to grow up with that kind of pain and end up like us. We know that we took all the substances, alcohol and drugs ... There was a bar here too, and the military as well. The whole time they would get drunk and us children would have to find a place to stay ... When men got drunk ... we would hide under houses.... Back then, the whole town would be drunk for a whole week or three days.[22]

---

21 Library and Archives Canada, RG 85, Northern Affairs Program, Series 1884-85, Vol. 1951, Files A-1000/169, pt. 1, item: F.H. Compton, Report on Trip to Frobisher, 31 January 1962, p. 9.

22 Testimony in Inuktitut.

From the beginning of the settlements, Inuit were aware of these problems. Some people attempted to control access to alcohol in their communities. Their success was limited, however, because they were only allowed to speak about rules around the product, not the programs needed to understand and address the full range of options concerning individuals, social conditions, and economic realities. Inuit laws, piqujait (rules of acceptable behaviour), and customs pittailiniq (refraining from doing what is not allowed) were challenged and mainly ignored in the settlement context. Inuit were expected to exercise self-control and to respect individual limits and rules consistent with Qallunaat social norms, even though they were given very little support to deal with the negative effects of alcohol use and they were living in a condition of dependency, subject to the paternalistic attitudes and policies of Qallunaat, which made them particularly prone to alcohol abuse.

SCHOOLING AND ITS EFFECTS ON INUIT CULTURE

In the 1950s, the Canadian government decided that all Inuit children needed to be given a formal education so that they could be brought into mainstream Canadian society and into the new jobs that an expanding northern economy was expected to provide. This decision, and the methods that were used to employ it, had profound consequences for the children, their families and communities, and Inuit culture. Some of these consequences were intentional, and some were not.

Before formal schooling was introduced, Inuit children learned the skills they needed to carry out their traditional roles by observation and practice. Inuit boys learned how to hunt, and thus feed and take care of a family, by accompanying their fathers on hunting trips. The knowledge and skills they acquired included understanding weather, navigation, and animal behaviour. Girls generally learned important skills, such as preparing food and skins, sewing clothing, making kamiks (skin boots), rearing children, and providing home care by watching and helping their mothers. As July Papatsie, an Inuit artist, told me: "We are very good with our hands because we had to be. That's why a man who did not know how to make an iglu could not marry a wife and a woman who could not sew could not marry a man."[23]

In the first sixty years of the twentieth century, attempts by outsiders to teach children reading, writing, and arithmetic were scattered and inconsistent. Following the Second World War this began to change, as informal networks of education were replaced by a new government program that aimed to make Inuit into full Canadian "citizens."

Government officials initially expected that Inuit could be convinced to place their children in school hostels for all or a portion of the school year, while parents and non-school-age siblings returned to their ilagiit nunagivaktangit. Officials were surprised to find that Inuit parents who agreed to schooling were not prepared to leave their children in the care of others. Families came to the settlement with their children, living in tents until housing was available. Gamailie Kilukishak of Pond Inlet was one of many parents who recalled: "I didn't really want to move but . . . I didn't want to be separated from my child."[24] Both the written record and Inuit testimony show that most Inuit had reason to believe that they would lose family allowances if they did not send their children to school. This was a very serious threat indeed, since family allowances had become essential to the survival of many families.

Some children were sent much farther away, to residential schools in Churchill (Manitoba), Chesterfield Inlet, Yellowknife, Inuvik, and Iqaluit. Others were sent to live with Qallunaat families in southern cities, such as Ottawa, Edmonton, and Halifax. This caused great anguish for both the

23 Testimony in Inuktitut.

24 Interview in Inuktitut.

parents and the children. Jacobie Panipak of Clyde River described watching children being taken away to Churchill:

> They had absolutely nothing, no suitcase ... They had a small, very small bag of belongings with them. I felt so much empathy for them when they left like that. I had so much love for them. I felt for them. They had hardly anything, maybe a few toys and a few belongings when they left.[25]

In the classrooms, children were taught a curriculum that often had no relevance to life in the North. Materials such as the "Dick and Jane" reading series, for example, described a world that was utterly strange to Inuit children, and one that they would likely never experience. Many who went through the educational system remembered being made to forget their Inuit roots. Kaujak Kanajuk of Pond Inlet remembers: "We weren't allowed to draw dogs or tell stories about them, anything that had something to do with being Inuk, about [iglus] or anything, as soon as we came here [to Pond Inlet]."[26]

As I mentioned, one of the goals of the education system was to allow Inuit to take their place in a new northern economy based on southern norms. Some Inuit parents agreed to have their children educated in the "Canadian" school system, believing that it would provide them with greater opportunities and prepare them for the new jobs they had been promised. This decision was not made lightly, especially since a child going to school would not have the time to acquire the knowledge and skills needed to live on the land. In practice, however, schools did not maintain the standards of southern institutions, and learning was often directed towards the limited opportunities in manual labour for men, or secretarial and institutional work for women. Even these initiatives often failed because the jobs were

---

25 Testimony in Inuktitut.

26 Testimony in Inuktitut.

too few, and the education prepared Inuit for little else within the broader world. There was no attempt to prepare Inuit for management roles so that they could participate as equals in northern development and take control of their own lives.

Another harmful element of the educational system concerned language. Children were taught exclusively in English. Many teachers saw it as an essential part of their job to forbid the use of Inuktitut both in and out of the classroom. I heard many sad and disturbing descriptions of physical and mental abuse in cases where a child was unable to learn English quickly enough, or when a child used Inuktitut among his or her peers. Geela Akulukjak of Pangnirtung wept as she related the account of her abuse:

> I was told to go to school here and I did my best to go to school. Ever since then I was scared of Qallunaat because a teacher I had would slap me, would slap the children who could not speak English, with a yard-stick; she was a woman. That always hurts me, because I couldn't speak English, she forced us to try.[27]

July Papatsie also told me of the abuse that was handed out in the school he attended:

> Children who spoke Inuktitut were punished. I remember their first punishment: They had to put their hands on the desk and got twenty slaps on the back of their hand. The second time they got thirty slaps on their bare bum in front of all the class. They were forced to eat a bar of soap. They would throw up for two or three days. They were told that it was because they spoke an evil language.[28]

---

27 Testimony in Inuktitut.

28 Testimony in Inuktitut.

The consequence of the school system was a deep cultural and generational divide between children and their parents. Children who had lost the ability to speak in Inuktitut could no longer communicate with parents and grandparents who knew little to no English. Equally serious was the loss of cultural teachings, beliefs, values, and skills, especially those needed for activities on the land. Children raised in schools with southern foods and values went home and viewed their parents' traditional values and habits with disdain, not understanding how difficult and challenging it was to make the transition from living on the land to settlement life, with all its disempowering influences. This was a cultural divide that often proved hard to repair. In the words of former residential school student Paul Quassa, "We lost that knowledge that we would have had if we had grown up with our parents." Many parents felt guilty that they had made the wrong decision by sending their children to school, since the education they received left them ill-prepared for a life of self-reliance and self-determination in either the modern wage economy or the traditional economy.

IMPORTANCE OF HUNTING

Hunting has always been a defining element of Inuit culture. Over countless generations, Inuit have developed a deep understanding of their environment and applied this understanding in laws, customs, and practices that would ensure the wise use of game resources, on which their survival depended. As one Inuit elder, Juda Taqtu, told me: "We used to have a system or rules that we had to follow within our own camp—we were told what to do, not to waste and how many to get, not to overdo it."[29]

However, these traditions were called into question as the Canadian government increased its presence in the North, and as Inuit were drawn into the settlements.

29 Testimony in Inuktitut.

In the 1950s, the government stepped up its enforcement of game laws in the Qikiqtani region. These laws addressed southern concerns about preserving and conserving species, rather than northern realities, and Inuit were not asked to contribute their extensive knowledge of Arctic game populations. The Canadian Wildlife Service (CWS) was very concerned that Inuit would overharvest animals in switching from traditional to modern technologies, including motorboats and rifles. Even though CWS officials did not have sufficient or reliable information about game populations, they developed laws with strict limits or prohibitions on the types and number of animals that could be taken, and restrictions on the dates when they could be hunted. Simeonie Kaernerk told me:

> We went through harder times when the government started controlling the wildlife we used as food and clothing. The Inuit people were told to start working. But the Inuit who went out hunting were able to go out hunting whenever they wanted. They caught whatever they saw. [Then] they were told not to do that anymore.[30]

As a result, Inuit often had to starve or hunt illegally, and hide their catches from the authorities, because otherwise they could face significant fines or threats of incarceration.

While game laws could sometimes be disregarded when required, the transition to settlement life threatened the Inuit hunting culture more profoundly. Many Inuit who came to the settlements wished to alternate wage work with periods of hunting, which would allow them to continue eating country foods and maintain their connections to the land. This meant keeping their qimmiit.

30 Testimony in Inuktitut.

KILLINGS OF QIMMIIT

Qimmiit were essential for Inuit life on the land. The care and management of a dog team was an integral part of Inuit culture, daily life, maturity, and survival. The closeness of this relationship is captured by the Inuktitut term for dog team, qimutsiit, which includes both the qimmiit and the hunter. Qimmiit allowed families to travel long distances as they moved between ilagiit nunagivaktangit. In winter, for example, they pulled hunters and their equipment for hunting and traplines; brought the game back to ilagiit nunagivaktangit or trading posts; helped locate game by scent; protected hunters against predators; assisted in polar bear hunts; and warned about sea cracks while travelling. In spring and summer they carried packs. In all conditions, they could find their way home in perilous weather and ice conditions.

Pauloosie Veevee of Pangnirtung was one of many witnesses who spoke eloquently about the importance of qimmiit:

> Not all Inuit men living in traditional camps had dog teams. If an Inuk man didn't have a team of his own, it was interpreted that he was yet not quite a man... An Inuk was judged in accordance with the dogs' performance, appearance, health, and endurance. If the dogs looked well-fed and well-mannered, the owner was seen as a great hunter and admired by others. If an Inuk man's dog team was notably happy and well-fed, they would be able to take him long distances [and were] aids to his independence and masculinity. That is how significantly important dogs were to Inuit.[31]

Between 1957 and 1975, there was a dramatic decline in the number of qimmiit in the Qikiqtani region. Many qimmiit died as a result of disease

31 Interview in Inuktitut.

outbreaks, in spite of a major effort made by the RCMP to inoculate and replace animals. Inuit knew, however, that disease could be expected and that teams could be reconstituted quickly with the remaining dogs after epidemics. Some hunters shot their qimmiit before moving into settlements, because they knew qimmiit were not allowed, or realized they would no longer have a use for them. Others abandoned their teams after they took work in the settlements, because they no longer had enough time to hunt or care for the dogs. In other cases, dog teams were left alone when their owners were suddenly sent south for medical treatment. Some qimmiit were taken over by other hunters who needed to replace their teams. The decline in the numbers of qimmiit was also due to increasing use of snowmobiles in the late 1960s, which allowed settlement-based hunters to travel greater distances in shorter times. It is also an undisputed fact that hundreds—perhaps thousands—of qimmiit were shot by the RCMP and other authorities in settlements from the mid-1950s onwards because Qallunaat considered the dogs to be a danger to inhabitants or feared they could spread dog diseases.

Although qimmiit are large and potentially dangerous animals, Inuit have successfully managed them for countless generations. In ilagiit nunagivaktangit, qimmiit were highly socialized with other qimmiit and with people. Inuit integrated qimmiit into the practices of everyday life, spirituality, and storytelling. Loose qimmiit knew their places among other dogs and within the ilagiit nunagivaktangat. They could protect themselves and others. Once they came into the settlements, however, qimmiit posed many problems. With so many families moving into the settlements with their teams, the sheer number of qimmiit was in itself challenging and problematic. Owners found it difficult to find time to hunt enough to feed the qimmiit, so the dogs often had to forage for themselves, well beyond the limits of their owner's house, either by scrounging for food at the dump or by stealing food. As anthropologist Toshio Yatsushiro noted in 1959, the decision of Inuit to let their qimmiit forage was "perfectly reasonable." Even though there was a high risk of the dogs being shot for being loose, if qimmiit could not forage for food, they would die anyway.[32]

Qallunaat had very little or no experience with working dogs, and were either fearful of or careless around loose qimmiit.[33] Qimmiit in turn did not adapt well to being around strangers or new qimmiit; they were more wary, and their behaviour became less predictable and potentially more dangerous. In addition, people living in the settlement were likely to be walking outside in store-bought clothes that offered no protection from dog bites.[34] Authorities—primarily RCMP members—responded to the perceived danger by shooting loose qimmiit, often without explanation or warning.

The killings took place under the authority of the Ordinance Respecting Dogs. This ordinance stated that dogs were not permitted to run at large in designated settlements, and that dogs in harness were permitted within a settlement only if they were muzzled or under the control of a person over sixteen years of age who was "capable of ensuring that the dog will not harm the public or create a nuisance." The owner had up to five days to claim the dog(s) and pay a fine. However, the Ordinance also provided that if a dog officer was unable to seize a dog that was running at large, or was otherwise in violation of the ordinance, he could destroy it, and no compensation would be provided.

These provisions were inappropriate, to say the least. Chains to secure the dogs were either not available or prohibitively expensive, and ropes

---

32 Autry National Center, Institute for the Study of the American West, Braun Research Library, Collection MS 212 (Toshio Yatsushiro), Box 2, File 44, transcript of interview with Joomii, E-7-444, July 26, 1959.

33 Both Inuit and Qallunaat believed that qimmiit sometimes interbred with wolves, contributing to a Qallunaat fear of this breed of dog. In addition, the RCMP warned that qimmiit should never be considered or owned as pets, as the risk of attack to humans, especially women and children, was unacceptably high.

34 Inuit traditional clothing made from furs and skins was sufficiently thick and strong to prevent most qimmiit bites from penetrating human skin.

were not a long-term solution, since qimmiit could easily chew through them. Muzzles would have prevented dogs from eating snow, which they need for hydration, and would not have allowed them to protect themselves from predators, such as bears, wolves, or even other loose dogs; nobody had time to supervise qimmiit all day, every day; and the supposed age of maturity, sixteen, was meaningless to Inuit. For Inuit, maturity was measured by abilities, not age. Many RCMP members, who were ex officio dog officers and assumed most of the burden of enforcing the Ordinance, did not bother trying to catch and impound a dog. There were a number of reasons for this: The dog would be difficult to catch, it might bite the officer, and once impounded, there was a good chance the dog would not be claimed by the owner because of the high cost of the fine.[35] In any case, many officers did not have access to dog pounds. It became easier to simply shoot qimmiit than to go through the process outlined in the Ordinance. Inuit also observed that dogs belonging to the RCMP, Inuit special constables, or Hudson's Bay Company (HBC) employees were rarely shot, and may not have fully understood that their owners had the means to keep teams under watch and chained when necessary. This special exemption often created animosity between Inuit whose dogs were killed and those whose dogs were always spared, even if they ran at large.

The policy of shooting qimmiit as a disease control measure was equally ill-considered. Authorities believed that killing all dogs that were sick or exposed to disease would prevent further spreading of disease. In fact, not all dogs would succumb to illness, and some that did would recover, allowing Inuit to reconstitute their dog teams with dogs that were likely to be very strong and healthy. It should also be noted that, despite the emphasis on killing qimmiit to control disease, there was a confusing contrary policy of having the police immunize dogs against disease and even import dogs to replace others lost in a canine epidemic.

---

35 The fine was not a lot of money by southern standards, but it was prohibitive for most Inuit, especially those on social assistance.

The killing of qimmiit has become a flash point in Inuit memories of the changes imposed on their lives by outsiders. In community after community that we visited, Inuit told me, often through tears, "I remember the day my dogs were shot," or "I remember when my father's dogs were killed." The pain still felt from these memories is a testament to the symbiotic relationship between Inuit and qimmiit, and to the fact that the loss of qimmiit was a stark challenge to their independence, self-reliance, and identity as hunters and providers for their family. Snowmobiles were not an option for many hunters—when they were first introduced, only a few Inuit who were employed and well-paid could afford the machines. It was often years after his qimmiit had been shot before a hunter was able to replace them with a snowmobile. Thomas Kublu underlined the enormity of the loss of a hunter's dogs in his testimony to the Commission:

> In the spring of 1965 while I was at work, all my dogs which were chained up were shot. I was not around when this happened . . . I never understood why they were shot. I thought, "Was it because my hunting was getting in the way of my time as a labourer?"
>
> This was very painful to me as I needed to hunt, and because I came from another community I was alone with no relatives to help me out with my responsibilities as a hunter and wage earner. The dogs were my only means of transportation and hunting since I had no snowmobile. I could no longer hunt or travel once my dogs were shot. Since I had grown up hunting with a dog team and I so enjoyed hunting, a major part of my livelihood was taken away from me, my identity and means of providing for my family.
>
> At this time the role of the Inuk male as a provider was the sole purpose of nurturing and protecting our family and community and that was very quickly obliterated with single gun shots held to

> our dogs, our only means of transportation and hunting. We took pride in our roles as hunter-gatherers and that was all we had left in our identities. Our mobility rights were taken away from us.[36]

Both hunters and their families suffered terribly as a result of the loss of qimmiit. There were not enough jobs in the settlements, and families became dependent on inadequate social assistance payments and expensive storebought food that was not sufficiently nutritious to meet their dietary requirements. Many Inuit told me they believed that the government was aware of the impact of the loss of qimmiit on Inuit culture, health, and well-being, but that it did nothing to ease the situation. They also blamed many of the killings on the ignorance of officials concerning the care and handling of qimmiit. Inuit were particularly critical of Qallunaat who had no knowledge of the negative impacts chaining had on the behaviour of working qimmiit. Inuit also expressed both frustration and remorse—frustration that they could not understand why so many qimmiit were shot, especially those in harnesses or those that in their opinion did not pose a real safety or disease threat and remorse that they did not do more to stop the killings. In many cases, their failure to act stemmed from ilira, a mixed feeling of awe and fear of Qallunaat, whose intentions and behaviour were not clear to Inuit.

The events described above have come to be called qimmiijaqtauniq, which means literally "many dogs (or dog teams) being taken away or killed," and is often translated as "the dog slaughter." Beginning in the late 1990s, a number of Inuit publicly charged that the dog killings were carried out by the RCMP under government orders, so that they would lose their mobility and any possibility of returning to their traditional way of life. In 2005, the federal government rejected a parliamentary committee's advice to call an independent inquiry into the dog killings, and instead asked the RCMP to investigate itself. The Qikiqtani Inuit were very reluctant to participate in

36 Testimony and submission in Inuktitut.

this investigation without assurances concerning the independence of the investigations and the handling of their testimonies.

The resulting *RCMP Sled Dogs Report* confirmed that hundreds and perhaps thousands of dogs were killed by RCMP members and other authorities in the 1950s and 1960s. However, as a detailed analysis of the resulting RCMP report prepared by this Commission points out, the RCMP took an overly legalistic approach to their investigation.[37] Their investigators only looked for evidence of a government conspiracy or unlawful behaviour in the actions of the RCMP in killing qimmiit. Unfortunately, they did not go beyond these two concerns to consider other issues such as the inappropriateness of the law under which qimmiit were killed, or the many ways in which the killings were related to the relocations that were occurring at the time. The authors also dismissed Inuit memories of the killings as false, or arising from faulty memories, and condemned Inuit leaders who brought the incidents to public notice as being motivated by a desire for monetary compensation.

As the QTC analysis of the RCMP report notes, Inuit had no access to decision-makers and limited access to local officials. As a result, in many cases Inuit were not given any reasons why their dogs were shot, and when explanations were provided they were likely to be incomplete and/or badly translated.[38] It was therefore quite reasonable for Inuit to draw a connection between the killing of their sled dogs and the detrimental effects of centralization, namely the loss of their ability to move back to the land; increasing reliance on a cash economy; and the exclusive concentration of services in settlements.

---

37 See *QTC Review of the RCMP Sled Dogs Report* (2006).

38 The *RCMP Sled Dogs Report* notes that: "Many former members reported instances where they gave a lengthy explanation to the Inuit for a decision being made, only to witness the interpreter reduce it to several sentences. The assumption by the members was that the interpreter conveyed only the decision, not the explanation." *The RCMP and the Inuit Sled Dogs* (*Nunavut and Northern Quebec: 1950–1970*), Royal Canadian Mounted Police, 2006, 46.

At the same time, the QTC study shows that the killings went on far too long to be the result of a secret plan or conspiracy, and that they began—in the mid-1950s in Iqaluit—several years before the federal government adopted a formal centralizing policy. However, the Ordinance was completely consistent with standard government policy that Inuit must, at their own expense, accommodate newcomers' needs and wants. While the law was clear to those who enforced it, to hunters it was illogical, unnecessary, and also harmful; in addition, it was not consistently or predictably applied. Inuit and dogs had existed together for uncounted generations without such restrictions being necessary. It is clear that the Government of Canada failed in its obligations to Inuit when it placed restrictions on their use of dogs without providing the means to make those restrictions less onerous and without involving Inuit directly in finding solutions.

HEALTH CARE AND THE SEPARATION OR LOSS OF FAMILY MEMBERS

Relocations to settlements were not the only moves that dislocated the lives of Inuit between 1950 and 1975. Medical strategies intended to improve Inuit health by removing patients to southern hospitals succeeded in their primary goal but inflicted lasting damage on many individuals and their families.

Before the Second World War, health treatment in the Qikiqtani region, other than traditional Inuit care, was limited to one small hospital at Pangnirtung, and otherwise to services provided by the RCMP, missionaries, the HBC, and annual visits by shipboard medical teams, primarily for injuries. The impetus for improvements in health services in the region arose from the general modernization of health care across Canada, as well as from the government's somewhat belated reaction to reports by missionaries, researchers, bureaucrats, and American military personnel about high mortality rates among Inuit. By the mid-1960s, nursing stations provided basic health care in all settlements and ever fewer visits to ilagiit nunagivaktangit.

After 1950, medical personnel on the new medical patrol ship the *C.D. Howe* screened Inuit for tuberculosis and other infectious diseases or ailments, and those found to be infected or sick were removed without notice for indefinite stays in southern hospitals. Individuals who refused to be screened or were known to be sick were sometimes tracked down at their ilagiit nunagivaktangat by the ship's helicopter. Those sent south for treatment often endured weeks on board the ship before they spent many months or years in treatment, far away from their families.

During the QTC hearings, many Inuit spoke of the terror and sadness they experienced when they were sent away to hospitals and sanatoria, often without being able to say goodbye to their families. Jonah Apak of Clyde River remembered:

> I was one of the people sent out by the *C.D. Howe* for TB. We had no choice but to go for medical purposes. At the front of the *C.D. Howe* ship, there was a section. They segregated the Inuit to the area where it was the bumpiest. We were treated like lower-class people. We were where there was a lot of movement. When we were in the middle of the sea, it was really dark at night.[39]

Like other Inuit children, Jonah was forbidden to speak Inuktitut in the school he attended while he was being treated. Children were essentially orphaned at the tuberculosis hospitals or sanatoria in the South. They were subjected to disciplinary measures, such as being spanked, hit, force-fed, or tied to their beds for hours on end, actions that they would never had experienced at home. On top of all this, officials and institutions also managed to lose or mix up records, which meant that some people—children and

39 Testimony in Inuktitut.

adults—were not returned to their ilagiit nunagivaktangat or their own districts. Children who returned had often lost their ability to speak Inuktitut, and were unable to communicate with their parents or grandparents. In some cases, children lost years of parental teachings that were necessary for survival on the land. The result was a profound sense of cultural shock and dislocation both down south and at home upon return, as Jonah explained:

> I was in a confusing situation. I was in two different worlds. I was treated like I was not Inuk ... I didn't know what I was.
>
> They sent us back to our camp. I thought I was a southerner. I didn't want to come back. I didn't like the tundra and the house ... I had to get to know my culture again.[40]

In some cases, the journey home was longer than the treatment itself. Some children never returned, or returned years later, when it was discovered that they had been kept by well-meaning hospital staff. Adults who returned from treatment were often unable to return to their former lives, and ended up dependent on government relief. While the government created "rehabilitation centres" to allow Inuit to be integrated—physically and socially—into communities in the Qikiqtani region, the programs of the centres could be more appropriately described as acculturation, not rehabilitation.

Another tragic aspect of the policy to send Inuit south, rather than to build facilities in the North, related to the deaths of patients and the treatment of their remains. Some relatives were never informed that a family member had died down south until long afterward—if at all. Jaykolasie Killiktee told us:

---

40 Testimony in Inuktitut.

> In those days, when my grandmother left on the ship, I think my whole clan—especially our grandfather—was going through stressful times. The only time we could see our grandmother was the next year, or as long as it took to heal. There were no airplanes, no means of mail, no means of telephone, no means of communication with our loved ones. I remember them crying, especially the old ones. It was very traumatic and it had a profound impact on our people. Even when my older brother left, it felt as if we had lost our brother because we knew we wouldn't be in touch—only on very odd occasions we would get a letter. When my grandmother passed away, we were never told if she passed away, or where she passed away.[41]

Inuit with family members who died down south are still hurting from never having had the proper closure that could come from knowing where their relatives are buried or being given the opportunity to visit the graves.

DEVELOPMENT AND EMPLOYMENT

Part of the Canadian government's plan for bringing southern standards of living to the Qikiqtani region was to encourage economic development and thereby raise Inuit standards of living. One government official saw "hope" in the employment of Inuit because, in his words, they would "form a stable and cheerful labour force, one that does not demand premium wages to work in this austere land."[42]

41 Testimony in Inuktitut.

42 Library and Archives Canada, RG 22, Indian and Northern Affairs, A-1-a, volume 1339, file 40-8-23, Report on Employment of Northern People, 1960.

The government looked primarily to mining and oil and gas production for future employment of Inuit, but the pace of development was very slow. By 1975, two mines on the Parry Channel were in the planning stages—Nanisivik and Polaris—and studies were also underway to exploit and ship oil and gas.

Officials and Inuit themselves also searched for development opportunities in the local economy. Cape Dorset provided an early example, which some other communities followed, of amassing earnings from carving and printmaking. Its West Baffin Eskimo Co-op also pioneered commercial hunting and fishing camps. Construction of infrastructure in the settlements, including housing, airfields, diesel power generation plants, and government buildings, provided some temporary manual labour jobs for men. Some Inuit women also found work as secretaries and clerks in government offices or as teacher assistants.

One important employment opportunity, albeit for a limited number of Inuit, was the position of special constable for the RCMP. Inuit special constables were crucial to the RCMP's work in the Qikiqtani region, acting as guides, hunters, and interpreters, and helping to bridge the gap between Qallunaat and Inuit culture. In addition to accompanying the RCMP on patrols, special constables were expected to work at the detachment, as were the rest of their families. Their wives would make and mend the officer's trail clothing, do household chores, and sometimes prepare meals. If they had children, they too would be expected to help with the post chores. While special constables received salaries, there is no indication that other members of their families were always paid for their work. In addition, family members had to cope without the support of their husbands and fathers while the special constables were away on patrol for extended periods.

Inuit expressed a number of different opinions about economic development during our hearings. Some spoke of the importance of even temporary wages for raising their standard of living. Mikisiti Saila of Cape Dorset described how he was encouraged to make carvings from walrus tusks: "I made a small ptarmigan and a couple of fish figures ... and brought it back. It felt like I had so much money when I sold it. He paid me $50 for that. My father and I were able to have tea and not just handouts. This was a great accomplishment."[43]

Others told me that they were mistreated or intimidated by managers and employers working for development enterprises and that some people were never paid for the manual labour or services, such as guiding or interpreting, provided to government. Ham Kudloo of Pond Inlet told me about his experience as an interpreter on the *C. D. Howe*: "I was thinking, 'Alright, I will be making money,' [but] I found out later it was voluntary ... I wasn't given one dollar ... a thank you ... When I got older, I was thinking 'Boy, I must have been very patient.'"[44]

Several people testified that they were sent south (sometimes repeatedly) for training, especially in trades, but had few opportunities to apply their skills to paid employment in their home communities. They faced returning to jobs that were either seasonal or depended on their acceptance of frequent moves to follow jobs across the territories. Some Inuit also spoke about the negative impact of intensive aerial surveys and development on wildlife.

Overall, while some new jobs were created between 1950 and 1975, most of these were in government services, and there were too few opportunities to employ all those who moved to the settlements. As a result, the region became a place of high unemployment where formerly self-sufficient families often had little choice but to become dependent on social assistance.

43 Testimony in Inuktitut.

44 Testimony in Inuktitut.

POOR COMMUNICATIONS AND CROSS-CULTURAL UNDERSTANDING

One characteristic of all the changes I have described is the poor communications between Inuit and Qallunaat about what was taking place or what the changes were intended to achieve.

The ability of Inuit and Qallunaat to communicate effectively was challenged by a lack of a common language, and by profound cultural differences based on distinct worldviews and experiences. Most Qallunaat went to the Arctic on short-term contracts, some for an adventure, but almost all as a way to advance their careers quickly. Very few stayed for more than two to three years. The high turnover rate meant that there was a continuous loss of corporate memory, including knowledge of which approaches or decisions were successful and which were not. Many employees did not stay long enough to see or be aware of the effects of their work, good or bad. Even though the environment and culture were completely foreign to them, most Qallunaat thought they knew better than Inuit, who lacked the perceived benefits of a southern education. Qallunaat had no need to learn Inuktitut and saw no benefit in doing so: English was the language of government, education, and business. Inuit, however, learned English, more often than not by necessity or through formal schooling, work, or southern medical treatment. Inuit had little power to make Qallunaat listen and were also less inclined, due to cultural norms, to challenge assumptions and opinions expressed by the dominant group. As Simeonie Akpalialuk of Pangnirtung told me:

> Our people were conditioned by the missionaries, by the RCMP, to feel inferior. They developed a superiority-inferiority complex. I don't know, maybe to control them. That's why you heard many times, "We grew up fearing the police, fearing the white person."

> Just the ordinary white person. We couldn't approach them. To us they were the big white man and that is the kind of conditioning and thinking we were brought up with.[45]

Qallunaat quickly learned to take advantage of this deference to authority in order to ensure Inuit acquiesced to their wishes. Even when Inuit clearly disagreed or refused the proposed request, Qallunaat would apply pressure tactics such as warnings and threats to obtain the desired results.

Very few police officers, government administrators, and bureaucrats charged with modernizing the Qikiqtani region from 1950 to the 1970s attempted to fully understand Inuit culture or even the Inuit language. Their efforts were generally limited to supervising the translation of rules and simple instructions into Inuktitut, with varying levels of effectiveness. RCMP officers gave translation roles to special constables who had a partial understanding of English and no experience with Canada's interrelated systems of government and justice. Inuit children were expected to translate foreign concepts and complicated documents for their parents. On many occasions, the government used Inuktitut to preach Canadian values to its internal colony. An ambitious effort was 1964's *Q-Book: Qaujivaallirutissat*, a complete reworking of the former *Eskimo Book of Wisdom*. It clearly placed Inuit experiences in the "old days" and instructed Inuit about Canadian habits and institutions.

Some government representatives made attempts to bridge cultural and linguistic divides by giving Inuit a voice in meetings with senior officials. However, for various reasons,[46] Inuit generally avoided participation in government-organized forums that followed perplexing rules of procedure, systemically favoured Qallunaat ideas, and predetermined government priorities and outcomes.

---

45 Testimony in English.

46 Including astute assessments of the wisdom of challenging authorities in public venues and avoiding the negative consequences that would inevitably result.

Throughout the period, Qallunaat demonstrated a sense of cultural superiority and a belief that their role was to lead Inuit as quickly as possible into the "modern" world. The patronizing position of Qallunaat, interspersed with actions that showed, at different times, hostility, indifference, or romanticism toward Inuit culture, made it very difficult to engage in meaningful dialogues about government policies that were having such a deep impact on Inuit lives. Given the lack of dialogue, it is not surprising that many Inuit drew their own conclusions about government intentions, policies, and actions, such as the widespread belief that the killings of qimmiit were part of a deliberate policy to force them to remain in the permanent settlements.

Saimaqatigiingniq: The Way Forward

As the Commission visited the communities in the Qikiqtani region, we heard strong messages—not only about traumatic past experiences, but also about the need for healing and reconciliation. Many participants recommended concrete steps that can and should be taken to allow Inuit to move forward into a more promising future.

After completing our first round of community visits, we held a workshop with staff and members of the Executive of the Qikiqtani Inuit Association (QIA), as well as the QTC's historical research team. This workshop identified a wide range of further recommendations. The main themes that emerged from both the workshop and our community visits were acknowledgement, historical awareness, healing, meaningful involvement, cross-cultural training, and better communication. These themes are organized into four categories of detailed recommendations, as presented below.

- The Government of Canada should acknowledge that the effects of many of its decisions led to unnecessary hardship and poor social, health, and education outcomes for Inuit, and both southern Canadians and younger Inuit should learn more about the changes that occurred in the 1950 to 1975 period in the Qikiqtani region. Concrete steps to promote healing for those affected by some important events in the period, including forced relocations and medical evacuations, are detailed in the section titled Acknowledging and Healing Past Wrongs.
- To reduce the likelihood of past mistakes being repeated, Inuit governance must be strengthened so that political, social, and economic decisions truly reflect Inuit culture and needs. Some of the ways this can be accomplished are detailed in the Strengthening Inuit Governance section.
- Despite many political, economic, and social changes in the twentieth century, Inuit have retained their distinct culture. As described in the Strengthening Inuit Culture section, they are one of the founding peoples of Canada with a culture that should be celebrated, strengthened, and made better known to other Canadians.
- The historical legacy in the Qikiqtani region includes a number of serious social ills, such as alcohol and substance abuse, unhealthy diets, high unemployment, low rates of graduation, high crime rates, and insufficient and substandard housing. The section on Creating Healthy Communities describes a variety of culturally appropriate steps that should be taken to improve the quality of Inuit life.

In presenting these recommendations, I am hopeful that the Qikiqtani Inuit Association will work with key stakeholders in communities and government to develop an effective implementation strategy and action plan, and that all levels of government will commit the necessary resources to achieve the agreed-upon objectives.

Acknowledging and Healing Past Wrongs

DIRECTIONS FOR CHANGE

- Ensure that the Government of Canada understands and acknowledges its role in events that have had—and continue to have—long-lasting, harmful effects on the lives of Inuit.
- Promote public understanding of the Qikiqtani region's history.
- Promote healing for families affected by forced relocations and medical evacuations.

CASE FOR CHANGE

Appearing before the QTC, whether in public or at home, was a painful experience for many Inuit. For some, the memories were so raw that they asked to tell their stories in private. Many others broke down as they spoke in the public sessions. However, over and over again, I was told that the hearings were the beginning of a healing process. People were greatly relieved at being able to express what they had kept hidden for so long.

Some Inuit found the courage to speak for the first time, while others retold well-known accounts about what happened to them. In all cases, people were strongly motivated by an opportunity to speak freely, without prejudice, within the context of an Inuit-led process. They expected their accounts to contribute to a more balanced historical account of the events that they had experienced as children, youth, and adults. They were also clear that what they experienced needed to be heard, not just by the Commission, but also by the Government of Canada.

Healing and reconciliation are only possible when the party responsible for past wrongs fully accepts its responsibility and commits to restoring the relationship with those who have suffered as a result of its actions. My first recommendation is that the Qikiqtani Inuit Association should present the full QTC report to the Government of Canada, and request a formal acknowledgement of the report's findings. Inuit are confident that a careful consideration of the report will lead the Government to re-examine its actions and acknowledge the impact of forced relocations, separations of families, inadequate housing, and the killing of qimmiit on Inuit. Inuit would also be receptive to a sincere apology for those acts, as long as that apology signals a willingness to work with Inuit in a respectful partnership that seeks to redress past and continuing wrongs. Inuit also seek to protect their unique culture through a continuing relationship to the land they have occupied for countless generations.

It would be fair to say that there is limited public awareness of the recent history of the Qikiqtani region on the part of southern Canadians. The region is geographically remote from most of the rest of Canada, and it generally receives media attention only with respect to issues that are on the agenda of southern Canadian politicians and opinion leaders, such as Arctic sovereignty or oil and gas exploration. The Canada's North Poll, conducted by Ipsos Reid on behalf of Inuit Tapiriit Kanatami in 2009, indicated that, of the more than one thousand Canadian respondents, one in three scored a D or failed a simple true-or-false quiz about Canada's Arctic. The average score was a C. Notably, 53% strongly or somewhat disagreed that they are "generally aware of the realities of life for the Inuit in the Canadian Arctic." It follows from this that Canadians are also relatively unaware of what has been happening in the North since the 1950s. Indeed, for most, the 50s, 60s, and 70s were decades of national optimism and relative prosperity, in stark contrast to the reality lived by most Inuit.

The work of this Commission is an opportunity to help increase public understanding of a dramatic transformation that happened within the lifetime of anyone over the age of thirty-five. It is equally important that all Inuit have access to the testimonies, documents, and reports of the Commission to understand the life stories of Elders. I therefore recommend that the Qikiqtani Inuit Association give priority to making the QTC's historical collection accessible to the widest possible audience.

In the first part of this report, I mentioned the key role played by Inuit special constables in guiding, hunting, and interpreting for RCMP members, and the unpaid work that their families contributed at the police detachments. RCMP members have been quick to acknowledge the importance of special constables. In 1995, a research group in British Columbia interviewed one hundred and fifty-seven former RCMP members who had served in the Qikiqtani region. Officers readily admitted how ill-prepared they were for northern service: "There was nothing in the manual. It was all learned by trial and error. Looking back, I probably wouldn't have survived there because you had to rely on other people. You could not be an individualist there."

While the contributions of a few special constables have been recognized by the RCMP, I believe that the RCMP with involvement of the Qikiqtani Inuit Association should prepare a formal recognition of the role of all Inuit special constables and their families. As Elijah Panipakoocho of Pond Inlet commented in his testimony:

> I think the government has to give a very big gesture of appreciation to the Inuit who gave most of their lives to assist [RCMP members] . . . if the RCMP had ever tried to do this without the assistance of Inuit they would have never survived, they would have been dead . . . Those people have to be recognized—without their efforts, Canadian sovereignty would not have progressed to the point where it has today.

In 1934, the Hudson's Bay Company, which was anxious to place posts in the High Arctic, obtained government permission to move fifty-two Inuit from three locations on Baffin Island to Dundas Harbour on Devon Island, where they were expected to trap and trade for two years. The relocation was not a success. Pangnirtung families were returned home, but Cape Dorset families were subjected to an additional three moves over the next dozen years.

The Dundas Harbour relocations are an early example of government action and perceptions about Inuit—they were adaptable and moveable. Additionally, the relocations provide evidence that the government was interested in developing the Arctic economically through the HBC, without providing any services. The effects were traumatic. For the rest of their lives, some relocatees longed for their families and ancestral homeland. Tagoona Qavavouq of Arctic Bay told me that her mother-in-law Ajau suffered great mental anguish after the relocations and died prematurely. She explained:

> When the elders are moved to a different area, when they return home, they can heal and feel better . . . Because they came from Cape Dorset, they were like orphans here [in Arctic Bay]. They were different, being different people from a different land, people did not really communicate with them in the same way.

The legacy of the relocations continues on both the northern and southern coasts of Baffin Island, especially in Cape Dorset and Arctic Bay. The children and grandchildren of those relocated, while closely connected to their current communities, want to learn more about family members living in other communities and experience the land that sustained their ancestors. Accordingly, I recommend that the Government of Canada set up a Dundas Harbour Relocation Trust Fund to allow descendants of families separated as a result of this relocation to travel between Cape Dorset and Arctic Bay for periodic family visits.

Three communities in the Qikiqtani region were closed with little or no notice or consultation in the period covered by the QTC mandate:

Kivitoo, Padloping, and South Camp. The closing of these communities and the centralization of services in larger settlements eased the government's administrative burden and reduced the cost of delivering services. The inhabitants, however, paid a high cost in personal suffering and a loss of deep connections to their home communities. As part of its acknowledgement of responsibility for the trauma caused by these closings, the Government of Canada should provide assistance for families to visit their former homes for on-site healing. This would provide closure for a healing project started several years ago.

The Government of Canada also has a responsibility to help Inuit locate and visit the burial sites of relatives who died in southern Canada during medical treatment. Many relatives were not even informed that a family member had died after being taken away. Thomas Kudlu of Igloolik told me: "It makes me realize that we Inuit were not important enough to be given the courtesy to be informed about the death of our father... The shock of learning about his death when we expected to welcome him home is one of my painful memories."

Finding and visiting the graves of loved ones would help provide closure for families, and the Government of Canada should provide financial assistance to make this possible.

RECOMMENDATIONS

1. The Qikiqtani Inuit Association should formally present the full QTC report to the Government of Canada and request a formal acknowledgement of the report's findings.
2. The QTC historical collection (reports, database, and testimonies) should be made accessible to all participants and anyone interested in understanding and presenting an accurate picture of the Qikiqtani region's history.

3. The QIA and the RCMP should formally recognize the contributions of Inuit Special Constables and their families to the work of the RCMP in the region.
4. The Government of Canada should set up a Dundas Harbour Relocation Trust Fund to allow descendants of families separated as a result of this relocation to travel between Cape Dorset and Arctic Bay for periodic family visits.
5. The Government of Canada should provide funding for on-site healing programs for the families affected by the closing of Kivitoo, Padloping, and South Camp (Belcher Islands) communities.
6. The Government of Canada should defray the costs of allowing Inuit to locate and visit the burial sites of family members who died in southern Canada during medical treatment, in order to provide closure for those families.

Strengthening Inuit Governance

DIRECTION FOR CHANGE

- Ensure that the Governments of Nunavut and Canada provide Inuit with the means and opportunities to see that their unique needs and cultural priorities are fully addressed when the Governments of Nunavut and Canada make political, social, and economic decisions affecting Inuit.

CASE FOR CHANGE

Qikiqtani Inuit were self-governing prior to centralization. Well into the twentieth century, Inuit could go about their day-to-day lives as hunters with limited exposure to Canadian laws and institutions. As we have seen, this situation changed dramatically following the Second World War. Decisions affecting every aspect of Inuit life, including hunting restrictions, compulsory schooling, and medical evacuations, were imposed through a new governance system that was completely foreign to Inuit. For many years, Inuit had no democratic representation or access to decision-makers. Keith Crowe, a scholar and bureaucrat fluent in Inuktitut, worked in the Qikiqtani region for many years. He summed up government decision-making during the 1960s as a "combination of southern speed and paternalism, or 'father knows best.'"

> Northern native people, divided into tribal and local groups, without a strong voice, have been over-run by organized southerners. The southern power groups did what was to their advantage and even did what they thought was best for the native people without discussing their plans or getting native approval.

Qikiqtani Inuit did obtain some input into territorial decisions after 1967, when a territorial legislative assembly was created in Yellowknife. By the 1970s, Inuit had also become involved in regional and local decision-making through their participation in the Baffin Regional Council, hamlet councils, and housing authorities. Inuit involvement was almost always limited to a small range of options acceptable to Qallunaat. The creation of the Inuit Tapirisat of Canada in 1971, which was the first Inuit land-claims organization and a forerunner of Inuit Tapiriit Kanatami, gave Inuit a stronger voice in Inuit and Arctic affairs. This was followed by the creation of the Baffin Regional (now Qikiqtani) Inuit Association in 1975, and then the Tungavik Federation of Nunavut in 1982, which was formed to negotiate the Nunavut Land Claims Agreement (NLCA).

The NLCA committed Inuit to agreeing with the formation of a new territory—Nunavut—that would have a public government without special status for Inuit but with provisions to protect Inuit language, culture, and interests. When the new territory came into being in 1999, there were high expectations that Inuit would finally gain control of their own futures. Mary Simon, Canada's Ambassador to the Circumpolar Arctic, commented:

> the very scale of the Nunavut undertaking means it cannot be overlooked . . . For the first time in Canadian history, with the partial exception of the creation of Manitoba in 1870, a member of the federal-provincial-territorial club is being admitted for the precise purpose of supplying a specific Aboriginal people with an enhanced opportunity for self-determination. This is groundbreaking stuff.

In the seventeen years since the ratification of the NLCA and eleven years since Nunavut's creation, the initial expectations have not been met. Paul Quassa, one of the negotiators of the NLCA, expressed his disappointment as follows:

> A lot of us Inuit thought that with Nunavut we would have a different system geared more toward Inuit. It would be a public government, but geared more toward Inuit and Inuit tradition. Even though our Legislative Assembly has more Inuit now, it is still operating in a Qallunaaq way, perhaps because we still have to be part of the political system.

I believe an important step toward redressing this situation should be a formal acknowledgement by the Nunavut Legislative Assembly that, in accordance with the intention of the Nunavut land-claims negotiation, Inuit goals and aspirations can and should be advanced through the Government of Nunavut, working collaboratively with Inuit organizations. Inuit make up about 85% of the population of Nunavut, and this fact should be reflected in a special status that also respects the needs and constitutional rights of the minority Qallunaat population. The same principle is applied in Quebec, where Francophone goals and aspirations are given priority because they constitute about 80% of the province's population.

It follows from this principle that the Government of Nunavut should conduct its day-to-day operations in keeping with its obligations and responsibilities to Inuit under the NLCA. One of these obligations, set out in Article 32, is that the Government must provide Inuit "with an opportunity to participate in the development of social and cultural policies, programs, and services, including their method of delivery," and that such policies, programs, and services must "reflect Inuit goals and objectives." Meaningful consultation and participation must be improved to fully implement this provision.

The Government of Nunavut also has special obligations to Inuit under Section 35 of the Constitution, which recognizes and affirms existing Aboriginal and treaty rights, and under subsequent Supreme Court of Canada decisions. Guerin (1984) and Sparrow (1990) created and described a duty of the Crown to act as a fiduciary in its dealings with Aboriginal peoples, and justify its conduct when protected rights are interfered with or infringed. The Court also emphasized that Aboriginal rights must be interpreted flexibly in a manner that is "sensitive to the Aboriginal perspective." These rulings underline the necessity for the Government of Nunavut to consult with and fully involve Inuit in all decision-making.

Under Article 23, the NLCA includes the objective of increasing Inuit participation in government employment to a representative level, which means about 85 percent Inuit employment in all occupational groupings and sector levels. This goal is very far from being met—the current level of Inuit representation is around 45 percent. If the Government of Nunavut is to be an effective advocate for Inuit interests in its day-to-day operations, this situation must be rectified.

Nunavut has talented Inuit who continue to champion Inuit causes at the regional, territorial, and federal levels. It is important for all Inuit to better understand how government functions, and how to become involved in decision-making. For example, while most Canadians find the division of responsibilities among orders of government, Aboriginal birthright corporations, and bodies created by land-claim agreements confusing, the problem is acute in Nunavut. For these reasons, I recommend that the Qikiqtani Inuit Association establish a governance education program that will help community members develop skills and share knowledge about the principles of governance, government, and Aboriginal rights. They can thereby strengthen their political and community engagement to achieve their aspirations.

Governance education needs to be complemented by a greater effort on the part of both the federal and territorial governments to make their programs and services accessible at the local level. It can be unduly challenging for citizens to find out what is available to them. Front-line staff often lack information and training. As a result they are unable to give answers to basic questions, and take no initiative to track down the person who can provide the help requested. A fundamental shift to a client-oriented work culture is needed to address this issue. In this connection, I am encouraged by the Government of Nunavut's recent hiring of Government Liaison Officers outside the capital to facilitate access to government services.

Public consultation also needs to be significantly improved so that Inuit are given adequate notice of opportunities for input into proposed policies and legislation, and are provided with solid and easily understood background information about issues and options. Many community members are frustrated by consultation meetings at which they are not provided enough information, and which are not attended by the officials or politicians who could answer their questions and commit to addressing their concerns. Furthermore, the communities know from past experience that their comments and concerns might not be considered or incorporated in the final decision. In fact, many community members believe that the government has a preferred outcome and only conducts the consultations because they are a legal requirement. It is also not uncommon for the territorial and federal governments to conduct separate consultations on the same issue. This fractured approach is seriously problematic on many fronts, including the duplication of effort and resources by different levels of government and Inuit organizations. There is an unreasonable expectation that community members will have the time and patience to participate multiple times with regard to the same issues.

To improve the quality of public consultation, I recommend that the Qikiqtani Inuit Association establish consultation guidelines for all private, public, and research agencies to use in conducting consultations with Inuit. These guidelines would address Inuit issues and concerns, such as the need to incorporate Inuit Qaujimajatuqangit (IQ) in decision-making.

Lack of understanding of Inuit culture and the Arctic environment contributed to mistakes made by Qallunaat in the Qikiqtani region in the period examined by the QTC. Given the large number of transient government employees in Nunavut, improved cross-cultural understanding is still a fundamental issue. Many public servants display a lack of awareness of Canadian Arctic history and Inuit culture, and of the day-to-day reality of Inuit lives. For these reasons, I recommend that the Governments of Nunavut and Canada, assisted by the Qikiqtani Inuit Association, develop and deliver cultural training to all government employees whose work affects Inuit.

Over the many centuries that Inuit have lived in the Arctic, they have acquired a profound understanding of their environment, and how to live successfully in that environment and with each other. From this experience they have developed a unique body of learning and understanding called IQ. It includes what is sometimes called Inuit Traditional Knowledge, or Traditional Ecological Knowledge, which is practical knowledge, such as how to navigate in a storm or identify a male or female polar bear by its tracks. IQ is more than this, however. It is "not only the action of doing things, but also why they are done as they are . . . [it is] the integration of [an] encompassing worldview, value-based behaviour, ecological knowledge, and environmental action." Given its past and present role in Inuit survival, I believe IQ and traditional knowledge must be respected and incorporated into all decision-making in Nunavut.

Finally, at the federal level, I believe Canada should formally demonstrate its commitment to the right to self-determination of all its Aboriginal peoples, including Inuit, by endorsing the United Nations Declaration on the Rights of Indigenous Peoples. Adopted by the United Nations General Assembly in 2007, the Declaration outlaws discrimination against indigenous peoples and promotes their full and effective participation in all matters that concern them, as well as their right to remain distinct and to pursue their own visions of economic and social development. Canada was one of only four states that voted against the Declaration in 2007. However, in the March 2010 Speech from the Throne, the Government of Canada announced its intention to endorse the Declaration "in a manner fully consistent with Canada's Constitution and laws." Given that the Declaration is, as the government itself has noted, an "aspirational" document, there is no impediment to endorsing it now without qualification, even if much remains to be accomplished before its goals are fully achieved in this country.

RECOMMENDATIONS

1. The Nunavut Legislative Assembly should formally assert that Nunavut and the Government of Nunavut were created by the Nunavut land-claims negotiations as vehicles for Inuit self-government, and, therefore, that Inuit goals and aspirations can and should be advanced through the Government of Nunavut working collaboratively with Inuit organizations.
2. The Government of Nunavut should conduct its day-to-day operations in keeping with its obligations and responsibilities under the Nunavut Land Claims Agreement and Section 35 of the Constitution.
3. The Qikiqtani Inuit Association should establish a program that will enable Inuit to develop and utilize the governance skills they will require to strengthen their political and community engagement in a civil society.
4. The governments of Nunavut and Canada should take all necessary action to make their programs and services for the people of Nunavut accessible at the local level.
5. The Qikiqtani Inuit Association should develop a framework (principles, policies, and techniques) for all private, public, and research agencies to use in conducting consultations with Inuit.
6. To ensure that Inuit culture is better understood by government employees whose work affects the Inuit, the Governments of Nunavut and Canada, assisted by the Qikiqtani Inuit Association, should develop and deliver cultural training to all such employees.
7. The governments of Nunavut and Canada, and all Inuit organizations, should respect and incorporate Inuit Qaujimajatuqangit and Inuit Traditional Knowledge in all decision-making in Nunavut.
8. The Government of Canada should immediately endorse the UN Declaration on the Rights of Indigenous Peoples without qualifications.

Strengthening Inuit Culture

DIRECTION FOR CHANGE

- Celebrate and strengthen Inuit culture, and make it better known to other Canadians.

CASE FOR CHANGE

Despite the dramatic changes in their way of life over the last half-century, Inuit have displayed remarkable resilience in adapting to their new circumstances without losing their language and traditions. In the 2001 census, 85.6 percent of Inuit identified Inuktitut as their first language, and 79.2 percent stated that Inuktitut was the only or main language spoken at home. Customary skills also continue to be widely practiced. For example, the 1999 Nunavut Community Labour Force Survey found that 78 percent of Inuit men aged fifteen to fifty-four participate in harvesting activity, at least occasionally. The importance of celebrating and strengthening Inuit culture should be self-evident, not only to Inuit themselves, but also to other Canadians. Inuit values and knowledge, which have allowed them to live successfully in the Arctic, are unique and irreplaceable. John Amagoalik eloquently expressed the importance of transmitting this heritage in an essay entitled "We Must Have Dreams:"

> We must teach our children their mother tongue. We must teach them what they are and where they come from. We must teach them the values which have guided our society over the thousands of years. We must teach them the philosophies which go back beyond the memory of man . . .

If Inuit culture is to thrive in the future, however, a number of challenges need to be addressed. One of these is the lack of effective instruction in Inuktitut. In his 2006 report, "The Nunavut Project," Thomas Berger identified a fundamental weakness of the current model of education, as well as its consequences. A lack of Inuit teachers and Inuktitut curriculum means that, with only a few exceptions, Inuit children are taught in Inuktitut until Grade 3, at which point English becomes the primary language of instruction for all subjects, and Inuktitut is taught only as a second language when teachers are available. Because they do not have a solid grounding in Inuktitut when they begin learning English, they can lose fluency in their mother tongue. This loss is not compensated for by advanced fluency in English; on the contrary, Berger noted, "They end up without fluency or literacy in either language."

The implications for the future survival of Inuktitut and Inuit culture are disquieting. As Berger comments:

> The Inuit of Nunavut are faced with the erosion of Inuit language, knowledge, and culture. Unless serious measures are taken, there will over time be a gradual extinction of Inuktitut, or at best its retention as a curiosity, imperfectly preserved and irrelevant to the daily life of its speakers.

Measures to ensure the continued transmission of Inuit values and IQ are equally essential. Incorporating IQ in the education curriculum is one such measure. Regrettably, as Heather McGregor has recently pointed out in *Inuit Education and Schools in the Eastern Arctic*, "the prioritization of cultural sustainability and IQ through education was not included in the land-claim agreement or in any other large-scale initiative associated with Inuit rights and benefits." The result of this oversight, in the words of Nunavut Tunngavik's 2007 "Report on Education in Nunavut," is that "Inuit culture in the Nunavut classroom still tends to be treated as décor and artifact rather than viewed as an integral foundation for all learning."

This situation is beginning to change. One important development is territorial legislation that addresses the importance of preserving IQ and Inuktitut. The 2008 Inuit Language Protection Act provides that the Government of Nunavut must "design and enable the education program to produce secondary school graduates fully proficient in the Inuit Language, in both its spoken and written forms." The Education Act, passed in the same year, proclaims as its first fundamental principle, "The public education system in Nunavut shall be based on Inuit societal values and the principles and concepts of Inuit Qaujimajatuqangit." It also stipulates that every student shall be given a bilingual education in an Inuit language and either English or French. The Department of Education has already issued a new curriculum framework based on the values and principles of IQ. This framework is the basis of a long-term project to develop a made-in-Nunavut curriculum and materials for kindergarten through to Grade 12. The projected completion date is 2018–2019. I recommend that the Department of Education distribute the components of this curriculum to all communities as they are completed, and direct school officials to implement them as soon as possible.

I also recommend that historical material from the QTC be included in the new Nunavut curriculum. Many witnesses who appeared before the Commission told me how reluctant they had been to tell their children about the traumatic events of the past, or how their own parents had kept silent. The lack of knowledge among Inuit youth about the events described in this report was clearly demonstrated in the sessions we held with secondary school graduates participating in the Nunavut Sivinuksavut program in Ottawa. These sessions also showed how interested young Inuit are in learning more about the events that changed the lives of their parents and grandparents and created the communities in which they now live.

Another complementary method of transmitting Inuit traditions and history between generations is through practice—by bringing Elders and others with Inuit knowledge together more often in places and contexts that make it possible to learn and share. Simonie Kaenerk of Hall Beach told me:

> We have to educate the younger people ... not just [about] hunting [but about] family life, how to get along with family members ... We have to get this information from the Elders. We are not asking Elders enough about what happened in the past; that is why we are losing our traditional way of life.

One way of increasing meaningful contacts between the generations is to bring Elders into schools as teachers. The Department of Education has already established a one-year Elders' Teachers' Certification Program, which will also have the benefit of increasing the number of Inuktitut-speaking teachers. There are a number of other creative possibilities, such as those recommended in a learning unit designed by two teachers in Igloolik, called *Anijaarniq: Introducing Inuit Landskills and Wayfinding*. In addition to interviews with Elders describing how they navigate, the unit emphasizes the importance of inviting Elders into the classroom to share their knowledge and experiences, and of going outside with them so that students can experience first-hand the skills they are describing.

Such activities complement other programs to take youth out on the land to learn traditional skills from Elders. The Qikiqtani Inuit Association's Traditional Camping Program provides this experience in thirteen communities. I recommend that the Government of Nunavut develop more programs such as these to ensure that young people continue to learn from Elders, and that Elders become more involved in the daily lives of communities.

If Inuktitut is to be entrenched as the dominant language of Nunavut, it is important that adults be given the opportunity to learn it. Unfortunately, there are fewer adult language classes available now than there were before the creation of the territory. A second-language Inuktitut program exists in Iqaluit, but the cost can be prohibitive. There is a very large disparity between federal funding of Inuktitut- and French-language programs. The federal Government annually funds French-language training at the rate of $3,400 per francophone in Nunavut, while Inuktitut receives only $48.50 per Inuk. I recommend that the governments of Canada and Nunavut work together to develop and adequately fund programs that will give all Inuit and Qallunaat the opportunity to learn Inuktitut.

Finally, I believe an effective way to celebrate Inuit history and culture and make it better known to all Canadians would be to create an Inuit History Month. The success of Black History Month has demonstrated the potential benefits of such an initiative. Fifty years ago, there was very little knowledge of the history and contributions of African-Canadians in Canada. Beginning in the 1950s, when various groups began to celebrate Black History Month, and particularly after 1995, when the Month was formally recognized by a resolution of the Canadian Parliament, that situation changed. Today, each February, a high proportion of Canadian schools have activities related to Black History Month, and the awareness of African-Canadian history and achievements has increased significantly. The rationale for the initiative, as set out by the Ontario Black History Society, is that:

> African-Canadian students need to feel affirmed; need to be aware of the contributions made by other Blacks in Canada; need to have role models; need to understand the social forces [that] have shaped and influenced their community and their identities as a means of feeling connected to the educational experience and their life experience in various regions in Canada. They need to feel empowered. The greater Canadian community needs to know a history of Canada that includes all of the founding and pioneering experiences in order to work from reality, rather than perception alone.

These words apply equally to Inuit and their experiences, and an Inuit History Month could produce a comparable increase in awareness on the part of Inuit and all Canadians. Accordingly, I recommend that the Qikiqtani Inuit Association develop a program of events for an Inuit History Month, which could be launched as a pilot in Nunavut, and then extended to all of Canada.

RECOMMENDATIONS

1. The Government of Nunavut's Department of Education should develop and distribute an Inuktitut- and Inuit-based curriculum to all communities and direct school officials to implement it as soon as possible.
2. The Government of Nunavut's Department of Education should include historical material from the QTC reports in the Nunavut education curriculum.
3. The Government of Nunavut should develop and deliver more programs that actively promote intergenerational experiences between Elders and Inuit children and youth to ensure that young people continue to learn from Elders, and that Elders become more involved in the daily lives of communities.
4. The Governments of Canada and Nunavut should work together to develop and fund Inuit Language programs that will ensure that all Inuit and Qallunaat in Nunavut have the opportunity to learn Inuktitut.
5. The Qikiqtani Inuit Association should initiate an Inuit History Month, launching the event in Nunavut and later extending it to all of Canada.

Creating Healthy Communities

DIRECTION FOR CHANGE

- Encourage healthy communities by adequately addressing intergenerational trauma caused by historical wrongs, through appropriate health, nutritional, housing, and environmental strategies.

CASE FOR CHANGE

Many of the changes introduced by the Canadian government in the Qikiqtani region between 1950 and 1975 were intended to improve the health and living conditions of Inuit. The results have been decidedly mixed. While rates of tuberculosis and infant mortality have been lowered, they are still unacceptably high relative to the rest of Canada. Poor nutrition has replaced periods of starvation as a major health concern. Today 70 percent of Inuit preschoolers in Nunavut live in homes where there is not enough food. Housing is in a state of crisis, and the territory is plagued by high rates of suicide, addiction, and incarceration. Indian and Northern Affairs Canada's most recent Community Well-Being Index shows a significant gap between the quality of life of Inuit communities relative to other Canadian communities. Inuit communities scored an average 62 out of a possible 100 points, in contrast to a score of 77 out of 100 for all other "non-Inuit" and "non–First Nations" communities. This disparity in well-being has narrowed since it was first calculated in 1981, but it is still unacceptably large.

If the killing of qimmiit is a flash point for Inuit memories of the changes to which they were subjected, suicide is one of the most disturbing consequences of those changes. Suicide was all but unknown among previous generations of Inuit. There was only one recorded suicide in Nunavut in the 1960s. Today, the territory averages twenty-seven suicides a year, and the suicide rate is about ten times the national average. The rate of death by suicide among 15- to 24-year-old Inuit men in Nunavut is twenty-eight times that of their peers Canada-wide. The Working Group for a Suicide Prevention Strategy for Nunavut comments, "The Inuit transition from a low-suicide society to a high-suicide society in a very short period of time is almost without parallel elsewhere on the planet." The factors influencing suicide rates are under intense scrutiny by academics in Canada and elsewhere, but it is plausible that Inuit youth are more vulnerable than many other groups due to the sheer number of factors —poverty, heavy drinking, cultural dislocation, low self-esteem, etc.—known to be associated with suicide.

I have already described how settlement life brought Inuit into contact with alcohol and drugs for the first time, in the absence of highly developed social controls that are taken for granted in the South. Given the ongoing cultural dislocation and lack of employment opportunities, it should be no surprise that substance abuse continues to be a serious problem in Inuit communities, along with its consequences, including domestic violence and health issues such as Fetal Alcohol Spectrum Disorder (FASD). Rates of heavy drinking in Nunavut are four times those in the rest of Canada. One 2001 report estimated that 30 percent of Nunavut's expectant mothers drank significant amounts of alcohol while pregnant, and that 85 percent of their children showed symptoms of FASD.

Smoking is another widespread addiction. An estimated 65% of Nunavummiut smoke daily—the highest rate in Canada. Smoking is a prime factor in Nunavut's high rate of lung cancer, and smoking by pregnant mothers is associated with the territory's high rates of infant mortality and low birth weight. Second-hand smoke contributes to the highest rate of lower respiratory tract infections among children in the world.

Links between substance abuse and high rates of incarceration in Nunavut are well-known. As the 2009 Government of Nunavut Report

Card points out, there are few culturally appropriate and local treatment facilities, and "with few diversion options, incarceration becomes the norm instead of the last resort." In addition, the Report Card notes that "long wait times for court, sometimes up to five years, creates stress in homes that are already riddled with problems." Several people interviewed for the report drew a link between waiting times for court and high suicide rates.

Earlier, I spoke of the need for the Government of Canada to formally acknowledge its responsibility for the harmful historical acts described in the first part of this report. I believe it is equally important that it accept responsibility for the ongoing consequences of those acts. Accordingly, I recommend that the Government of Canada formally acknowledge that the high rates of suicide, substance abuse, incarceration, and social dysfunction among Inuit are in part symptoms of intergenerational trauma caused by historical wrongs. This symbolic first step will clearly signal its commitment to help correct the mistakes it made over many decades.

As also noted earlier, the original intention of government planners was to bring the standards of living of the South to the North. Many actions and policies were inadequately resourced and poorly planned. They were destructive of Inuit culture and they rarely achieved the more laudable goals of improving material and health conditions. I believe the Government of Canada, as well as the Government of Nunavut, should commit to ensuring that all government health, social, and education programs and services are available to the people of Nunavut on a basis equivalent to those taken for granted by Canadians in the South. As a recent editorial in the *Globe and Mail* rightly said, "Every Inuit life should be precious, as precious as the lives of other Canadians."

There is widespread recognition that the problems I have described above need urgent attention. The Government of Nunavut has approved a comprehensive Addictions and Mental Health Strategy, but as the 2009 Report Card comments, the strategy remains largely unimplemented. More specifically, the report notes, "Communities perceive government inaction in the provision of mental health programs and services, largely because of the lack of mental health nurses in most communities." Community consultations for the Suicide Prevention Strategy also highlighted the need for "more mental health positions, and greater efforts to attract and retain staff for the existing positions." An additional concern is that few of the current mental health care workers are Inuit. As Nunavut Tunngavik's 2008 report on the Nunavut health system points out, "Inuit wish to incorporate traditional practices and the wisdom of Elders into most aspects of contemporary health care, particularly those intensely personal conditions such as childbirth and mental health." This requires training and hiring more Inuit for such positions. I recommend that the governments of Canada and Nunavut take the necessary steps to ensure that sufficient Inuit social, mental health, and addiction workers and programs are available to meet the needs of all Nunavut communities.

One of the inducements that brought Inuit into settlements during the 1950s and 1960s was the promise of free or low-rent housing. Many discovered that the number of houses was inadequate, most houses were too small, quality was poor, and the costs increased. These problems have not gone away—on the contrary, they have now reached crisis proportions. Housing is expensive and in short supply. Statistics Canada reports that 54 percent of Nunavut residents live in "crowded" conditions, compared to the Canadian average of 7 percent. Overcrowding, combined with building design flaws and the fact that houses are kept virtually airtight to conserve heat, contributes to the transmission of respiratory and other diseases. As NTI's report on the Nunavut health system notes, overcrowding can also contribute to high rates of violence in Inuit communities. In addition to overcrowding, the list of problems compiled by the 2009 Government of Nunavut Report Card includes "long waiting lists for houses . . . unaffordable rents, the poor condition of the housing stock, houses that are unsuitable for the elderly or people with disabilities, and new housing designs that do not meet the needs of communities."

Hundreds of people live without adequate housing in the Qikiqtani region. As the 2009 Report Card notes, the Nunavut Housing Corporation can supply the necessary expertise to plan and build the housing the territory requires, but the majority of funding will need to come from the federal government. The consequences of not committing the necessary money would be grave. "The housing problems will continue to grow and become even more detrimental to the social and economic foundation of Nunavut communities, and to Inuit self-reliance." I therefore recommend that the governments of Canada and Nunavut address Inuit housing needs through the provision of short-, medium-, and long-term funding to guarantee adequate and safe homes for all.

Despite the transition of Inuit to settlement life and a wage economy, the traditional land-based economy has not disappeared in Nunavut, and there are a number of important reasons why it should be encouraged to grow. One is that hunting and harvesting are essential components of Inuit culture and identity, as I have already discussed. Another is that country foods can contribute greatly to food security and better nutrition for Nunavummiut. Statistics Canada reports that in 2001, virtually half (49%) of all Nunavut households experienced food insecurity, defined as "not having enough food to eat due to lack of money." This is seven times the rate for Canada as a whole. In low- and lower-middle income Nunavut households, the rate for food insecurity is 68%. Those who lack food security are compelled to buy low-cost, nutritionally poor food that is contributing to increasing rates of obesity, diabetes, and high blood pressure. In contrast, as the Government of Nunavut's Framework for Action on Nutrition notes, "Inuit traditional foods have outstanding nutritional value and continued reliance on food from the land can help improve food security by providing a higher-quality diet at lower cost." Finally, hunting and harvesting can provide significant support to local economies, and reduce dependence on government jobs and income support programs. In 2001, the Conference Board of Canada estimated that the traditional land-based economy was worth between $40 and $60 million annually. For all these reasons, I recommend that the Government of Nunavut and the Qikiqtani Inuit Association work together to facilitate and promote Inuit participation in hunting, fishing, and gathering practices. This should include greater efforts to publicize the harmful effects on Inuit of the 2009 European Union ban on seal imports, and to appeal that ban to the World Trade Organization.

Over the last decade, it has become increasingly apparent that Inuit and the Arctic environment are facing multiple threats from climate change and contaminants. Each year, permanent Arctic sea ice coverage has been decreasing, reducing access to game and generating concerns about longer-term consequences such as flooding of communities from rising sea levels. While Inuit know (and archaeologists have confirmed) that their ancestors adapted to changes in game availability and distribution resulting from climate shifts, a recent study of climate change impacts on Inuit in Nunavut points out, "The mobility that Inuit once possessed to move in response to shifts in the pattern and state of their resource base is no longer possible." Inuit now live in permanent settlements. One of the resulting dangers is that they will become increasingly dependent on expensive and less nutritious store-bought food because country food cannot be secured.

The problem of environmental contaminants continues in the Arctic, both from southern sources and from resource development in the North. Living beings, including Inuit and Arctic land and marine mammals, have some of the world's highest levels of exposure to mercury and other toxic chemicals, including DDT and PCBs. These contaminants accumulate in the fat of animals at the top of the food chain, which are then consumed by Inuit. Normal freeze-and-thaw cycles release toxins gathered in annual snow accumulations into the same waters where Inuit hunt and fish. Resource development carries further environmental risks that Inuit are working to understand and manage.

There are powerful reasons—economic, scientific, cultural, and practical—for Inuit and southern scientists to cooperate in studying the

Arctic environment. As anthropologist Peter Bates explains in a recent article, Inuit and scientific approaches are markedly different in some respects, but each can complement the other. Both sets of knowledge are often needed for broad environmental studies in the Arctic, especially when the interpretation of natural events and causal analysis concerning Arctic animals is contemplated or when health studies are designed or interpreted.

As a result, the possibilities for meaningful collaborations between Inuit and scientists will increase. I would add that, for this to occur, the exchange needs to be two-way: Inuit need to be better informed about what science can offer in addressing issues such as the effects of toxic contaminants, and Qallunaat scientists need to understand the beneficial role that Inuit and their knowledge can contribute to scientific studies. It is also possible for scientific research to offer something that both the government and Inuit were seeking from the beginning of the modernizing period—local jobs for educated Inuit. I therefore recommend that the governments of Canada and Nunavut provide training and other support that will allow Inuit to actively participate in Arctic environmental studies and activities. Such training will not only add trained scientists and observers, but also provide additional employment opportunities for Inuit in communities and better research results.

RECOMMENDATIONS

1. The Government of Canada should formally acknowledge that the levels of suicide, addiction, incarceration, and social dysfunction found in the Qikiqtani region are in part symptoms of intergenerational trauma caused by historical wrongs.
2. The governments of Canada and Nunavut should ensure that sufficient Inuit social, mental health, and addiction workers and programs are available to meet the needs of all Nunavut communities.

3. The governments of Canada and Nunavut should make sure that government health, social, and education programs and services are available to the people of Nunavut on a basis equivalent to those taken for granted by Canadians in the South.
4. The Governments of Canada and Nunavut should address Inuit housing needs through provision of short-, medium-, and long-term funding to ensure adequate and safe homes for all.
5. The Government of Nunavut and the Qikiqtani Inuit Association should work together to facilitate and promote Inuit participation in hunting, fishing, and gathering practices that will sustain and strengthen Inuit culture and food security, improve nutrition, and support local economies.
6. The governments of Canada and Nunavut should provide training and other support that will allow Inuit to actively participate in Arctic environmental studies and activities.

Conclusion

I hope that this Commission marks the beginning of a new relationship, of saimaqatigiingniq, in which the two sides meet in the middle and are reconciled. This relationship must be between equal partners, who share the goal of ensuring the well-being of the Qikiqtani Inuit, and it must be built upon mutual respect and ongoing consultation. Only through continuous dialogue and engagement on all issues that could potentially impact the lives of Inuit can we achieve healing and reconciliation between the North and the South, governments and Inuit.

Thanks to the initiative and constant support of QIA, Inuit have had the opportunity to share their often painful experiences with fellow Inuit and southern Canadians, and to understand better how and why the historical failure of the Canadian government to consult Inuit before imposing new and often inappropriate policies and practices in the North has completely transformed their way of life.

My recommendations outline some key steps that I believe are required to build this new relationship. The first is awareness and acknowledgement of past wrongs, and commitment on both sides to collaborate in building a better future. The recommendations I have made on ways to strengthen Inuit culture and governance, and to ensure healthy communities, are based on the principle that the Qikiqtani Inuit must be fully empowered to decide their own future. They can find strength and resilience in their heritage of Inuit Qaujimajatuqangit, and they must be given the capacity to decide for themselves how this heritage will shape their communities and their ways of life. At the same time, the governments of Canada and Nunavut must ensure that Inuit have the modern supports and services that will help heal Nunavut's social and economic ills. For we must remember: Achieving saimaqatigiingniq is in the interests not just of Inuit but of all Canadians who value this unique culture and wish to see it thrive.

Endnotes

ANALYSIS OF THE *RCMP SLED DOGS REPORT*

The Minister's letter does not define "history," but it must mean something more comprehensive than the "chronology" that she also asked for.

In the absence of either a chronology or an analytical history of the dog killings, it is important to note that neither the Standing Committee nor the Minister called for reconciliation between Inuit and the RCMP. This silence may in effect have judged in advance that the RCMP would find that the dog killings were legal.

In drawing attention to prestige as a factor promoting ownership of dogs, Van Norman missed the underlying importance of sled dogs in Inuit culture; these are explored in Francis Lévesque, "Les Inuit, Leurs Chiens Et L'administration," 139–75.

Figures in this chapter are derived from appendices in the annual report by the Advisory Committee on Northern Development on *Government Activities in the North.*

The question of whether there is "wrongdoing" without a breach of statutes or ordinances is one on which the QTC research team and the RCMP Review Team would probably not agree. The position adopted in this book is that when people in authority perform lawful acts in an arbitrary or disrespectful manner or without regard for harm done to individuals, a wrong has occurred, even if no specific law has been broken.

Wrongdoing does not necessarily leave a paper trail. Only if record creation and retention rules were strictly followed can the integrity of the whole record be guaranteed. The official record would be unreliable if decisions were made in person or on the telephone, if correspondence was treated as personal, failed to be placed on any official file, or was subsequently removed by any person.

Until 1966, departments could consult a Public Records Committee, which oversaw the destruction or preservation of records referred to it. From 1966 to 1987, a Treasury Board directive, the Public Records Order, required departments to consult the Dominion Archivist before destroying their own records.

For sources of other quotes, please see the complete notes provided online.

THE OFFICIAL MIND OF CANADIAN COLONIALISM

The definition of the contact zone is offered by Pratt, *Imperial Eyes*, 7.

The progressive extension of broadcast services into the Arctic was reported on annually in *Government Activities in the North*, the regular roll-up of all departmental activities published by the Advisory Committee on Northern Development.

Phillips wrote of the typical Mountie, "his objective at first was simply to exist," *Canada's North*, 126.

E. Rheaume is quoted from a telephone interview with QTC researchers and staff, March 8, 2010.

For sources of other quotes, please see the complete notes provided online.

ILLINNIARNIQ: SCHOOLING IN QIKIQTAALUK

The Northern Services Officer is quoted from Flucke, "Wither the Eskimo," 17.

Grantham is quoted from LAC, RG 22, Indian and Northern Affairs, accession A-1-A, volume 805, file 40-8-9, part 1, Education of Eskimos, "Minutes of the Fifth Meeting of the Sub-Committee on Eskimo Education," October 29, 1954.

Mosesee Qappik's experiences are shared in QTC, May 15, 2008.

The quote on rapid urbanization in the Arctic District is from LAC, RG 22, Indian and Northern Affairs, volume 1331, file 40-2-136, part 5, "Director of Deputy Minister Gordon," February 15, 1968.

Gamailie Kilukishak is quoted from QIA, July 1, n.y.

Ooloosie Kopalie is quoted from QIA, March 23, 2005.

Jeannie Mike's experiences are found in QTC, May 14, 2008. She is quoted from the same source.

Kaujak Kanajuk is quoted from QIA, n.d.

The former teacher is quoted from NWT Archives, collection 331, Northwest Territories Department of the Executive fonds, accession G-1988-004, box 8, Oral History—Transcripts Teachers (Harper), "Interview with Kenn Harper," May 31, 1979.

For Jenness' figures and subsequent quote, see Jenness, *Eskimo Administration II*, 129.

Taqtu is quoted from Innuksuk and Cowan, *We Don't Live in Snow Houses Now:* 97.

Quppirualuk Padluq is quoted from QTC, January 30, 2008. Geela Akulukjak is quoted from QTC, May 14, 2008. July Papatsie is quoted from QTC, November 27, 2008.

Elizabeth Kyak is quoted from QTC, December 10, 2008.

Mick Mallon is quoted from Dorais, *The Language of Inuit*, 195.

John J. and Irma Honigmann are quoted from Honigmann, *Eskimo Townsmen*, 157.

The "fundamental rights" denied to Inuit parents is a reference to Article 13 of the United Nations International Covenant on Economic Social and Cultural Rights.

Louis Uttak is quoted from QTC, September 12, 2008. Jeannie Mike is quoted from QTC, May 14, 2008.

For the discussion of ilira, see Kuptana, "Ilira, or Why it was Unthinkable," 7.

Mary Battye is quoted from QTC, May 14, 2008. Elisapee Ootoova is quoted from QTC, December 11, 2008. Peterosie Qarpik is quoted from QIA, April 11, 2005. Annie Paingut Peterloosie is quoted from QIA, n.d.

The 1962 and 1970 figures are from MacPherson, *Dreams and Vision*, 207. Figures for 1979 (including hostels) are from a recruiting pamphlet, Northwest Territories Department of Education, "Teach in Canada's Arctic" (Yellowknife, 1980).

NUUTAUNIQ: MOVES IN INUIT LIFE

Brody, *Living Arctic*, 83.

Concepts

Robert Williamson is quoted from Royal Commission on Aboriginal Peoples (RCAP), *The High Arctic Relocation*, 11.

The term "ilagiit" is discussed in Trott, "Ilagiit and TuqΠuraqtuq.

Quoted material is taken from McElroy, *Nunavut Generations*, 87; and M'Donald, *A Narrative of Some Passages in the Life of Eenoolooapik*, 5.

Moved Groups

R.A.J. Phillips, *Canada's North*, 80–81. Susan Singoorie is quoted from QTC, November 27, 2008; Rhoda Tunraq is quoted from QTC, March

23, 2008; Tagoona Qavavouq is quoted from QTC, April 23, 2008; and Pauloosie Kaujak is quoted from QTC, April 23, 2008.

Samwillie Elijasialak is quoted from RCAP, *The High Arctic Relocation*, vol 1, 43–44.

Norman Komoartuk is quoted from QTC, May 13, 2008. Leah Evic is quoted from QTC, May 14, 2008.

The official record was used in Damas, *Arctic Migrants/Arctic Villagers*, 142–49.

Moving Individuals

Gene Rheaume is quoted from QTC, March 16, 2010, (telephone interview); Walter Rudnicki quoted from QTC, November 25, 2008; Jonah Akpak is quoted from QTC, September 9, 2008; Bryan Pearson is quoted from QTC, July 17, 2008; and Thomas Kublu is quoted from QTC, January 26, 2009.

The QTC gratefully acknowledges David King's generosity in making available his research notes and draft of an unpublished scholarly paper on Inuit education and his copies of archival documents related to all communities in Qikiqtaaluk.

Ruth Sangoya is quoted QTC, April 8, 2005; Gordon Rennie is quoted from QTC, June 18, 2008; Annie Shappa is quoted from QTC, May 17, 2008; Paul Quassa is quoted from QTC, September 12, 2008; and Thomasie Panniluk is quoted from QTC, September 9, 2008.

Moses Kasamak is quoted QIA, February 17, 2005; Peter Akpalialuk is quoted from QIA, March 1, 2006; and Juda Taqtu is quoted from QIA, n.d.

Mina Eyaituq is quoted from QTC, March 4, 2008; Lottie Arragutainaq is quoted from QTC, March 4, 2008; Annie Appaqaq-Arragutainaq is quoted from QTC, March 5, 2008; and Emily Takatak is quoted from QTC, March 5, 2008.

PALIISIKKUT: POLICING IN QIKIQTAALUK

Elijah Panipakoocho is quoted from QTC, December 19, 2008.

Brody explains ilira in the context of Inuit relations with RCMP in *The Other Side of Eden*, 43.

Amagoalik and McComber, *Changing the Face of Canada*, 19.

Taissumani Nunamiutautilluta, 1920 to 1945

Joshua Idlout is quoted from QTC, n.d.

Grant is quoted from her work, *Arctic Justice*, 20.

Arrival of the RCMP in Qikiqtaaluk

Hildebrandt is quoted from his work, *Views from Fort Battleford*, 36.

Mckay, "Maintain the Right?" 4.

For the purposes of the QTC reports, the English term "camp" has been dropped in favour of the term "ilagiit nunagivaktangat" (plural "ilagiit nunagivaktangit"). The choice of the term was determined through a terminology/linguistics workshop organized by the QTC in April 2010.

Morrison is quoted from his work, *Showing the Flag*, 2.

Hugh Fagan is quoted from *Qimmit*, film, directed by Ole Gjerstad and Joelie Sanguya (Montreal, National Film Board of Canada, 2010).

The former RCMP officers are quoted from *Qimmit*. Mosha Akavak is quoted from QTC, July 2008. Sam Arnakallak and Timothy Kadloo are quoted from Grant, *Arctic Justice*, 232.

Sangussaqtauliqtilluta, 1945 to 1960

Terry Jenkin is quoted from QTC, November 26, 2008.

The Fox-3 quotation is from LAC, RG 22, Indian and Northern Affairs, series A-1-a, volume 833, file 40-8-24, part 1, Eskimo Women (Relations

With), "Letter to Minister of Northern Affairs from A. DewLiner, re: Eskimos on DEW Line," October 1, 1958.

John Amagoalik is quoted from Amagoalik and McComber, *Changing the Face of Canada*, 36.

The quotation on carrying out the work of other departments is from Morrison, *Showing the Flag*, 152.

The quotations on the role of the NSO and tensions between AANDC and the RCMP are from NWT, 263, Alexander Stevenson fonds, series N-1992-023, box 42, file 5, Royal Canadian Mounted Police 1949–1973, Letter to Nick Nickels from C. M. Bolger, re: Igloolik, November 24, 1961.

The Calvin Alexander quotations are from *Qimmit*.

Joe Tikivik is quoted from QTC, May 17, 2008.

Nunalinnguqtitauliqtilluta, 1961 to 1975

Duffy is quoted from his work, *The Road to Nunavut*, 196–97.

The 1962 government quotation is from LAC, RG85, Northern Affairs Program, series 1884-85, volume 1951, file A-1000/169, part 1, "Report on Trip to Frobisher," by F. H. Compton, Frobisher Bay, NWT, January 31, 1962.

The quotation on the Cape Dorset petition is from Kulchyski and Tester, *Kiumajut (Talking Back)*, 262.

July Papatsie is quoted from QTC, November 27, 2008.

Yatsushiro, "The Changing Eskimo," 23-24.

T. E. R. Lysk is quoted from LAC, RG18, RCMP series 1985-86/048, volume 55, file TA 500-8-1-5, Memo to Officer Commanding, Frobisher Bay, from E. R. Lysk, June 5, 1964.

Inuit Special Constables and Intercultural Interpretation

Mosha Akavak is quoted from QTC, July 2008.

Ejesiak Padluq is quoted from QTC, January 24, 2008.

Terry Jenkin is quoted from QTC, November 26, 2008.

The quotation from the 1978 report to the Commission of the NWT is from RCMP Archives Management Section, volume 1, file T-125-1, supp A, Territorial Policing Agreement—Non-Police Duties, Memorandum from A. H. Buttler, Chief Superintendent, G Division to Commissioner, re: attached letter regarding Territorial Policing Agreement, June 2, 1978.

Dog Ordinance and the Killing of Qimmiit

Quassa and McComber's, *We Need to Know Who We Are*, 38.

Jacopoosie Peter is quoted from QTC, June 18, 2008.

Mosesee Qiyuakjuk is quoted from QIA, April 2006.

Joshie Teemotee Mitsima is quoted from QTC, n.d.

Yatsushiro quotes an Inuk on the control of qimmiit but also of Inuit in "The Changing Eskimo," 20–21.

July Papatsie is quoted from QTC, November 27, 2008.

Elisapee Ootoova is quoted from QTC, December 11, 2008.

Joshua Idlout is quoted from QTC, n.d.

Kutsiz, "An Elder Offers Advice," 12.

PIVALLIAJULIRINIQ: ECONOMIC DEVELOPMENT IN QIKIQTAALUK

Cultural Constraints—Government Assumptions

The policy statement on economic and cultural change is taken from Canada, Department of Northern Affairs and National Resources (NANR), Advisory Committee on Northern Development, "Government Activities in the North, 195." (Ottawa: Department of Northern Affairs and National Resources, 1957).

Lachlan Burwash is quoted from his 1924 *Toronto Star* interview in LAC, RG85, volume 755, file 4687.

Elder Naki Ekho is quoted from McElroy, *Nunavut Generations*, 87.

Long-Range Goals of Government and Inuit Organizations

AANDC's objectives are quoted from *Department of Indian Affairs and Northern Development, Canada's North, 1970–1980*, 24, 31.

Tungavik Federation of Nunavut, "An Inuit Response," *CARC—Northern Perspectives*, 17, no. 1 (1988).

Preparing Individuals For Economic Development

The 1955 departmental statement is quoted from Department of Northern Affairs and National Resources (NANR), *Annual Report Fiscal Year 1954–1955 and Human Problems in the Canadian North* (Ottawa: NANR, 1955), 10.

Muckpaloo is quoted from Innuksuk and Cowan, *We Don't Live in Snow Houses Now*; 175.

Samson Meeko Sr. is quoted from QTC, 4 March 2008.

Employment

Inuit wage employment statistics are taken from Mitchell, *From Talking Chiefs*, 147.

Pond Inlet statistics are taken from Bissett, *Northern Baffin Island*, 164.

George Wenzel is quoted QTC, June 18, 2009; Henry Boaz is quoted from QTC, n.d.; Manasie Amagoalik is quoted from QTC, December 19, 2008; and Ham Kudloo is quoted from QTC, December 19, 2008.

Community-Focused Development

For the Cape Dorset story, see Houston, *Confessions of an Igloo Dweller* and Ryan, *Cape Dorset Prints*.

Mitchell, *From Talking Chiefs*, 22.

Mining, Oil, and Gas

The 1950 survey was published in Dunbar and Greenway, *Arctic Canada from the Air*.

Wenzel's findings and quote on the Inuit employment at the mine are taken from Wenzel, "Remote Site Labour," 89.

Specific information on how money from mining was spent in communities is from McPherson, *New Owners in their Own Land*, 106.

IGLULIRINIQ: HOUSING IN QIKIQTAALUK

Brody, *The People's Land*, 127.

Sarah Amgoalik is quoted from Tester and Kulchyski, *Tammarniit (Mistakes)*, 182.

The quote about extras that go with a house is from Hamilton, *Arctic Revolution*, 211.

Gamailie Kilukishak is quoted from QIA, n.d.

Peter Awa is quoted from QIA, July 8, 2004.

Alicee Joamee is quoted from QTC, June 17, 2008.

Rachel Panipakoocho is quoted from QTC, December 19, 2008.

The 1955 government plans are quoted from HBC Archives, RG 7, 1, 1753, "R. G. Robertson to R. H. Chesshire," 22 April 1955.

Eskimo Housing Loan Program, 1959 to 1965

Emily Takatak is quoted from QTC, March 5, 2008.

Elizabeth Kyak is quoted from QTC, December 10, 2012.

Juda Taqtu is quoted from QIA, n.d.

Eskimo Rental Housing Program, 1965 to 1968

Elijah Padluq is quoted from QTC, September 16, 2008.

Ham Kudloo is quoted from QIA, February 21, 2005.

Johanasie Apak is quoted from QIA, April 2, 2004.

Julia Amaroalik is quoted from QTC, September 11, 2009.

Mary Battye is quoted from QTC, May 14, 2008.
Moses Kasarnak is quoted from QIA, February 17, 2005.

Continuing Challenges

Elisapee Arreak is quoted from QIA, March 25, 2004.
Leah Okadlak is quoted from QTC, April 21, 2008.
Elijah Padluq is quoted from QTC, September 16, 2008.
Jaypeetee Kudlualik is quoted from QTC, October 1, 2008.
Alooloo Kautauk is quoted from QTC, September 9, 2008.
Markosie Sowdluapik is quoted from QTC, May 14, 2008.
Apphia Killiktee is quoted from QTC, December 11, 2008.
Leah Evic is quoted from QTC, May 14, 2008.
Quppirualuk Padluq is quoted from QTC, January 24, 2008.
Emily Takatak is quoted from QTC, March 5, 2008.
Iqaluk Juralak is quoted from QTC, n.d.
Leah Okadlak is quoted from QTC, April 21, 2008.
Damas, *Arctic Migrants*, 122.

Northern Rental Purchase Program

Pearson's arguments are taken from Pearson, personal papers, "NWT's native homes subject of concern," from unknown newspaper (c. 1974), and Pearson, personal papers, "Build houses here, North told," from unknown newspaper (c. 1974).

The 1958 quote is from, LAC, RG 22, Indian and Northern Affairs, accession A-1-a, volume 335, file 40-8-23, part 1, Housing Program—Criticism of the Department Re: Treatment of Eskimos (Attacks on the Department re: Eskimos).

Population statistics are taken from Wally Firth, MP, as quoted in Duffy, *The Road to Nunavut*, 46.

AANIAJURLIRINIQ: HEALTH CARE IN QIKIQTAALUK

Miluqtitutttuq Akesuk is quoted from QTC, n.d.

Wenzel, "Inuit Health and the Health Care System: Change and Status Quo," *Études/Inuit/Studies* 5, no. 1 (1981): 13.

Taissumani Nunamiutautilluta

Kudjuarjuk is quoted from Bennett and Rowley, *Uqalurait*, 212.

Edith Prudence Hockin is quoted from Cowall, "Puvaluqatatiluta, When We Had Tuberculosis," 46.

Sangussaqtauliqtilluta

Dr. Moore is quoted from LAC, RG 85, volume 1348, file 1000/150, part 2, Letter to Director, Northern Administration and Lands Branch from Dr. P.E. Moore, Director, Indian and Northern Health Services, October 29, 1957, in Tester, *Health and Medical Care*, 12.

The quotation on public health education is from "Disease and Death in Canada's North," (paper presented at the WHO Conference on Medicine and Public Health in the Arctic and Antarctic, Geneva, August 1962). An Inuit Elder is quoted on the nurse-patient relationship from Canitz, "Nursing in the North," (1990).

C.D. Howe

Elijah Padluq is quoted from QTC, September 16, 2008.

Walter Rudnicki is quoted from QTC, November 25, 2008.

Minister Jean Lesage is quoted from Nixon, "Percy Elmer Moore," (1989), 167.

Criticisms of Inuit conditions on the *C.D. Howe* are from Grygier, *A Long Way from Home*, 93, 97.

Centralization

DNHW, "Health Services for Small Population Groups," (1963), 1.

The young patient is quoted from an uncited letter from a sanatorium in Tester, McNicoll, and Irniq, "Writing for our Lives," 131.

The 1950 article is "The Surprising Eskimo," *Canada's Health and Welfare* 13, no. 110 (December 1955): 2–3.

Jonah Kelly is quoted from QTC, June 18, 2008.

Sytukie Joamie is quoted from QTC, May 17, 2008.

Baird, "The Eskimo Woman: Her Changing World," *The Beaver* (Spring 1959): 51.

Collins is quoted from his work, "The Puzzling Plight of the Eskimo," *Imperial Oil Review* (October 1960), 16.

The Impacts of Care and Evolving Concerns, 1960–1975

Duffy, *The Road to Nunavut*, 80–81.

Jeetaloo Kakee is quoted from QTC, June 18, 2008.

Martha Idlout is quoted from QTC, April 14, 2008t.

Levi Evic is quoted from QTC, May 15, 2008.

Apphia Agalakti Awa is quoted from Wachowich, *Saqiyuq*, 42.

Leah Otak is quoted from QTC, September 12, 2008.

Nutrition, Food Security, and Diet

Kokiapik, "Between Two Worlds," *Canadian Woman Studies/Les Cahiers de la Femme* 14, no. 4 (1994): 21.

Dr. G. E. Gaulton is quoted from Duffy, *The Road to Nunavut*, 75.

David Kalluk is quoted from QTC, April 23, 2008.

Shorty Shoo is quoted from QIA, n.d.

Solomonie Qiyutaq is quoted from QTC, March 2006.

Dr. Curson is quoted from Eber, "Baffin Island's Flying Dentists," *North* 19, no. 1 (1972): 2.

Moller, "A Problem of the Government?" 58.

Rhoda Katsak is quoted on the subject from Wachowich, *Saqiyuq*, 176.

Mental Health

Vallee, "Eskimo Theories of Mental Illness," 56.

Frank Tester is quoted from QTC, November 28, 2008.

Laimiki Innuaraq is quoted from QTC, September 12, 2008.

Alicee Joamie is quoted from QTC, June 17, 2008.

Thomas Kublu is quoted from QTC, January 26, 2009.

Annie Shappa is quoted from QTC, May 18, 2008.

Lotz, "Social science research and northern development," Arctic 21, no. 4 (December 1968): 291–94.

ITK is quoted from their Department of Health and Social Development vision statement, https://www.itk.ca/about-itk/dept-health-and-social-development.

Wenzel, "Inuit Health," 7.

Inspector H.A. Larsen is cited from LAC, RG18, RCMP fonds, box 42, file D-1512-2-4. The comment about the value of the Family Allowances was made with respect to Arviat in 1951.

Willis, "Northern Health," 22.

Robertson, "The Coming Crisis in the North," 44–52.

O'Neil, "Self-Determination, Medical Ideology and Health Services in Inuit Communities," 33–50.

Mary Iqaluk is quoted from QTC, January 20, 2009.

QIMMILIRINIQ: INUIT SLED DOGS IN QIKIQTAALUK

Pauloosie Veevee is quoted from QIA, July 2006.

The 1956–57 formal statement on policy is from the Advisory Committee on Northern Development, "Department of Northern Affairs and National Resources: Northern Administration and Lands Branch. Arctic Division," Government Activities in the North, 1956 (Ottawa, 1957).

Understanding Qimmiit

Unless otherwise noted, the data used in this section comes from MacRury, *The Inuit Dog*; Montcombroux, *The Canadian Inuit Dog*; Freuchen, "The Eskimo Dog" in *Mammals*, 141–87.

Hazards and Socialization

Kananginaaq Pootoogook is quoted from QTC, January 30, 2008.

Simonie Michael is cited from QIA, January 26, 2005.

Ikey Kugitikakjuk is quoted from QIA, n.d.

David Mickiyuk is quoted from QTC, January 20, 2009.

Qimmiit in the Traditional Inuit Economy

Isaac Shooyook's experiences are recorded in QTC, April 22, 2008.

Peter Akpalialuk's experiences are found in QIA, March 1, 2006.

Pauloosie Ekidlak is quoted from QIA, February 19, 2004.

Myths and Symbolic Culture

Simonie Michael's recollection about naming puppies is from QIA, January 26, 2005.

Jimmy "Flash" Kilabuk's recollection of qimmiit as family members is from QIA, December 2, 2004.

The description of qimmiit as "everything" is from Pauloosie Ekidlak, QIA, February 19, 2004, and Peter Akpalialuk, QIA, March 1, 2006.

Laws Affecting Qimmiit

The section allowing the destruction of dogs by the RCMP can be found in Northwest Territories, Council of the Northwest Territories, "An Ordinance Respecting Dogs," chapter 2, 1949 (Ottawa: King's Printer, 1950).

Qimmiq Diseases

Simonie Michael is quoted from QIA, January 26, 2005.

Jacobie Iqalukjuak remembers the effects of rabies in QIA, March 23, 2004.

The term "niaqqirilutik" for distemper is from Johnasie Apak, QIA, April 2, 2004. The term "niaqunngujuq" for distemper is from Agiaq in Oosten and Laugrand, *Travelling and Surviving on Our Land*, 61.

Neomi Panipakutuuk's experiences are quoted from QIA, February 17, 2004.

Ipeelie Koonoo's recollections about rabies and distemper are quoted from QIA, n.d..

Elijah Mike discusses the seriousness of rabies in QIA, January 25, 2005.

Neomi Panipakutuuk is quoted from QIA, February 9, 2004.

The term "qimmiijaqtuq" is from Agiaq in Oosten and Laugrand, *Travelling and Surviving on Our Land*, 60.

Attacks by Qimmiit

Rosie Katsak is quoted from QTC, December 19, 2008.

Milton Freeman is quoted from QTC, June 4, 2009.

Frank and Anita Vallee are quoted from RCMP, "The RCMP and the Inuit Sled Dogs," (2006), 474–76, which cites 1963-02-15 "A Dog's World," Frank and Anita Vallee Povungnituk Newsletter #7.

Gordon Rennie is quoted from QTC, June 17, 2008.

W. G. "Moose" Kerr is quoted from RCMP, "The RCMP and the Inuit Sled Dogs," (2006), 225.

The RCMP report is quoted from LAC, RG18, RCMP fonds, 1985-86/048 55, volume 55, file TA 500-8-1-12, Conditions Amongst Eskimos—Generally, by D.S. Moodie, July 12, 1955.

Pauloosie Veevee is quoted from QIA, July 1, 2006.

Mosesee Qiyuakjuk is quoted from QIA, April 1, 2006.

Levi Evic is quoted from QTC, May 15, 2008.

Louis Uttak is quoted from QIA, July 12, 2004.

Ejetsiak Peter is quoted from QTC, January 31, 2008.

Nuna Parr is quoted from QTC, January 30, 2009.

RCMP member Al Bunn is quoted from RCMP, "The RCMP and the Inuit Sled Dogs," 534–35.

Taqialuk Temela is quoted from QIA, August 24, 2004.

Dr. H. G. Ross is quoted from RCMP, "The RCMP and the Inuit Sled Dogs," 474.

R. D. Van Norman is quoted from RCMP, "The RCMP and the Inuit Sled Dogs," 363-65.

F. J. G. Cunningham is quoted from RCMP, "The RCMP and the Inuit Sled Dogs," 210.

P. Godt is quoted from LAC, RG85, Northern Affairs Program, series D-1-A, volume 1473, file 201-1-8, Report by P. Godt, Acting Chief, Co-operative Development, re: Trip to Cape Dorset, May 21, 1959.

F. Delaute is quoted from NWT Archives, Northern Affairs Branch, series G-79-003, box 163, file 4, Memo from J. F. Delaute to Administrsator of the Arctic, re: shooting of the dogs by the RCMP, June 22, 1959.

Yatsushiro, "The Changing Eskimo," 21–22

Levi Evic is quoted from QTC, May 15, 2008.

For both quotations from Adamie Veevee, see QTC, May 15, 2008.

Jacopie Nuqingaq is quoted from QTC, September 30, 2008.

Leah Nuqingag is quoted from QTC, September 30, 2008.

Meeka Kakudluk was interviewed during preparation of Gleeson, "Reliving the Relocation: Residents Return to Camps they Once Called Home," *Northern News Services*, August 2, 1999.

For Jacopie Koosiaq, see his "Letter to the Editor," *Inukshuk*, April 10, 1975.

Jason Palluq is quoted from QTC, September 8, 2008.

Joanasie Illauq is quoted from QTC, September 8, 2008.

Tester, "Inuit Sled Dogs," 40.

Paomee Komangapik is quoted from QTC, December 19, 2008.

For Rosie Katsak, see QTC, December 19, 2008.

Mucktar Akumalik is quoted from QIA, n.d.

Milton Freeman is quoted from QTC, June 4, 2009.

Simon Idlout it quoted from QTC, April 14, 2008.

Ludy Padluk is quoted from QTC, April 16, 2008.

Thomas Kublu is quoted from QTC, January 26, 2009.

Eugene Ipkamak is quoted from QIA, August 19, 2004.

Peter Awa is quoted from QIA, July 9, 2004.

Jake Ikeperiar testified about shooting dogs in QTC, September 9, 2008.

Moses Allianaq is quoted from QIA, February 25, 2004.

Celina Irngaut is quoted from QTC, September 12, 2008.

Both quotations from Pauloosie Ekidlak are from QIA, February 19, 2004.

Akeeshoo Joamie is quoted from QIA, n.d.

Abraham Ulayuruluk is quoted from QTC, September 12, 2008.

Who Killed the Qimmiit?

Mucktar Akumalik is quoted from QTC, April 22, 2008.

George Wenzel is quoted from QTC, June 18, 2009.

Goteleak Judea is quoted from QTC, September 15, 2008.

Inuit Perspectives

Pauloosie Veevee is quoted from QIA, July 1, 2006.

For "passive resistance" see Jack Grabowski, quoted in RCMP, "The RCMP and the Inuit Sled Dogs," 435–46.

Simon Idlout is quoted from QTC, April 14, 2008.

Quotation from the QTC final report is from p. 16.

Snowmobiles

Jaykolasie Killiktee is quoted from QTC, December 10, 2008.

Mary Iqaqrialuk is quoted from QIA, March 30, 2004.

Technical and statistical information in this section is collected mainly from two publications: Smith, "The Mechanical Dog Team," (1972), and Ingham, *As the Snow Flies*, 155–63.

Inuit Inquiries

Yatsushiro, "The Changing Eskimo," 19–26.

Bryan Pearson was quoted in Stewart, "The shameful way we treat our Eskimos," *Star Weekly*, June 25, 1966, and repeated his observations in Northwest Territories, "Debates: Official Report," 212–13.

For an example of the silence created by shame and hurt, see Eena Angmarlik, QTC, May 15, 2008.

QTC, *Achieving Saimaqatigiingniq*, 45.

ACHIEVING SAIMAQATIGIINGNIQ

For the purposes of the QTC reports, the English term "Inuit sled dogs" has been dropped in favour of the Inuktitut term "qimmiit."

The term "poverty" should be considered in the context of the period. It was possible for Inuit families in ilagiit nunagivaktangit to feel they were living comfortably, even though they had very little income and would be considered extremely poor by Western standards. Inuit in settlements, however, needed cash income from wage employment or social benefits to meet daily needs.

Some of the recommendations made by witnesses at our hearings did not fall within our mandate, and so could not be included.

For sources of other quotes, please see the complete notes provided at www.qia.ca or www.qtcommission.com.

References

Please note that the following reference list has been abridged for the printed publication. For additional notes on each chapter, visit www.qia.ca or www.qtcommission.com.

Baird, Irene. "The Eskimo Woman: Her Changing World." *The Beaver* (Spring 1959), 51.

Bates, Peter. "Inuit and Scientific Philosophies about Planning, Prediction and Uncertainty." *Arctic Anthropology* 44, no. 2 (2007).

Bennet, John and Susan Rowley. *Uqalurait: An Oral History of Nunavut.* Montreal: McGill–Queen's University Press, 2004.

Bissett, Don. *Northern Baffin Island: An Area Economic Survey.* Department of Indian Affairs and Northern Development, Industrial Division. Ottawa, ON: 1974.

Boas, Franz. *The Central Eskimo.* Nebraska: University of Nebraska Press, 1964.

Bonesteel, Sarah. *Canada's Relationship with Inuit: A History of Policy and Program Development.* Prepared for Indian and Northern Affairs Canada, June 2006.

Brody, Hugh. Living *Arctic: Hunters of the Canadian North.* Vancouver: Douglas & McIntyre, 1987.

Brody, Hugh. *The Other Side of Eden: Hunters, Farmers, and the Shaping of the World.* New York: North Point Press, 2000.

Canitz, Brenda. "Nursing in the North." *Northern Perspectives* 17, no. 3 (August–October 1989).

Clancy, Peter. "The Making of Eskimo Policy in Canada, 1952–1962." *Arctic* 40, no. 3 (1987): 194–195.

Coates, Kenneth. *Canada's Colonies: A History of the Yukon and Northwest Territories*. Toronto: Lorimer, 1985.

Coates, Kenneth, W. Lackenbauer, W. Morrison, and Greg Poelzer. *Arctic Front: Defending Canada in the Far North*. Toronto: Thomas Allen, 2008.

Collins, Robert. "The Puzzling Plight of the Eskimo." *Imperial Oil Review* (October 1960), 16.

Cowall, Emily. "Puvaluqatatiluta, When We Had Tuberculosis." PhD diss., McMaster University,

Damas, David. *Arctic Migrants/Arctic Villagers: The Transformation of Inuit Settlement in the Central Arctic*. Montreal: McGill–Queen's University Press, 2002.

Davis-Putt, Betty-Anne. "Rights of Passage in the North: From Evacuation to the Birth of a Culture." In Mary Crnkovitch, ed. *Gossip: A Spoken History of Women in the North*. Ottawa: Canadian Arctic Resources Committee, 1990.

Dick, Lyle. *Muskox Land: Ellesmere Island in the Age of Contact*. Calgary: University of Calgary Press, 2001.

Diubaldo, Richard. *The Government of Canada and the Inuit, 1900–1967*. Ottawa: Indian and Northern Affairs Canada, 1985.

Dorais, Louis-Jacques. *The Language of Inuit: Syntax, Semantics, and Society in the Arctic*. Montreal: McGill–Queen's University Press, 2010.

Dunbar, Moira and Keith Greenaway. *Arctic Canada from the Air*. Ottawa: Defence Research Board, 1956.

Duffy, R. Quinn. *The Road to Nunavut: The Progress of the Eastern Arctic Inuit Since the Second World War*. Montreal: McGill–Queen's University Press, 1988.

Eber, Dorothy. "Baffin Island's Flying Dentists." *North* 19, no. 1 (1972): 2.

Egeland, Grace M. et al. "Food insecurity among Inuit preschoolers: Nunavut Inuit Child Health Survey, 2007–2008." *Canadian Medical Association Journal* 182, no. 2 (2010).

Ehrlander, Mary. "The History and Roots of a Frontier Alcohol Culture: Alaska and Northern Canada." *The Northern Review* 32 (2012): 63–103.

Elton, Charles. "Epidemics Among Sledge Dogs in the Canadian Arctic and their Relation to Disease in the Arctic Fox." *Canadian Journal of Research* 5, no. 6 (1931): 673–692.

Flucke, A. F. "Wither the Eskimo." *Northern Affairs Bulletin* 10, no. 1 (1963): 17.

Fortier, Y. O. "Activities of the Geological Survey of Canada in the Arctic Islands, 1947–1953." *The Arctic Circular* 8, no. 3 (1954): 25–33.

Grant, Shelagh. *Sovereignty or Security: Government Policy in the Canadian North 1936–1950*. Vancouver: University of British Columbia Press, 1988.

Gleeson, Richard. "Reliving the Relocations: Residents Return to Camps they Once Called Home." *Northern News Services* (August 2, 1999).

Grygier, Pat Sandiford. *A Long Way From Home: The Tuberculosis Epidemic Among the Inuit*. Montreal: McGill–Queen's University Press, 1994.

Hamilton, John David. *Arctic Revolution: Social Change in the Northwest Territories, 1935–1994*. Toronto: Dundurn Press, 1994.

Harper, Kenn. "Writing in Inuktitut: An Historical Perspective." *Inuktitut* 53 (1983): 19–24.

Harper, Kenn. "Taissumani: The Closing of Padloping." *Nunatsiaq News*, October 31, 2008.

Hicks, F. J. "The Eastern Arctic Medical Patrol." *Canadian Medical Association Journal* 100, no. 11 (1969): 537–38.

Hinds, Margery. *High Arctic Venture*. Toronto: Ryerson Press, 1968.

Hobart, C. W. "Inuit Employment at the Nanisivik Mine on Baffin Island." *Inuit Studies* 6, no. 1 (1982): 53–74.

Honigmann, John and Irma. *Eskimo Townsmen*. Ottawa: Canadian Research Centre for Anthropology, University of Ottawa, 1965.

Houston, James. *Confessions of an Igloo Dweller*. Boston: Houghton Mifflin, 1995.

Hunt, Constance. "The Development and Decline of Northern Conservation Reserves." *Contact: Journal of Urban and Environmental Affairs* 8, no. 4 (1976): 30–75.

Ingham, L. Allister. *As the Snow Flies: A History of Snowmobile Development in North America*. Lanigan, SK: Snowmobile Research Publishing, 2000.

Innuksuk, Rhoda and Susan Cowan. *We Don't Live in Snow Houses Now: Reflections of Arctic Bay*. Ottawa: Canadian Arctic Producers, 1976.

Ittinuar, Peter Freuchen. *1950—Teach An Eskimo How to Read... Conversations with Peter Freuchen Ittinuar*. Edited by Thierry Rodon. Iqaluit: Language and Culture Program, Nunavut Arctic College, 2008.

Jennes, Diamond. *Eskimo Administration II: Canada*. Technical paper no. 14, Arctic Institute of North America, Montreal, 1964.

Jull, Peter. "Inuit Politics and the Arctic Seas." In Franklin Griffiths, ed., *Politics of the Northwest Passage*. Montreal: McGill–Queen's University Press, 1987.

Katerberg, William H. "A Northern Vision: Frontiers and the West in the Canadian and American Imagination." *American Review of Canadian Studies* 33 (2003): 554–56.

Kokiapik, Rhoda. "Between Two Worlds." *Canadian Woman Studies/Les Cahiers de la Femme* 14, no 4 (1994): 21.

Kulchyski, Peter Keith and Frank J. Tester. *Kiumajut (Talking Back): Game Management and Inuit Rights, 1900–70*. Vancouver: UBC Press, 2007.

Kuptana, Rosemarie. "Ilira, or Why It Was Unthinkable for Inuit to Challenge Qallunaat Authority." *Inuit Art Quarterly* 8, no. 3 (1993): 7.

Kutsiz, Mary Anulik. "An Elder Offers Advice." *Inuktitut* 79 (1995): 12.

Laugrand, Frédéric and Oosten Jarich. *Inuit Shamanism and Christianity: Transitions and Transformations in the Twentieth Century*. Montreal: McGill–Queen's University Press, 2010.

Loomba, Ania. *Colonialism/Postcolonialism*. London and New York: Routledge, 1998.

Lotz, J. "Northern Alternatives." *Arctic* 28, no. 1 (1975): 4–5.

Lotz, J. "Social science research and northern development." *Arctic* 21, no. 4 (December 1968): 291–294.

Lyall, Ernie. *An Arctic Man: Sixty-Five Years in Canada's North*. Edmonton: Hurtig Publishers, 1979.

MacPherson, Norman. *Dreams and Visions: Education in the Northwest Territories*. Yellowknife: Northwest Territories Education, 1991.

MacRury, Ian. *The Inuit Dog: Its Provenance, Environment and History*. Cambridge: University of Cambridge, 1991.

Marcus, Alan R. *Out in the Cold: The Legacy of Canada's Inuit Relocation Experiment in the High Arctic*. Copenhagen: IWGIA, 1992.

Matthiasson, John. *Living Off the Land: Change Among the Inuit of Baffin Island*. Peterborough, Ontario: Broadview Press, 1992.

Mayes, Robert G. "The Creation of a Dependent People: The Inuit of Cumberland Sound, Northwest Territories." Ph.D. dissertation, McGill University, 1978.

McElroy, Ann. *Nunavut Generations: Change and Continuity in Canadian Inuit Communities*. Long Grove, Illinois: Waveland Press, 2008.

McGregor, Heather. *Inuit Education and Schools in the Eastern Arctic*. Vancouver: UBC Press, 2010.

McPherson, Robert. *New Owners in their Own Land: Minerals and Inuit Land Claims*. Calgary: University of Calgary Press and Arctic Institute of North America, 2003.

Mitchell, Marybelle. *From Talking Chiefs to a Native Corporate Elite*. Montreal: McGill–Queen's University Press, 1996.

Moller, Helle. "A Problem of the Government? Colonization and the Socio-Cultural Experience of Tuberculosis in Nunavut." Master's thesis, Copenhagen University, 2005.

Monk, Lindsay. "Decolonizing Home: A Reconceptualization of First Nations' Housing in Canada." Master's thesis, University of Victoria, 2006.

Montcombroux, Geneviève. *The Canadian Inuit Dog: Canada's Heritage*. Winnipeg: Whipoorwill Press, 2002.

Morey, D.F. and K. Aaris-Sørensen. "Paleoeskimo Dogs of the Eastern Arctic." *Arctic* 55, no. 1 (2002): 44–56.

Morrison, William. *Showing the Flag: The Mounted Police and Canadian Sovereignty in the North, 1894–1925*. Vancouver: University of British Columbia Press, 1985.

Nicholson, L.H. "The Problem of the People." *The Beaver* (1959): 20–21.

Nixon, P.G. "Early Administrative Developments in Fighting Tuberculosis Among Canadian Inuit: Bringing State Institutions Back In." *Northern Review* 2 (1988).

Nungak, Zebedee. "Experimental Eskimos." *Inuktitut* 87 (2000): 16.

O'Neil, John. "Self-Determination, Medical Ideology and Health Services in Inuit Communities." In *Northern Communities: The Prospects for Empowerment*, eds. Gurston Dacks and Ken Coates. Edmonton: Boreal Institute for Northern Studies, 1988, 33–50.

Oosten, Jarich and Frédéric Laugrand. *Travelling and Surviving on Our Land: Inuit Perspective on the 20th Century*. Iqaluit: Nunavut Arctic College/Nortext, 2001.

Paine, Robert. *The White Arctic: Anthropological Essays on Tutelage and Ethnicity*. St. John's: Memorial University of Newfoundland, 1977.

Phillips, R.A.J. *Canada's North*. Toronto: Macmillan of Canada, 1967.

Phillips, R.A.J. "The Opening Door." *North* 8, no. 1 (1961): 12–13.

Platts, R.E. "The Angirraq: Low Cost Prefabrication in Arctic Houses." *Arctic* 19, no. 2 (1966).

Pratt, Mary Louise. *Imperial Eyes: Travel Writing and Transculturation*. London and New York: Routledge, 2008.

Robertson, R. Gordon. "The Coming Crisis in the North." *North* 14, no. 2 (1967): 44–52.

Quassa, Paul and Louis McC*omber.* We Need to Know Who We Are: The Life Story of Paul Quassa. Iqaluit: Nunavut Arctic College, 2008.

Quinn, R. Quinn. *The Road to Nunavut: The Progress of the Eastern Arctic*

Inuit since the Second World War. Kingston: McGill–Queen's University Press, 1988.

Posen, Claire. "20 Years of Co-operation in Canada's Arctic." *North* 16, no. 3 (1979): 2–7.

Royal Commission on Aboriginal Peoples. *The High Arctic Relocation: A Report on the 1953–55 Relocation*. Ottawa: Royal Commission on Aboriginal Peoples, 1994.

Ryan, Leslie Boyd. *Cape Dorset Prints: Fifty Years of Printmaking at the Kingnait Studios*. San Francisco: Pomegranate, 2007.

Smith, Lorne. "The Mechanical Dog Team: A Study of the Ski-Doo in the Canadian Arctic." *Arctic Anthropology* 9, no. 1 (1972): 8.

Sparham, Desmond. "Education at Cape Dorset: An Evaluation." *Eskimo* 31, no. 7 (1974): 12–14.

Tester, Frank James, Paule McNicoll, an dPeter Irniq. "Writing for our Lives: The Language of Homesickness, Self-Esteem and the Inuit TB Epidemic." *Études/Inuit/Studies* 25, no. 1–2 (2001): 122–23.

Thomas, D.K. and C.T. Thompson. *Eskimo Housing as Planned Social Change*. Ottawa: 1972.

Trott, Christopher. "Ilagiit and Tuq½uraqtuq: Inuit Understandings of Kinship and Social Relatedness." Paper prepared for First Nations, First Thoughts conference at the Centre of Canadian Studies, University of Edinburgh, 2005.

Tungavik Federation of Nunavut. "An Inuit Response." *Northern Perspectives* 17, no. 1 (1988).

Vallee, Frank. "Eskimo Theories of Mental Illness in the Hudson Bay Region." *Anthropologica* 8, no. 1 (1966): 56.

Vestey, Jennifer. "Igloolik Eskimo Settlement and Mobility, 1900–1970." Master's thesis, McGill University, 1973.

Wachowich, Nancy. *Sagiyuq: Stories from the Lives of Three Inuit Children*. Montreal: McGill–Queens University Press, 1999.

Wenzel, George. "The Integration of 'Remote' Site Labor into the Inuit Economy of Clyde River, NWT." *Arctic Anthropology* 20, no. 2 (1983): 79.

Wenzel, George. "Inuit Health and the Health Care System: Change and Status Quo." *Études/Inuit/Studies* 5, no. 1 (1981): 13.

Willis, John S. "Northern Health: Problems and Progress." *Northern Affairs Bulletin* 6, no. 5 (1959): 21.

Yatsushiro, Toshio. "The Changing Eskimo." *The Beaver* (1962): 23–24.